Wounds of History

Wounds of History takes a new view in psychoanalysis using a transgenerational and social/political/cultural model looking at trauma and its transmission. The view is radical in looking beyond maternal dyads and Oedipal triangles and in its portrayal of a multi-generational world that is no longer hierarchical. This look allows for greater clinical creativity for conceptualizing and treating human suffering, situating healing in expanding circles of witnessing.

The contributors to this volume look at inherited personal trauma involving legacies of war, genocide, slavery, political persecution, forced migration/unwelcomed immigration and the way attachment and connection is disrupted, traumatized and ultimately longing for repair and reconnection.

The book addresses several themes such as the ethical/social turn in psychoanalysis, the repetition of resilience and wounds and the repair of these wounds, the complexity of attachment in the aftermath of trauma, and the move toward social justice. In their contributions, the authors remain close to the human stories.

Wounds of History will be of interest to psychoanalysts, psychologists and other mental health professionals, as well as students or teachers of trauma studies, Jewish and gender studies and studies of genocide.

Jill Salberg, PhD, ABPP, is clinical adjunct associate professor of psychology, faculty member and clinical consultant/supervisor at the NYU Postdoctoral Program in Psychotherapy and Psychoanalysis, and faculty and supervisor at The Stephen Mitchell Relational Study Center and the Institute for Contemporary Psychotherapy. She has contributed to and is editor of *Good Enough Endings: Breaks, Interruptions and Terminations from Contemporary Relational Perspectives*. She co-edits a new Routledge book series, Psyche and Soul: *Psychoanalysis, Spirituality and Religion in Dialogue*. She is in private practice in Manhattan.

Sue Grand, PhD, is clinical adjunct associate professor of psychology, faculty member and clinical consultant/supervisor at the NYU Postdoctoral Program in Psychotherapy and Psychoanalysis including their couples and family specialization, faculty at the trauma program at the National Institute for the Psychotherapies, The Stephen Mitchell Relational Study Center, and a fellow at the Institute for the Psychology of the Other. She is the author of *The Reproduction of Evil: A Clinical and Cultural Perspective* and *The Hero in the Mirror: From Fear to Fortitude*. She is in private practice in NYC and Teaneck, NJ.

RELATIONAL PERSPECTIVES BOOK SERIES

LEWIS ARON & ADRIENNE HARRIS
Series Co-Editors

STEVEN KUCHUCK & EYAL ROZMARIN
Associate Editors

The Relational Perspectives Book Series (RPBS) publishes books that grow out of or contribute to the relational tradition in contemporary psychoanalysis. The term *relational psychoanalysis* was first used by Greenberg and Mitchell[1] to bridge the traditions of interpersonal relations, as developed within interpersonal psychoanalysis and object relations, as developed within contemporary British theory. But, under the seminal work of the late Stephen Mitchell, the term *relational psychoanalysis* grew and began to accrue to itself many other influences and developments. Various tributaries – interpersonal psychoanalysis, object relations theory, self psychology, empirical infancy research, and elements of contemporary Freudian and Kleinian thought – flow into this tradition, which understands relational configurations between self and others, both real and fantasied, as the primary subject of psychoanalytic investigation.

We refer to the relational tradition, rather than to a relational school, to highlight that we are identifying a trend, a tendency within contemporary psychoanalysis, not a more formally organized or coherent school or system of beliefs. Our use of the term *relational* signifies a dimension of theory and practice that has become salient across the wide spectrum of contemporary psychoanalysis. Now under the editorial supervision of Lewis Aron and Adrienne Harris with the assistance of Associate Editors Steven Kuchuck and Eyal Rozmarin, the Relational Perspectives Book Series originated in

1 Greenberg, J. & Mitchell, S. (1983). *Object relations in psychoanalytic theory.* Cambridge, MA: Harvard University Press.

1990 under the editorial eye of the late Stephen A. Mitchell. Mitchell was the most prolific and influential of the originators of the relational tradition. He was committed to dialogue among psychoanalysts and he abhorred the authoritarianism that dictated adherence to a rigid set of beliefs or technical restrictions. He championed open discussion, comparative and integrative approaches, and he promoted new voices across the generations.

Included in the Relational Perspectives Book Series are authors and works that come from within the relational tradition, extend and develop the tradition, as well as works that critique relational approaches or compare and contrast it with alternative points of view. The series includes our most distinguished senior psychoanalysts, along with younger contributors who bring fresh vision.

Vol. 76
Demons in the Consulting Room: Echoes of Genocide, Slavery and Extreme Trauma in Psychoanalytic Practice
Adrienne Harris, Margery Kalb and Susan Klebanoff

Vol. 77
The Ethical Turn: Otherness and Subjectivity in Contemporary Psychoanalysis
David M. Goodman and Eric R. Severson

Vol. 78
Talking About Evil: Psychoanalytic, Social, and Cultural Perspectives
Rina Lazar

Vol. 79
Two Languages of Love: Contemporary Psychoanalysis and Modern Jewish Philosophy
Michael Oppenheim

Vol. 80
Psychoanalysis, Trauma and Community: History and Contemporary Reappraisals
Judith L. Alpert and Elizabeth R. Goren

Vol. 81
Body–Mind Dissociation in Psychoanalysis: Development after Bion
Riccardo Lombardi

Vol. 82
Wounds of History: Repair and Resilience in the Trans-Generational Transmission of Trauma
Jill Salberg and Sue Grand

Vol. 83
Trans-generational Trauma and the Other: Dialogues across History and Difference
Sue Grand and Jill Salberg

Wounds of History

Repair and Resilience in the
Trans-Generational Transmission
of Trauma

Edited by Jill Salberg and
Sue Grand

Routledge
Taylor & Francis Group
LONDON AND NEW YORK

First published 2017
by Routledge
2 Park Square, Milton Park, Abingdon, Oxon OX14 4RN

and by Routledge
711 Third Avenue, New York, NY 10017

Routledge is an imprint of the Taylor & Francis Group, an informa business

© 2017 Selection and editorial matter, Jill Salberg and Sue Grand; individual chapters, the contributors

The right of the editor to be identified as the author of the editorial matter, and of the authors for their individual chapters, has been asserted in accordance with sections 77 and 78 of the Copyright, Designs and Patents Act 1988.

All rights reserved. No part of this book may be reprinted or reproduced or utilized in any form or by any electronic, mechanical, or other means, now known or hereafter invented, including photocopying and recording, or in any information storage or retrieval system, without permission in writing from the publishers.

Trademark notice: Product or corporate names may be trademarks or registered trademarks, and are used only for identification and explanation without intent to infringe.

British Library Cataloguing in Publication Data
A catalogue record for this book is available from the British Library

Library of Congress Cataloging in Publication Data
Names: Salberg, Jill, editor. | Grand, Sue, editor.
Title: Wounds of history : repair and resilience in the trans-generational transmission of trauma / edited by Jill Salberg and Sue Grand.
Description: Abingdon, Oxon ; New York, NY : Routledge, 2017. | Series: The relational perspectives book series | Includes bibliographical references and index.
Identifiers: LCCN 2016011484 | ISBN 9781138807495 (hardback : alk. paper)
Subjects: LCSH: Psychic trauma. | Psychic trauma–Treatment. | Intergenerational relations–Psychological aspects. | Resilience (Personality trait) | Psychoanalysis.
Classification: LCC BF175.5.P75 W68 2017 | DDC 155.9/3–dc23LC record available at https://lccn.loc.gov/2016011484

ISBN: 978-1-138-80749-5 (hbk)
ISBN: 978-1-138-80750-1 (pbk)
ISBN: 978-1-315-75106-1 (ebk)

Typeset in Times New Roman 11/14
by Wearset Ltd, Boldon, Tyne and Wear

This book is dedicated to our husbands, Michael A. Salberg and Bernard Rous, whose support, encouragement and love sustained us and helped make this work possible. Each of them in their own way share our quest for truth, compassion and work that helps to heal a broken world.

Contents

Notes on Contributors   xii

Editors' Introduction   1
JILL SALBERG AND SUE GRAND

PART I
Massive Trauma: Attachment Ruptured, Attachment Repaired   7

    Introduction   9
    GEORGE HALASZ

1 Listening to My Mother's Testimony   18
    DORI LAUB

2 Arrival At Auschwitz: Traumatic Rupture and Empathic Containment in the Joint Narrative of a Mother and a Daughter who Survived the Holocaust Together   39
    JOHANNA BODENSTAB

3 The Rhythm of Resilience: A Deep Ecology of Entangled Relationality   60
    KAREN HOPENWASSER

4 The Texture of Traumatic Attachment: Presence and Ghostly Absence in Transgenerational Transmission   77
    JILL SALBERG

PART II
Repetitions of Violence, Antidotes to War — 101

History Making — 103
RACHAEL PELTZ

5 Has Sexuality Anything to Do with War Trauma? Intergenerational Transmission and the Homosexual Imaginary — 109
STEVEN BOTTICELLI

6 Repairing an Immigrant Chinese Family's "Box of Terrible Things" — 125
AMY KLATZKIN, ALICIA F. LIEBERMAN, AND PATRICIA VAN HORN

7 Enduring Mothers, Enduring Knowledge: On Rape and History — 149
JUDITH L. ALPERT

PART III
Persecution and Otherness: Different Subjectivities and the Restoration of Trust — 163

Introduction — 165
SAMUEL C. GABLE AND DAVID M. GOODMAN

8 Collectively Creating Conditions for Emergence — 169
KATIE GENTILE

9 Trauma and Recovery: A Legacy of Political Persecution and Activism Across Three Generations — 189
JUDITH LEWIS HERMAN

10 In Shadows of Terror: An Intergenerational Tale of Growing Up in the Old Left — 204
LISA S. LYONS

11 To Unchain Haunting Blood Memories: Intergenerational Trauma among African Americans — 226
KIRKLAND C. VAUGHANS

PART IV
Fragmented Legacies, Healing Narratives   243

Introduction   245
JILL SALBERG

12 Historical Trauma Among Indigenous Peoples of the Americas: Concepts, Research, and Clinical Considerations   250
MARIA YELLOW HORSE BRAVE HEART, JOSEPHINE CHASE, JENNIFER ELKINS, AND DEBORAH B. ALTSCHUL

13 Growing Up Armenian   268
ERIC V. HACHIKIAN

14 Things They Carried: Leaving Korea   286
MARIE MYUNG-OK LEE

Index   **290**

Contributors

Judith L. Alpert, PhD, a psychologist and psychoanalyst, is Professor and Clinical Consultant at New York University's Postdoctoral Program in Psychotherapy and Psychoanalysis. She is also Professor of Applied Psychology and former Co-Director of the Trauma and Violence Transdisciplinary Studies Program at New York University. She is founder and past president of the Division of Trauma Psychology of the American Psychological Association and served as Co-Chair of the American Psychological Association's Working Group on Recovered Memories. Her publications, including four edited books and over 200 articles, focus mainly on trauma and memory for traumatic events. She maintains a private practice in New York City.

Deborah B. Altschul, PhD, is a psychologist, faculty member and Deputy Director of the University of New Mexico Department Of Psychiatry's Division of Community Behavioral Health. Her research is largely focused on examining the connection between behavioral health disparities, cultural competency, consumer outcomes, and evidence-based practice. She is currently working with the State and several tribal communities on their implementation and evaluation of Systems of Care mental health initiatives. Prior to working in New Mexico, Dr. Altschul worked at the University of Hawai's Department of Psychology's Mental Health Services Research, Evaluation, and Training Program where she worked on the state's cultural competency plan, and a project making cultural adaptations to evidence based practices for Native Hawaiian, Pacific Islander, and Asian populations. Dr. Altschul completed a postdoctoral fellowship with the National Association of State Mental Health Program Directors aimed at improving racial and ethnic disparities in mental health services, and worked with the State of Colorado to develop their cultural competency plan.

Johanna Bodenstab, PhD, was an author, translator, and independent researcher. She held an MA in German literature and theater from Freie Universität Berlin, Germany. She was a graduate of the "Psychoanalysis for Scholars" program at Western New England Society for Psychoanalysis in New Haven, CT. She held a PhD from Universität Kassel, Germany for her work with survivor testimonies and on mother–daughter relationships during the Holocaust. She passed away on April 23, 2015.

Steven Botticelli, PhD, is on the faculty of the NYU Postdoctoral Program in Psychotherapy and Psychoanalysis, where he serves as co-chair for the Independent track. He is a contributing editor for *Studies in Gender and Sexuality* and the Division/Review, and a contributor to the Psychoanalytic Dialogues blog. He co-edited (with Adrienne Harris) *First Do No Harm: The Paradoxical Encounters of Psychoanalysis, Warmaking and Resistance* (Routledge, 2010). He practices in New York City.

Maria Yellow Horse Brave Heart, PhD, (Hunkpapa/Oglala Lakota), is Associate Professor of Psychiatry/Director of Native American and Disparities Research at the University of New Mexico (UNM) Department of Psychiatry and Behavioral Sciences, Division of Community Behavioral Health. She has been founding President/Director of the Takini Network/Institute, based in Rapid City, South Dakota, a Native collective devoted to community healing from intergenerational massive group trauma. She is Chair of the Special Interest Group on Intergenerational Trauma and Resilience for the International Society for Traumatic Stress Studies. In 1992, she founded the Takini Network and developed the *Historical Trauma and Unresolved Grief Intervention* (HTUG), recognized as an exemplary model, in a special minority initiative, by the Center for Mental Health Services in 2001. In 2009 HTUG was selected as a "Tribal Best Practice" by the First Nations Behavioral Health Association, the Pacific Substance Abuse and Mental Health Collaborating Council, and the Substance Abuse and Mental Health Services Administration (SAMHSA). Currently, she is Principal Investigator for a NIMH-funded R34 pilot study *Iwankapiya-Healing: Historical Trauma Practice and Group IPT for American Indians*. The goal of *Iwankapiya* is to examine the effectiveness of the HTUG intervention combined with group Interpersonal Psychotherapy (IPT) for American Indian adults with depression and related disorders. She is also Principal Investigator of the *New Song Mountain Tribal Preventive and Early Mental Health Intervention Project* focusing on Southwestern reservation youth, funded by the National Institute for Minority Health and Health Disparities, part of the UNM Center for the Advancement of Research, Engagement, and Science on Health Disparities.

Josephine Chase, PhD, (Mandan/Hidatsa – Ihunktawan/Hunkpapa), is Faculty at Oglala Lakota College (OLC), Social Work Department. She has been the Associate Director of the Takini Network/Institute, based in Rapid City, South Dakota, a Native collective devoted to community healing from intergenerational massive group trauma. Since 1992, she has collaborated in the development of the *Historical Trauma and Unresolved Grief Intervention* (HTUG), recognized as an exemplary model, in a special minority initiative, by the Center for Mental Health Services in 2001. In 2009 HTUG was selected as a "Tribal Best Practice" by the First Nations Behavioral Health Association, the Pacific Substance Abuse and Mental Health Collaborating Council, and the Substance Abuse and Mental Health Services Administration (SAMHSA). Currently, she is Principal Investigator at the Tribal site in South Dakota for a NIMH-funded R34 pilot study *Iwankapiya-Healing: Historical Trauma Practice and Group IPT for American Indians*. The goal of *Iwankapiya* is to examine the effectiveness of the HTUG intervention combined with group Interpersonal Psychotherapy (IPT) for American Indian adults with depression and related disorders. She is also Co-Principal Investigator of the OLC American Indian Higher Education Consortium Behavioral Health Research Project funded by the Native American Research Centers for Health, under an initiative to create Behavioral Health research and curricula at Tribal Colleges and Universities.

Jennifer Elkins, Faculty, University of Georgia School of Social Work.

Samuel C. Gable, MA, is a doctoral candidate of counseling psychology at the University of Massachusetts Boston. His current research addresses health disparities and community interventions through computerized neuropsychological assessment, as well as explorations in the moral reasoning of bystanders to sexual assault. His clinical work resides at the interface of trauma and legal advocacy for asylum-seeking individuals.

Katie Gentile, PhD, is Professor of Interdisciplinary Studies and Director of the Gender Studies Program at John Jay College of Criminal Justice and on the faculty of New York University's Postdoctoral Program in Psychotherapy and Psychoanalysis. She is the author of *Creating Bodies: Eating Disorders as Self-destructive Survival* (2007) and *The Business of being Made: The Temporalities of Reproductive Technologies in Psychoanalysis and Culture* (2016), both from Routledge. She is the editor of the Routledge book series *Genders & Sexualities in Minds & Cultures*, co-editor of the journal *Studies in Gender and Sexuality*, and on the editorial board of *Women's Studies Quarterly*.

David M. Goodman, PhD, is the Associate Dean of Academic Affairs and Student Services at the Woods College of Advancing Studies at Boston College, the Director of *Psychology and the Other*, and a Teaching Associate at Harvard Medical School/Cambridge Hospital. He has written over a dozen articles on continental philosophy, Jewish thought, social justice, and psychotherapy. His recent book *The Demanded Self: Levinasian Ethics and Identity in Psychology* (Duquesne University Press, 2012) considers the intersection of psychology, philosophy, and theology as it pertains to narcissism, ethical phenomenology, and selfhood. Additionally, he co-edited a book (with Mark Freeman), *Psychology and the Other: A Dialogue at the Crossroad of an Emerging Field* (Oxford University Press, 2015), which features some of the conversations from the first *Psychology and the Other* conference in 2011. He is also a licensed clinical psychologist and has a private practice in Cambridge, MA.

Sue Grand, PhD, is faculty and supervisor at the NYU Postdoctoral Program in Psychotherapy and Psychoanalysis; faculty, the couples and family therapy program at the NYU Postdoctoral Program in Psychotherapy and Psychoanalysis; faculty, trauma program at the National Institute for the Psychotherapies; faculty, The Mitchell Center for Relational Psychoanalysis; visiting scholar at the Psychoanalytic Institute of Northern California; fellow, The Institute for Psychology and the Other. She is the author of *The Reproduction of Evil: A Clinical and Cultural Perspective* (Routledge, 2002) and *The Hero in the Mirror: From Fear to Fortitude* (Routledge, 2011). She is co-editor with Jill Salberg of the book *Trans-generational Trauma and the Other: Dialogues Across History and Difference* (Routledge, 2017). She is an associate editor of *Psychoanalytic Dialogues* and *Psychoanalysis, Culture and Society*. She is in private practice in NYC and in Teaneck, NJ.

Eric V. Hachikian is an Armenian-American composer, whose music has been hailed by the *New York Times* as "lovely and original," and his compositions can be heard in a variety of major motion pictures (*The Night Before*; *Fury*; *Get Hard*; *Ferrell Takes The Field*; *The Place Beyond The Pines*; *Charlie Countryman*; *Better Living Through Chemistry*; *Project X*; *50/50*; *The Wrestler*) and network television shows (Netflix's *Marco Polo*; ABC's *Mixology & Revenge*; Fox's *The Mindy Project*; CBS's *CSI: Crime Scene Investigation*; HBO's *Silicon Valley*, *Entourage* & *How To Make It In America*; Showtime's *Homeland* and *The Big C*; FX's *Tyrant* and *The Strain*; The Discovery Channel's *LIFE: The Series*). As Creative Director and co-founder of Soundcat Productions, a boutique music company with studios in New York City and Los Angeles, he has written and produced music for numerous national and international ad campaigns. He has also written for Off-Broadway productions, and the Los Angeles Philharmonic, the New York Pops Orchestra, the Baltimore Symphony, and the Boston Pops Orchestra have performed his compositions. A classically trained composer, as well as a self-taught DJ and perpetual student of world music, his musical instincts have no boundaries, and his multi-genre interests result in a unique and personal sound. He studied Nadia Boulanger's methods in Paris, France, and has also studied composition and audio engineering at the Aspen and Tanglewood Music Festivals. He received his Bachelor of Music with highest honors from the University of Michigan, and his Master of Arts from New York University.

George Halasz, MD, is a consultant child and adolescent psychiatrist and adjunct senior lecturer, School of Psychology and Psychiatry, Faculty of Medicine, Nursing and Health Sciences, Monash University, in Australia. He has written extensively on the experiences of the "second generation" of the Holocaust and is a contributor to Kathy Grinblat's *Children of the Shadows: Voices of the Second Generation* (University of Western Australia Press, 2002), and Nancy R. Goodman and Marilyn B. Meyers's *The Power of Witnessing: Reflections, Reverberations, and Traces of the Holocaust* (Routledge, 2012). He has co-written and edited three books, and a number of chapters and journal articles that deal with a range of developmental and psychiatric conditions. He served on the Editorial Board of the *Australian and New Zealand Journal* *of Psychiatry* (1992–2004) and is currently on the editorial board of *Australasian Psychiatry* (2005–current). From 2007–2010 he served on the Steering Committee for the Cunningham Dax Collection and working group for the exhibition, "Out of the Dark – The Emotional Legacy of the Holocaust." Current book-in-progress on Intergeneration Relational Trauma and Repair (2015–2016).

Judith Lewis Herman, MD, is Professor of Psychiatry *Emerita* at Harvard Medical School. For 30 years she was Director of Training at the Victims of Violence Program at The Cambridge Hospital, Cambridge, MA. She received her medical degree at Harvard Medical School and her training in general and community psychiatry at Boston University Medical Center. She is the author of two award-winning books: *Father-Daughter Incest* (Harvard University Press, 1981) and *Trauma and Recovery* (Basic Books, 1992). She has lectured widely on the subject of sexual and domestic violence. She is the recipient of the 1996 Lifetime Achievement Award from the International Society for Traumatic Stress Studies and the 2000 Woman in Science Award from the American Medical Women's Association. In 2007 she was named a Distinguished Life Fellow of the American Psychiatric Association, and in 2011 she received the Lifetime Achievement Award from the Trauma Psychology division of the American Psychological Association.

Karen Hopenwasser, MD, is Clinical Associate Professor of Psychiatry at the Weill Cornell College of Medicine in New York City. She is a psychiatrist in private practice with a subspecialty in the treatment of adults severely traumatized as children. Her publications and presentations have focused on the clinical and neurobiological understanding of posttraumatic states, with special attention to innovative and integrative techniques for healing. Her current exploration of the relationship between rhythmic entrainment and attunement in therapeutic healing is deeply informed by a lifelong involvement in music study and performance. Along with clinical practice she is also involved in addressing global mental health issues and is a member of the NGO Committee on Mental Health in Consultative Relationship with the United Nations.

Amy Klatzkin, MA, LMFT, trained at UCSF Child Trauma Research Program. She is currently a child and family psychotherapist in private practice in San Francisco.

Dori Laub, MD, was born in Cernauti, Romania on June 8, 1937. He is currently a practicing psychoanalyst in New Haven, CT who works primarily with victims of massive psychic trauma and with their children. He is Clinical Professor of Psychiatry at the Yale University School of Medicine and Co-Founder of the Fortunoff Video Archive for Holocaust Testimonies. He obtained his MD at the Hadassah Medical School at Hebrew University in Jerusalem, Israel and his MA in Clinical Psychology at the Bar Ilan University in Ramat Gan, Israel. He was Acting Director of the Genocide Study Program (GSP) at Yale for the years of 2000 and 2003. Since 2001, he has also served as Deputy Director for Trauma Studies for the GSP. He has published on the topic of psychic trauma, its knowing and representation in a variety of psychoanalytic journals and has co-authored a book entitled, *Testimony-Crises of Witnessing in Literature, Psychoanalysis, and History* with Professor Shoshana Felman (Routledge, 1991).

Alicia F. Lieberman, PhD, is Irving Harris Endowed Chair in Infant Mental Health, Professor and Vice Chair for Academic Affairs at the University of California San Francisco Department of Psychiatry. She is director of the Child Trauma Research Program at the San Francisco General Hospital.

Lisa S. Lyons, PhD, is a psychoanalyst and psychologist. She is on the faculties of the Stephen Mitchell Center for Relational Studies, the National Institute for the Psychotherapies Program in Integrative Psychotherapy, the Institute for Contemporary Psychotherapy, and the Center for Psychoanalysis and Psychotherapy of New Jersey. She has published and presented on the Intergenerational Transmission of Trauma, Political Repression, Dreams, Reverie and Waking Dreams, Psychoanalysis across Cultures, and Integrating Relational Psychoanalysis and Dialectical Behavior Therapy. She is in private practice in New York City and Teaneck, NJ.

Marie Myung-Ok Lee is a novelist whose next novel, on the future of medicine, is forthcoming with Simon & Schuster. She writes regularly for the *New York Times*, *Slate*, the *Guardian*, the *Nation*, the *Atlantic*, *Five Chapters*, and *Salon*. She was the first recipient of a creative writing Fulbright Fellowship to South Korea, was a judge for the National Book Awards and the PEN/E.O. Wilson Literary Science Writing prize, and won the Richard Margolis award for social justice reporting, and was a finalist for the United States Artists Fellowship. She is an Adjunct Professor at Columbia University, where she was the Writer-in-Residence for the MFA program. Previously, she taught at Brown and Yale.

Rachael Peltz, PhD, is a Training and Supervising Analyst and Faculty at the Psychoanalytic Institute of Northern California, Supervising Analyst at the Massachusetts Institute of Psychoanalysis and Access Institute. She is Past President of Section 9 – Psychoanalysis for Social Responsibility, Division 39, APA. She has published papers in *Psychoanalytic Dialogues, Fort Da, Rivista Di Psicoanalisi, Mind and Human Interaction, Psychotherapy and Politics International* and the book, *Psychoanalysis, Class and Politics: Encounters in the Clinical Setting* co-edited with Lynne Layton, Nancy Caro Hollander and Susan Gutwill (Routledge, 2006). Her clinical practice with adults, adolescents, couples and families is in Berkeley, CA.

Jill Salberg, PhD, ABPP is a clinical adjunct associate professor of psychology, faculty member and clinical consultant/supervisor at the New York University Postdoctoral Program in Psychotherapy and Psychoanalysis, faculty and supervisor at the Stephen Mitchell Center for Relational Studies and the Institute for Contemporary Psychotherapy. Her papers have been published in *Psychoanalytic Dialogues, Studies in Gender and Sexuality* and *American Imago* and she has chapters in *Relational Psychoanalysis Vol. 5: Evolution of Process* (Routledge, 2011), *The Jewish World of Sigmund Freud* (McFarland, 2010), and *Answering a Question with a Question: Contemporary Psychoanalysis and Jewish Thought* (Academic Studies Press, 2013). She is a contributor to and the editor of the book *Good Enough Endings: Breaks, Interruptions and Terminations from Contemporary Relational Perspectives* (Routledge, 2010). She is co-editor with Sue Grand of the book Transgenerational Trauma and the *Other: Dialogues Across History and Difference* (Routledge, 2017). She has conceived of and co-edits the book series, *Psyche and Soul: Psychoanalysis, Spirituality and Religion in Dialogue* at Routledge/Taylor & Francis Group and is on the editorial board of the Psychoanalysis and Jewish Life Book Series of the Academic Studies Press. She is in private practice in Manhattan.

Patricia Van Horn, JD, PhD (d. 2014), was Clinical Professor at the University of California San Francisco Department of Psychiatry, Director of the Division of Infant, Child and Adolescent Psychiatry at

San Francisco General Hospital, and Associate Director of the SFGH Child Trauma Research Program.

Kirkland C. Vaughans, PhD, is a licensed clinical psychologist and a psychoanalyst with a private practice in New York City. He is the founding editor of the *Journal of Infant, Child, and Adolescent Psychotherapy* and first-editor of the two-volume book, *The Psychology of Black Boys and Adolescents* (Praeger, 2014). He is a senior adjunct professor of psychology at the Derner Institute of Advanced Psychological Studies at Adelphi University and faculty member of their Postgraduate Program in Child and Adolescent Psychotherapy, a clinical supervisor at the National Institute for Psychotherapies, and visiting faculty member at IPTAR. He is a school psychologist at Hempstead High School and the former Regional Director of the defunct New Hope Guild Centers of Brooklyn. He has published articles on the intergenerational transmission of trauma among African Americans and presented widely on topics affecting Black male youth. He also serves on the Board of Directors for the Harlem Family Psychoanalytic Institute. He is also an Honorary Member of the Institute for Psychoanalytic Training and Research (IPTAR).

Editors' Introduction

Jill Salberg and Sue Grand

This book has had a rich gestational history. Several years ago, Salberg and Grand met to discuss mutual interests in political/social violence, the trans-generational transmission of trauma and the themes of attachment that have been focal to contemporary psychoanalysis. This inspired us to organize a conference at NYU, entitled The Wounds of History: Repair and Resilience in the Trans-generational Transmission of Trauma. Blessed with a wonderful committee,[1] we brainstormed about how to address diverse Big Histories, their intra-psychic, inter-subjective and social legacies. Our particular emphasis was on repairing wounds and arresting painful repetitions, in both intimate and social registers. This mission awakened us to something that has been missing from the trans-generational literature: the transmission of strength, resourcefulness and resilience, that operates in tandem with the transmission of wounds. We wanted to attend to the dual edge of history's legacy: the ways it can take shape in an ethos of *care*, as well as in varieties of (self/other) destruction. This thrust us, of course, into the mysteries of the human condition: why do some of us metabolize trauma with concern for the other, while we also persist in the repetition of our own wounds. We have found no answers. However, what we did find is a common thread running through all of the trans-generational literature to date: that is, the disintegrative effects of trauma on attachment bonding. In this book, we highlight this theme, theorize it and make it explicit; but we also highlight the miracle of *enduring attachment* that is often threaded through encounters with trauma. In this book, we do not split, or bifurcate, these attachment motifs – but find them to be inter-penetrating. Nonetheless, we think that they offer commentary on the vicissitudes of concern, resilience *and* repetitive destruction, which are the legacy of historical trauma. Gathering together as a committee, we believed that a conference on these issues would speak to many clinicians, academics and activists.

The study of trans-generational transmission of trauma began with a look at Holocaust trauma. Rich work in this field continues (Gerson, 2009; Grand, 2009; Grand & Salberg, 2015; Guralnik, 2014; Richman, 2006, 2014). It has been in the past 20 years that scholarship on witnessing, testimony and trans-generational transmission have extended beyond the Holocaust, to other political and social traumas and genocides. Thus, we have work by Apprey (2003), Gump (2010) and Leary (1997) on the legacy of African-American slavery in subsequent generations; Davoine and Gaudillière (2004) linked the inchoate memory of WWII with psychosis in subsequent generations; Faimberg's idea of "telescoping of generations" and Reis' (2005) efforts to expand analytic conceptions of the patient's history past consideration of a person's developmental course to include the shaping force of events in creating culture or the very subjects that experience culture and cultural events. Recently, Grand (2015b) has examined the racial legacy of Native American "vanishing" in the United States, and linked this to African-American slavery. Vaughans (2015) has written about the long-term effects of slavery naming it as a "cultural introject" affecting the lives of blacks and whites today. Grand (2000) has also examined the legacy of the Armenian genocide, as well as the trans-generational transmission of genocide through the perpetration of sexual abuse on succeeding generations. While Salberg (2015) has written how the attachment relationship is the mode of trans-generational transmissions and carries the presence and absence of parental dysregulation resulting from traumatic experiences.

Nonetheless, to date, the literature is largely missing an explicit look at the *strengths* transmitted to subsequent generations, and the enduring capacities for love, bonding, devotion and activism that we often find in succeeding generations. To transmute violent repetitions into repair, these capacities need to be illuminated. Thus, in inviting our authors to contribute to this volume, we asked them to address several themes: a diversity of Big Histories; the repetition of both *resilience* and *wounds*; the repair of these wounds; and the complexity of attachment in the aftermath of trauma. Ultimately, the authors in this volume share a common goal. We want to expand the social/ethical turn in psychoanalysis (Goodman, 2012; Layton & Goodman, 2014; Layton, Hollander & Gutwill, 2006), and facilitate the I–Thou capacity that is nascent in all of us.

The Trans-Generational Model

As we immersed ourselves in this shared project, new questions emerged for us. These questions intrigue us, and we hope to engage our readers in playing with them, as some of our authors are doing. In particular: *who constitutes the psychoanalytic family?* To date, the trans-generational "turn" has been *added on* to our existing notions of the family. Regardless of our theoretical persuasion, our theories have always been grounded in models of mommy, baby, and daddy – regardless of what sex, gender identity or sexual orientation this "mommy" or "daddy" has. Our intra-psychic and inter-subjective models always circulate around dyads and triads, in a hierarchical model that is largely absent of siblings. But we are beginning to suspect that the *trans-generational turn* can radically test this conception of family. In doing so, this turn potentially de-stabilizes the bedrock of our theories. We now understand that psychic influence extends well beyond maternal dyads and Oedipal triangles. In the trans-generational model, the psyche is constituted by a much larger object world. This world is more multi-generational. It is also no longer exclusively hierarchical but is horizontal: inclusive of the *communal cohort* effect of massive trauma. This look allows for greater clinical creativity for conceptualizing and treating human suffering. It expands our psychic world *and our relational resources*, as we also integrate the social/political/cultural markers of collective trauma.

This shift can also call upon us to ask: what happens to psychoanalytic theory when the psychoanalytic family grows beyond maternal dyads and Oedipal triads? If trans-generational transmission enters the core of psychoanalysis, would it transform much of our thinking? Will it expand our understanding, as did the findings of attachment research and neuroscience? How are we altering our further understanding of the self-in-relation? What about our concepts of subjectivity, if we are to view subjectivity as marked by the personal *and* the collective, without privileging one in lieu of the other? Then, too, this shift complicates *parental authority, and hierarchical structures.* Salberg (2007) has queried how Freud, in his singular emphasis on Oedipus as the over-arching mythic master story, overlooked his own Jewish biblical myths of profound sibling rivalry. She notes that the first murder recorded in the Bible was of Abel by Cain, a sibling murder, not a patricide. Mitchell (2003) has written extensively about the way our theory omits siblings and peers.

Despite her contribution, siblings remain marginal to our discourse. What happens to the psyche when the family becomes more multi-generational *and* more horizontal? What happens to psychoanalysis? Mitchell has argued that sibling and peer relations are an important locus for critical thinking and social justice, allowing us to think, and bond, outside parental authority. This opens up the capacity to *resist and question hierarchical authority*. As long as *one child* is double teamed by two parental authorities, it is difficult for this space to open up.

In the recent ethical/social turn of psychoanalysis, we are all trying to locate social justice at the core of psychoanalysis. In linking global violence and social justice to the trans-generational turn, we cannot help wondering if this effort has been limited, or constrained, by a theory that excludes siblings and peer relations. Like all psychoanalysts, the authors in this volume comment little on sibling relations – a flaw that we hope will be countered in the future. Nonetheless, the cohort of violence is *ever-present*: we view this peer group as an important locus of bonding; solidarity; of mutual care and holding, repair and mentalization. Furthermore, it is an important site of *social consciousness and social activism*. We have tried to articulate, and perform, the power of these witnessing circles in a recent issue of *Contemporary Psychoanalysis* (Grand & Salberg, Special Editors, 2015).

We have highlighted the above inquiries, and we are sure the reader will discover others. Together, we all want to think about how these shifts can be utilized to facilitate the repair of our shared history of violence. How can this look contribute to individual healing and to the empowerment of social justice? In examining these questions, we believe that psychoanalysts can contribute to stopping the cycle of violence that is too often produced by trans-generational transmission.

The Wounds of History: Repair and Resilience in the Transgenerational Transmission of Trauma addresses both individual and cultural problems while attempting to examine and open up many of the questions we have laid out. Throughout the essays in this book, this reconceived family provides our leitmotif: it is the ruptured *site* of the trans-generational wound; it is the inchoate locus of transmission; *and* it holds the potential for repair. Additionally, *attachment theory* will be central to our argument, and to the essays in this book. Unlike other books already published on this topic that focus on war, or trauma (see Davoine & Gaudillière, 2004; Goodman & Meyers, 2011; Epstein, 1979; Schore, 2001), our book will be addressing multiple dimensions – the personal as affected by the interpersonal, the familial across generations across historical eras and political climates while viewing the body and the mind as receptors and metabolizers of trauma with capacities within individuals, families and cultures for resilience and repair.

Further, in our view we must privilege the telling and listening of stories, otherwise we can easily reproduce trauma in the retelling of trauma stories. Instead, in aiming for reparative forms these stories must be held, and mediated, by empathic witnesses, and an "imaginative witness" (see Grand, 2009; Reis 2015) who engage its aesthetic while containing its aggression. We need to do this, knowing that aggression keeps escaping this container. And we need to recognize that our best efforts to address diversity are also limited: there are so many histories that are not included in this volume. This absence should not be read as disavowal or inattention, but, rather, as a sign that this volume is a beginning. Furthermore, we hope that our readers will continue testing, challenging and expanding psychoanalytic theory without alienation, or cognitive distance.

Note

1 Judith Alpert, Melinda Gellman, Elizabeth Goren, Deborah Liner, Jan Lobel, Lu Steinberg, Isaac Tylim, Barbara Waxenberg and Deborah Waxenberg.

References

Aprrey, M. (2003). "Repairing History: Reworking transgenerational trauma." In: *Hating in the First Person Plural*. Pg. 3–29. Ed. D. Moss. New York: Other Press.
Davoine, F. & Gaudillière, J. M. (2004). *History Beyond Trauma: Whereof One Cannot Speak, Thereof One Cannot Stay Silent*. New York: Other Press.
Epstein, H. (1979). *Children of the Holocaust: Conversations with Sons and Daughters of Survivors*. New York: Putnam.
Gerson, S. (2009). "When the Third is Dead: Memory, mourning, and witnessing in the aftermath of the Holocaust." *International Journal of Psychoanalysis*, 90: 1341–1357.
Goodman, D. (2012). *The Demanded Self: Levinasian Ethics and Identity in Psychology*. Pittsburgh, PA: Duquesne University Press.
Goodman, N. R. & Meyers, M. B. (eds.). (2011). *The Power of Witnessing: Reflections, Reverberations, and Traces of the Holocaust*. New York and London: Routledge.
Grand, S. (2000). *The Reproduction of Evil*. Hillsdale, NJ and London: Analytic Press.
Grand, S. (2009). *The Hero in the Mirror: From Fear to Fortitude*. London: Routledge.
Grand, S. (2015a). "Circles of Witnessing: On hope and atrocity." *Contemporary Psychoanalysis: Special Issue: The Evolution of Witnessing: Emergent Relational Trends in Holocaust Studies*, 51 (2): 262–275.

Grand, S. (2015b). "The Other Within: White racial shame and the Native American genocide." Psychology and the Other conference, Boston.

Grand, S. & Salberg, J. (2015) Co-editors: Special Issue: "The Evolution of Witnessing: Emergent relational trends in Holocaust studies." *Contemporary Psychoanalysis*, 51 (2): 185–194.

Gump, J. (2010). "Reality Matters: The shadow of trauma on African-American subjectivity." *Psychoanalytic Psychology*, 27 (1): 42–54.

Guralnik, O. (2014). "The Dead Baby." *Psychoanalytic Dialogues*, 24 (2): 129–145.

Layton, L. & Goodman, D. (2014). Editors' introduction to special issue: "Psychology and the Other: The historical-political in psychoanalysis' ethical turn." *Psychoanalysis, Culture and Society*, 19 (3): 225–232.

Layton, L., Hollander, N. C. & Gutwill, S. (2006). *Psychoanalysis, Class and Politics: Encounters in the Clinical Setting.* London: Routledge.

Leary, K. (1997). "Passing, Posing and 'Keeping it Real'." *Constellations*, 6 (1): 85–96.

Mitchell, J. (2003). *Siblings, Sex and Violence.* Cambridge, UK: Polity Press.

Reis, B. (2005). "The Subject of History/The Object of Transference." *Studies in Gender and Sexuality*, 6: 217–240.

Reis, B. (2015). "How Deep the Sky: Discussion of special issue on the evolution of witnessing: emergent relational trends in Holocaust studies." Co-edited by Sue Grand & Jill Salberg, *Contemporary Psychoanalysis*, 51 (2): 333–347.

Richman, S. (2006). "Finding One's Voice: Transforming trauma into autobiographical narrative." *Contemporary Psychoanalysis*, 42: 639–650.

Richman, S. (2014). *Mended by the Muse: Creative Transformations of Trauma.* London: Routledge.

Salberg, J. (2007). "Hidden in Plain Sight: Freud's Jewish identity revisited." *Psychoanalytic Dialogues*, 17 (2): 197–217.

Salberg, J. (2015). "The Texture of Traumatic Attachment: Presence and ghostly absence in trans-generational transmissions." *Psychoanalytic Quarterly*, LXXXIV (1): 21–46.

Schore, A. N. (2001). "The Effects of Early Relational Trauma on the Right Brain Development, Affect Regulation, and Infant Mental Health." *Infant Mental Health Journal*, 22: 201–269.

Vaughans, K. (2015). "To Unchain Haunting Blood Memories: Intergenerational trauma among African Americans." In: *Fragments of Trauma and the Social Production of Suffering: Trauma, History and Memory.* Pg. 277–290. Ed. M. O'Loughlin & M. Charles. Lanham, MD: Rowman & Littlefield.

Part I
Massive Trauma
Attachment Ruptured, Attachment Repaired

Introduction

George Halasz

Freud's construct of 'psychic apparatus' and 'psychic reality' (Laplanche & Pontalis, 1983) became the foundation of the science 'psychoanalysis'. These constructs remained the centerpiece of the various schools of psychoanalysis and dynamic psychotherapy for most of the twentieth century. Contemporary psychoanalysis confronts the unprecedented challenges to these constructs posed by the neurosciences heralding the current paradigm change, powerfully driven by advances in the understanding of the neurobiology of trauma.

The current paradigm has transformed neuroscience's earlier focus on the synapse – the 'chemical imbalance theory of mental symptoms and illness' – to advance the centrality of dysregulated neural networks as the preferred model. Schore's extensive body of work offers a coherent formulation of the neurobiological mechanisms of relational trauma (2012) expanding his earlier (2001) observation that for relational trauma '[T]here is no one objective threshold at which all infants initiate a stress response; rather, this is subjectively determined and created within a unique organismic-environmental history' (p. 206). Furthermore Schore (2001) posed critical questions to which we now have emerging answers:

> What if the brain is evolving in an environment of not interpersonal security, but danger? Is this a context for the intergenerational transmission of psychopathology, and the origins of maladaptive infant health? Will early trauma have lasting consequences for future mental health, in that the trajectory of the developmental process will be altered?
>
> (p. 207)

Questions like these resonate at the heart of Part I, seeking further clarification to the likely mechanism accounting for transmitted intergenerational trauma (see Salberg). Some psychoanalysts have rejected the challenges posed by neuroscience (Blass & Carmeli, 2007) while others eagerly embraced the opportunities offered (Baradon, 2010). Part I also confronts neuroscience's paradigm change, specifically applied in the specialized field of massive trauma, offering innovative new concepts, clinically useful ideas and original research using video excerpts from Holocaust testimonies. Lastly, there are implications as to how later generations can further their own resilience (see Hopenwasser) helping repair the generational and historical trauma wounds.

As entry to these chapters, I believe it is crucial first to address the central ongoing concern within psychoanalysis that I first mentioned. The nature and status of the construct of 'psychic trauma', which resides within Freud's 'psychic reality', alongside the complex human experiences that constitute the 'reality' of any trauma is as relevant and debated today as it was in Freud's time. To clarify the complex issues at the heart of trauma transmission further, I will contrast two unique brief case studies. While both vignettes concern psychoanalysts impacted by the Holocaust trauma and both involve issues of trauma between a parent and child(ren), yet, as they are separated by more than half a century, they underline how professional attitude changes to trauma are influenced by their personal circumstances, in these two cases, prominent leaders within psychoanalysis.

I hope this approach might serve to highlight how psychoanalysis, the profession, has adapted, or failed to adapt, to the advances in trauma research over the last half century; to underscore the hegemony of trauma; and to provide the context for the sense of urgency we face to clarify the distinction between 'psychic' and 'real' trauma and its transmission. I am concerned that to ignore this challenge risks the credibility of psychoanalysis as a science of the mind still relevant in the twenty-first century.

At present, it seems that the proliferation of terms to describe the experience of trauma include, but are not limited to, 'relational trauma', 'attachment trauma', 'vicarious trauma', 'emotional trauma', 'developmental trauma', 'complex trauma' and the persistence of 'psychic equivalence' of trauma. The difficulty for clinicians and researchers is the added burden that these terms are sometimes used interchangeably. Thus the ambiguity attached to the term 'trauma' and its usage, past and present, impacts on both the credibility and status of the profession and the personal identity of the professionals. As therapists, we daily face the clinical challenge to choose between focusing on either 'psychic' or 'real' trauma with our patients. How we choose to respond to the moment-to-moment encounter clinically is problematic.

How we distinguish between our use of these two terms for trauma, on the one hand 'real' childhood 'developmental' and/or infantile 'relational' trauma, while on the other, to contrast both these real traumas with 'psychic trauma' and/or 'psychic equivalence' will, to a great degree, shape our understanding and response to the question of how trauma is passed on. Especially important within the question of transmission is the 'vicarious' trauma transmission that occurs daily during our therapy sessions – trauma transmission to-and-from patient and therapist.

Rather than trying to find immediate answers to these pressing concerns, Salberg, in her chapter, offers another possibility. Drawing upon the work of Robert Prince (2009) she argues that psychoanalysis itself is 'a survivor of the Holocaust'. She further elaborates utilizing the work of Aron and Starr, Davoine and Gaudillière, and Kuriloff,

> it often takes the passage of some time before processing [of trauma] can take place. Time was certainly needed for metabolizing the trauma of the Holocaust in order to be able to study it, and perhaps this further delayed a more generalized transgenerational transmission study of other historical traumas.
>
> (p. 82)

The concept that psychoanalysis itself is 'a survivor of the Holocaust' suggests that the responsibility for the delay in sorting out the definition and mechanisms of trauma transmission rests within the profession, with the psychoanalysts themselves. Just as other Holocaust survivors brought their particular survival instincts and attitudes – including the survival defense of dissociation – to bear their own trauma, so would have survivors who were psychoanalysts.

To explore this issue, we gain some critical insights from Hartman's (2014) recent reconstruction of Anna Freud's complicated mourning process in the context of the Holocaust. We glean how, as the inheritor of her father's legacy, Freudian psychoanalysis, she deployed the Freudian concept of trauma for her own self-understanding. According to Hartman, Anna Freud's self-analysis, including dreams, led to her self-definition that today would undoubtedly be defined as her double exposure to trauma (first, direct trauma, while at the same time, the recipient of transferred trauma from her survivor father), yet back then, the very idea that her father's Holocaust trauma was transmitted to her was not yet conceivable. It took another half a century to advance trauma studies to the point where Schore (2001) introduced the seminal concept of 'relational trauma', and mechanism to account for such family trauma transmission.

Hartman's (2014) review of this unique father–daughter relationship serves to illustrate several key points regarding the fate of Freud's construct of 'psychic trauma' in the post-Holocaust world of psychoanalysis. The unique transmission of psychoanalysis and its constructs from Sigmund Freud and his daughter Anna, at that time in her early forties, included the entwined texture of her traumatic attachment embracing the transmission of the very concept of 'trauma' itself. As father and daughter together left Vienna on 4 June 1938, the question whether Holocaust trauma transmission might have occurred between them at that time was an impossible question to formulate, as the atrocities of the Holocaust had yet to be fully witnessed. But could that question have been posed after the events of the Holocaust, after 1945?

In his article, Hartman affords a special, albeit brief section of two paragraphs to 'Trauma' (pp. 1203–1204). This brevity textually underlines the contrast between Anna Freud's otherwise original and prodigious output on a wide range of psychoanalytic topics and her apparent avoidance and/or reluctance to address the topic of trauma in her in-depth self-analysis. Hartman notes that Anna Freud's contribution to a symposium on trauma in 1964 centered on the

> definition of trauma that closely followed her father's notion of the breaching of the stimulus barrier and the inability of the ego to cope with stimuli from within or without. She sought to restrict the term to this experience rather than the broader concepts like cumulative trauma, strain trauma, retrospective trauma and other related broader concepts. She felt that the definition of trauma had been mistakenly broadened to include any circumstance that contributed to psychopathology. In Anna Freud's view, for something to be considered

traumatic the stimulus barrier had to be breached and the ego knocked out of commission however briefly. By this definition the youngest concentration camp survivors did not suffer trauma but rather severe developmental interference. Also by her definition, she could not be considered to have suffered trauma because her stimulus barrier was not breached and her ego functioning remained intact during her ordeal with the Nazis and when she was informed of her aunts' deaths.

(pp. 1203–1204)

While Hartman's reconstruction of this father–daughter loyalty with respect to psychoanalytic theorizing on trauma is a single case, an anecdote, it carries a profound message related to the issue we confront – namely the possible reasons and motivations for the delay by psychoanalysis and psychoanalysts to recognize the phenomenon of trauma transfer.

Alternatively, in our current zeitgeist see in Salberg's chapter how she introduces the metaphor, 'the texture of traumatic attachment', thus offering a framework and language to begin to unravel the complex pattern woven by the verbal threads of 'psychic' and 'real' trauma, and its relationship to 'traumatic attachment' as these relate to trauma transmission.

Fast-forward nearly half a century. Child survivor and distinguished professor of psychiatry and training and supervising psychoanalyst Henri Parens (2012) reflected on his struggles to come to terms with the impact of his Holocaust trauma on his wife and sons. Parens introduced his struggles in the context of contemporary neuroscience, using another term for trauma – traumatism. Parens offered an explanation for the apparent irreversibility of his traumatism due to '[I]ts inscription in the amygdala and forged pathways to the frontal cortex [which] I believe cannot be totally metabolized (i.e., totally suppressed and overridden by new neural pathways) by in-depth analytic working through' (pp. 97–98). Parens further adds,

Kandell's important findings and theorizing on synaptic formation and the possibility of overriding old neural pathways by new ones is limited – while I do believe that we should not abandon trying to do so until long-term analytic efforts seem to hit the brick wall of indelibility.

(p. 98)

I found Parens' metaphor the 'brick wall of indelibility' an echo of earlier metaphors like 'dead mother', 'abyss', 'black hole', 'empty circle' used in psychoanalytic narratives suggestive of the apparent limitation of reparation of trauma. More correctly, stated in the context of relational trauma, it amounts to, or at least is suggestive of, the closure of opportunities for further reparative moments that can, and does, take place in focused trauma informed therapy. Metaphors carry an inherent and attendant risk of reification. The 'brick wall of indelibility' may represent that fleeting moment of collision between the 'old' paradigm of psychic trauma and its transmission with the 'new' paradigm 'relational trauma' that offers an opening, letting in new possibilities beyond the 'brick wall'. I wondered whether Parens had 'real' or 'psychic' trauma in mind, as clearly his theorizing centered on the amygdala and neural synapses, it suggested a model of 'real' traumatic imprints.

Hopenwasser (2008) introduced 'dissociative attunement' as an exciting new dimension to the phenomenon of dissociation. In her chapter, she elaborates how 'Each of us brings into the therapeutic process memories that have fallen off the arrow of time … Hidden within this narrative history is an epigenetic transformation of our selves' (p. 60). Alluding to the reality of the 'very expression of our genes' it behooves us to refine our usage of the term 'trauma' as the future links may well be forged between that experience we term 'trauma' corresponding with its specific epigenetic switches.

Both Laub's and Bodenstab's chapters powerfully focus, from very different perspectives, on critical moments in excerpts from joint videos between next-of-kin. These chapters carried special significance for me as my own research of trauma transmission between my mother and I is based on close analysis of a split screen, split between her video testimony and the analysis of my moment-to-moment responses (Halasz 2012). Bodenstab microanalyzes two excerpts of a mother, Rosalie, and her daughter, Jolly, testimony that lasts less than four minutes. Yet painstakingly she captures there 'an almost iconic historical moment and, at the same time, mark a distinctive narrative turn' (p. 000). As her part of her research, Bodenstab reconstructs their moments of arrival at Auschwitz, on the ramp, at the selection. There she explores the central role of their relationship, also to highlight that contrast of the apparent clarity of vision of the researcher with the 'opacity' of the actual witness.

This theme is further explored, with additional self-analysis, in Laub's chapter.

Laub's pioneering work established in 1979 the first video archives of Holocaust survivor's testimonies, now at Yale University. His chapter confronts his own past through a unique and extraordinary act of multiple perspectives in self–other witnessing as he extends his earlier work on this essential subject (Laub, 1992). This time Laub returns after a period of 26 years, to witness the 'testimonial relationship' between his mother and himself. He describes this monumental task entailing

> multiple relational shifts here, as I take multiple positions: I am one of the interviewers; I am present as my mother's son; I am a co-survivor; I interject commentary during her testimony; and I am watching this video 26 years later, in a process of self-analysis.
>
> (p. 20)

There is no introductory comment that I can offer to do justice to this Olympian effort.

Lastly Salberg's chapter, as it dovetails past and present struggles to unravel the mysterious processes that underpin trauma transmission between the generations, highlights how past epochs have overcome their challenges, collisions between 'old' and 'new' paradigms. Her work, and the others in Part I, have led me to offer an interim conclusion: that as our current neuroscience culture transforms the paradigm within psychoanalysis, so this part applies these paradigm changes to our thinking about and understanding of the impact of massive trauma and intergenerational trauma transmission, if we wish to allow ourselves this opportunity. Today, the collisions we face are pithily summarized by Schore's (2012) critical observation, that the current paradigm shift in psychoanalysis is a 'shift from a focus on cognition to one of affect [that] also includes a shift in clinical work from solely a repression based theoretical foundation to recognition of the survival strategy of disassociation' (p. 17).

Throughout reading this part, I was wondering about our ethical mandate, to do no harm. How do we fulfill this requirement today? I believe that during this paradigm change it requires of us to re-analyze our own clinical practice, its theoretical and conceptual underpinnings and, if found wanting, modify our techniques where our patients' presentation includes massive trauma. I turn to Frances Tustin's (1994) brutally honest final publication, and, to paraphrase her sentiment, I gleaned from her wisdom that we should aim not to perpetuate the error of a narrow-minded and dogmatic adherence, even to time-honored wisdom, if that tends to be detrimental to our patients', and our own, welfare.

Acknowledgment

I thank Dr Vicki Gordon and Shraga Lewitan for helpful comments on an earlier version of this chapter. I also thank my mother, Alice Halasz, who pays special attention to review all my manuscripts, a process known as my 'Mum Test', which can be more rigorous than the usual editorial reviews.

References

Aron, L. & Starr, K. (2013). *A Psychotherapy for the People: Toward a Progressive Psychoanalysis.* London: Routledge.

Baradon, T. (ed.). (2010). *Relational Trauma in Infancy: Psychoanalytic, Attachment and Neuropsychological Contributions to Parent-Infant Psychotherapy* (e-Library). London: Taylor & Francis e-Library 2009.

Blass, R. B. & Carmeli, Z. (2007). The case against neuropsychoanalysis. *International Journal of Psychoanalysis*, 88, 19–40.

Davoine, F. & Gaudillière, J. M. (2004). *History Beyond Trauma: Whereof One Cannot Speak, Thereof One Cannot Stay Silent.* New York: Other Press.

Halasz, G. (2012). Psychological witnessing of my mother's Holocaust testimony. In: Goodman, N. R., Meyers, M. B. (Eds), *The Power of Witnessing: Reflections, Reverberations, and Traces of the Holocaust. Trauma, Psychoanalysis, and the Living Mind* (pp. 145–157). New York: Routledge.

Hartman, J. J. (2014). Anna Freud and the Holocaust: mourning and survivor guilt. *International Journal of Psychoanalysis*, 95, 1183–1210.

Hopenwasser, K. (2008). Being in rhythm: dissociative attunement in therapeutic process. *Journal of Trauma and Dissociation*, 9, 349–367.

Kuriloff, E. (2010). The Holocaust and psychoanalytic theory and praxis. *Contemporary Psychoanalysis*, 46, 395–422.

Laplanche, J. & Pontalis, J.-B. (1983). *The Language of Psycho-Analysis.* London: Hogarth Press.

Laub, D. (1992). Bearing witness, or the vicissitudes of listening. In Felman, D., Laub, S. (Eds), *Testimony: Crisis of Witnessing in Literature, Psychoanalysis, and History* (pp. 57–74). New York: Routledge.

Parens, H. (2012). A Holocaust survivor's bearing witness. In Goodman, N. R., Meyers, M. B. (Eds), *Power of Witnessing: Reflections, Reverberations, and Traces of the Holocaust. Trauma, Psychoanalysis, and the Living Mind* (pp. 87–103). New York: Routledge.

Prince, R. (2009). Psychoanalysis traumatized: the legacy of the Holocaust. *American Journal of Psychoanalysis*, 69, 179–194.

Salberg, J. (2015). The Texture of Traumatic Attachment: Presence and Ghostly Absence in Transgenerational Transmission. *Psychoanalytic Quarterly*, Volume LXXXIV, Number 1: 21–46.

Schore, A. N. (2001). The effects of relational trauma on right brain development, affect regulation, and infant mental health. *Infant Mental Health Journal*, 22, 201–269.

Schore, A. N. (2012). *The Science of the Art of Psychotherapy*. New York: W.W. Norton.

Tustin, F. (1994). The perpetuation of an error. *Journal of Child Psychotherapy*, 20, 3–23.

Chapter 1

Listening to My Mother's Testimony

Dori Laub

Testimony and Psychoanalysis – Theoretical Considerations

Testimony is a meeting place for the mutual witnessing and repair of trauma induced fragmented memories and psychic disruption. The testimonial intervention is responsive to and addresses what has been left deeply wounded, that which has not found an opportunity to heal, in the trauma survivor. A psychoanalytic understanding of the interviewer and interviewee relationship during the testimonial intervention can not only vastly contribute to our understanding of the traumatic damage, but also informs us as to the healing processes that need to be set in motion to repair it.

The uniqueness of the testimonial intervention lies in the fact there is always an event, an experience, even if it covers a lifetime, that is known to be there, even if it had hitherto not been consciously formulated. It is thus information that has yet to be recorded, brought to an addressee, to a party interested in receiving it. Testimony is therefore, a transmittal of information and there is an internal unrelenting pressure to convey as well as an external readiness and eagerness to receive it.

When such transmittal has been accomplished, the survivor no longer is or feels alone with the inexpressible extreme experience. She is less helplessly prey to its devastating impact. The internal cauldron of sensations and affects has been put into the frame of a sequential narrative. They are now remembered, transmitted and can also be forgotten. Such narrative is however never complete and highly charged blank spots of the inexpressible (almost unimaginable) experience persist, exerting their magnetic power on the survivor, who feels compelled to endlessly revisit them while at the same time she constantly flees their proximity.

Reprinted with Kind Permission:
Laub, D. (2015). Listening to My Mother's Testimony. *Contemporary Psychoanalysis*, 51 (2): 195–215.

It is these intense affect laden voids of memory, which to begin with, can obliterate the traumatic experience in its entirety, that constitute the power source that drives testimony and exerts the pressure for its deliverance. This holds true for a broad range of experiences of extreme trauma. In more recent observations, cancer survivors, when feeling safe in the company of other survivors, are also driven to "tell their story" of their encounters with death. A group of chronically hospitalized "psychotic" Holocaust survivors, interviewed in Israel in recent years, experienced the same internal pressure to bear witness. Unfortunately their capacity to symbolize, free associate, reflect and verbalize has been so profoundly damaged by the chronicity of their condition (lasting for decades), their social isolation and their somatic treatments (insulin shock, ECT, and psychotropic medication), that all they were able to create was a constricted, static and fragmented narrative.

The goal of traditional psychoanalysis, on the other hand, is to allow for the emergence of the unconscious through the method of free association and the elucidation of the transference experience. There is no particular force, no inner compulsion that drives it, no story that reaches for words. It is rather a surrender to the wanderings of the mind, while feeling protected by the analyst's nonjudgemental presence and neutrality. It has a rhythm set by the frequency of the sessions and it lacks an endpoint in time. Dreams, parapraxes and transference experiences and enactments, and last but not least, remembrances, provide the scaffolding along which the analytic narrative unfolds. Although there is no explicit addressee in traditional analysis, the analyst's emotional presence implicitly fulfills that function, thus becoming the equivalent of the testimonial "thou".

Psychoanalytic literature is indeed replete with reference to the internal good object, usually highlighting the infant's relationship with the mother. Beginning with Freud's (1930) concept of the oceanic feeling – being one with the universe – that arises from the oneness with the mother, and continuing with Margaret Mahler's (1963) developmental phase of symbiosis, Winnicott's (1953) "transitional space", Henry Parens' (1970) "inner sustainment", Mahler's (1975) "object constancy", and Kohut's (1971) "self object" – all the above deal with processes that are essential for internal representation and symbolization to occur. The latter constitutes core components of the testimonial intervention.

Within the spectrum of psychoanalytically informed therapeutic interventions, the testimonial process possesses three unique elements: the internal pressure to transmit and tell, the real story that is "there", and the yearning for and the presence of a listener who receives it.

On closer scrutiny these three elements do not place testimony in a category that is separate from psychoanalysis. Both processes – testimony and psychoanalysis are in essence dialogic. The analysand does not speak to a void, even if he speaks to himself. It is his own internal good object, projected onto the analyst that he addresses in such case. In both processes, the narrative deepens and branches out, taking turns that may come as a surprise to the narrator. Freud's (1933) dictum "where id was, there the ego shall be" applies to both, although in the lengthier psychoanalysis this can go much further than in the single session testimony (p. 30). Furthermore, a process is set in motion in both, which can continue on its own, far beyond the time frame of the psychoanalytic or the testimonial event. This process includes, but is not limited to, symbolization, self reflection and remembering. While it is not a particular event that serves as an organizing principle like in testimony, psychoanalysis too leads to the recovery of memories that may emerge as organizing principles and thus become building blocks of the psychoanalytic narrative. What may remain, the basic difference between testimony and traditional psychoanalysis, may be limited to the inner intense pressure to transmit and the experience of transmittal itself, which are at the center of the testimonial intervention. The latter can, therefore, be seen as a piece of psychoanalytic work that is limited in scope and that does not include parapraxes, transference or dream work.

The testimonial momentum may be also operative, in traditional psychoanalysis, when traumatic experience is involved. At such a juncture it becomes the process that fuels the therapeutic action and provides the impetus for clinical movement and flow. It would be methodologically very difficult to isolate and study it in the context of such traditional psychoanalyses; therefore, the nontraditional modality of the testimonial intervention is needed in order to provide the most suitable research setting that can capture the testimonial momentum for its in depth investigation.

In this paper, I will trace the testimonial relationship as it appears in my mother's testimony. This tracing follows multiple relational shifts here, as I take multiple positions: I am one of the interviewers; I am present as my mother's son; I am a co-survivor; I interject commentary during her testimony; and I am watching this video 26 years later, in a process of self-analysis.

My Mother's Testimony

As I listen to my mother's testimony, I am struck by the first words she utters "This hurts so much" (das tut so weh). I feel very shaken. I can feel her pain shooting through me. This is a glimpse, a flash back of how she experiences herself, of how she feels, looking back on her life. It is the moment she is most open with herself and with me. Several times during the testimony, when I urge her to describe the pictures she sees on the screen of her memory – she simply refuses, and proceeds to talk about events as facts "I do not want to, I never think about this ... It is indescribable.... Jews from all over the city, trying to reach the Ghetto as ordered that very day, before 6 p.m. – the curfew time. They are carrying their belongings, their bedding wrapped around their neck. Some not making it, remain lying in the street."

She quickly reined in her pain and began discussing with me the mechanics of the interviews: where should she look when she was talking, should she take off her glasses, would she have an opportunity to correct what she had said. She seemed very anxious, unsure of herself, eager to be doing the right thing and uncertain she would be capable of achieving that goal. She indeed began talking in a very scripted, restrained manner, but loosened up considerably, when invited to speak about her "Sunny" childhood memories in the little village of Banilla (now in the Ukraine), where she was born. She had the biggest red apple and the nicest dress for the Jewish Holiday Simchat Torah. Her parents' home was the center of intellectual, Jewish-Zionist life in town, and visitors would join the evening meal for passionate debates on relevant topics. There was a special room with a Sefer Torah, where on Shabbat and on holidays, services were regularly held. She always attended the prayers. She had this very exceptional grandmother who was an expert in everything, from German literature to gardening. One cannot help but be impressed by the self-awareness and intense participation of the little girl in the life she lived. She was on par with the grown-ups, yet cherished so much the privileged child position.

On viewing the tape I wonder whether my mother needed to remember her early childhood as so sunny because of what followed. At age 6, the whole family including grandmother, who was in her eighties, had to flee the advancing Russian troops, who had brutalized the village during an earlier occupation. It was a year into WWI. The whole family wandered on foot through Eastern and Central Europe until they reached the Sudetenland in Czechoslovakia (that had large Jewish graveyards but only few living Jews because of earlier pogroms), where they settled for nearly two years. When they returned to Banilla, they found that their home had been destroyed.

My mother gave her testimony to the Fortunoff Video Archive on November 8, 1986. Larry Langer and I became her interviewers because she wanted to speak in German. I first viewed her testimony in November 2012. For this presentation I have not only revisited my mother's story of survival, which is also my own, but I have also revisited my own work as an interviewer of Holocaust survivors and as a psychoanalyst.

The following event which she describes in her testimony, and which I remember in detail, illustrates my mother's unique ability to fully grasp the danger inherent in a particular situation, and make a split second decision that saved our lives.

It was the day on which our camp, the "Cariera de Piatra," was to be liquidated. German SS arrived in trucks in order to transport the nearly 2,000 inmates across the river Bug (which was several hundred yards away) to the German occupied portion of the Ukraine, where Einsatzgruppe (Death Squad) "D" operated, and where they faced certain death. During the preceding week, an attorney by the name of Stoller collected money in order to bribe the Romanian commandant. A list was compiled of people, which the latter would claim were necessary for the upkeep of the camp, and were therefore to be protected from being taken by the Germans. After a nearly sleepless night, all the camp inmates were arranged at dawn in groups of 30 on the big central square. My father was the leader of such a group. Attorney Stoller and his family, who belonged to our group, were standing nearby, and my mother was watching closely what he was doing. Suddenly he picked up his luggage, starting to move away with his family. My mother took me by my hand and did the same, summoning my father to join. Stoller challenged her, insisting that only he had been called, to which she responded that she had been called too. My father reluctantly joined us, as he felt he could not abandon the group he was in charge of. After walking for several hundred yards, with Romanian and German soldiers not stopping us, we arrived at a wooden hut, where the Jews that "were on the list," were hiding. The door was locked from inside and my mother banged on it. According to her testimony she was asked if she was on the list, and when she responded in the affirmative, she was allowed in. I remember the hut being packed with people, standing very quietly. We could hear a lot of commotion outside – cars driving, people screaming. Hours passed. Suddenly we heard Germans shout "Jews out!" My father started to say goodbye to my mother, embraced her, and gave her his wristwatch. Somehow the commandant was notified, appeared on the scene, and insisted that these were "his Jews." The Germans relented and left. More hours passed. As the evening set in, things quieted down outside. The door was opened and we were allowed to leave and to return to our barracks. The place was completely deserted and it was a clear night. We could see the stars in the sky and hear the echoes of our footsteps. I turned to my father and asked him how deep the sky was. He understood my question which really was how far away was God. His answer to me was: "Roosevelt and Churchill are not going to let this happen."

Nothing else needed to be said.

Being in the Lead

As long as my mother's testimony related events that preceded my own conscious memories, I could listen to it as if it were any other testimony of a Holocaust survivor. The moment she started talking of events of which I had my own clear and conscious memories, my listening changed. These were now like composite memories I was hearing, constructed from her memories and from my own. I could no longer *imagine* what I heard because I had been there myself. My own memories felt to me to be more immediate and more specific and I often filled in the "gaps" in her testimony.

There was something very reassuring for me in experiencing the convergence of our testimonies, hers and mine. I was not alone with my memories. But in fact I had never been alone with my memories. I experienced my mother as always present with me. As always, she was in charge and in the lead and things were going to turn out well, as she had promised.

She had assumed that role shortly after WWII started. Both her parents were sick, her child was little and her husband was at risk, because men were more easily targeted. All the family wealth had been stripped away by the Soviets, who had briefly occupied Czernowitz, the town we lived in in 1940. They slated both her father and husband for deportation to

Siberia. After the Romanian and German forces reoccupied the city in 1941, she faced a trial in a military tribunal for leaving the Ghetto without permission, which carried a mandatory death sentence. She knocked on every door and was able to procure German witnesses, who lied on her behalf, and she was acquitted. She told no one in the family about it.

She found herself to be in the lead in the daily struggle for survival, and felt that she had to do that alone and on her own. She could not share her terror, her worries, her unrelenting search for nearly impossible solutions to life threatening situations, with other family members. She had to appear steadfast and self-assured so as to keep their spirit up, to keep them from surrendering to fate, even when she felt the ground under her feet was giving away.

Moreover, the rules of engagement had drastically changed. Benevolence, tolerance and solidarity were all but gone. One could no longer rely on having the status and the rights of a citizen, a refugee or even a human being, whose life was guaranteed. No promises and no agreements were being kept. The perpetrator could carry out at will acts of reckless violence and of brutality that had no limit. Killings, beatings and robbings were the order of the day. Merciless, whimsical and ever-changing edicts were as random as were bullets. The Ukrainian bystanders, yesterday's neighbor, partook in the atrocities. And the fellow Jewish victims ruthlessly competed for the scarce chances of survival. My mother had to learn and master the unprecedented new landscape, and often had to do so in a split second, incessantly, and while on the run. She had to constantly be on the alert and, forcefully suppress her yearnings to return to normalcy, to "the way things were." She could do so as long as my father was by her side. "It was war and the war will be over one day." All she had to ensure was surviving the war.

When my father was no longer by her side, she shriveled inside. She continued to ferociously protect her child, but no longer had hope. Deep down she realized that for her, "normalcy" will never be there again. She stopped hoping for the return of the life she once had, even though upon her return to her hometown, after the war ended, she found to her delight, that both her parents were alive. What took the place of the return to normalcy, was her yearning to be again the child she remembered. It was as though the regressive pull, that had to be so tightly suppressed during the fight for survival, could be allowed back into consciousness, now that the war was over. Needless to say, this was expressed as a feeling and never enacted. As her son I found it difficult to empathically respond to this wish. It either threatened my position as the child in the dyad, or I found it unsafe and premature, because both as a survivor myself and as her child, I was far from certain that the war had indeed ended.

It was about a year after we returned from the camps that my mother took ill and was bedridden for over six months. Many doctors examined her and there were multiple diagnoses. Some thought it was her heart and others called it a form of rheumatism. In retrospect, I think it was a depression with many somatizations. She had at least one bout of anger, for no apparent reason, during which she screamed at me and beat me. After years of self restraint, she finally gave in to the suppressed, pent-up rage for what was done to her and to the pain for the losses she had suffered.

I could not forgive her for that. For about 10 years, until my maternal grandmother died in 1956, I did not disclose to my mother. After my grandmother died, I realized that it was only she and I now, and we were both alone. I made my peace with her and told her about my long silence, without giving a reason for it.

Now as I watch the testimony unfolding, I realize the centrality of my position in my mother's life, in her survival, and in her memory. Her story is frequently interspersed with dialogues and arguments she had with her little boy. Our relationship was the context through which *she remembered and narrated her story of the camp.* I more and more came to realize that this is a testimony of a mother about her child, in the presence of her child, a survivor himself, who at the same time is also the interviewer; the receiver of the testimony.

Shifting Time Frames of Memory

As her testimony moves through different periods of time, mutual remembrance grows and shifts.

There is the portion of her life she lives, in which I am not included. A lot happened in her life before I was born; her own childhood years in the village of Banilla; the family flight and exile during WWI; the return home and the move to the city of Czernowitz; accumulating wealth and marrying my father. I know from her about the good life my family was living but also about the clouds of the impending war that were gathering on the horizon.

Then there are the years of anti-Semitic persecution preceding the deportation. I have quite a few memories of that time but her story and my story are still quite separate. I vaguely remember the Soviet occupation and the terror that reigned in our home. I have no memories of the Ghetto experience, which for my mother seems to have been her first encounter with the "extreme." Curiously, many of my own memories, separate from my mother's, come from the time we spent in the camps. Examples of such memories are: My sitting with a little girl on the banks of the river Bug, arguing whether one could or could not eat grass, and my watching through a large window Romanian and German troops advancing to the front and from a particular day onwards, moving in the opposite direction, as their retreat began. I remember occasional fights she had with my father, once even throwing a boot at him, to get him to step out of line, do what she felt was needed to save our lives.

But the moment we were seized to be deported, it becomes more a joint story. Her testimony keeps unfolding through her frequently resorting to describing interactions with me and through talking about me. Examples of such "joint stories" will be given later in this essay.

All of the above created multiple perspectives that exist side by side with my mother's testimonial narrative of and about her five year old son. These perspectives existed in the original process of testimony, as I moved through the positions of interviewer and participant during the videotaping. Now, as I watch this anew, these perspectives are complicated by new layers of time and development in my own life. What follows is a list of these perspectives. In describing them I shall refer to myself in third person. So as to preserve my role as witness and observer of the testimony and of myself.

1   *The boy of whom the mother talks*, sometimes telling of an event through her dialogue with him. He is depicted as precociously aware of the grim reality of the unfolding events. He knows that the uniformed men came to take them to the camps and insists on joining his parents and not remain with his maternal grandparents at home; he knows of the compulsory yellow star and insists on wearing it, although as a child he is exempt; he refuses conversion to Christianity for the whole family – all of the above because he is a proud Jew.

    She also speaks of the child before the persecution started. Whatever he had, it was only the best. His toys were the most sophisticated ones, like electric trains. His clothes were imports from the United Kingdom. And what she didn't mention in her testimony was that he had a full-time governess, an Arian for that matter. It was a German woman, Bertha Stark, who raised him from age 1 to age 3, at which point she was involuntarily repatriated to Germany. She spoke of his early childhood with the same glow, perhaps glitter, that she spoke of her own. This "glow" most likely became the central building block of the resilience she was able to mobilize, during the hardships of our deportation.

2   *The adult who has his own very explicit and vivid memories of the events he has lived through,* of which his mother speaks. He often remembers details she does not, and has memories of other events, his mother does not mention. At times he does not, or only vaguely remembers, events that his mother expands on. The memories that are his own include his incessant desire to run away from his parent to better able to hide because he was so little.

3   *The interviewer of the testimony who listens to both his mother's memories and his own* and uses the latter to bring her back to the narrative thread she frequently loses, to offer further details to what she tells, and to draw her attention back to events she has omitted. He thus functions as an orienting, guiding map as well as a propelling force, to his mother's narrative. The interviewer who listens to himself – to the cognitive and affective responses he had as he experienced the events, as they came to be memories that remained vivid and intense after the decades, and as he listens to them in his mother's testimony. What he hears through these three complimentary channels informs how he conducts the interview, how he proceeds witnessing the unfolding testimony of his mother.

4   *The psychoanalyst who has reflected on the place his mother filled and on the role she played in his becoming who he was, as a child, as an adolescent, and as a grown up,* who built a family of his own and embarked on a professional career. With all this in mind, he picks up multiple cues from his mother and from himself, during the interview and while viewing it again, allows such cues to reverberate in him, until they fall into place and are integrated into a fresh coherent insight of all the information he has absorbed.

5   *On viewing the testimony multiple times, the interviewer listens both to what the witness, his mother, tells, and to how he responds to it now.*

He pays close attention to his first responses and to his responses on subsequent viewings. He reflects on his mother's life and on her death (1994), and on his own life with her, as they both resonate with his responses listening to her testimony. A reflective space is created and maintained, in which these various perspectives can coalesce, can complement each other, and can eventually become a multifaceted "whole."

The Protected Child Inside

In my mother's testimony it is as though physical reality matters little, as long as human ties are preserved. Bitter cold, severe hunger, typhus and other life-threatening illnesses, as well as bullets that can hit at any moment, matter little, as long as the child has the protective space provided by his own parents. When this occurs, there is even the possibility of optimism and laughter.

I think this protected space, that she carried within herself, was the source of her resilience, initiative and the immense courage she displayed time and again, during the two years we spent in the camps. She knew very well what the reality was. In her testimony she states that less than 170 people survived from the 6,000 that comprised the three transports that had been sent to the camps from Czernowitz on June 7, 14, and 28, 1942. But her suffering does not come through in her testimony. Her primary and most coveted wish was to protect her child from experiencing the harsh reality they all lived in. She carried her "sunny" childhood inside herself. It was perhaps her most cherished possession, made into an impenetrable enclosure, that was wrapped around her son. She spared no effort to make this safety zone, his own. She literally force-fed him, when she herself remained hungry. He was the apple of her eye, and she wanted to preserve his carefree childhood world, modeled on the memories of her own childhood, at all cost. She put everything she had into her only child, trying not only to provide for him, but also to create for him the opportunities to explore and find pleasure in life. Years later, when he was a university student, she sent him on trips throughout Europe, when she herself was uncertain, where the next meal would come from.

Interestingly, she succeeded in her endeavor to instill this sense of safety in me. When I wanted and even tried to run away from my parents,

I did not doubt for a moment that I will be able to successfully hide, survive the war, and live a life that would be as beautiful as the life they had lived before. An example of this unconditional protectiveness follows.

"So we climbed into a cattle car, some people had big packages, some small ones. We had the least because we had no time to pack. It was terribly crowded. There was no place to sit or to stand. My child immediately stated – "Where is my little bed, where will I sleep?" So I told him in order to calm him. I saw that there were very many intellectuals. I thought a physician would be considerate. So he lay down on my child. Dr., Dr. let me. The child cannot breathe. There was no place available. They pushed in as many as they could. My child started to cry – where will I sleep, where is my little bed? I said Dori, I'll buy you another bed. He said but you have no money. Muti, where will you take money to buy me a bed? So I could not calm him even with this. He cried. We continued our journey.

DR. LAUB: Do you remember what you answered me?
CLARA LAUB: What I answered you: That shall buy you another little bed.
DR. LAUB: How?
CLARA LAUB: I'll sell something.
DR. LAUB: That you have two coats and you'll sell one coat and buy me a bed.
CLARA LAUB: Yes, I answered after he said that I do not have money to buy him a bed [I said] I have two coats and I shall sell one and buy him a bed."

Hers was a promise that, of course by far exceeded the promise for a place to sleep, which indeed she kept. In the camp I always slept between my mother and my father, insulated from the bitter cold, physical discomfort, and above all from the never-ending terror that prevailed. My plea for the little brass bed was indeed a plea for safety and her promise to me was one of safety and I understood it, and always remembered it as such. This brief exchange is paradigmatic of her life during the two years we spent in the camps. Curiously during her testimony, the situation was reversed: It was I who promised her safety in her journey back into her traumatic memories.

Dealing With Terror

When it comes to the terror of everyday life, facing death at every turn, my mother becomes either matter of fact, treating experiences as mere fact, speaking without affect in a blunted, constricted almost robotic manner, or simply refuses to think or speak of events. Little horror comes through as she speaks of people being shot on her left and on her right; of having to be completely quiet, for 2–3 days in a sealed cattle car, standing in the train station Lipcani, Bassarabia, on her way to the camps, lest the German soldiers milling around, would discover that the cargo of those wagons were Jews, and shoot them on the spot; or when she escapes the deportation of the camp inmates to the German occupied Ukraine, to their certain death. The same is true for many other moments, when she summoned the courage to decisively act.

The terror of the situations she describes, facing death every day, comes through only indirectly, through losing the thread of her thought or forgetting to speak about terrifying events I know about and had to direct her to. I am in the unique position of knowing many of the events because I have lived through them myself, and because my own internal witnessing – created and maintained vivid and detailed memories of those events. As her interviewer I could thereby offer a safe, reliable, holding environment for the traumatically broken narrative my mother provided. Sometimes I could offer details to statements she made, as illustrated in the earlier shown video excerpt about the boy who was crying for his little brass bed.

What I experienced in my earlier viewings as blunted affect, or "keeping her distance," in my mother's testimonial discourse, and later on wondered about as dissociative elements, came to look on further introspection as something much more profound. My mother was less there – both to her story and to herself, while describing very critical moments – such as facing a military trial for leaving the ghetto, on finding the door to the hut where inmates were hiding while the rest of the camp was being transferred across the River Bug, to be locked from inside – she was partially absent in her affect. The most poignant term for this state, I find in Giorgio Agamben's notion of the "lacunae," which are at the core of every attempt at telling the Holocaust experience. Her vitality, her color, her strength had been drained from her narrative. I was surprised at my remembering those moments as the clearest. I most likely complemented the affective lacunae in her experience and in her memory, through my experiencing, through my memories and through my imagination. In her testimony I literally brought her back to those moments. I knew what she had left out and occasionally verbalized it. The excerpt that follows exemplifies such a situation. I literally had to remind her to talk of the episode that follows:

Tape II 37:33–39.50

"We went, all three of us, and the officer already had the money and could not get rid of us. Where should he take us? He did not have where. So he had started shooting people. This one does not walk in an orderly way, here there was loud talking. Here, there was too much. I know, he always he looked for something, to shoot people. All of a sudden he aimed his rifle, I did not know – did he aim at my son or at my husband? It was aimed at us but not at me personally. I was afraid ... And there were 3–4 soldiers who guarded us – As he was aiming the weapon to shoot again, I jumped [at it]. I did not not think for a moment what I was doing, but I jumped at the gun, so that he should shoot me and not my husband or my child. He was perplexed and stopped. This had not happened to him before that Jews revolted. They have to go like sheep. And as I jumped at him, I said to him in Romanian, "Sir it is war now, you too have family and you are not certain if you will see your family again. You can have more mercy with these unfortunate people." He grasped it very well. The whole thing lasted perhaps a minute, and I did not think ahead of time what I was doing, what I was saying. Instead of shooting me he was so confused and confounded. He was afraid the others will revolt too and he will be killed – that he took out a leather whip and started hitting me on my head. I felt the first blow, the others not anymore.

I broke down and was lying for weeks, it probably was meningitis – with fever and unconscious, but my husband was still alive, so he still could hand me something."

I have no memory of what followed her being beaten unconscious. I was unable to imagine and remember that my mother was gone, and that I was left alone, without her protection. In this, as well as in other episodes, I did, however, remember details that markedly varied from the ones she related in her testimony. I knew that the gun was not pointed at me but only at my father. My father and I were not even standing close by together. I knew that the woman behind the locked door did not politely ask my mother whether we were on the list, and when my mother answered in the affirmative, opened the door. I remembered my mother banging on the door and threatening that if they did not open the door, she would turn all the occupants of the hut, over to the Germans. Is it possible that I sensed that at such moments she had reached the limits of her endurance and therefore I took over the function of observing and judging events so as to be able to act, that I created my own stable boundaries when I sensed that the protective space she continuously offered, was wearing thin?

I find this to be a par excellence example for the *intergenerational transmission of trauma, in the making*. I knew exactly how great the terror that lurked behind the courageous behavior was, because I had been there myself. I had learned from her the strategy that worked: to observe in detail, to reflect and be able to act. I employed it myself at moments I felt she could no longer handle it. That was how my memories of such moments came to be so precocious, vivid and detailed. Yet I was always absolutely certain that she would come back. Alone and by myself, I could not carry this on. She would always be there and guarantee life, guarantee the future.

I wondered by the same token whether it *was I*, who had become the repository of the feelings of terror my mother was able to refuse, so as to continue being able to act. Let me quote from a semi-autobiographical essay I recently published, to further illustrate this point.

"When I review the pages that I have just written, what stands out glaringly to me is what I have left out. A pervasive experience, I omitted from what I previously wrote, was an almost continuous sense of dread. My days in the camp were times of sheer terror. I knew quite accurately what was happening. My so-called composure was both real and a façade – a thin exterior veil over an inner life flooded by dread. There were moments when it was obvious that something was imminent, that something new was going to happen. I could envision the gray uniformed soldiers and their helmets. My vision was mostly of their legs, strutting by, raised high up with their knees unbent, marching. This is probably what I saw as a child; my gaze was focused on their shiny boots. When I looked up, I saw baby faces topped by steel helmets. I can remember their heavy belts, their shiny helmets tightly fitted on their heads, and their rifles loosely hanging on their shoulders. These soldiers were going to come and do something to us, with the bayonets stuck on top of their rifles. I did not allow myself to feel any further. I could feel an overwhelming sense of terror piercing through my body, almost paralyzing me. I can almost feel it now when I merely think about it. It travels to my fingertips and is accompanied by a weird sense of numbness. I can hardly move. Some sounds are droning in my ears. I am almost outside myself. I am nauseated and start to retch. I may have screamed while retching. I was terrified that they were coming."

On Countertransference Analysis

While repeatedly viewing my mother's testimony, I found that examining my own evolving responses to it, to be invaluable in understanding certain life-long traits in myself, traits that reflected my responses to the manifest and to the latent deeper meanings her testimonial statements contained. It is through this approach, I believe, that the analysis of the countertransference transcends the intergenerational transmission of trauma – through providing a scaffold whereby the complex intrapersonal and interpersonal dynamics that occur in such transmission, can be more fully explicated and understood in depth.

Examining my own responses to my mother's testimony, I noticed remarks she made, which triggered feelings of resentment in me. This was particularly so when she spoke of the biggest disappointment of her life, which was – how vicious people (and by that she meant fellow Jews) could be towards each other. She felt betrayed by her former friends, who turned their back on her, when she tried to tell them of her sufferings in the camps. I also felt resentment when she spoke of still wanting to be the child she once was. It was difficult for me to hear her plea for being cared for and for being parented. I was angered by her presenting herself as the victim. To me she had always been the lioness-mother and I did not want to release her from that position; that is to lose her. Moreover, I refused to offer the mothering she pleaded for, that is, to make it a two-way street between the two of us, to exchange places with her. All my adult life, I repeatedly watched her getting hurt, getting turned down by friends and relatives, who refused to reciprocate her offers to share. I always tried to alert her, to warn her, to be more discriminating as to whom she engaged with. I always tried to protect her from pain and sometimes even fought her battles. Yet I always hated doing that, resented being invited to be her parent. I had no difficulties doing that very same thing for others – to make it the core of my identity as a healer. As an analyst, I could accompany my patients into the darkest, most terrifying places. I could be totally present and regulate their pace, so that they could continue moving, not fall or break apart. With my mother, I refused to engage her pain. Did she not know better, was she not the extraordinarily courageous and fearless woman, who banged on the locked door and leaped on the gun that was aimed at my father?

I remember that later in life I felt so abandoned and so enraged by her readiness to give in to her pain. I felt it to be such a betrayal, and I wanted to have nothing to do with it.

I realized that examining my countertransference feelings after my earlier viewings, helped me listen better on subsequent viewings. I therefore decided to resume scanning comments she made, that irritated me. I found myself bristling at her repeatedly expressing her belief that events hit her harder, wounded her more deeply, because she was so completely unprepared for them. She had been raised as the most special, beloved and indulged child and daughter, by her protective parents and grandparents. She had led the most sheltered life – therefore the abyss she fell into, was so much steeper. Was she not a refugee child during WWI, between ages 6 and 8? Did she not lose an older sister to diphtheria during that exile? Did she not find a home that had been destroyed, when she returned to Benilla? Was that presumed innocence and naiveté the very reason for exposing herself to being repeatedly hurt throughout her life? I found her claim to shelteredness to be the breeding ground for the ultimate big disappointment later in her life. For me it also detracted from the truthfulness and the authenticity of the horror she lived through. I felt it to be a self-indulgent privatization of her pain.

I realized that indeed, with the onset of the war, and particularly with the deportation to the camps, there was a pervasive drop in status in my mother's life. Her whole world came crushing down. She plummeted from being a wealthy, sheltered wife and daughter, whose major task was to be beautiful, elegant, sociable and entertaining, to a woman (and eventually a widow) who was no longer wealthy, and had no means to support herself and her family. She had no one to lean on except for her husband who believed the world could be safeguarded by hard work and following orders. She was encumbered by two ailing parents she had to take care of and by a five year old boy for whom she struggled to bring normalcy back. I realized all that, but I felt that that alone, did not warrant her surrender to her pain. This was particularly so, because she had already demonstrated how ferociously she could fight back.

Further Reflections on Countertransference Analysis

I am trying to continue writing about my mother's testimony, and find myself staring at a blank space, unable to come up with a new thought. Feelings of boredom alternate with a sensation that I am facing a solid concrete wall. Is there anything more, anything new that I have to say? Does not a vast literature already exist, on the transgenerational transmission of trauma? What if anything can I add to it? Yet I feel that something is in abeyance, waiting, wrapped in terror. What I am facing when I try to move, is a solid impenetrable barrier; I do not possess the strength to inch myself forward.

Then it strikes me, as if I have peeped behind the curtains. I had just re-read something I had written about testimony more than ten years ago – about the testimonial "camaraderie," that allows for the shared realization that the lost ones are not coming back; the realization that what life is all about is precisely to live with an unfulfilled promise, an unfulfilled hope. *No context exists that demonstrates* this *more powerfully than surviving the Holocaust*. I feel that my mother's life is the very testimony to exactly that. I understand now her opening comment "This hurts so much." A friend, herself a child of survivors and a trauma researcher, who had met my mother, calls at this moment and I pass this idea by her. She is completely on the same page. The damage my mother suffered and lived through had never been repaired. She did not find a soul mate with whom she could rebuild her life. She did not remarry, have more children, and reinvent her life. The losses she sustained remained losses, to the very end. She learned, to value close familial ties and therefore nurtured both her parents, until they died. She put everything she had into me, her only child. When her financial situation stabilized and her son married and had children, she still did not have a home, a family. He left for a distant continent, taking her first grandchild which she so doted on, away from her. The grandchildren she had did not compensate for her losses. She had a feather stuffed quilt sown for him, so that he would keep warm in the cold wintry nights.

I knew of her anguish and did whatever I could to lessen it. I was cognizant of her pain, of her unending mourning for her own blissful childhood, for the time in her life when she still had a close companion – my father. No deprivation was too much, no effort seemed too hard for her, at that time. I realized that nothing I could do could reverse the destruction – make her life whole again. I realized that *the Holocaust is a wound that does not heal*. I had to face my own limitations, my own failure to fulfill the grandiose expectations I had, to be able to heal her pain. The best I could do was to face together with her the destruction, which allowed for no genuine hope, for no light at the end of the tunnel. Her unalleviated pain, however, placed a big burden on me, which I often resented.

In the last video excerpt I am going to show, I challenge the illusory, frozen imbalance between her experience and mine – her having lost everything and my having retained my wholesomeness, re-found what I cared for most. Such imbalance could potentially undermine my ability to witness her testimony.

Tape III, 06:32–07:59

I came into our home. Actually I should have been happy because I came back from the camp, but there was such poverty ... that – no curtains, no rugs, nothing, so poor, so dry. My son ran first. He remembered that he had special closet where his toys were. The first thing he did was run to his closet. It was true, my parents did not sell anything of his things. He had electrical trains. He already had at that time, the toys you see today. This technology. Everything was in his place and he was so joyful. My father approached him very quietly, so that I should not hear – "Dori have you seen a louse? Do you remember?" He said: What is that OPA, what is that? But I really kept him clean.

DORI LAUB: Yes, but I remember the toy closet, it was a grey bluish closet. I think, I opened the door and there were hardly any toys.
CLARA LAUB: There were enough. May be not all [the toys were there]
DORI LAUB: The closet looked to me to be empty.
CLARA LAUB: Then you are right.
LARRY LANGER: You are saying empty and your mother says full
DORI LAUB: There were a few toys
LARRY LANGER: Not all

This excerpt is of such importance because it demonstrates how the totality of the destruction she experienced is addressed both by her and by me. Although to her surprise, she finds both her parents alive, everything feels so hopeless, so bleak. She tries to balance the sense of doom with the illusion of my refinding all my toys intact. My contradiction not only deprives her of that illusion, but also informs her, in a voice that is completely separate and my own, that already at that time, I had stopped being the child that had to be kept "happy." On the contrary, I had been and continued to be fully present and informed of the irreversible destructiveness we had both experienced. She seemed to have been relieved by my contradicting her and promptly informed me of that by saying *"Then you are right."*

Concluding Remarks

As earlier mentioned, the multiple viewings of my mother's testimony created and maintained an enhanced reflective space which allowed the overwhelming identifications with the experiences she relates, the unending grief and pain and the unfulfillable wishes she expresses to become more and more contextualized. The survivor, the son and the listener to her testimony, feels less and less overwhelmed, helpless, enraged and paralyzed, and can empathically hear and accept the enormity of the pain that she feels, the rage she suppresses, and the unrelenting terror she does not and cannot let herself feel, and does not let herself know of.

Listening to the contextualized identification with her plight allows for feelings of authentic empathy to emerge that no longer are a frozen reflexive response. Movement and imagination, as well as language and narrative become possible, allowing for traumatizing affects to persist as signal affects, thus preventing them from colonizing completely the space available for experience – in essence from hijacking life.

Bibliography

Agamben, G. (1999). *Remnants of Auschwitz: The Witness and the Archive.* Translated by Daniel Heller-Roazen. Zone Books, New York, p. 33.

Fortunoff Video Archive for Holocaust Testimonies at Yale., L. Klara HVT777, 1986. German, Excerpts a.) Tape II 06:18 to 07:55, b.) Tape II 37:33 to 39:50, c.) Tape III 06:34 to 07:59.

Freud, S. (1930). *Civilization and its Discontents.* SE 21. London: Hogarth Press, pp. 57–146.

Freud, S. (1933). *New Introductory Lectures on Psycho-Analysis*. SE 22. London: Hogarth Press, pp. 3–182.

Kohut, H. (1971). *The Analysis of the Self*. New York: International Universities Press.

Mahler, M. S. (1963). Thoughts about Development and Individuation. *Psychoanalytic Study of the Child*, 18, 307.

Mahler, M., Pine, F., & Bergman, A. (1975). *The Psychological Birth of the Human Infant: Symbiosis and Individuation*. New York: NY: Basic Books.

Parens, H. (1970). Inner Sustainment: Metapsychological Considerations. *Psychoanalytic Quarterly*, 39, 223–239.

Winnicott, D. W. (1953) Transitional Objects and Transitional Phenomena. *International Journal of Psychoanalysis*, 34, 89–97.

Chapter 2

Arrival at Auschwitz
Traumatic Rupture and Empathic Containment in the Joint Narrative of a Mother and a Daughter who Survived the Holocaust Together

Johanna Bodenstab

This chapter is based on two excerpts from the joint video testimony of a mother and a daughter who survived the Holocaust together. It examines the narrative dissonance, which occurs when both women relate their arrival at the concentration camp of Auschwitz. The two emerging narrative perspectives are reflective of two strikingly different emotional positions taken during the actual event: while the daughter slid into a traumatic position, which was dissociated and stripped of any psychic ability to relate to self or other, the mother was able to hold an empathic position, which remained connected and provided structure for their experience. In the context of the daughter's trauma the relationship to mother emerges both as a containing reality (for the daughter) and as a connection with an internal object (for the mother). In the context of the devastating external reality of the Holocaust which led to a massive destructuralization both of the environment and of the psyche and to psychic equivalence which blurred the distinction between external and internal realities, the structuring qualities of the mother–daughter relationship became essential in dealing with the dissociative effects of traumatic experience. Though the relational structure provided by the mother as an empathic other could not undo the trauma of the daughter, it certainly provided an experiential context to contain the traumatic experience.

Reading Along Broken Lines

The reality of the Holocaust as captured in the testimonies of survivors who remember it is very often in total violation of the average expectable environment. This violation implies a range of disparities, which not only places the testimonial endeavor well in a position of "probing the limits of representation" but also results in narratives deeply "wounded by reality" and shaped by massive trauma.[1]

For the survivors themselves this disparity can play out as a biographical rift opening between who they have become since the Holocaust and who they were made to be during their persecution. There is no certainty how to place their Holocaust experience within the continuity of their lives after the Holocaust. Can the narrating "I" in a testimony, indeed, speak for one's "Auschwitz double"; or can it speak because it keeps "that other, the Auschwitz one" separate from the speaker?[2]

As an experiential gap, however, the disparity between the average expectable environment and a traumatic event of massive proportions also poses methodological challenges. Obviously anyone today can, for example, know much more about the arrival at the Auschwitz ramp and the selection process following it than did many of the people who actually arrived at that very ramp. But what use to make of this knowledge? When does it facilitate the ability to listen and comprehend and when does it serve as a protective shield fending off unbearable memories? If what can be told depends largely on a matching ability to listen and to understand, this experiential gap may well challenge the very possibility of the testimonial endeavor.[3]

Posthumous knowledge of the Holocaust and its overarching grasp of a situation suggest a command of events and a certainty of perspective unavailable to the survivor as the actual experience occurred. Claude Lanzmann became acutely aware of this qualitative gap while working on his documentary "Shoah." Initially what the survivors were telling him seemed not to match the knowledge the filmmaker had acquired in preparation for his interviews with them. Surprisingly his knowledge did not facilitate a better understanding but caused him profound confusion instead. It was only after visiting the actual locations of the survivors' memory that Lanzmann grasped the awkwardness of his acquired knowledge: by putting himself geographically and physically in the same spot with them, as it were, he came to realize how little resemblance the places of today carry with the remembered places of the Holocaust. There is literally no common ground with the experience of the survivors. Any understanding can only weave around this gap.[4] This means that a testimony must be considered as an authentic eyewitness account even though in extreme cases the experience as it is narrated in a testimony may well contradict the posthumous knowledge of an event.[5]

The gaps and rifts listed above point to rupture as an organizational principle, both of experience and of narrative. Survivors, analysts, and researchers have to come to terms with rupture as a dimension of experience and as a structural element in their very different ways. In this context knowledge poses a problem not only because of its shielding potential but also because of its unbearable intensity. In fact, at a time when our general knowledge about the Holocaust has grown considerably, survivors themselves have increasingly begun to negotiate the gap between immediate experience and posthumous knowledge. While this newly introduced knowledge may be of great help in structuring their narratives, it can easily become a protective shield against vulnerability in the face of painful experience.[6]

The testimonies of Holocaust survivors carry what French novelist Soazig Aaron has termed "extreme knowledge",[7] an "intimate knowledge of death",[8] or of absolute contingency that is totally unbearable because it eradicates meaning, devours structure, and kills certainty and reliability even as one listens to it 65 years after the end of World War II. This knowledge is further intensified by its proximity to trauma, which shapes the narrative of so many Holocaust testimonies. Due to the extreme nature of the underlying experience and the trauma it has caused in a survivor, she may not be able "to find categories of thought or words for [her] experience. That is, since neither culture nor experience provide structures for formulating acts of massive aggression, survivors cannot articulate trauma."[9]

Although the emotions evoked in a listener by the testimonies can at times be overwhelming, they create a useful link to extreme knowledge.[10] Psychoanalytic literature has described the intensity of countertransference feelings in the presence of severe trauma but also their utmost importance as an invaluable link to a traumatized patient.[11] Likewise, the emotions and affects aroused by a testimony can become meaningful as indicators of trauma, as an echo of a traumatic experience that at the time of the narrative could not be communicated through the words of the narrating "I" because at the time of the Holocaust the affected subject could psychologically not contain her experience. Even in retrospect a survivor may not be able to reflect upon the pain she has suffered because she remains dissociated from her original experience and cannot claim the pain as her own.[12]

This emotional connection of a listener to the trauma narrative of a survivor is, at first, a terrible one – disturbing, unwanted and, yet, invaluable, for it is perhaps the only one possible in the presence of total rupture caused by massive destruction, by "disarticulation" of psychic structure,[13] and by the loss of the self as "interpreter of experience" and as "maker of meaning."[14] However, this connecting to rupture by means of countertransference is by no means a reparative act. It is rather a process of immersion, which makes it possible to capture that something could not be symbolized due to the particular nature of traumatic memory.

From a psychoanalytic point of view the Holocaust can be understood as an external reality, which is so unreal in its extreme violence that it becomes hard for a person exposed to such reality to distinguish whether she lives through a terrifying fantasy or actual reality. This blurring of the spheres of emotional and external reality is paralyzing: reality has not only lost its familiarity but also its meaning as a sphere shared with others that defines the limits of one's inner world. One's sense of being in the world is radically changed when the habitual order of inside and outside is violated. "This means that the external event and the internal event are simultaneous, synchronous or the same thing, or that there is no longer an outside from which [something] came or an inside which can register [that something]."[15] Ultimately rupture as the organizational principle, both of experience and of narrative, is indicative of a massive destructuralization, which not only affected the relationship between "inside" and "outside" but psychic structure itself.[16] Therefore, any interpretive endeavor struggling to grasp trauma narratives must renounce claims to wholeness and can only offer a reading oriented toward rupture or a reading along broken lines.[17]

T-34 (Rosalie W. and Jolly Z., 1979), a Mother–Daughter Testimony[18]

The problem of the dissociating forces of trauma and of the struggle or failure to connect is also at the core of this essay. How can connection be sustained in the face of total rupture? How can psychic structure be maintained in the face of massive trauma? I will address this tension in the context of a mother–daughter relationship, which survived the Holocaust. What follows is a section taken from a larger work-in-progress on mother–daughter relationships during the Holocaust. This project is based on video-testimonies from the Fortunoff Video Archive at Yale University. None of the survivors whose testimonies I have studied was questioned about their relationships to mother or to child/daughter in a systematic fashion. My data is circumstantial and therefore very often incomplete, opening at least as many questions as are answered. Faced with this situation the testimony of Rosalie W. and Jolly Z. is a particularly valuable source because mother and daughter survived the Holocaust together and were interviewed together, which gives their relationship central meaning regarding their survival as well as the structure of their narrative. While there is trauma present in Rosalie's and Jolly's joint testimony, their relationship allows them to negotiate an elaborate narrative that is extremely contained and reflective of the ongoing emotional connection between mother and daughter.

In this essay I offer a close reading of two excerpts, which add up to less than four minutes chosen from an interview with a total recording time of one hour and 40 minutes. However, these four minutes seem to capture an almost iconic historical moment and, at the same time, mark a distinctive narrative turn. First, they both relate to a situation, which seems strangely familiar to anyone: in retrospect the arrival at Auschwitz has become a paradigmatic situation. But while it may be what first comes to mind when thinking about "the Holocaust" it is important to realize that the ramp in Auschwitz was really only a detail in a vast picture of destruction and that many more scenarios of persecution did exist as part of the genocide against the European Jews. In view of the iconic status of the arrival at Auschwitz it is equally helpful to place the particular arrival of Rosalie and Jolly in its historical context: Both women were deported from Hungary to Auschwitz in May 1944 and survived together until their liberation in Bergen-Belsen in April 1945. The deportation of the Hungarian Jews has been termed "The Last Chapter" by the German historians Gerlach and Aly because it occurred relatively late during World War II, between May and July 1944.[19] The destination of the trains was Auschwitz, where most of the arriving people were selected to the gas chambers. Within seven weeks more than 430,000 Jews were deported – that was approximately half of the Jewish population of Hungary at that time.[20] Rosalie and Jolly were the only members of a family of more than 40 people to enter the camp. Everybody else was gassed upon arrival.

At the time of their arrival at the Auschwitz ramp Rosalie (the mother) was 43 years old and Jolly (the daughter) was 17. This particular difference in age would have made their separation during the selection inevitable: in

Auschwitz, children looking younger than the age of 13 were sent to the gas-chambers upon arrival and typically the mothers accompanying them were sent with them to avoid the upheaval and disorder separations might have provoked. Women looking older than 40 years were likewise selected for instant murder. They were deemed too old to withstand the camp conditions for any time.[21] This means that teenage girls arriving in Auschwitz would mostly have lost their mothers upon arrival.[22] Indeed, this is exactly what happened to Rosalie and Jolly. Only this mother managed to undo her separation from her daughter thus escaping her own death in a gas chamber.

In this context the central role of the relationship between Rosalie and Jolly will come into focus.[23] We shall see that both women, in accordance with their relationship as mother and daughter, developed emotional strategies and behaviors to deal with and master the unknown situation at the ramp. In the joint testimony of mother and daughter their relationship is present both as a lived reality and as an emotional space. This structural duality had to gain particular importance in a situation like the Holocaust, when experience reached psychotic levels[24] and a reliable distinction between emotional and external realities became increasingly difficult. Boulanger has described the mental state corresponding to this blurring of reality spheres as one of "psychic equivalence" when "the psyche is overwhelmed by external horrors that find their equivalents in the unconscious" and when "the psychic space in which reflection can occur has been foreclosed."[25] The relationship between Rosalie and Jolly provided structure for an experience that was both extremely unstructured and shattering. This became particularly meaningful in the context of the traumatic aspects of their experience.

A second important reason for choosing these excerpts is that they stand out from the narrative structure of the joint testimony, which, generally speaking, has a beautiful narrative flow produced by the voices of a mother and a daughter who are intimately connected yet distinctive and strong in their own rights. Their perspectives are interweaving to create a multifaceted narrative filled with great detail. However, there are several moments when this harmonic narrative interaction is interrupted and gives way to dissonance and contradiction, when an underlying struggle becomes palpable and the security of the mother–daughter bond is in suspension. None of these are moments of intense affect or aggression. Typically, neither of the two testifying survivors even acknowledges that they disagree with each other. Rather than rejecting these moments as incoherent and contradictory, I understand them as particularly dense moments of testimony when the impact of their experience threatens to rupture their relationship and when the relationship the two women share can be witnessed in action to maintain itself.

The Daughter Remembers the Selection/Jolly Z. (00:44:22)

> And we were standing in rows of five and as we approached the officer who was doing the selection – just with his finger [*demonstrating*]: "Right." "Left." – Ah, he sent my mother to one side [*points to the right*] and me to another side [*points to the left*]. And we had no idea what it means. Somehow instinctively we came back and met in front of him and my mother held onto me and she said in German: "Bitte, lassen Sie mich mit meiner Tochter." Which means: "Please, let me stay with my daughter." And he noticed how nice she speaks German. He says: "How come you speak German?" She says: "Well, I went to German school." He said: "Well, get lost." And he didn't tell us to the right or to the left. But instinctively we went to the side where it meant life. But we could as well have gone to the other side.
>
> (44:22 to 45:21)

It is quite striking that a situation, which seems rather clear from the perspective of the researcher, is rendered with so much opacity by an actual witness. Jolly's description of the selection process seems frozen and hermetic. It has an almost hypnotic quality as if what really happened had unfolded with the inevitability of a dream following its own enigmatic rules and brimming with meaning yet to be grasped. The finger of the German officer is ticking like a metronome and mother and daughter follow its rhythm spinning to opposite sides. But like in a mirroring choreography they are separated only to come together again. After an unreal conversation about the mother's knowledge of German both women are dismissed and find their way to the side "*where it meant life.*"

If we did not know what Rosalie's and Jolly's separation implied, we would be left with the impression of a hypnotic ballet executed with the precision of a mechanism. There seems to have been no agency or any power to act on the daughter's part. The explanation she offers to explain how she and her mother remained together is utterly primitive and not an explanation at all: "*Instinctively*" mother and daughter came back and met in front of the German; "*instinctively*" they went to the side that meant life. "Instinct" supposedly guided both women like an internal compass helping them to steer the course of their relationship despite the selection.

But it seems that Jolly is strangely displaced as a narrator not only vis-à-vis the event but also vis-à-vis herself. The daughter gives testimony in the absence of an "observing ego", which is reflected in the absence of a narrating "I" in the entire passage.[26] The operational mode of her account is a "we" which is rather undifferentiated. At first it refers at least to all the women and children in her family ("*we were standing in rows of five*"). Then this entire family has vanished from the testimony and Jolly herself is present solely as a (grammatical) object: she is sent to one side by the officer, held by her mother, and talked about in their conversation. Beyond that she has merged into a "*we*" with Rosalie and eventually both mother and daughter form an indistinguishable unit inevitably gravitating to the good side.

It is thanks to an intervention by the interviewer that the daughter's account reluctantly gains some transparency and is forced into differentiation. The hypnotic union with mother related by Jolly becomes transparent for Rosalie's active role during the selection.

INTERVIEWER: Who pulled whom?
JOLLY: Well, I really don't remember. We just both walked over.
INTERVIEWER: Maybe your mother does?
JOLLY: I think my mother tells me now that she wanted to go where the young people were sent because somebody in the ghetto, I understand an SS in the ghetto told her that whenever a selection is taking place she should go where young and capable people are sent. That means we'll be able to go to work.

(45:29 to 46:04)

While Jolly may have had the impression during the selection that she and her mother were moving in unison and were guided by their instincts she has found out from Rosalie since that her mother had some information that helped her to orient herself during the selection. Given this information it becomes evident that while Jolly's testimony seems to speak for both women, her narrative not only denies the separation from her mother (that did occur), but posits that the relationship with her mother inevitably had to hold. In doing so it erases the mother as a separate entity: at the time of the selection Rosalie knew something that her daughter had no idea about. To understand this seeming denial of experience and of separateness better, it is helpful to turn to Rosalie's account of the selection:

The Mother Remembers the Selection/Rosalie W. (00:51:00)

INTERVIEWER: And you walked off the train...
ROSALIE (MOTHER): Yeah.
INTERVIEWER: What next? Next moment?
ROSALIE (MOTHER): No. We went in a place...
INTERVIEWER: Oh, no!
JOLLY (DAUGHTER): (*to her mother*) The selection.
INTERVIEWER: Next moment.
JOLLY (DAUGHTER): (*to her mother*) The selection.
ROSALIE (MOTHER): Oh, when Mengele ... the selection!
JOLLY (DAUGHTER): (*cues her mother*) We came down from the train. Then we...
ROSALIE (MOTHER): ...so we went. He was there and he looked: who was young was on the right side – who was old or with children on the left side.
JOLLY (DAUGHTER): And then we were...
ROSALIE (MOTHER): This was it. [*does not hear Jolly*] And I went to him.
JOLLY (DAUGHTER): We were separated...
ROSALIE (MOTHER): Hm?
JOLLY (DAUGHTER): We were separated...
ROSALIE (MOTHER): We was separated and I looked at her. She looked at me: "Ma!" [*mimics the pleading gesture of her daughter*] And I went to him and I said to him:
JOLLY (DAUGHTER): We met before him. [*to the interviewers*]
ROSALIE (MOTHER): "Gentleman, please, let me to my daughter." He said: "From where you speak so good German?" I said: "I have German

schools." And he asked me how old I am. At that time I was 43 – and I don't know – somebody told me – and I said "38." When I would say the true, I would go on the left side. I said 38. Maybe my mother was there.

JOLLY (DAUGHTER): [*smiling, to the interviewers*] She means her mother from heaven.

ROSALIE (MOTHER): We were kissing and crying. We are together. And then they took us to cut out the hair and to take away the clothing, everything.

(51:00 to 52:19)

Compared with the inevitable mechanics of the selection process related by the daughter, the mother's account is strikingly emotional and reveals the intense drama of the selection. She relates not only the great relief after they had overcome their involuntary separation ("*We were kissing and crying*"), she also remembers her daughter's despair when standing alone on the other side. The mother's narrative "*we*" readily surrenders to the fact of her separation from her daughter. It remains transparent for two women and their difference: a younger one pleading in anguish and an older one daring enough to defy the flow of the selection process. Unlike Jolly's testimony Rosalie's relates both to herself and to her daughter at the ramp. She was able to respond to Jolly's crisis with the protectiveness of a mother. The daughter's undifferentiated use of the pronoun "we" may well invoke a persistent emotional bond with Rosalie. But it is only the mother's testimony that speaks from a position of empathy – a position that is grounded in concern for an other and at the same time in self-reference.[27] Her empathy enabled Rosalie to respond to Jolly's need and to fulfill her daughter's expectation that her mother help her. The fundamental importance of this maternal action fully comes to light when one considers that "[i]n the concentration camps, the sadistic, bureaucratic killing disproved this basic expectation" of an empathic response to one's needs.[28] In an environment where "the simple assumption of life is destroyed [so that] being alive is no longer natural",[29] Rosalie's action became more than a maternal gesture in that it maintained a vital investment in human interactions and relationship. The empathic position of the mother is in contradiction of an "indifferent [external] reality" and the total annihilation it implies.[30]

Jolly's Dissociation and the Concreteness of the Maternal Body

Another important piece of information we can glean from Rosalie's account refers to her daughter and sheds an entirely new light on Jolly's opaque account of the selection. Only through her mother do we learn that Jolly was pleading with Rosalie to join her. The mother's testimony speaks for her daughter and relates an experience beyond her own. It is thanks to her perspective that we get a glimpse of how the selection affected the daughter. Since Jolly herself makes no reference to her emotional state, one might wonder whether the hypnotic gestalt of her narrative during this particular passage can be understood as evidence of the dread she experienced during the selection. This would mean that while her fear remains absent in contents from her account, it is inscribed in her testimony without being mediated by the narrating "I." Due to the traumatic dissociation suffered during her arrival at Auschwitz, Jolly is not able to describe herself explicitly in relationship to her experience during the interview; however, her narrative is shaped by the unsymbolized dread she experienced during the selection.

As I mentioned above, in the daughter's account of the selection there is not only an absence of self-reference but connected to it there is her absence as a witness to her mother. Jolly's perception of Rosalie seems to be defined entirely by her need. Mother matters as a holding presence for her daughter and as emotional scaffolding for her narrative. If it was not for the "we" shared with Rosalie, Jolly would hardly have a story to tell. One might try to explain this dependence on mother as an adolescent gesture, however, such a developmental assessment can easily lose sight of the enormous pressure of the external situation bearing on both mother and daughter. I would argue that Jolly was not simply reaching out like a child for her mother but that – as her agency, cohesiveness, and sense of self faltered due to intense external pressure – she was desperate for someone in whose presence she could remember herself.[31] In her physical presence Rosalie literally fleshed out what seemed increasingly unimaginable in the face of the indifferent reality of total annihilation. The concreteness of her presence and the physicality of the maternal body had to gain particular importance in the context of psychic equivalence as they sustained an emotional reality of relatedness to self and object in the flesh. Rosalie took on the role of an environment – a maternal function described by Winnicott in the context of early infancy, which in the context of the selection carried meaning as embodiment of the reality of connectedness and belonging thus providing as external reality the emotional space her daughter was losing.[32] Only with Rosalie's physical presence serving as a concrete reminder of a reality not defined by the ramp and the selection process could Jolly eventually realize that she was part of something other than annihilation. The recourse to the maternal flesh, then, is here not as much an indication of regression as it hints at a collapse of symbolization brought on by trauma.[33]

The joint testimony of mother and daughter reveals how closely Jolly came to a state of traumatic dissociation during the selection, which is revealed by her inability to relate the reality surrounding her and to locate herself within the situation. With the loss of self-reference, the psychological prerequisite of perception of self is lost and there is no more psychological space to imagine the other person. This is the traumatic position when experience cannot be owned as part of one's own story and the self can no longer function as the interpreter of one's experience.[34] The word has to become flesh to carry any meaning at all.[35] Jolly's testimony relates to a moment that she could not fully grasp and to which she could be present only in as much as she felt the physical connection with her mother.[36]

Traumatic Loss of Structure and the Structuring Power of a Mother–Daughter Relationship

To understand the traumatic scope of Jolly's and Rosalie's situation it is helpful to consider the circumstances surrounding the arrival at Auschwitz as a traumatic sequence. Jolly was not only affected by the separation from her mother: the family arrived in Auschwitz after a four-day journey in overcrowded cattle cars. Indeed, Jolly is commenting on her sense of humiliation due to the lack of privacy:

> You know: it was a very conservative, conventional group and here you have to eat whatever you have – you have to eliminate right there, standing next to each other ... I mean, this was a cargo of human beings and life went on, the natural processes went on. And this was just a most dehumanizing experience to be so close and all this to happen.

One can only assume how deeply the emotional chaos of this loss of social structure must have affected the teenage girl.[37] Although Jolly carefully avoids putting faces and names to that human cargo, her sense of shame and bewilderment is palpable. Her testimony seems to protect the modesty of the group with whom she traveled – people who at some point during the journey would have to relieve themselves in the absence of the privacy of a bathroom. It is more than likely that many of these people were Jolly's relatives since she mentions elsewhere that they arrived in a group of more than 40 relatives, her parents among them. Therefore, "the demolition of shame barriers, the elimination of privacy,"[38] and the loss of control over bodily functions was not an anonymous occurrence but happened between close relatives. The complex and subtle relationships between several generations of the same family were shattered by the regressive, undifferentiated behaviors induced in grown-ups exposed to extremely primitive circumstances. Not only were generational and personal boundaries violated, a reduction to the physical aspects of human existence and a loss of control over her own body also occurred. This implies a blow to Jolly's physical cohesion and introduces an additional level of vulnerability as her internal world representations were brutally deconstructed.[39]

The humiliating deportation was followed by the arrival in the unknown: *"And we had no idea where we are. We had no idea what's coming. We still tried to keep together because that was always the most important part."* At the ramp the family was torn apart in a sequence of separations all of which remain shrouded in an amorphous "we." Only the last contact with her father stands out. There is no indication in the testimony that Jolly had anybody with her on her side of the selection. She was completely isolated from everybody she knew and had to face the unknown completely alone. She found herself in an emotional place of "catastrophic loneliness" where she could no longer be known.[40] Jolly may not have known that the selection was really a prelude to the killing process in Auschwitz but with all her connections to the known world being cut off one after the other, she underwent a process of annihilation, dying a slow psychogenic death.[41]

Rosalie was not only the last remaining link to the world Jolly had known but the last person to know Jolly. By heeding her daughter's plea, by meeting her need, the mother kept the possibility of relatedness alive in a moment of near apocalyptic destruction of human bonds. This destruction was manifest in the selection process resulting in the physical loss of Jolly's entire family and had its emotional impact on the daughter sliding into the dissociative state of the traumatic position. Rosalie's gesture did not only restore the reality of the mother–daughter relationship but at the same time it maintained the emotional reality of relatedness to oneself and to the world outside.[42] The traumatic reality of the Holocaust is often understood as eclipsing the other in her empathy and as a source of hope. At the core of trauma lies an experience of what Laub and Auerhahn have called "failed empathy", which effaces "the link between self and other." A failure of empathy does not only destroy "hope of communication with others …, it also diminishes the victims' ability to be in contact and in tune with themselves, to feel that they have a self." For these authors the essence of Holocaust trauma ultimately lies in "the breakdown of the communicative dyad in the internal, representational world of the victim."[43]

Therefore it is important to grasp Rosalie in her double role: while her protective gesture was deeply grounded in her mother–daughter relationship with Jolly, it carries a psychologically much deeper meaning in the context of the Holocaust. It may well be that Jolly's plea "*Ma!*" activated Rosalie so that both women in their separate roles as mother and daughter could take recourse to their relationship. But in doing so they held on to an idea of an other that could save and be saved – they maintained their relatedness both as a reality and as an emotional connection in an environment that was shattering connections through its absolute indifference and murderousness. This does not only suggest that the relationship was meaningful as structure holding mother and daughter in place vis-à-vis each other while it became increasingly difficult for the self to locate herself in reference to external as well as to internal reality. It also means that the empathic position Rosalie maintained toward her daughter counteracted her traumatic position. And while it would certainly be overstated that their relational ties provided Rosalie and Jolly with a full protection against trauma, it is obvious that during the selection the mother's presence seems to have mitigated "the most pernicious effects of traumatic dissociation" for Jolly.[44] Of course, this hardly explains Rosalie's astonishing ability to maintain her own relational ties. She carried the full burden of the asymmetry of the dyad – according to her protective role as mother she had to take full responsibility for her daughter. How did the structuring power of the mother–daughter relationship become relevant in her case?

The Mother in the Mother (Rosalie's Good Object)

Perhaps the most surprising part of Rosalie's exchange with the German is the question about her age. How could she possibly have known what the German wanted to hear? Of course, we could argue that on the basis of the little knowledge she had about selections she was smart enough to figure out that it was her age that had separated her from Jolly. But that is not how she herself describes it. She depicts her answer as coming from a part of herself that is puzzling and wondrous. Somebody must have told her what the right answer would be: "*Maybe my mother was there.*" Obviously she cannot find a reason within herself to explain how she thought of the right answer. Instead, she takes recourse to her own mother and tries to explain her action by relating to her protective presence. However, Rosalie's reaching out for her mother is entirely different from Jolly's pleading call during the selection.

First of all, at the time of the selection the presence of Rosalie's mother could only have been an internal reality for Rosalie, for as Jolly explains in utter amusement to the interviewers, Rosalie "*means her mother from heaven.*" But why is this deceased mother, who was never deported to Auschwitz, invoked in her daughter's testimony? What does it mean that she comes to mind when Rosalie remembers the selection? The presence of the maternal figure in Rosalie's version of the selection allows the survivor to talk both as a mother and as a daughter. In her testimony Rosalie can present herself as someone in need of protection and as someone protective of another person. In other words, both positions of the dyad are present in Rosalie's testimony. The dyad marks the emotional space of the early relationship between a primary caregiver and a child, but it can also be understood as a relational matrix since the ability to relate to oneself and to others is formed largely in the early exchanges with one's mother/primary caregiver.[45] In this respect Rosalie's reference to her mother can be understood as the emergence of her good object, which is as much an inner representation of the maternal figure as it is part of Rosalie's self. This suggests that, unlike Jolly, Rosalie was able to sustain an inner dialogue with herself during the selection. This inner dialogue had her good maternal object as emotional reference point. She was not only responsive to her daughter's need but could handle a moment of her own helplessness. If we assert with Kirshner that the good object "is essential to the capacity for emotional participation in the world of others",⁴⁶ it would seem that Rosalie's self-reference, which she expresses through the emotional bond with her internal mother, mirrors her relatedness with Jolly. Her ability to stay connected with her daughter and to relate to Jolly's terror hinges upon her ability to relate to herself.

The Trauma of Annihilation

At this point we have to remind ourselves that Rosalie's empathic response to her daughter, which provided structure for Jolly and averted her fragmentation did occur in the context of genocide. The *"other side"*, which Jolly cautiously juxtaposes with *"the side where it meant life"*, meant death. The testimony is very clear about the fact that both women only found out what the chimneys meant after they had spent a couple of days in Auschwitz. It remains, however, unclear when they realized that all the other members of their family had been murdered upon arrival. During the interview this painful knowledge moves Rosalie to tears while her own encounters with death during the selection remain far removed from her narrative. (A) Her account of the selection implies that she, too, had been selected to go to the gas chambers, but there is no reflection on her narrow escape from her own death. (B) The selection also brought the separation from her husband, but while Rosalie's narrative repeatedly touches upon her arrival in Auschwitz she never mentions her separation from him. It is Jolly, who in the presence of her mother manages to narrate the good-bye with her father.⁴⁷

But while Rosalie's empathic response helped to avert Jolly's psychic death at the Auschwitz ramp there is no such maternal gesture available in the face of the violent death of their husband/father. It seems that the posthumous knowledge about death as the underlying meaning of the selection process can hardly be negotiated in this testimony. During the Holocaust both women seem to have resisted the idea that their husband/father was dead. Whenever he figured in their conversations or their minds he was a living memory. I understand this denial of death as part of their self-sustaining effort to avoid the reality of murder going on around them and its emotional impact on them as much as necessary for their own survival. During the interview the loss of their husband/father is one of the few events that causes a breakdown of narrative with both women struggling for composure and for words. However, this pain only surfaces retrospectively after the full realization of their loss and is part of their mourning and of their posthumous surrender to the reality of his death. In the face of this death neither of the two women is able to hold an empathic position for the other. There is no comfort, no perception of each other's suffering, there is nothing but pain. With Charlotte Delbo we have to acknowledge that ultimately "there [is] no possible getting away from [the murderous reality of Auschwitz]" and that even the survival of their relationship will ultimately never nullify the trauma they lived through.[48]

Conclusion

It was in the context of Rosalie's and Jolly's mother–daughter relationship that we could grasp the deep connection between empathy and trauma. While the traumatic position is marked by a state of dissociation and thus a loss of psychic structure, the empathic position is grounded in a texture of relationships with self and others, allowing for dialogue both with the external reality and with oneself. This means not only that these two positions are extreme opposites of one another but also that one can be the undoing of the other: trauma implies a failure of empathy as experienced through another person as well as a lack of empathy due to a loss of self-reference and the observing ego, while empathy has the potential to contain the fragmentation caused by trauma and to offer relatedness where context is lost both internally and on the outside.

I suggest considering the selection at the Auschwitz ramp as a potentially total loss or "disarticulation" of structure both on a social and on a psycho-emotional level, "so that the parts are no longer in relation to each other and functioning as a whole".[49] If we assume with Jonathan Cohen "that psychic structure depends for its maintenance on environmental support throughout life",[50] we begin to grasp fully not only the catastrophe of psychic equivalence as described by Boulanger but also the crucial importance of Rosalie's physical presence to Jolly. Even the posthumous interview resonates with the wholeness of their relationship: as I have shown, Jolly's version of the selection is a piece of unmediated testimony speaking to the horror of her arrival to Auschwitz without naming it explicitly. This can be fully appreciated only because her version is contained by her mother's version. One narrative perspective embraces and holds the other thus forming a joint testimony structured according to the psychological dynamics of the relationship between mother and daughter. While one must acknowledge that neither of the two testimonial versions of the selection can fully explain why Jolly and Rosalie stayed together, it is striking to trace the structuring power of their relationship and its effect on self-perception and identity, on the ability to witness, to empathize, and ultimately to act, but also on the way both women are able to shape their personal narratives.

Notes

1 Both formulations are borrowed from other authors: Friedlander (1992); Boulanger (2007).
2 Delbo (1990), p. 3.
3 This is true for the specific dynamics of any given interview – see Felman and Laub (1992), Chapter II: Bearing Witness or the Vicissitudes of Listening, pp. 57–74 – and also for the socio-historical context in which testimony occurs – see Wieviorka (2006).
4 See Lanzmann (2007), see esp. pp. 38–39.
5 Felman and Laub (1992), pp. 59–63; and more recently and extensively Laub (2009a).
6 See Laub and Bodenstab (2008), esp. pp. 392–393.
7 Aaron (2002).
8 Boulanger (2007), p. 36 and also pp. 30–39.
9 Laub and Auerhahn (1993), here p. 288.
10 Re "The Hazards of Listening" see Felman and Laub (1992), pp. 57–74.
11 See e.g. Wilson and Lindy (1996), pp. 1–62, 249–263, and 389–394; Kogan (2004); and also Boulanger (2007), Chapters 6–9.
12 The idea that traumatic experience cannot be claimed by the person who was exposed to it follows Caruth (1996).
13 Tarantelli (2003), here p. 923.
14 Boulanger (2005), here p. 24.
15 Tarantelli (2003), p. 919.
16 See Laub and Auerhahn (1989).
17 I am indebted to Prof. Andreas Hamburger (Berlin) who suggested the German concept "bruch-orientierte Lektüre" in a conversation on testimony.
18 Rosalie W. and Jolly Z. Holocaust Testimony (T-34), Fortunoff Video Archive for Holocaust Testimonies, Yale University Library.
19 See Gerlach and Aly (2002).
20 See Gerlach and Aly (2002), p. 275.
21 See Gerlach and Aly (2002), pp. 291–292.
22 Compare for example the memoirs of Fried (1990) and Ornstein (2004).
23 For a discussion of the psycho-emotional dynamics of Rosalie's and Jolly's relationship compare Bodenstab (2004).
24 Ilse Grubrich-Simitis (1981) has spoken of "the realization of a psychotic universe" in the context of Holocaust related trauma; see also Boulanger (2007), p. 3 who in the context of Holocaust survivors mentions "a psychotic experience anchored in reality events" (quoting Jonathan Cohen).
25 Boulanger (2005) p. 22.
26 Laub and Auerhahn (1993), p. 295.
27 Re the importance of empathy (a) in the context of trauma, see Laub and Auerhahn (1989), pp. 377–400 and (b) in sustaining the testimonial effort, see Felman and Laub (1992) pp. 71–72.
28 Laub and Auerhahn (1989), pp. 378–379.

29 Tarantelli (2003) p. 925.
30 Boulanger (2007), p. 59.
31 Boulanger (2007) speaks about "the relational self in crisis" in the context of trauma and about the importance of the presence of another person for survival, pp. 95–99.
32 Compare Ogden (1985), esp. p. 355.
33 Re the break-down of symbolization due to trauma see among others Ilse Grubrich-Simitis (1984), here pp. 305–309 and more recently Laub (2005).
34 See Boulanger (2005), p. 24.
35 This concreteness or literalness in the context of trauma has been described by DesPres (1976), p. 205 and more recently by Laub (2009b).
36 For a discussion of the importance of the maternal presence, both real and symbolic, in the context of trauma see Laub and Auerhahn (1989), pp. 387–390 and Laub and Auerhahn (1993), pp. 287–288, and more recently Brown (2005), here pp. 400–401.
37 Re the humiliating effects of the arrival procedure in concentration camps, see Amesberger, Auer, and Halbmayr (2004), pp. 70–79, re violation of personal boundaries esp. p. 73.
38 Grubrich-Simitis (1984), p. 307.
39 Compare Boulanger (2007) who describes the loss of physical cohesion as a dimension of trauma, pp. 85–89.
40 Grand (2000), p. 4.
41 With Tarantelli (2003) we can understand trauma as psychogenic death; Grand (2000) speaks of a death "without dying" in the context of trauma.
42 Compare note 36.
43 Laub and Auerhahn (1989), pp. 379–380.
44 Boulanger (2007), p. 97.
45 See Boulanger (2007), p. 96, but also Ogden (1985), pp. 354–362.
46 Kirshner (1994), here p. 283.
47 In a second testimony which Jolly gave four years later without her mother she is trying to evade the separation from her father and talking about it eventually causes her deep emotional pain; Jolly Z. Holocaust Testimony (T-220), Fortunoff Video Archive for Holocaust Testimonies, Yale University Library.
48 Delbo (1990), p. 2.
49 Tarantelli (2003), p. 920.
50 Cohen (1985), here p. 166.

References

Aaron, Soazig (2002): *Le Non de Klara*, Paris (Maurice Nadeau) [Klara's "No"].
Amesberger, Helga, Auer, Katrin, & Halbmayr, Brigitte (2004): *Sexualisierte Gewalt. Weibliche Erfahrungen in NS-Konzentrationslagern*, Vienna (Mandelbaum Verlag) [*Sexualized Violence: Female Experience in NS Concentration Camps*].
Bodenstab, Johanna (2004): Under Siege. A Mother–Daughter Relationship Survives the Holocaust, *Psychoanalytic Inquiry* 24/5, pp. 731–751.
Boulanger, Ghislaine (2005): From Voyeur to Witness. Recapturing Symbolic Function After Massive Psychic Trauma, *Psychoanalytic Psychology* 22, pp. 21–31.
Boulanger, Ghislaine (2007): *Wounded by Reality. Understanding and Treating Adult Onset Trauma*, New York and London (Psychology Press).
Brown, Lawrence (2005): The Cognitive Effects of Trauma. Reversal of Alpha Function and the Formation of a Beta Screen, *Psychoanalytic Quarterly* 74, pp. 397–420.

Caruth, Cathy (1996): *Unclaimed Experience. Trauma, Narrative, and History*, Baltimore (MD) and London (Johns Hopkins University Press).
Cohen, Jonathan (1985): Trauma and Repression, *Psychoanalytic Inquiry* 5, pp. 163–190.
Delbo, Charlotte (1990): *Days and Memory*, translated and with a Preface by Rosette Lamont, Marlboro, Vermont (Marlboro Press).
DesPres, Terence (1976): *The Survivor. An Anatomy of Life in the Death Camps*, New York (Oxford Press University).
Felman, Shoshana & Laub, Dori (1992): *Testimony. Crises of Witnessing in Literature, Psychoanalysis, and History*, New York and London (Routledge).
Fried, Hedi (1990): *The Road to Auschwitz. Fragments of a Life*, edited and translated from the original Swedish by Michael Meyer, Lincoln (NE) and London (University of Nebraska Press).
Friedlander, Saul (Ed.) (1992): *Probing the Limits of Representation. Nazism and the "Final Solution"*, Cambridge (MA) and London (Harvard University Press).
Gerlach, Christian & Aly, Götz (2002): *Das letzte Kapitel. Realpolitik, Ideologie und der Mord an den ungarischen Juden 1944/1945*, Stuttgart and München (Deutsche Verlags-Anstalt).
Grand, Sue (2000): *The Reproduction of Evil. A Clinical and Cultural Perspective*, Hillsdale (NJ) (Analytic Press).
Grubrich-Simitis, Ilse (1981): Extreme Traumatization as Cumulative Trauma, *Psychoanalytic Study of the Child* 36, pp. 415–450.
Grubrich-Simitis, Ilse (1985): From Concretism to Metaphor. Thoughts on Some Theoretical and Technical Aspects of the Psychoanalytic Work with Children of Holocaust Survivors, *Psychoanalytic Study of the Child* 39, pp. 301–319.
Kirshner, Lewis A. (1994): Trauma, the Good Object, and the Symbolic. A Theoretical Integration, *International Journal of Psycho-Analysis* 75, pp. 235–242.
Kogan, Ilany (2004): The Role of the Analyst in the Analytic Cure during Times of Chronic Crisis, *JAPA* 52/3, pp. 735–758.
Lanzmann, Claude (1995): *Shoah. The Complete Text of the Acclaimed Holocaust Film*, New York (Da Capo Press).
Lanzmann, Claude (2007): Site and Speech. An Interview with Claude Lanzmann about Shoah by Marc Chevrie and Hervé Le Roux, in: Liebman, S. (ed.): *Claude Lanzmann's Shoah. Key Essays*, Oxford and New York (Oxford University Press), pp. 37–49.
Laub, Dori (2005): Traumatic Shutdown of Narrative and Symbolization. A Death Instinct Derivative? *Contemporary Psychoanalysis* 41, pp. 307–326.
Laub, Dori (2009a): On Holocaust Testimony and Its Reception Within Its Own Frame, as a Process in Its Own Right, *History and Memory*, 21/1, pp. 127–150.
Laub, Dori (2009b): Hastorf Lecture (unpublished manuscript).
Laub, Dori & Auerhahn, Nanette (1989): Failed Empathy. A Central Theme in the Survivor's Holocaust Experience, *Psychoanalytic Psychology*, 6/4, pp. 377–400.
Laub, Dori & Auerhahn, Nanette (1993): Knowing and Not Knowing. Forms of Traumatic Memory, *International Journal of Psycho-Analysis* 74, pp. 287–302.
Laub, Dori & Bodenstab, Johanna (2008): Wiederbefragt. Erneute Begegnung mit Holocaust-Überlebenden, in: von Plato, Alexander, Leh, Almut & Thonfeld, Christoph (eds): *Hitlers Sklaven. Lebensgeschichtliche Analysen zur Zwangsarbeit im internationalen Vergleich*, Wien, Köln and Weimar (Böhlau Verlag), pp. 389–401.
Ogden, Thomas H. (1985): The Mother, the Infant and the Matrix. Interpretations of

Aspects of the Work of Donald Winnicott, *Contemporary Psychoanalysis* 21, pp. 346–371.

Ornstein, Anna (2004): *My Mother's Eyes. Holocaust Memories of a Young Girl*, Cincinnati (OH) (Emmis Books).

Tarantelli, Carole (2003): Life within Death. Towards a Metapsychology of Catastrophic Psychic Trauma, *International Journal of Psycho-Analysis* 84, pp. 915–928.

Wieviorka, Annette (2006): *The Era of the Witness*, translated from French by Jared Stark, Ithaca (NY) and London (Cornell University Press).

Wilson, John P. & Lindy, Jacob D. (eds) (1996): *Countertransference in the Treatment of PTSD*, New York and London (Guilford Press).

Chapter 3

The Rhythm of Resilience
A Deep Ecology of Entangled Relationality

Karen Hopenwasser

> There's something happening here
> What it is ain't exactly clear.
> (Stephen Stills 1967)

Something happens between us, between clinician and patient, something happens over time in treatment that takes such great effort to describe. Sometimes we do not even know that this is a particular experience to be described. The felt sense of trauma resonates through generations. Each of us brings into the therapeutic process memories that have fallen off the arrow of time; memories from our individual histories, embodied and dissociated memories from parents, grandparents, great-grandparents.

The brilliantly talented, deaf percussionist Evelyn Glennie so beautifully states that to truly listen we must use our bodies as resonating chambers (Glennie 2007). But because our bodies *are* resonating chambers, we are always listening, with, or without, cognitive awareness. Intergenerational transmission of traumatic experience tells the story of information flow through our bodies which themselves are embedded in a resonant world.

The stories that we hear and the stories that we feel shape a narrative history each one of us carries through life. Hidden within this narrative history is an epigenetic transformation of our selves. From generation to generation stress alters the very expression of our genes, so that ultimately it is possible to inherit the consequences of trauma without any stories, without conscious awareness of what came before.

Understanding just a bit about the biophysics of communication and the molecular chemistry of epigenetics offers us an opportunity to listen beyond words. Translation from the biophysics of what we perceive to the cognitive meaning of what we know remains tricky and for that reason I hold as a mantra a byte from the poet Muriel Rukeyser:

Time comes into it.
Say it. Say it.
The universe is made of stories,
not of atoms.
    ("The Speed of Darkness")

Storytelling Without the Words to Say It

In our clinical work it is a challenge to hold in our minds an awareness of information that is dissociated and discontinuous (Bromberg 1998, 2006, 2011). It is even more difficult to hold in awareness information that is known through a felt sense, or a feeling state, that is not cognitively connected to the story (Hopenwasser 2008). I grew up in a family where the stories began in 1910 or 1915. The top layer of felt sense was as if life began in the new world and the life left behind never happened. But I have found clues to deeper, discontinuous layers of felt sense. I will share a personal experience of storytelling that was both discontinuous and traumatizing and will compare that experience with a kind of storytelling that is healing and builds resilience.[1]

When I was as a young child, my mother told me the story of her arrival in New York. She was born in Montreal, where her family had settled at the turn of the twentieth century. History tells me her parents were running from repression and the impending pogroms in Kishinev, Russia, though I would never have known that on her account. As a five-year-old French- and Yiddish-speaking child she arrived illegally across the border from Canada into New York, a time when it was not so difficult to enter the United States illegally. The story told once, was that in the car, hiding in the "boot" was my Uncle Dave. I don't remember why he had to be hidden and not my mother, or why he would not have been easily found. I just remember that is how they came to the United States. It never occurred to me to question the story. Really? Immigrants with limited means driving a car from Canada in 1920? Years later when I asked again about this the story was brushed aside. Not exactly denied. More like I don't remember.

While my father was a lively raconteur, mostly tales of his adventures riding the rails as a young man during the depression, my mother said nothing about her childhood. Her father died on my fourth birthday and her mother was gone by the time I was eight. It never occurred to me, growing up, to notice that there were no stories about her childhood being told.

For me it was a different kind of storytelling that left a footprint on my psyche. My mother was anxious and claustrophobic. By the time I could remember much she was depressed and would often fall asleep reading on the couch. Even though she was an avid reader, I do not have any memory of her reading to me. It was my intellectually precocious much older brother who would come each night and read to me – sometimes the age-appropriate stories of Lewis Carroll, often the less appropriate Sir Arthur Conan Doyle's Sherlock Holmes and even less appropriate stories and poems of Edgar Allen Poe. This must have been the first words I heard of "The Tell Tale Heart":

> TRUE! – nervous – very, very dreadfully nervous I had been
> and am; but why *will* you say that I am mad? The disease
> had sharpened my senses – not destroyed – not dulled them.
> Above all was the sense of hearing acute. I heard all things in
> the heaven and in the earth. I heard many things in hell.
> How, then, am I mad? Hearken! and observe how
> healthily – how calmly I can tell you the whole story.

And then the end:

> "Villains!" I shrieked, "dissemble no more! I admit the deed! – tear up the planks! here, here! – It is the beating of his hideous heart!"

My recall suggests that I was too young to understand all the words being read. But I have a felt sense memory of fear. I can see in my child mind an image of a heart beating under the floor boards (which I remember as being in the wall) conflated with the sound of another Poe creation, "The Bells":

> The tintinnabulation of the bells, bells, bells, …
> Oh, the bells, bells, bells!
> What a tale their terror tells
> Of Despair!

These nighttime tales were my first lesson about the power of storytelling in the lives of children.

I will probably never get to know more details of my mother's early life, as she died before I realized this was something I needed to know. And while it remains conjecture, I will also continue to believe that my older brother's fascination with the macabre was somehow a manifestation of a dissociated inheritance. I watched my brother pass this sensibility on to his children, while I took the opposite route of, at first avoidance (oh how I despise the writings of Poe) and then, processing this particular felt sense within a trauma wise psychoanalytic psychotherapy.

The Rhythm of Identity

> The rhythms of life churn us like a great sea churns under a rising full moon.
> (Roberta Hill (Oneida poet) 1998, p. 73)

For many families, stories pass down from generation to generation locking in a narrative that may or may not be accurate, but serve to heal, comfort or build a sense of community. Native American poet Luci Tapahonso tells the story of a brutal, failed, forced assimilation of Navajo people in New Mexico from 1864 to 1868 in her poem "In 1864". It is a narrative poem that tells the story of telling stories about remembering.

> My aunt always started the story saying, "you are here because of what happened to your great-grandmother long ago".
> (Tapahonso 1993, p. 7)

And Native American poet Simon Ortiz, in his story/poem, "Time as Memory as Story", writes about the movement of memory through time and compares the felt sense of either time standing still or the passage of time as if it were a trek toward finding oneself (Ortiz 2002).

In a European postmodern view of trauma and time, Pat Barker, in her novel, *Another World*, tells the story of three generations of trauma in a British family. She compares the passage of time to the flow of blood and describes how trauma causes coagulation, ultimately stopping the flow (Barker 1999).

Extreme traumatic experience in childhood has a profound impact on an individual's embodied, neurophysiologic processing of time. While each day our body ages, never defeating death, neurophysiologically we seem to function more like a quantum computer, with the strange "spooky action" of entanglement and a posttraumatic difficulty distinguishing between past, present and future.

> One of the hallmarks of posttraumatic adaptation is the belief that what happened in the past will happen in the future. And one of the hallmarks of dissociative adaptation is the belief that what happened in the past will happen in the future even when there is no narrative memory of what actually happened.
> (Hopenwasser 2009, p. 72)

Even when there is little or no narrative memory of past trauma often the next generations carry this belief that what happened in the past will happen in the future.

I first understood how we can learn about this fragmentation of the lived past through poetry and fiction while reading Ann Michaels' poetic novel, *Fugitive Pieces*, a fictional memoir of a holocaust survivor poet. In the first pages of *Fugitive Pieces* we are swallowed by the tale of a Polish boy hiding in a bog. He had witnessed through sound, hiding behind the wallpaper in a cupboard, Nazi soldiers murder his parents and drag away his 15-year-old sister. The boy is wrapped in darkness and filled with the sound of this overwhelming trauma. Later in the novel Michaels writes in her poetic voice how the dead entered into those who were forced to dig mass graves. Like Pat Barker she describes the flow into their blood streams and through them into future generations (Michaels 1997).

What Michaels writes as poetic metaphor is actually more than metaphor and near truth. Our stressful, traumatic experiences in childhood actually alter gene expression (through a process called DNA methylation) which is then transmitted onto future generations (Dietz et al. 2011; Malan-Muller et al. 2014; Skelton et al. 2012; van der Knapp et al. 2014). It has been shown that the offspring of male mice exposed to early traumatic experience show behavioral changes similar to those in the parent mice. This is thought to be secondary to changes in non-coding RNAs (Gapp et al. 2014). And recent research on the glucocorticoid receptor gene in children of Holocaust survivors reveals that paternal PTSD leads to hypermethylation while maternal PTSD has the opposite effect (Yehuda et al. 2014) with implication for differential symptomatology of PTSD, dissociation and depression. Chronic activation of stress hormones alter protein synthesis and so memorialize our traumas within our bodies.

Sometimes, storytelling serves not to remember, but the purpose of forgetting. Gabriele Schwab, who grew up in West Germany post WWII, describes being told the dissociated stories of horrible war trauma, only later to realize the purpose of these stories to camouflage a profound very personal trauma. She writes:

> As a child I thus became the silent witness to these war stories, the one not allowed to ask questions or interrupt the flow of words. Yet I became much more. I became an empty vessel to hold a deeper terror that remained untold, a silence covered by words, a history condemned to secrecy, a deadly guilt and mute shame handed down as shards of splintered affect.
>
> (Schwab 2010, p. 43)

If our bodies are in fact a resonant chamber, this sense of empty vessel is a disavowal of her inherited trauma, an attempt to make it not me. She goes on to say:

> Yet, even as a child, I picked up on something amiss in these stories. That, more than anything else, left me confused. It was as if the words themselves were emptied of the very feelings invoked in me when I was confronted with the facts of horror. It was not that the stories were devoid of emotions but rather that words and emotions did not quite fit together; words echoed falsely. Children have a sense of this discrepancy but do not understand it. Today, I am convinced that I picked up on something untold, silenced, violently cut out. At the time, I was just confused and mortified by a silent terror that lay under the surface of what was told. It upset my trust in words, I think, as well as my sense of attunement. It complicated how I related to those I was supposed to trust, my parents and my grandmother. Words could be split into what they said and what they did not say.
>
> (p. 43)

The key word here is attunement. What is the difference between a healing, reparative storytelling and this more dissociated transmission of horror? Perhaps the difference is the relation of embodiment and environment. Perhaps the difference can be found in the rhythmic and resonant flow of memory between past and future. While Schwab is recognizing that "[w]ords could be split into what they said and what they did not say" we can also recognize that both cognitive and affective information is also transmitted without words. Information flows through deeply ecological and embodied processes shaping which storytelling fosters resiliency and which re-traumatize.

We are born into rhythm and music, we communicate through rhythm and music and we heal through rhythm and music. As W.E. Du Bois wrote about the precursor to the sorrow songs of slavery:

> The child sang it to his children and they to their children's children, and so two hundred years it has travelled down to us and we sing it to our children, knowing as little as our fathers what its words may mean, but knowing well the meaning of its music.
> (1909/2012, p. 120)

Music (song) moves through time. It is the flow of knowing from generation to generation. It is the anti-coagulant for terrible events that stop the flow of time in our minds. It is both words and the music itself that carries information from generation to generation. And it is the experience of music and rhythm in a relational context that offers the possibilities of healing and builds resilience. Gratier and Trevarthan "have identified the motives and emotions for culture in narratives of mother–infant vocal interaction" and believe "that writing the story of life needs the sense of belonging to a community and that this is vital for well being" (2008, p. 151). From the very start in life the resonance of rhythmic pulse embeds us within a relational universe. And as we develop through childhood it is the coherence of rhythmic neuronal oscillations multiplexing in the brain that allows us each a sense of continuity in our personal identity (Watrous et al. 2013). When trauma disrupts this coherence, fragments of memory fall off the arrow of time. What happened then, years ago, is happening now. And in ways that are so difficult to understand, what happened a century ago is also still happening now.

Our minds and bodies are rhythmic entities that resonate within nesting hierarchies of dyads, families, communities, cultures and an ecosphere. I stop short of saying the Universe, because that would slip into a spiritual realm to which I allude but goes beyond the scope of this chapter. What a challenge to separate sound and vibration from spirituality. This is very much illuminated in the teachings of the very early twentieth century Sufi Master Hazrat Inayat Khan, who equates all vibration as music, who has said: "Rhythm is life disguised in motion" and that "time is the rhythm that is in the whole universe" (1991, p. 151). Spiritual resonance through generations of storytelling can be found in the deeply spiritual poetry of Lucille Clifton, who traced her ancestry through slavery in Virginia to the African kingdom of Dahomey, a region known for its female warriors and writes:

> in populated air
> our ancestors continue
> i have seen them.
> i have heard
> their shimmering voices
> singing.
> ("Two-Headed Woman")

It is through sound and music that I have come to understand the biology of resilience. Sound (or the resonant feel of sound) and rhythm are what give us strength and continuity in the face of fragmenting violence. It is the congregation singing in synchrony while worshiping or mourning, in the aim of healing. It is the platoon singing and marching together in time, in the aim of destroying disguised as protecting (McNeill 1995).

Early in the film *12 Years a Slave*, based upon the life of Solomon Northup, we see Northup's intense emotional struggle with his loss of freedom. Standing at a graveside with other slaves, we watch him listening but resisting participation in the song "Roll Jordan Roll". Slowly the song rises up from within him until we see him sing forcefully in unison with the others. At that moment we can appreciate the power of communal voices in building resilience and supporting survival. Elsewhere in the film we see the same impact of humming – fostering resilience and survival. The musical complexity of this film addresses the dialectics of slave songs as both resistance and "imagined reconciliation" (Powers 2013).

How ironic that song and rhythm are not more appreciated in our psychoanalytic work with adults, that we are in a way constrained by language and silence. Anything else would break a frame, whatever variation of frame you chose. Though of course, this frame is broken anyway. Look at the work of Haidee Faimberg. Despite her strict adherence to a particular language, she describes how there is always another frame, one not noticed, not seen. She may choose not to use the terms trauma, or dissociation, or transgenerational, but she knows there is transmission of information going unspoken. She knows to listen to the listening, which means to use awareness for the knowing of the embodied and embedded (Faimberg 1988).

In recent years there has been increasing interest in the rhythmic pulse of therapeutic interaction (Nebbiosi & Nebbiosi 2007; Knoblauch 2011) but in psychotherapeutic work we seem to have forgotten one of the most powerful tools available: the management of pain through rhythm and sound. How complicated it might be if we brought song into the treatment. Perhaps too close, too intimate for comfort. At least for me too close for comfort.

I have never sung a song with even my most traumatized patients, and instead choose to use a Tibetan singing bowl to do the singing. It works extremely well without the feeling of boundary loss that singing together might create. The sound is balancing for the autonomic nervous system, soothing for all but the very most severely traumatized and the feeling of its vibration can facilitate a biological integration that has to be experienced to appreciate fully. In an exploration of the neurobiological nature of feelings, Damasio and Carvalho describe the evolutionary and neurobiological origins of feelings. They make a cogent argument for feelings as an emergent property for adaptation and survival. They present a view that the "felt experience" predates the evolution of humans and that much of the felt sense comes from a synchronization of pulses traveling in the body, not necessarily through direct neuronal synaptic pathways with which we are most familiar, but instead through something called ephaptic transmission, an electrochemical flow leaking between cells (Damasio & Carvalho 2013). When I use my Tibetan singing bowl I am also thinking about this ephaptic resonant pulsation. Used at the right moment, the singing bowl facilitates not just the integration of felt sense with cognitive coherence but also facilitates the entrainment of two humans pulsing together in an empathically shared felt sense.

The singing bowl does not distinguish between therapist and patient. The sound permeates and envelopes. Just as Solomon Northup was drawn into the shared energy of singing a spiritual, we are pulled into a vibrational sphere that quietly communicates a shared vulnerability as well as strength. No words are needed. How powerful that can be when the anguish of trauma obliterates the words to say it.

If we are going to understand ourselves as embodied, embedded cognitive process with a felt sense of suffering, then we need to expand our concepts of transference and countertransference to include an embodied ecology. Biophysicists Farnsworth, Nelson and Gershenson state: "that life is an informational phenomenon, at every level of organization, from molecules to the global ecological system ... living is information processing, in which memory is maintained by both molecular states and ecological states" (2013, p. 203). In clinical work with traumatized patients and their descendants, dissociative attunement[2] becomes an emergent phenomenon, a frame not noticed, and a communication of information that is known through a dissociated process that can be experienced as intuition.

The Deep Ecology of Entangled Relationality

We don't always talk about dissociation when we talk about trauma, but neurobiologically, discontinuous bits of traumatic memory are inherently dissociated. And dissociation is a concept that leads us into complexity, the non-linear dynamics of information flow. For some it is a large leap from storytelling to complexity theory, but we cannot understand intergenerational transmission of trauma without expanding our knowledge base to neurophysics and perhaps even more broadly, to biophysics and deep ecology.[3] Our appreciation of relationality is tied to the emergence of non-linear dynamics as it interweaves with phenomenology. From our earliest moments in life we are a biological system nested within larger systems. Sander writes in his exquisite integration of non-linear dynamics with developmental theory: "The living system is a symphony of biorhythmic systems within systems" (2002, p. 22). These biorhythmic systems, from cells, to neural networks, to the emergent property of mind are the essence of the deep continuity of mind and life (Thompson 2010).

Florence Chiew asks, in "Neuroplasticity as an Ecology of Mind: 'Where does the Neurobiological End and the Sociopolitical Begin?'" (2012). She reminds us of the work of Gregory Bateson, his understanding that "the mind is an ecological 'tangle'"; tangle, taken from the mathematics of Bertrand Russell and Alfred North Whitehead. To understand the flow of traumatic, embodied information through generations, we might need to understand entangled, a quantum physics term taken from the work of Schrodinger, Einstein, David Bohm, John Steward Bell, et al. Quantum entanglement, a phenomenon Einstein called "spooky action at a distance" refers to information that is non-local, information transmitted and experienced simultaneously despite physical separation. Yes, Einstein, Bohm and Bell are referring to nuclear particles, such as electrons. But current discussions on quantum entanglement extend to macroscopic systems (Vedral 2008), physical, biological and social, and have emerged in what is called quantum information theory. The philosophical meaning of this is that over time information becomes increasingly diffuse but never disappears. Anyone wanting to know more about quantum information flow can look at the work of physicist Sean Carroll (2010), who offers an accessible discussion of memory, quantum physics and the arrow of time. While the most speculative application of quantum computation concepts to the brain, literally to brain matter, is the proposal that microtubules (resonating cytoskeletal proteins) are a physiological substrate of consciousness (Hameroff & Watt 1982; Hameroff & Penrose 1996), less controversial applications are growing in the cognitive sciences (Wang et al. 2013; Loewenstein 2013).

It is at the intersection of physics and the sociopolitical that we find complexity, the self-organizing systems of an ecosphere. From our anthropocentric view we are primarily concerned about how *we* humans feel, how *we* humans think, how *we* humans know. But we humans remain embedded in an ecosphere within which we evolved. The Georgian ethnomusicologist Joseph Jordania traces the evolutionary importance of humming (song without words), comparing its function to that of the bird's sentinel song (a form of communication that the moment is safe) as well as a means for managing fear and anxiety (Jordania 2010). We hum when we feel well. We hum when we need to feel better. And we hum when the silence of helplessness would otherwise be lethal. The precursor of sorrow songs, in the various languages of enslaved Africans, evolved into the sorrow songs of slavery, the gospel, blues, the jazz of postbellum America and the freedom songs of the American Civil Rights Movement. Freedom Singer Bernice Johnson Reagon says: "When we sing, we announce our existence"... "Singing is running this sound through your body. You cannot sing a song and not change your condition".

The sorrow songs of slaves incorporated West African polyrhythmic call and response patterns into secular and religious spirituals that were complex expressions. These were work songs, songs of protest, and songs encoded with secret messages (Wright 2006). As Frederick Douglass described in his writings, "A keen observer might have detected in our repeated singing ... something more than the hope of reaching heaven. We meant to reach the *north* – and the north was our Canaan" (Douglass 1994, p. 308).

In Haiti, the unique evolution of voodoo cult songs were instrumental in the organization and execution of the only fully successful revolution against slavery, which was launched through the Bois Caïman ceremony in 1791. In Brazil, where nearly 40 percent of African slaves disembarked, and the last place in the Americas to abolish slavery (on May 13, 1888), the jongo, an African-based dance/song ritual also served a similarly complex purpose and now represents an intergenerational movement in Brazil. It has been said about the jongo that

> those who recorded the *jongo* during the nineteenth century failed to grasp what these slave meetings really entailed, that is, oral histories versified in music containing the ironic criticisms of their masters, mistresses, and foremen; internal disputes; reverence for the past, and respect for Africans and their ancestors. Proverbs, metaphorical images, and coded messages were neither perceived nor mentioned by travelers.
> (Mattos & Abreu 2013, p. 80)

And through both protest song and jazz one finds the web of sound linking the American civil rights movement with the South African anti-apartheid movement, in the jazz of Hugh Masekela and the songs of Miriam Makeba and the evocative motif of Max Roach and Oscar Brown's 1960 collaboration *We Insist! – Max Roach's Freedom Now Suite*.[4]

The Dialectical Relationship of Memory and Resilience

For me the memory of frightful stories at bedtime mingle with the memory of my mother's love of music – the Saturday afternoon opera on the radio, the Beethoven symphonies and the voice of Paul Robeson singing the Negro Spiritual, "Sometimes I Feel Like a Motherless Child". Along with the felt sense of Edgar Allen Poe, I remember the felt sense of this sorrowful song. Too young to understand the metaphor within, I experienced a literal resonance. Sometimes I felt like a motherless child. And sometimes I felt like music was my mother. This was my own experience of resilience born from within vulnerability and in that dialectic lay the seeds of empathy and joy. For most people this dialectic is dependent upon acceptance into and participation in a community. For some people this requires a de novo creation of community.[5]

When we use our own personal narratives to understand the reverberations of pogroms, holocausts, middle passage, colonial oppression, the tyranny of fascism, we do not always find the sameness in our differences. Storytelling does not always bring us together. With few exceptions (there are some significant cultural differences in tonal systems), music and rhythm seem to be a universal language of healing. As psychologist and infant researcher Colwyn Trevarthan says:

> [m]usic is therapeutic in a more fundamental way than talk because it attunes to the essential efforts that the mind makes to regulate the body in both its inner processes and in its purposeful engagements with the objects of the world. It is also a direct way of engaging the human need to be sympathised [sic] with – to have what is going on inside appreciated by another who may give aid and encouragement.
> (Trevarthan 1999–2000, p. 198)

The sound and rhythm of drumming, humming, shouting and dancing together entrains us as a group. This entrainment, or synchronization of biological rhythms, boosts our immune system, improves heart rate variability and can create a trance-like sense of well-being. While the felt sense of well-being may be transient, the physiological changes over time are persistent. Studies in neonatal intensive care units show the sustained, positive impact of live music not seen when the music played is a recording (Arnon et al. 2006; Gilad & Arnon 2010). We need living, breathing social contact to entrain and that is one reason why social support boosts resilience. When I use the Tibetan singing bowl in my office with a patient I am facilitating entrainment. And perhaps in our clinical work, as our bodies entrain in a psychotherapeutic rhythm, we are having an epigenetic impact for generations to come.

Notes

1 The term resilience has become something of a buzzword. The American Psychological Association brochure on resilience states,

> Resilience is the process of adapting well in the face of adversity, trauma, tragedy, threats or significant sources of stress – such as family and relationship problems, serious health problems or workplace and financial stressors. It means "bouncing back" from difficult experiences. Research has shown that resilience is ordinary, not extraordinary. People commonly demonstrate resilience.
> (www.apa.org/helpcenter/road-resilience.aspx)

However, resilience is not simply about bouncing back. In a world challenged by deforestation, water scarcity and overpopulation, resilience has become a way of thinking about the biosphere. The Stockholm Resilience Center defines resilience as

> The capacity of a system – be it a forest, city or economy – to deal with change and continue to develop; withstanding shocks and disturbances (such as climate change or financial crises) and using such events to catalyse renewal and innovation.
> (www.stockholmresilience.org/download/18.10119fc11455d3c557d6 d21/1398172490555/SU_SRC_whatisresilience_sidaApril2014.pdf)

It is this concept of renewal and innovation that feels most relevant to the intergenerational transmission of trauma and resilience.
2 "Dissociative attunement is another way of talking about conscious, unconscious, embodied and embedded flow of information, addressing the physiological, neurobiological and mental synchronization of information processing within the therapeutic dyad" (Hopenwasser, 2016).
3 Deep Ecology is a term associated with the Norwegian philosopher Arnie Næss, referring to the interrelatedness of all systems on Earth as well as a belief that anthropocentrism is misguided. The concepts of deep ecology are well covered by Fritjof Capra in *The Web of Life: A New Scientific Understanding of Living Systems*.
4 In *We Insist!* the album opens with "Driva Man", in which Abby Lincoln sings a tale of slavery with tambourine and then rimshot starkly marking the sound of the whip. In "Triptych: Prayer, Protest, Peace", Lincoln sings a wordless song including shouting and screaming and humming. The final track, "Tears for Johannesburg", was written in response to the famed Sharpeville massacre in South Africa in 1960.
5 For example, Sidiki Conde, a Guinean born paraplegic drummer and dancer, along with other disabled performers, founded *Message de Espior* (The Message of Hope) in Conakry the capital city of Guinea. He is the subject of a documentary film, *You Don't Need Feet to Dance*.

References

Arnon, S., Shapsa, A., Forman, L., Regev, R., Bauer, S., Litmanovitz, I. & Dolfin, T. (2006) Live Music is Beneficial to Preterm Infants in the Neonatal Intensive Care Unit Environment, *Birth*, 33(2), pp. 131–136.
Barker, P. (1999) *Another World*, New York: Farrar Straus Giroux.
Bromberg, P. (1998) *Standing in the Spaces*, London: Routledge.
Bromberg, P. (2006) *Awakening the Dreamer*, London: Routledge.
Bromberg, P. (2011) *The Shadow of the Tsunami*, London: Routledge.
Capra, F. (1997) *The Web of Life: A New Scientific Understanding of Living Systems*, Norwall, MA: Anchor.

Carroll, S. (2010) *From Eternity to Here: The Quest for the Ultimate Theory of Time*, Boston, MA: Dutton Adult.

Chiew, F. (2012) Neuroplasticity as an Ecology of Mind, *Journal of Consciousness Studies*, 19(11–12), pp. 32–54.

Clifton, L. (1980) *two-headed woman*, Amherst, MA: University of Massachussetts Press.

Damasio, A., Carvalho, G.B. (2013) The Nature of Feelings: Evolutionary and Neurobiological Origins, *Nature Reviews Neuroscience*, 14, p. 149.

Dietz, D.M., LaPlan, Q., Watts, E.L., Hodes, G.E., Russo, S.J., Feng, J., Oosting, R.S., Vialou, V., Nestler, E.J. (2011) Paternal Transmission of Stress-Induced Pathologies, *Biological Psychiatry*, 70, pp. 408–414.

Douglass, F. (1994) *Autobiographies: Narrative of the Life of Frederick Douglass, an American Slave/My Bondage and My Freedom/Life and Times of Frederick Douglass Henry Louis Gates*, New York: ed. Library of America.

Du Bois, W.E. (2012) *The Souls of Black Folk*, digireads.com.

Faimberg, H. (1988) The Telescoping of Generations: Genealogy of Certain Identifications, *Contemporary Psychoanalysis*, 24(1), pp. 99–118.

Farnsworth, K.D., Nelson, J., Gershenson, C. (2013) Living is Information Processing, from Molecules to Global Systems, *Acta Biotheoretica*, 61(2), pp. 203–222.

Gapp, K., Jawaid, A., Sarkies, P., Bohacek, J., Pelczar, P., Prados, J., Farinelli, L., Miska, E., Mansuy, I.M. (2014) Implication of Sperm RNAs in Transgenerational Inheritance of the Effects of Early Trauma in Mice, *Nature Neuroscience*, 17, pp. 667–669.

Gilad, E., Arnon, S. (2010) The Role of Live Music and Singing as a Stress-Reducing Modality in the Neonatal Intensive Care Unit Environment, *Music and Medicine*, 2(1), pp. 18–22.

Glennie, E. (2007) www.ted.com/talks/evelyn_glennie_shows_how_to_listen.

Gratier, M., Trevarthan, C. (2008) Musical Narrative and Motives for Culture in Mother–Infant Vocal Interaction, *Journal of Consciousness Studies*, 15(10–11), pp. 122–158.

Hameroff, S., Marcer, P. (1998) Quantum Computation in Brain Microtubules? The Penrose–Hameroff "Orch OR" Model of Consciousness, *Philosophical Transactions: Mathematical, Physical and Engineering Sciences*, 356(1743), Quantum Computation: Theory and Experiment, pp. 1869–1896.

Hameroff, S., Penrose, R. (1996) Orchestrated Reduction of Quantum Coherence in Brain Microtubules: A Model for Consciousness, *Mathematics and Computers in Simulation*, 40(3), pp. 453–480.

Hameroff, S., Watt, R. (1982) Information Processing in Microtubules, *Journal of Theoretical Biology*, 98, pp. 549–561.

Hill, R. (1998) Immersed in Words, in Ortiz, S.J., *Speaking for the Generations: Native Writers on Writing*, Tucson, AZ: University of Arizona Press, pp. 73–91.

Hopenwasser, K. (2008) Being in Rhythm: Dissociative Attunement in Therapeutic Process, *Journal of Trauma and Dissociation*, 9(3), pp. 349–367.

Hopenwasser, K. (2009) Bearing the Unbearable: Meditations on Being in Rhythm, *Voices, The Journal of the American Academy of Psychotherapists*, 45(2), pp. 67–73.

Hopenwasser, K. (2016) Dissociative Attunement in a Resonant World, in Howell, E., Itzkowitz, S., *Psychoanalysis and the Dissociative Mind*. Oxford: Routledge, pp. 175–186.

Jordania, J. (2010) Music and Emotions: Humming in Human Prehistory, Proceedings of the International Symposium on Traditional Polyphony, held in Tbilisi, Georgia in

2008. International Research Center for Traditional Polyphony of Tbilisi State Conservatory.

Kaufman, J., Herzog, A. (2006) *The Collected Poems of Muriel Rukeyser*, Pittsburgh, PA: University of Pittsburgh Press.

Khan, H.I. (1996) *The Mysticism of Sound and Music*, Boulder, CO: Shambhala Press.

Knoblauch, S.H. (2011) Contextualizing Attunement within the Polyrhythmic Weave: The Psychoanalytic Samba, *Psychoanalytic Dialogues*, 21, pp. 414–427.

Loewenstein, W.R. (2013) *Physics in Mind: A Quantum View of the Brain*, New York: Basic Books.

McNeill, W. (1995) *Keeping Together in Time: Dance and Drill in Human History*, Cambridge, MA: Harvard University Press.

Malan-Muller, S., Seedat, S., Hemmings, S.M.J. (2014) Understanding Posttraumatic Stress Disorder: Insights from the Methylome, *Genes, Brain and Behavior*, 13, pp. 52–68.

Mattos, H., Abreu, M. (2013) *Jongo*, Recalling History, in Monteiro, P.M. and Stone, M., *Cangoma Calling, Spirits and Rhythms of Freedom in Brazilian Jongo Slavery Songs*, www.laabst.net/.

Michaels, A. (1997) *Fugitive Pieces*, New York: Alfred Knopf.

Nebbiosi, G., Nebbiosi, F. (2007) "We" Got Rhythm: Miming and the Polyphony of Identity in Psychoanalysis, in Anderson, F., *Bodies in Treatment: The Unspoken Dimension*, London: Routledge, pp. 213–236.

Ortiz, S.J. (2002) Time as Memory as Story, in *Out There Somewhere (Sun Tracks)*, Tucson, AZ: University of Arizona Press.

Powers, A. (2013) NPR music blog, www.npr.org/blogs/therecord/2013/11/12/244851884/12-years-a-slave-is-this-years-best-film-about-music.

Rukeyser, M. (2006) The Speed of Darkness, in *The Collected Poems of Muriel Rukeyser*, Pittsburgh, PA: University of Pittsburgh Press.

Sander, L.W. (2002) Thinking Differently: Principles of Process in Living Systems and the Specificity of being Known, *Psychoanalytic Dialogues*, 12(1), pp. 11–42.

Schwab, G. (2010) *Haunting Legacies: Violent Histories and Transgenerational Trauma*, New York: Columbia University Press.

Skelton, K., Ressler, K.J., Norrholm, S.D., Jovanovic, T., Bradley-Davino, B. (2012) PTSD and Gene Variants: New Pathways and New Thinking, *Neuropharmacology*, 62, pp. 628–637.

Tapahonso, L. (1993) *Sáanii Dahataati: The Women are Singing*, Tucson, AZ: University of Arizona Press.

Thompson, E. (2010) *Mind in Life: Phenomenology and the Sciences of Mind*, Cambridge, MA: Belknap Press.

Trevarthan, C. (1999–2000) Musicality and the Intrinsic Motive Pulse: Evidence from Human Psychobiology and Infant Communication, *Musicae Scientia*, Special Issue, pp. 155–215.

van der Knaap, L.J., Riese, H., Hudziak, J.J., Verbiest, M.M., Verhulst, F.C., Oldehinkel, A.J., van Oort, F.V. (2014) Glucocorticoid Receptor Gene (NR3C1) Methylation following Stressful Events between Birth and Adolescence, *Translational Psychiatry*, 4, p. e381.

Vedral, V. (2008) Quantifying Entanglement in Macroscopic Systems, *Nature*, 19 June, pp. 1004–1007.

Wang, Z., Busemeyer, J.R., Atmanspachaer, E.P. (2013) The Potential of Using Quantum Theory to Build Models of Cognition, *Topics in Cognitive Science*, 5, pp. 672–688.

Watrous, A., Tandon, N., Conner, C.R., Pieters, T., Ekstrom, A.D. (2013) Frequency-Specific Network Connectivity Increases underlie Accurate Spatiotemporal Memory Retrieval, *Nature Neuroscience*, 16(3), pp. 349–356

Wright, J. (2006) Songs of Remembrance, *Journal of African American History*, 91(4), pp. 413–424.

Yehuda, R., Daskalakis, N.P., Lehrner, A., Desarnaud, F., Bader, H.N., Makotkine, I., Flory, J.D., Bierer, L.M., Meaney, M.J. (2014) Influences of Maternal and Paternal PTSD on Epigenetic Regulation of the Glucocorticoid Receptor Gene in Holocaust Survivor Offspring, *American Journal of Psychiatry*, 171, pp. 872–880.

Copyright information

"For What It's Worth". Words and Music by Stephen Stills. Copyright © 1967 (Renewed) COTILLION MUSIC INC., TEN EAST MUSIC, SPRINGALO TOONES and RICHIE FURAY MUSIC. All Rights Administered by WARNER-TAMERLANE PUBLISHING CORP. All Rights Reserved. Used By Permission of ALFRED MUSIC.

"The Speed of Darkness" by Muriel Rukeyser, Used by Permission. All rights reserved.

From Sáanii Dahataal/The Women Are Singing: Poems and Stories by Luci Tapahonso. © 1993 Luci Tapahonso. Reprinted by permission of the University of Arizona Press.

Copyright © 1980 by Lucille Clifton. Now appears in The Collected Poems of Lucille Clifton 1965–2010 by Lucille Clifton, published by BOA Editions. Reprinted by permission of Curtis Brown, Ltd.

1991 PBS program, THE SONGS ARE FREE, www.pbs.org/moyers/journal/11232007/profile3.html.

Chapter 4

The Texture of Traumatic Attachment
Presence and Ghostly Absence in Transgenerational Transmission

Jill Salberg

When I was five or six years old, I had a recurring dream, actually more a nightmare. I dreamt that I was with my parents and older sister in what looked like a smoke-filled saloon from a 1950s Hollywood Western. The atmosphere was tense and I was aware of a legend about a witch who had a brown paper bag filled with cancer. If she put it under your chair, you would die. The witch entered the saloon and placed the bag under my chair. I would wake up terrified, paralyzed with fear. I never understood why I kept dreaming this dream. In time it faded.

I was fortunate to know my grandparents as an adult. One day, in speaking with my mother's mother, she told me of a recent nightmare she had had. She said she dreamt it often. She dreamt that she would walk out of the subway in Brooklyn and not know where she was. She would feel terrified in the dream – not just lost, but terrorized by *lostness*. As she told me this dream, I could sense her real panic, her terror at being alone in the world. I was in my thirties and wanted to reassure my terrified, beloved grandmother; I tried, although I was not sure I could.

I did not yet know my grandmother's trauma – her own mother's death during childbirth when my grandmother was just four years old – or how to understand its entrance into my childhood and my dreamscape. It was only during a second analysis, one more open to the occurrence of transgenerational transmissions, that I came to know and understand that multiple generations and their trauma histories inhabited my world, my nightmare. It was only then that the witch with death in a paper bag stopped haunting me.

How does one explain the occurrence of anxieties, terrors, and nightmares that inhabit the children and grandchildren of trauma survivors (who

Reprinted with kind permision:
Salberg, J. (2015). The Texture of Traumatic Attachment: Presence and Ghostly Absence in Trans-Generational Transmission. *Psychoanalytic Quarterly*, LXXXIV (1): 21–46.

have been called the second and third generation) when the content fits the actual experience of the first-person trauma survivor? The process, as discussed in the literature, sounds almost magical: passage from grandparent to parent to child, extruding unconscious toxic contents. It feels mystifying.

I propose that the mode of transmission is much more understandable if we utilize the lens of attachment theories and research as a through line to weave together multiple literatures. The intersection that I want to focus on is how a person carries within his or her mind and inscribed on his or her body numerous histories of experiences within the family's legacy of traumas and losses, along with the family's culture and external world. How do trauma survivors transmit these unspoken fragments to their children? Given my dream, this question was deeply personal, a psychological imperative for me. However, I came to believe that it was also an imperative for psychoanalysis.

The growing literature on transgenerational transmission of trauma has begun to provide a much-needed expansion of the psychoanalytic field. Ogden (2008), in writing about Bion's ideas on cognition, suggests that one of Bion's central ideas was that "it requires two minds to think one's most disturbing thoughts" (p. 20). I would elaborate on this, drawing on Faimberg's (2005) idea that what occurs is a history of identifications, what she has termed a *telescoping of generations*, and I would suggest that it may take three generations to contain disturbing feelings and events. This has been a central feature in the concept of the transmission of traumatic experience from the first to the second or third generation: that parents extrude the traumatic contents of their minds into their children.

The work on transgenerational transmission of trauma often refers to these unspoken stories, but the mode of transmission has been shadowy and poorly defined. In proposing attachment as the mode of transmission, I hope to integrate theories and thus clarify our own and our patients' experiences. Understanding the role of attachment and the mutual regulation and/or dissociation of affects within human relationships opens the door to deepening our conception of how transmissions occur implicitly and explicitly. Parents and children form an attachment unit that allows for deep unconscious communication of fear and safety, of anxiety and security, of closeness and distance, love and hatred, and so much more. All of this is often transmitted through the registers of attunement and misattunement and the active processes of self-other regulation of affects.

Children are constantly observing their parents' gestures and affects, absorbing their parents' conscious and unconscious minds. In the shifting registers of attunement and misattunement, children adjust and adapt to the emotional presence and absence of their caregivers/parents, always searching for attachment. These searches begin at birth and occur before there are words, when there are gazes, stares, sounds, and touch – as well as the absence of these. This is how stories are told, even when not spoken, in the nonverbal and preverbal affective realms – silent and vocal, yet played out in subtexts, often on the implicit level.[1]

My own thinking reflects a zeitgeist shift in the field from the nuclear orbit of the primal oedipal family – two parents and a child, in what I would term a *one-generation model* – to a broader view that incorporates the influences of disrupted attachment across multiple generations. Additionally, the burgeoning field of epigenetics, which looks at the "bidirectional interchange between heredity and environment" (Gottlieb 1991, p. 33), offers much-needed explanatory power as to how environmental factors and historical time may affect gene expression and possible inheritable aspects of these expressions. For example, recent research in neuroscience suggests that epigenetics may account for some of the findings of transgenerational transmission of stress as measured by increased cortisol levels. Lyons-Ruth (2002) writes that findings from the research literature on rats

> ... converge with findings from human attachment studies that have also documented the link between disorganized attachment strategies and elevated Cortisol levels to stressors. In addition, human attachment studies have documented the inter-generational transmission of attachment strategies over two and three generations.
>
> (pp. 108–109)

Kohler (2012), in summarizing research findings on the effects of environment on epigenetics, writes:

> Some epigenetic "marks," i.e., specific chemical attachments such as a methyl group, can be transgenerationally transmitted.... In the context where epigenetic changes can be inherited and passed on to subsequent generations, the "nurture" of one generation contributes to the "nature" of subsequent generations.

In this way, I believe we must conceptualize transgenerational transmissions in multiply determined and nonlinear ways: transmissions are always multigenerational and richly influenced by context, both historical and personal, and are carried in the mind and in the body. No one theory can begin to explain this, and for that reason we must draw from many sources and interweave various points of view to understand the complexity of experience.

Tracing History, Emerging Themes

I have come to realize that I think of psychoanalysis today – and what may someday be referred to as the *transgenerational turn* – as a kind of paradigm shift. Until recently, psychoanalytic focus had been on intrapsychic and interpersonal relationships, often evolving its ideas split off from the applied world of psychoanalysis – the world of cultural, political, historical, and trauma studies. Psychoanalysis has simultaneously addressed and denied the *wounds of history*, thereby enacting what Herman (1992) termed our "episodic amnesia" (p. 8) about trauma. We are now at a moment when theories of transgenerational transmission of traumas, formed through the epochs of great wars, famine, dislocation, the Shoah and other genocides, slavery, immigration, and now climate catastrophes, coincide with the volumes of scholarship within individual psychoanalysis, attachment research and theories of attachment disorders, and studies on the neurobiology of the mind–body experience, along with our contemporary understanding of dissociation and affect regulation.

Psychoanalysis has always been divided in conceptualizing the genesis of human suffering. I think of Charcot's work studying the enigma of hysteria and Freud's brief time studying in Paris before taking his ideas back to Vienna, first to Breuer, then Fliess – while Janet's work on dissociation remained separate, taken up again only recently (Davies 1996). There was Ferenczi's pioneering work on trauma and mutual analysis, and his prescient understanding of dissociative phenomena, all of which put him at great odds with Freud. His work clearly demonstrated that he understood a child has had to bear two traumas (Ferenczi 1932), the first of which is the pain of an actual reality event. Ferenczi's focus on real acts carried out by grownups put him in opposition to Freud's insistence on unconscious fantasy, as did his resolve about the harm caused by adults' disavowal and denial.

Ferenczi's focus on real events and the refusal of acknowledgment by those whose care matters the most to the child is what I would term a *failure of witnessing* and the serious damage that it causes. Freud's reaction against Ferenczi's ideas (and the forces that Ernest Jones would later bring to bear) allowed the suppression of Ferenczi's work for many decades after his death. This permitted psychoanalysis to develop without a recognition of the significance and reality of trauma, while trauma studies and the intergenerational transmission of trauma evolved as an isolated area of study outside the field of psychoanalysis. Imagine our historical course if Ferenczi's work had entered mainstream psychoanalysis in 1932.

The arrival of Bowlby's work (1958) stands as a watershed moment to many in the attachment field, with his understanding of the traumatic effects of children's enforced separations from their mothers during hospital stays. While in supervision with Klein, Bowlby became interested in a mother's extremely anxious state and its impact on the child. Despite Klein's absolute indifference to this, Bowlby forged ahead in exploring the "intergenerational transmission of attachment difficulties and how unresolved issues in one generation can be visited on the next" (Coates 2004a, p. 577). Nonetheless, a rift was apparent, and instead of allowing an interpenetration of ideas, the British Psychoanalytical Society alienated Bowlby, viewing his ideas as nonpsychoanalytic.

I imagine that Bowlby's rift with Klein was seen as a betrayal not only of Klein's ideas, but also of the entire psychoanalytic enterprise. Klein's dedication was to expanding Freud's intrapsychic developmental vision to early infancy. It is interesting to note that Klein's alignment with Freud in drive theory – specifically, the death instinct and internal phantasy over reality/trauma – was antithetical to the view of her first analyst, Ferenczi.[2] However, her persistence in disregarding the actual mother and the real environment were directly in opposition to Bowlby's experiences during the war years, when he helped evacuate children out of London. Anna Freud and Dorothy Burlingham were also part of this group aiding children; they allowed for what Fonagy (1999) referred to as *multitrack* developmental networks.

Bowlby believed that there had been clear evidence that a singular focus on internal phantasy without regard for the mother or the context was misguided. Despite the lack of support from the British Society (Holmes suggests that Bowlby was "virtually airbrushed out of the psychoanalytic record," 1995, p. 20), Bowlby maintained that his work on attachment as a separate and primary motivational system was indeed psychoanalytic.

Concurrent with some of these developments in England was the work being done in the United States by Sullivan (1953), whose interest in cultural forces and the immediate interpersonal interaction held sway over the intrapsychic. The toxic effect of the mother's anxiety on the child was critical in the development of Sullivan's ideas about defensive operations – specifically, personifications of *good-me*, *not-me*, and *bad-me*. Although not a direct theory of multiple self-states or an explicit study of attachment, this conception of Sullivan's is a clear precursor to what we now call *relational trauma*.

Intersecting all these streams of thought were the great societal changes and historical upheavals of the twentieth century. It is undoubtedly an understatement to say that both World War I and World War II massively disrupted tens of thousands of lives. Psychoanalysis has been altered in ways that have taken decades for us to begin to comprehend. Prince (2009) believes that, here in the United States, "psychoanalysis is a survivor of the Holocaust" (p. 179), and that many of our analytic ideas reveal a delayed or incomplete mourning. Also in this vein, Kuriloff (2010) wrote about the silence that ensued after postwar analysts – many of whom were Jews who had been subjected to great hardship – fled Europe and immigrated to the Americas. She noted that our analytic theories show a lack of evidence of – or perhaps it is more appropriate to say a *missing presence* of – what had just transpired and been endured.

Aron and Starr (2013) also investigated the flight of Jewish analysts from Europe and the ensuing silence regarding the trauma they and their patients had endured. Aron and Starr extended Prince's (2009) idea of psychoanalysis itself as a trauma survivor, arguing that it was born out of trauma to begin with and grown during the developing seeds of virulent anti-Semitism in a Europe pervaded by enduring racism, misogyny, and homophobia.

It is interesting to posit that, with any trauma, it often takes the passage of some time before processing can take place. Time was certainly needed for metabolizing the trauma of the Holocaust in order to be able to study it, and perhaps this further delayed a more generalized transgenerational transmission study of other historical traumas. Davoine (2007) believes that it takes half a century to process a war, suggesting an even longer gestational period of silence. Analysts did not start writing about the effects of World War II and Holocaust-related trauma on psychoanalytic theory and practice for quite some time – until, as Laub and Auerhahn (1993) suggest, subsequent analytic generations started to metabolize this wound of history. Bergmann and Jucovy (1982) located the earliest writings in psychoanalysis regarding the effects of the Holocaust on its survivors in the early 1960s and on the second generation several years later.

In 1967, the International Psychoanalytical Association held the first symposium on this topic, entitled "Psychic Traumatization through Social Catastrophe." Early contributors found common features in survivor families. Kestenberg (1972) investigated the effects of the Holocaust on the second generation and was instrumental in highlighting the idea that survivor-parents can transmit conflict and psychopathology to their offspring as a result of their own trauma incurred during the Holocaust. Kestenberg, along with Epstein (1979), initiated scholarship on the transgenerational transmission of Holocaust-related traumas to subsequent generations.

The focus of the early transgenerational literature was on the transmission of one person's experience to his or her child or grandchild, whether positive or negative. This process has felt static to me, limiting our view of the nuanced and fluid dance that actually occurs between parent and child. In moving to an attachment-based theory focusing on mutual affect regulation between mother and child, we can more easily recognize the constant interchange between parent and child around mood, affects, and their intensities. This process, and the ways in which it penetrates the clinical situation, have been explored by the Boston Change Process Study Group (2010).

The Impact of Trauma and History

Laub (1998), director and primary investigator for the video testimony project at Yale University's Genocide Studies Program, coined the poignant phrase *the empty circle*, drawing on a dream element of one of his patients. The motif of *the empty circle* captured "the absence of representation, the rupture of the self, the erasure of memory, and the accompanying sense of void that are the core legacy of massive psychic trauma" (p. 507). Despite knowledge of their parents' trauma, the children of trauma survivors experience a hole, an absence, in their family member survivors, Laub found. I would add that this hole or absence is part of the traumatizing effect on the child. I wonder, what does it feel like for a child to attach to a parent with a hole, an *empty circle*? Laub's *empty circle* affectingly captures the oddness of these traumatic transmissions from parent to child. There is a strange amalgam here of absence – of a gap of knowledge and of emptiness, simultaneously mixed with over-fullness or an excess of certain affects: often fear, dread, and even terror.

What are the affective aspects and psychic consequences for the child of an emotionally absent or fragmentary parent? Green (1972) was the first to describe a version of this experience for the child. He termed this kind of absent parent a *dead mother* – someone alive but not present, once enlivened but now, due to depression, lost to the child in what must seem an inexplicable way. Does the child feel fear? Longing? Grief? Green terms this a *psychosis blanche* – a blank or white state, absent anxiety, or mourning. This state of blankness causes the child's premature disillusionment with the mother. In Winnicott's (e.g., 1953) terms, this is *the catastrophe*, while for Green it entailed a further loss of meaning. The child detaches from this *dead mother* while simultaneously identifying with her. In the unconscious psyche, deadness and the loss of meaning are now installed.

In the past ten to fifteen years, this scholarship has been extended to other political and social traumas and genocides, as evidenced by the work on war by Davoine and Gaudillière (2004). Apprey (1996, 2003) and Gump (2000, 2010) have specifically added a great deal to our understanding of the traumatic legacies of slavery for African Americans. Grand (2000) wrote movingly about the experience of trauma survivors, enabling us to feel firsthand the moment of *dying without dying* that the survivor has felt and the awful sequelae of loneliness. She traced how trauma is then "reproduced" and visited on the next generation: "Evil is an attempt to answer the riddle of catastrophic loneliness. Unlike all other forms of human interaction, evil alone bears witness to the contradictory claims of solitude and mutuality that haunt traumatic memory" (p. 5). Grand helped us see how children become trapped in their parents' pain and trauma, endlessly seeking a parent who remains just out of reach.

Children are hungry for emotional/psychological contact with their parents, whether this is conceptualized as their being compelled to seek safety (Bowlby, e.g., 1958) or as their having a kind of attachment imperative (Bromberg 2011). In line with Grand, I believe the child will need to seek out even the parent's traumatized self. In this vein, Laub's *empty circle* can be seen as a form of Harlow's wire monkey (Harlow 1959). I believe that in the absence of a fully emotionally vital and present parent, the child nonetheless attaches not only to what is present, but also to what is absent – what is alive as well as what is deadened. This is Gerson's (2009) significant contribution: helping us understand that the imprint of absence on the child, the legacy of the trauma and loss without someone to empathically witness these experiences, becomes what Gerson termed – referencing Green (1972) – a *dead third*. He noted that the final experience for such a child is a "not-there-ness [that] constitutes both the 'gap' or absence as well as what fills the absence" (p. 1347).

While working in Israel, Gampel (1996) described losses that could not be symbolized and were not put into narrative form, becoming what she termed *psychic holes*. Perhaps even worse than Laub's *empty circle*, these empty internal spaces may then be filled with "only some radioactive remnants that can't be transformed into memory" (Gampel and Mazor 2004, p. 547). Given the lengthy half-life process for metabolizing trauma, likened to the time it would take for radioactive material to decay, we might expect that multiple generations will inevitably be exposed to some derivative of the trauma.

Faimberg (2005), in writing about this type of transmission, this *telescoping of generations* from parent to child, found in her patient Mario someone absent from his own life and experience – while he was in fact present in the secret lives of his parents prior to his own birth. However, for Faimberg, the interior of the child of a trauma survivor is not so much empty as it is filled with a condensed history of the parent, causing an "alienated identification" in the child. She writes, "The identifications constitute a 'link between generations,' which are alienating and opposed to any psychic representation" (p. 15). Furthermore, Faimberg believes that the child inhabits an unacceptable part of the parent, an unconscious *not-me* experience.

This is quite close to what Bromberg (1994, 2006, 2011) explicates in his work on dissociative experience, attachment, and relational trauma. Both Faimberg and Bromberg utilize and extend Sullivan's (1953) early concept of *not-me* personifications to highlight and explain dissociative transmissions. Undergirding this is Sullivan's early focus on transmissions of anxiety through the mother–child bond, starting in infancy. Sullivan, in focusing on anxiety as a key stressor in the early bonds of childhood, asserted that anxiety was inevitably transmitted from mother to child and was the key disruptive force. I believe this occurs to an even greater degree if trauma underpins the anxiety and becomes part of the fabric of the mother–child attachment.

Trauma work continued to be split off from mainstream psychoanalysis for many decades and, as a result, the prevailing analytic model was a *one-generation* model. We are often taught to ask our patients about early experiences in growing up with their parents, but we are not necessarily encouraged to look further back than one generation, resulting in a kind of myopia that limits our field of vision. It is interesting to note that, even with the paradigm shift from a one-person to a two-person psychology/model of mind, our discipline did not make a naturally analogous shift to a multigenerational model. It is very possible that ideas about transgenerational transmission of trauma could not enter into psychoanalytic thought until the field became more expansive, embracing new configurations of family, cultural issues, and problems with attachment. Reis (2007) reminded us that "American analytic literature continues to fail to bear full witness to the gravity and meaning of catastrophic world history" (p. 623).

With this in mind, how are we to understand the kind of behavior exemplified by the individual who tattooed his upper arm with an image of the Armenian flag and the number of people killed in the Armenian genocide of the early twentieth century, or a young man in Israel tattooing his grandparent's number from Auschwitz on his wrist? Rudoren (2012) suggests, "The ten tattooed descendants interviewed for this article echoed one another's motivations: they wanted to be intimately, eternally bonded to their survivor-relative" (p. 1). How are we to think about a desire to be, as those interviewed reported, "eternally bonded" to a parent or grandparent, particularly when trauma is part of their lives? How can we begin to understand how a horrific trauma, one that for many could not be talked about yet was never forgotten, now appears in this form of remembrance – a kind of skin memorialization, a sign of attachment and love? Apprey (1996, 2003) has written extensively on the transformation of negative forms of degradation from African American slave generations (tattoos, piercings) into similar practices found in modern black ghetto culture.

I think that, for the most part, we now accept the notion of unconscious transmission of trauma, but how do we understand how trauma, once it has been transmitted to successive generations, can be transmuted into positive experiences grafted onto attachment phenomena? What happens transgenerationally to diffuse or transmute what once was horrific – concretely embodied on an arm by a number denoting how many died, or a concentration camp number – into something to be desired and perpetuated by a family member of a subsequent generation?

Young (1993) highlighted an important distinction between memorials and monuments: "We erect monuments so that we shall always remember and build memorials so that we shall never forget" (Danto quoted by Young, p. 3). Perhaps we can think of such a tattoo as a skin memorialization – one that, in never allowing us to forget, keeps in check the destructive aggression of the trauma, but additionally celebrates survival and even resilience.

Alternatively, Abraham and Torok (1975; see also Torok 1968) described a place of internal memorialization that they termed a *crypt*, inside of which is a beloved corpse. Although their work is not explicitly focused on attachment, the search for the lost bond is at its core. Might this explain the new generation's tattoos as an externalization onto the skin, the body ego – like a carving on a headstone? Harris (2007) invokes Abraham and Torok (1975) in discussing Davoine's (2007) therapeutic work that tracks history, war, and multiple internal worlds. She writes:

> Once you begin to think this way about the shadowy line between the living and the dead, about the active absence and presence of spectral figures in our consulting rooms, in our dream lives, and in our lives, a rich experience of self and others opens up.
> (Harris 2007, p. 663)

Ghostly Attachments: The Vehicle of Transmission

I want to try to unpack how a child inevitably becomes intertwined with, and then comes to bear and live out, the family's trauma legacy. Bowlby's (1958) original work on attachment and the subsequent literature that elaborated his ideas have long shown the primary need for children to have a safe base in order to establish secure attachment, and how this underlies later social development. However, if a parent has self-states that are dysregulated or even dissociative, I think we can assume that he or she will be in some way emotionally compromised, and thus at times inaccessible to the child to help with self-regulation, self-soothing, and mentalization of feelings and thoughts.

As early as 1975, Fraiberg, Adelson, and Shapiro described trauma transmission in the attachment relationship between mothers and their children. These authors identified cases that included multigenerational trauma histories with dysregulated affect and problematic mother–infant attachments. In what I read as a description of the early treatment of transgenerational attachment trauma, Fraiberg, Adelson, and Shapiro offered the traumatized parent a deeply empathic witness in the form of a therapist who could allow the parent/patient to slowly come out of dissociation and become able to experience pain, grief, and terror for the first time. Furthermore, what was demonstrated was how this kind of therapeutic intervention around transgenerational transmission of attachment trauma allows for resilience to be fostered in the mothers.

More recently, Schore (2001) and Fonagy (1999) have written at great length regarding the necessary function that caregivers provide to the emotional and cognitive growth of children. When there are absent parts of the parents that the child cannot emotionally touch, what might a child have to do to attach to the parent? Grand (2000) wrote about the child's craving to connect to the absent space in the traumatized parent, speaking explicitly to a nexus of attachment, absence, embodied transmission, and unconscious fantasy. She described the resultant holes in parental bonding and the second generation's search for the parents' traumatized and pretraumatized selves. As she put it:

> To search for one's parent and to find fear in a handful of dust: such a dilemma precipitates a hunger for visceral contact with the parent's traumatized self.... To bond with the survivor's state of infinite nullification, the child may attempt to meet his parent in the intimate specificity of bodily torment.
>
> (pp. 25–26)

Gerson's (2009) further elaboration and contribution to these ideas help us understand the nature of the imprint of absence on the child. How does this child find a way to attach and feel connected to the parent who has had to detach from his or her own experience and mind?

I propose that we turn to the knowledge gained from attachment theory and infant research (Beebe and Lachmann 2013; Coates 2004a, 2004b, 2012, in press; Lyons-Ruth 2002, 2003; Slade 2014; Steele and Steele 2008; and others) and our relatively new emphasis on empathic attunement (as described by the Boston Process Change Group 2010), as well as work on relational trauma (Bromberg 1994, 2006, 2011; Schore 2001).

Absence, deadness, and dysregulated attachment are common features of survival, as discussed by Bergmann and Jucovy (1982), Faimberg (1996, 1998, 2005), Gampel (1996), Grand (2000), Davoine and Gaudillière (2004), and Laub (1998). We can now apprehend the dilemma of second and third generations who, from birth, have been cared for by parents with dysregulated affects and possibly dissociative self-states.

As a consequence of the unmetabolized trauma of actual events, attachment is inevitably affected, and what we have come to call *relational trauma* ensues (Coates 2004a, 2004b, 2012, in press; Fonagy 1999). In their primary attachment relationships, these children have had to manage fragmentation resulting from parental traumatization. (The caveat here is that this is not true of *all* such children, since survival resilience can also be transmitted.)

In longitudinal work, Lyons-Ruth (2003) has researched and documented the effects of contradictory maternal behaviors with infants who show disorganized attachment behaviors. She has found that:

> To the extent that the parent cannot acknowledge and respond to affectively salient aspects of experience, and to the extent that those aspects cannot be integrated into a verbal and interactive exchange with the child, dissociative lack of integration will occur.
> (pp. 900–901)

Lyons-Ruth likens her findings to what Bromberg (1994) argued: that dissociative states are the result of the parent's nonrecognition of the child's feelings – what Bromberg, drawing on Sullivan, calls the *not-me*. It is this fragmentation directly resulting from the parent's incapacity that is transmitted to the child, who must not know what he/she actually does know.

Additionally, Slade (2014) argues that we need to rediscover Bowlby's clear emphasis on *fear* as the motivational basis for attachment and a significant factor in the organization of internal psychic experience. This is key, Slade believes, to understanding the biological underpinnings that Bowlby tried to integrate. It is *fearful arousal* that propels the child to seek the mother for safety, both physical and relational. Bowlby felt this was a reciprocal system: the complement to the child's need is the caregiver's response. When caregivers fail to soothe, do not reassure, or are in fact abandoning or in some way scary, the child's attachment suffers.

Slade urges us to keep in mind that since fear is so primal in our evolutionary biological/social being, anything that increases fear is problematic. Trauma clearly complicates attachment, and when it is transmitted transgenerationally, the person of safety may also be the person to be feared.

Lieberman (2014) underscores this, writing:

> Dysregulated and traumatized parents can be very frightening to their children.... They transmit their internal disorganization to their children, not only by directing their anger, punitiveness, and unpredictability towards the child but also by exposing them to a cacophony of daily, real-life situations that are helplessly witnessed or experienced by the child.
>
> (p. 278)

Halasz (2011) utilized the techniques of infant–mother attachment research on himself and his mother. Using a split-screen format, he videotaped his own reactions while he watched his mother's Holocaust testimony. Tracking subtle changes in his facial expressions, gaze, voice, and breathing patterns, Halasz made evident the ongoing attachment mechanisms involved in trauma transmissions from parent to child. Drawing on the work of Bromberg and Schore, Halasz argued that the changes he saw in himself on video revealed his emotional movement from moments of matching his mother's affective states to moments of detaching from her states. He believes that his facial expressions were suggestive markers of his attunement and dissociation.

Harris (2014) incorporates Slade's underscoring of fear in attachment with Bromberg's development and elaboration on dissociative self-states. She writes, "The intergenerational transmission of trauma in which fear states linked often to unrecognized experiences of disrupted safety in one generation leak into and terrorize the next, often in nonverbal and early unmetabolized forms" (p. 270). Halasz's work demonstrates this so well.

When the traumatized parent remains resilient and alive, this state-shifting or fragmentation may be tolerable and fleeting for the child. I suggest that, in order to bond and attach in ever-more dysregulated circumstances, the child must attune to procedural communications about the trauma story, much as Halasz learned to do. The child must do this in order to have an attachment relationship, thereby becoming attached to a parent's presence and absence.

The matching and tuning "dance" done by the child is often what attachment researchers like Lyons-Ruth (2002, 2003) consider a form of role reversal – that is, the child is attempting to affectively regulate the parent in lieu of the parent regulating the child. I believe this is the child's ongoing attempt to repair the parent from the outside – a repair that can never be complete since the damage is actually on the inside. This will become the *texture of traumatic attachment* – how it feels to this child to feel connected to the parent. This textured affective experience is one in which the child shapes him-/herself to fit a parent's wound of history, be it war, rape, slavery, death – the list goes on. This may also be the place in which the child grows a kind of resilience, since in role reversal, the child is called upon to grow up sooner and to be, in a precocious manner, the more affectively regulated one.

Fundamentally, attachment is the oxygen of our emotional lives, serving to create a feeling of safety and security, allowing us to learn how to be socially human and operationally teaching us how to self-regulate our affective lives. It is because of attachment's primal aspect in our psyches that trauma and its impact constitute massive disruption and disorganization of the parent–child bonding system. When trauma revisits us transgenerationally through disrupted attachment patterns, it is within the child's empathic attunement and bond that the mode of transmission can be found.

The parent's deep bond and affective intensity may be generated from within an unmetabolized trauma scene. As a consequence, the child – in order to attach to this parent and get this parent attached to her/him – will need to enter and become enmeshed in the trauma scene. Through empathic mirroring and what Hopenwasser (2008) called *dissociative attunement*, the parents' trauma story enters the child's cellular makeup before there are words, and thus before a narrative can be told.

Harris (2006), in writing about ghosts, captures the haunting quality of transgenerational transmissions and believes that ghosts always suggest where mourning has not occurred. Much in line with Harris, and with Coates (2012) and Fraiberg, Adelson, and Shapiro (1975), I believe that these transmissions, our "ghosts," will always involve textured attachment patterns that then encode the wound of history.

My Ghosts, My Story

I return now to my recurring nightmare from childhood. I am making this dream a focus now because it clearly haunted my childhood, was briefly discussed in a first analysis, and returned as material in my second analysis. My first analysis began in the mid-1970s and continued through the 80s as part of my analytic training. This analysis in many ways focused on classic oedipal themes, with this dream as one of many pieces that my first analyst believed elucidated and gave form to the shape of oedipal dynamics in my family. Deep understanding led to many changes in my life, and by the end of that analysis, I hardly recalled the dream. It became more completely part of the past, belonging to childhood, as so many things do post-analysis. Or so I believed.

A decade and a half later, I decided to enter a second analysis, and my dream resurfaced and allowed me to see it as a focal point of transgenerational transmission work yet to be done. I can no longer recall the order in which I learned the following facts about my own birth and my grandmother's mother's death. I had known that my mother had hemorrhaged a great deal in giving birth to me. She was kept in the hospital for nine days, and once home she suffered from a serious postpartum depression. Within weeks of my birth, her parents – my grandparents – suggested that she go away with them on a vacation. She agreed and left me with a baby nurse, departing with her parents, my father, and my older sister. My father returned after two weeks, but my mother was probably away for a month during the first two months of my life.

These are details I have now been told, although on the implicit procedural level, I believe I had always experienced and known of this maternal abandonment and the difficulty my mother consequently had in attaching to me. (I have found it oddly interesting that my mother never spoke about this.) One way of my "knowing" – in Bollas's (1989) term, an *unthought known* – was an extremely unsettling, physically experienced anxiety that I have repeatedly felt around certain separations. The experience was so intense that at times it destabilized me, and I now more fully understand that these events specifically corresponded in some direct manner to my original abandonment and attachment trauma. The story continues.

My maternal grandmother, the person with whom I began this paper, was someone I often talked with when I was in my thirties. By this time,

I had my own children, and I had learned from my grandmother that her own mother had died in childbirth when my grandmother was only four years old. (I also have found it oddly interesting that my mother never spoke about this.) The family lived in a *shtetl* outside Krakow, Poland. Since they were poor, I suspect their home was small, and my grandmother could have heard what was happening at this very young age; she may even have suffered the shock of seeing her mother die. This would have been terrifying.

My grandmother's father was then in mourning and left with three daughters, ages four, three, and two. I do not know who helped care for my grandmother and her younger sisters until their father remarried. I do not know when he remarried, although I suspect that, given Eastern European *shtetl* life, it was sooner rather than later. I do know that my grandmother's stepmother would soon have five children of her own. Who could this four-year-old have turned to for comfort while grieving, for mothering and reparative soothing? Eventually, my grandmother came to the United States with her father, before World War I. Both she (who would have been between the ages of twelve and fourteen) and her father worked in garment-industry sweatshops, sending money back to the old country to bring the rest of the family over – a typical immigrant story.

My grandmother often awoke screaming from her dreams, I have been told, although she never recalled, or at least did not tell her children, what the nightmares were about. She did tell me a recurring dream from later in her life in which I sensed her panic and terror, as described earlier. I know that somehow I recognized a terror in it that I intimately knew as well. Bromberg (2013) believes that recurring dreams are less dreams in the sense we typically think of them than they are actual dissociated states of experience – that is, unmetabolized experiences of great fear, loss, or terror.

Richman (2006, 2009) movingly detailed how writing her memoir had helped transform her, restoring her voice by reclaiming what trauma had silenced. Writing my own memoir piece (Salberg 2005) had its own deeply therapeutic space in which the connection between my grandmother's anxiety dream and my own recurring nightmare has come more clearly into focus – that is, the link between her own mother's death, her experience of abandonment that deadened something in her, her decisive role in my mother's reenactment of maternal abandonment (these grandparents suggested and invited my mother to go away with my father and sister to "get over" postpartum depression), and my own childhood dream of death at the hands of a witch/mother.

The many levels of repetition and reliving of traumatic maternal loss are hard not to see in my personal history, and yet in my first analysis all this remained in the background. I have come to realize that there was a ghost in my primal life and attachment experience. I can see how my mother's abandonment of me as a newborn was a death within a family trauma story that was being relived in some compulsory way. I now believe that my early nightmare carried the trauma of my mother's postpartum depression (a deadened mother as witch) and her abandonment of me as an infant, along with her anxious attachment to her own traumatized mother, and, finally, my grandmother's early trauma of her own mother dying in childbirth along with a dead baby (death in a paper bag). Generations of death in a paper bag were delivered to me in my infancy.

I have been haunted by and have continued to live out a familial history of traumatic attachment and loss. If the primary evolutionary purpose of attachment is protection, my grandmother's early loss was traumatizing and violating of secure attachment, as was my own early experience of abandonment by my mother. Of significance is that my grandmother, whose own mother died when she was four years old – at an extremely young age, and in a world without resources to help her mourn this loss – then invited and became the agent of my mother's abandonment of her own newborn to effect her recovery. It is this kind of unconscious enactment of trauma that is reproduced across generations, often without reflection or questioning. Further, I have come to realize that the attachment/loss trauma in my family history has penetrated and altered what attachment feels like and how it was mediated in my family.

In this way, I believe that enacting trauma is less a discrete event and becomes more of what we refer to as relational trauma, and what I have been referring to as the *texture of traumatic attachment*. We can sometimes err on the side of believing that transgenerational transmission is a clear transmission of something, be it content or experience. Perhaps we need to think of it more as the sequelae of a traumatized person's fragmented states of mind, a person who is then parenting a child. It is the dysregulated affective states of the parent that infuse the child's attachment experience and can evoke fantasies of the parent's missing stories. There are often missing pieces of the trauma: sometimes it is the narrative, sometimes the affect, and sometimes both.

This is for me the nexus of where trauma meets attachment theories. The child needs to feel that he or she has access to and can live inside the mind of the parent. If part of that mind is deadened, hidden, and/or dissociated, the search for the parent becomes dire. In many ways it is a search for a missing bond, an attachment to an absence (Gerson 2009; Grand 2000). Both my grandmother's and my own recurrent nightmares recall states of abandonment and early terror: a child searching for the absent or dead mother (Green 1972).

In preparing to write about the ghosts in my life, I asked my mother for more information from that time. What I learned was another story of trauma and ruptured attachment, but also a story of possible mutual repair. I was born in December 1952, and most likely my mother's month away took place in early January. In the summer of 1953, no longer as depressed as she had been, she moved upstate with my sister and me to spend the summer with her parents, my father commuting on weekends. She hired a nanny to help take care of me: a Polish woman in her early thirties, tall with blonde hair and not Jewish like my family. She had left Poland after the war to immigrate to the United States. During the war, she had been forced into a death march in an attempt to escape the Nazis, and her baby daughter died. One can only imagine the wound inside this woman.

The nanny spent four months caring for me, and I have recently learned that she then met and married the local baker; she stayed in this town and went on to have another child. All of this I have been told, none of which I can remember. However, I am left wondering if in some crucial way, the nanny found a baby to love and to come back to life with, and I found a maternal figure whom I could revive.

Did we heal each other? I cannot really say for sure or know how important an event this was for me. I would like to believe that this young woman's caretaking of me helped restore her so that she could now imagine loving, marrying, and having another child. Perhaps it altered something in me, left a seed or kernel of the capacity from which healing grows. I believe that disrupted attachment marked by loss and trauma needs to be healed through reparative actions and experiences, through holding, witnessing, and recognizing attachments. I know that caring for someone or something restores all of us in untold ways.

We need to keep ourselves alert to how we can foster testimonies and narratives, as Laub (1998) has created, that will undo the silencing enforced by trauma. Psychoanalysis has begun to integrate trauma into its theories and methodologies. However, historical trauma – both outside and inside psychoanalysis – still needs to be witnessed so that we can move from absence into presence in our theories and praxis. In doing so, we will all be better equipped as witnesses for each other and our patients, nurturing seeds of resilience where we least expect to find them. Ultimately, we need each other to share, live out, and transform our stories.

Acknowledgments

The author wishes to thank Sue Grand, Adrienne Harris, and Carole Maso for their generous help and support.

Notes

1 A vast literature on this topic includes contributions by the following: Ainsworth (e.g., Ainsworth et al. 1978), Beebe and Lachmann (2013), The Boston Change Process Study Group (2010), Bowlby (e.g., 1958), Coates (2004a, 2004b, 2012, in press), Fonagy (1999), Hesse (1999), Lyons-Ruth (2002, 2003), Main and Solomon (1986), Seligman (2000), Slade (2014), and Tronick (1989).
2 Early deaths of siblings cast shadows over Klein's life, as was also the case for Freud. Although not within the purview of this paper, I wonder about how the disavowed traumatic losses in both Freud's and Klein's early lives may have contributed to a refusal to incorporate trauma into their theories.

References

Abraham, N. & Torok, M. (1975). The lost object-me: notes on endocryptic identification. In *The Shell and the Kernel: Renewals of Psychoanalysis*, ed. & trans. N. T. Rand. Chicago, IL/London: Univ. of Chicago Press.

Ainsworth, M., Blehar, M., Waters, E. & Wall, S. (1978). *Patterns of Attachment.* Hillsdale, NJ: Erlbaum.

Apprey, M. (1996). *Phenomenology of Transgenerational Haunting: Subjects in Apposition, Subjects on Urgent/Voluntary Errands.* Ann Arbor, MI: UMI Research Collections.

Apprey, M. (2003). Repairing history: reworking transgenerational trauma. In *Hating in the First Person Plural: Psychoanalytic Essays on Racism, Homophobia, Misogyny, and Terror*, ed. D. Moss. New York: Other Press.

Aron, L. & Starr, K. (2013). *A Psychotherapy for the People: Toward a Progressive Psychoanalysis.* London: Routledge.

Beebe, B. & Lachmann, F. M. (2013). *The Origins of Attachment: Infant Research and Adult Treatment.* London/New York: Routledge.

Bergmann, M. S. & Jucovy, M. E. (1982). *Generations of the Holocaust.* New York: Columbia Univ. Press.

Bollas, C. (1989). *The Shadow of the Object: Psychoanalysis of the Unthought Known.* New York: Columbia Univ. Press.
Boston CHANGE Process Study Group (2010). *Change in Psychotherapy: A Unifying Paradigm.* New York: W. W. Norton.
Bowlby, J. (1958). The nature of the child's tie to his mother. *Int. J. Psychoanal.*, 39:350–373.
Bromberg, P. (1994). "Speak, that I may see you": some reflections on dissociation, reality, and psychoanalytic listening. *Psychoanal. Dialogues*, 4:517–547.
Bromberg, P. (2006). *Awakening the Dreamer: Clinical Journeys.* London/New York: Routledge.
Bromberg, P. (2011). *The Shadow of the Tsunami and the Growth of the Relational Mind.* London/New York: Routledge.
Bromberg, P. (2013). Personal communication.
Coates, S. (2004a). John Bowlby and Margaret S. Mahler: their lives and theories. *J. Amer. Psychoanal. Assn.*, 52:571–601.
Coates, S. (2004b). The role of maternal state in mediating trauma and resilience in preschool children after September 11. Paper presented to the Jewish Board of Family and Children Services, October.
Coates, S. (2012). The child as traumatic trigger: discussion of Laurel Silber's "Ghostbusting Transgenerational Processes." *Psychoanal. Dialogues*, 22:123–128.
Coates, S. (in press). Can babies remember trauma? Pre-symbolic forms of representation in traumatized infants. *J. Amer. Psychoanal. Assn.*
Davies, J. M. (1996). Linking the "pre-analytic" with the postclassical: integration, dissociation, and the multiplicity of unconscious processes. *Contemp. Psycho-anal.*, 32:553–576.
Davoine, F. (2007). The characters of madness in the talking cure. *Psychoanal. Dialogues*, 17:627–638.
Davoine, F. & Gaudillière, J. M. (2004). *History Beyond Trauma: Whereof One Cannot Speak, Thereof One Cannot Stay Silent.* New York: Other Press.
Epstein, H. (1979). *Children of the Holocaust: Conversations with Sons and Daughters of Survivors.* New York: Putnam.
Faimberg, H. (1996). Listening to listening. *Int. J. Psychoanal.*, 77:667–677.
Faimberg, H. (1998). The telescoping of generations: genealogy of certain identifications. *Contemp. Psychoanal.*, 24:99–117.
Faimberg, H. (2005). *The Telescoping of Generations: Listening to the Narcissistic Links between Generations.* London/New York: Routledge.
Ferenczi, S. (1949). The confusion of the tongues between the adults and the child. *(The Language of Tenderness and of Passion) Int. J. Psychoanal.*, 30:225–230, 1949.
Fonagy, P. (1999). *Attachment Theory and Psychoanalysis.* New York: Other Press.
Fraiberg, S., Adelson, E. & Shapiro, V. (1975). Ghosts in the nursery: a psychoanalytic approach to the problems of impaired infant–mother relationships. *J. Amer. Acad. Child & Adolescent Psychiatry*, 14:387–421.
Gampel, Y. (1996). The interminable uncanny. In *Psychoanalysis at the Political Border*, ed. L. Rangell & R. Moses-Hrushovski. Madison, WI: Int. Univ. Press.
Gampel, Y. & Mazor, A. (2004). Intimacy and family links of adults who were children during the Shoah: multi-faceted mutations of the traumatic encapsulations. *Free Associations*, 11:546–568.
Gerson, S. (2009). When the third is dead: memory, mourning, and witnessing in the aftermath of the Holocaust. *Int. J. Psychoanal.*, 90:1341–1357.

Gottlieb, G. (1991). Epigenetic systems view of human development. *Developmental Psychol.*, 27:33–34.

Grand, S. (2000). *The Reproduction of Evil.* Hillsdale, NJ/London: Analytic Press.

Green, A. (1972). The dead mother. In *On Private Madness.* London: Rebus Press.

Gump, J. (2000). A white therapist, an African American patient – shame in the therapeutic dyad: commentary on paper by Neil Altman. *Psychoanal. Dialogues*, 10:619–632.

Gump, J. (2010). Reality matters: the shadow of the trauma on African American subjectivity. *Psychoanal. Psychol.*, 27:42–54.

Halasz, G. (2011). Psychological witnessing of my mother's Holocaust testimony. In *The Power of Witnessing: Reflections, Reverberations, and Traces of the Holocaust*, ed. N. R. Goodman & M. B. Meyers. New York/London: Routledge.

Harlow, H. F. (1959). Love in infant monkeys. *Sci. Amer.*, 200:68, 70, 72–74, June.

Harris, A. (2006). Ghosts, unhealable wounds and resilience: commentary on papers by Sandra Silverman and Maureen Murphy. *Psychoanal. Dialogues*, 16:543–551.

Harris, A. (2007). Analytic work in the bridge world: commentary on paper by Françoise Davoine. *Psychoanal. Dialogues*, 17:659–669.

Harris, A. (2014). Discussion of Slade's "Imagining Fear." *Psychoanal. Dialogues*, 24:267–276.

Herman, J. (1992). *Trauma and Recovery: The Aftermath of Violence – From Domestic Abuse to Political Terror.* New York: Basic Books.

Hesse, E. (1999. The adult attachment interview: historical and current perspectives. In *Handbook of Attachment: Theory, Research, and Clinical Applications*, ed. J. Cassidy & P. Shaver. New York: Guilford, pp. 395–433.

Holmes, J. (1995). Something there is that doesn't love a wall: John Bowlby, attachment theory, and psychoanalysis. In *Attachment Theory: Social, Developmental, and Clinical Perspectives*, ed. S. Goldberg, R. Muir, & J. Kerr. New York: Analytic Press, pp. 19–45.

Hopenwasser, K. (2008). Being in rhythm: dissociative attunement in therapeutic process. *J. Trauma Dissociation*, 9:349–367.

Kestenberg, J. (1972). Psychoanalytic contributions to the problem of children of survivors from Nazi persecutions. *Israel Ann. Psychiatry & Related Disciplines*, 10:311–325.

Kohler, B. (2012). Relational psychosis psychotherapy: a neuropsychoanalytic model. Paper presented at a meeting of the Amer. Assn. of Psychoanal. Physicians, Washington, DC.

Kuriloff, E. (2010). The Holocaust and psychoanalytic theory and praxis. *Contemp. Psychoanal.*, 46:395–422.

Laub, D. (1998). The empty circle: children of survivors and the limits of reconstruction. *J. Amer. Psychoanal. Assn.*, 46:507–529.

Laub, D. & Auerhahn, N. C. (1993). Knowing and not knowing massive psychic trauma: forms of traumatic memory. *Int. J. Psychoanal.*, 74:287–302.

Lieberman, A. F. (2014). Giving words to the unsayable: the healing power of describing what happened. *Psychoanal. Dialogues*, 24:277–281.

Lyons-Ruth, K. (2002). The two-person construction of defenses: disorganized attachment strategies, unintegrated mental states, and hostile/helpless relational processes. *J. Infant, Child & Adolescent Psychother.*, 2:107–119.

Lyons-Ruth, K. (2003). Dissociation and the parent–infant dialogue: a longitudinal perspective from attachment research. *J. Amer. Psychoanal. Assn.*, 51:883–911.

Main, M. & Solomon, J. (1986). Discovery of an insecure disoriented attachment pattern: procedures, findings, and implications for the classification of behavior. In *Affective Development in Infancy*, ed. T. Brazelton & M. Youngman. Norwood, NJ: Ablex, pp. 95–124.

Ogden, T. H. (2008). Bion's four principles of mental functioning. *Fort Da*, 14B:11–35.

Prince, R. (2009). Psychoanalysis traumatized: the legacy of the Holocaust. *Amer. J. Psychoanal.*, 69:179–194.

Reis, B. (2007). Witness to history: introduction to symposium on transhistorical catastrophe. *Psychoanal. Dialogues*, 17:621–626.

Richman, S. (2006). Finding one's voice: transforming trauma into autobiographical narrative. *Contemp. Psychoanal.*, 42:639–650.

Richman, S. (2009). Secrets and mystifications: finding meaning through memoir. *Psychoanal. Perspectives*, 6:67–75.

Rudoren, J. (2012). Proudly bearing elders' scars, their skin says "never forget." *NY Times*, Oct. 1, Section A, pp. 1, 6.

Salberg, J. (2005). Etudes on loss. *Amer. Imago*, 62:435–451.

Schore, A. N. (2001). The effects of early relational trauma on the right brain development, affect regulation, and infant mental health. *Infant Mental Health J.*, 22:201–269.

Seligman, S. (2000). Clinical implications of current attachment theory. *J. Amer. Psychoanal. Assn.*, 48:1189–1194.

Slade, A. (2014). Imagining fear: attachment, threat, and psychic experience. *Psychoanal. Dialogues*, 24:253–266.

Steele, H. & Steele, M., eds. (2008). *Clinical Implications of the Adult Attachment Interview*. New York: Guilford.

Sullivan, H. S. (1953). *The Interpersonal Theory of Psychiatry*. New York: W. W. Norton.

Torok, M. (1968). The illness of mourning and the fantasy of the exquisite corpse. In *The Shell and the Kernel*, by N. Abraham & M. Torok, ed. & trans. N. T. Rand. Chicago, IL/London: Univ. of Chicago Press.

Tronick, E. Z. (1989). Emotions and emotional communication in infants. *Amer. Psychol.*, 44:112–119.

Winnicott, D. W. (1953). Transitional objects and transitional phenomena: a study of the first not-me possession. *Int. J. Psychoanal.*, 34:89–97.

Young, J. E. (1993). *The Texture of Memory: Holocaust Memorials and Meaning*. New Haven, CT: Yale Univ. Press.

Part II

Repetitions of Violence, Antidotes to War

Part II

History Making

Rachael Peltz

On any given day in the year 2015, reading the morning newspaper over a cup of coffee is likely to fill one with anguish. Or so we hope. The absence of anguish would surely mean blankness, that apocalyptic state beyond the psychic threshold in which the full apprehension of reality can be taken in.

There is no shortage of devastation in today's world. There will be no shortage of ghostly passages from one generation to the next. We look for any glimmer of light or color amidst the grey newsprint. And sometimes we find it.

Mostly, I am sorry to say, we in the helping professions have our work cut out for ourselves. Any tools we collect in these times of wreckage are tools we will need. In that spirit, with tools in hand we must roll up our sleeves and do what we can. I believe this book was written with that work in mind.

These three chapters offer us more tools. They address the rather large domain of the making of history in the therapeutic setting, the sphere of critical social theory and our personal lives. They all address the travesties of war and the twisted ways war leaves its victims bewildered and unknowing where to look. History is made when the facts of history are realized in the lives of the people who carry it. We all carry history in our bones. But if it remains only in our bones we are more likely doomed to repeat it.

So, much of what we hope for in the therapy setting today pertains to releasing our patients from the clutches of the unspoken history in their bones. We in the profession, write about the unconscious transmission of trauma across the generations. We aim to locate ourselves with our patients in those – yes – prehistoric moments in which what we share is the immediacy of our embodied and timeless presences – together. Those presences appear as strange encounters, flashes, incongruous somethings. The possibilities are endless. But, that is how the unconscious (those timeless repositories of trauma) speak. They do not speak English, French, Urdu, Hebrew or Arabic. They speak the language of now. Catch me if you can. And our method is call "serious noticing."[1] James Wood coined this phrase while describing the kind of noticing involved in writing fiction. He asks,

> what do writers do when they seriously notice the world? Perhaps they do nothing less than rescue the life of things from their death ... the fading reality that besets details as they recede from us – the memories of our childhood, the almost-forgotten pungency of flavors, smells, textures: the slow death that we deal to the world by the sleep of our attention. By congested habit, or through laziness, lack of curiosity, thin haste, we stop looking at things."
>
> (p. 58)

Wood maintains that "the writer's task is to rescue the adventure from this slow retreat: to bring meaning, color and life back to the most ordinary things" (p. 59).

We therapists are all writers of fiction in this way. We must rescue the lives of our patients by seriously noticing what happens – what appears and disappears – when we are with them. That is how we make history together. That is how the facts that situate their lives become narratives. Our theories tell us how the capacity for *story making* rests on the internalization of embodied *story holding* presences. In other words, we must establish palpable contact with our patients for any hope of history making. The capacity to weave any kind of narrative is really quite an achievement and requires very devoted and engaged listeners.

These three chapters direct our attention to the ways the consequences of history are embedded in silence, omission and slippage. In "Repairing an Immigrant Chinese Family's 'Box of Terrible Things'", Klatzkin, Lieberman and Van Horn present the account of the child–parent psychotherapy (CPP) of Rose (mom) and Sophia (four year old). Rose is part of a Chinese family who immigrated to the US in the early 1990s, after which time her children (Sophia and her brother) were born. The authors navigate the story of this therapy through emergent "ports of entry"; beginning with the perception that both Sophia and her mother needed help calming down. They needed someone to help them breathe. That was the first order of business. Receiving that guidance signaled them that someone was "seriously noticing" and willing to step in to gently and firmly "hold" them as they learned to regulate their emotional rhythms. Furthermore it reminds us that sometime we have to move in close, in very real and embodied ways. When we do we become vitalizing presences that convey that the person we are trying to reach "matters."

Once equipped with calming tools, both mother and child were able to enter into their respective capacities for meaningful emotional work. This allowed for the beginning of narrative snippets culminating in the therapist's acute awareness of "facts of history" – that is, the impact of the Cultural Revolution and subsequent massacres in Tiananmen Square in China in 1989, to the discovery of a "box of terrible things" that held the links between the terror of the past and multiple anxieties in this family's present life.

In this account we are the beneficiaries of the wisdom that came of the experience of working with this family. This was a "no holds barred" approach in which the therapist felt free to "use all there is to use" to establish emotional contact, and locate the necessary facts which allowed a very deeply personal history to emerge.

In a move of "Nachtraeglichkeit" (Freud, 1896), this kaleidoscopic history-making process points toward the progressive possibilities in which present experience allows for the discovery of an unassimilated, not yet constituted experience from the past. Faimberg (2005) introduces the term "historicization" as the process by which historical events can be re-signified as a consequence of psychic re-working. This critical concept reminds us that like the events of a person's individual and familial life, the historical events that take place in society at a given time require psychic and social re-working.

In the next two chapters, Judith L. Alpert and Steven Botticelli locate themselves at this period of history as the outcome of such historicization. In each of these chapters transmission (trans-generational trauma) is written on the body, decoded through the body and repaired through attentiveness to the body transcripts.

In "Has Sexuality Anything to Do with War Trauma? Intergenerational Transmission and the Homosexual Imaginary," Steven Botticelli offers a complex analysis of how sexuality is recruited in the aftermath of wartime violence with regard to what he calls the homosexual imaginary. And lastly Judith L. Albert shares with us the making of her own history in which she conveys the story of three generations haunted by trauma beginning with Judith's grandparents in Russia.

We are reminded in these three chapters that it is precisely the history in our bones, foundational yet out of sight, that we sometimes know the least about. Like buildings in disrepair that remained standing yet invisible as monuments to unnamed wars, we hold within us living, invisible monuments, making their presences felt as mental and physical calcifications accumulated over generations of silence. These pieces of history are not among the stories we tell our children as they have not been sufficiently witnessed and remain un-signified – not-yet-thoughts without a thinker. "Yet, in the psyche," writes Eva Hoffman, reminiscent of Freud's own discovery, "time moves slowly, if at all." In that sense, it is never too late. The timelessness of unconsciousness could be said to preserve history in its wake. The human mind and its capacity for dynamic unconscious perception serves as a guardian for the history we have within us. The incongruities we perceive without knowing – about ourselves, our relationships and our societies – timelessly, and sometimes urgently, press to be discovered.

As therapists we are in the privileged position of being players and witnesses – players, co-creating the ever shifting field of psychotherapy and analysis in the cultural and historical here and now; and witnesses to the unconscious fleeting encounters of evidences of history yet to be constituted.

When we keep in mind the importance of historical events, modalities, social dynamics and places as they emerge in the field of therapy, we are going against one current in psychoanalysis that creates a false divide between external reality and its psychic inscriptions. Why are the events of history important as threads in the complex tapestry we weave with our patients? Because they belong to us, they shape our ancestral fate and our own sensibilities. And, because it is only out of constituting history, that we hold the hope of learning from it.

Among the psychoanalytic "objects" – good, bad, autistic, analytic, evocative, transformational, generational and so on – are historical objects. Laplanche and Pontalis (1973) define object relationships as "interrelationship(s), involving not only the way the subject constitutes his objects but also the way these objects shape his actions" (p. 278). Historical and cultural objects are no less composed of these interrelationships.

Eva Hoffman writes of how, in some instances, what we inherit are not experiences, but shadows. Each of these chapters speak to shadow dimensions. Hoffman goes on to say that "wrestling with shadows can be more frightening, or more confusing than struggling with solid realities" (p. 66). We could also say that the absence of acknowledgment of painful emotional experiences in one generation, leads to solidified petrification of unprocessed experience in the next generation. No longer encoded in what Bion referred to as a beta screen or rigidly constructed organization that aims to organize the chaos of traumatic past events, a re-transcription similar to Judith's and examples in Steve's chapter becomes possible.

If we are called to inquire carefully into a moment in history, as these three authors do, that calling will lead us in the direction of the unconscious object of analysis at that moment. For me, receptivity to these callings is the order of the day – hearing the sounds of unconscious reverberations as they emerge, in some instances as though we are tripping through the topographies of named and unnamed monuments to history – disjointed topographies of terror.

The forces of history in which each of our stories are interwoven demand no less effort, to make sense of the world in which we are thrown. For that to happen we need the help of cultural forms and institutions – what I have elsewhere (2005) called "social containers." This is a large topic, so I will limit my discussion to what societies deem significant enough to memorialize, and disturbing enough to disavow. We all need social containers. Indeed sometimes they are *actual* containers of history – the archives, monuments, museums, libraries – we rely on to help us locate ourselves and our relationship to the events of history and our ancestors. We need those social containers to help us make history out of the events of the past, and it is the job of a good-enough society to provide them. Unfortunately, what societies choose "to collect" in the process of collective memory is highly subject to the winds of politics and privilege.

To what register do these decisions belong? Public acknowledgment – allowing a collective opportunity for truth and reconciliation – or nameless disavowal?

The aftermath of such events is as uncertain as what leads to them. But what we know for sure is that people need to know the truth in history and need others to help them render it meaningful once they do.

Note

1 A term coined by James Wood (2015) in his beautiful essay entitled Serious Noticing in *The Nearest Thing to Life*.

References

Faimberg, H. (2005) *The telescoping of generations: Listening to the narcissistic links between generations*. London: Routledge, Taylor & Francis.

Freud, S. (1896) letter 52 (6 December 1896) In Extracts from the Fleiss papers. *The Standard Edition of the Complete Psychological works of Freud* (1950–74) 1. London: Hogarth Press.

Hoffman, E. (2004) *After such knowledge: Memory, history and the legacy of the holocaust*. New York: PublicAffairs.

Laplanche, J. and Pontalis, J.-B. (1973) *The language of psychoanalysis*. New York: W.W. Norton and Co.

Peltz, R. (2005) The manic society. *Psychoanalytic Dialogues*, 15:321–346.

Peltz, R. (2008) Learning from history: An interview with Robert Jay Lifton. *Psychoanalytic Dialogues*, 18:710–734.

Woods, J. (2015) *The nearest thing to life*. Waltham, MA: Brandeis University Press.

Chapter 5

Has Sexuality Anything to Do with War Trauma?

Intergenerational Transmission and the Homosexual Imaginary

Steven Botticelli

I invoke the title of Andre Green's (1995) famous jeremiad against the supposed disappearance of sexuality from psychoanalysis not in his tone of shrill indignation but in a spirit of curiosity about the appearance of homosexual themes in some psychoanalytic and other accounts of soldiering and its aftermath. Indeed Green might have been pleased at my discernment of sexuality in a place where its presence is not often noted or theorized.

I want to consider how sexuality, particularly certain forms of homosexuality, could become the channel through which traumatic pain undergone in war expresses itself, in intergenerational and other transfers. On the most fundamental level, this homosexualization would seem to represent the projection of the experience of passivity that is in the nature of trauma onto another man. Beyond this, what I will call the homosexual imaginary shares a number of salient features with the traumatic experience of killing in war, which might help us to understand the connections between the two that appear in the source material I will be presenting here.

By homosexual imaginary I am referring to the universe of ideas about and representations of homosexuality that circulate in the culture. These include culturally prevalent homophobic images, representations and formulations that nevertheless do not wholly constitute it, and which may or may not overlap with the lived sexual experience of gay men. They form a powerful ideality that shapes experience both within and between individuals of any and all sexualities. As new ideas, images, etc. about homosexuality come into being, as they have in recent years, it is in the nature of this unconscious cultural formation that I am describing that these become agglomerated onto already existing structures, rather than supplanting them.

Reprinted with kind permission:
Botticelli, S. (2015). Has Sexuality Anything to Do with War Trauma? Intergenerational Transmission and the Homosexual Imaginary. *Psychoanalytic Perspectives*, 12 (3): 275–288.

I believe these shared features, detailed below, may help account for the co-incidence of certain manifestations of homosexuality with war trauma, and may help explain how the psychological aftermath of wartime violation recruits sexuality for its expression. Both homosexuality and traumatic violence in war are lived or imagined as involving a penetration of a stimulus barrier that is not supposed to be breached; an experience of excess, of overstimulation; a transgression of limits that constitutes a violation of the social order (even if, in war, this limit has sanction to be breached). Leo Bersani (1987) writes of the "self-shattering" (p. 222) effect of passive anal sex, a useful experience, to his mind; trauma, of course, entails a shattering of self of a rather different sort. Homosexuality and trauma share a reputed quality of unrepresentability (homosexuality as "the love that dare not speak its name;" trauma as that which cannot be symbolized by the mind), and are things that adults keep secret from children. Thinking about violence and sexuality together, I am put in mind of the enigmatic message, Jean Laplanche's (e.g., 1997) conception of the manner in which sexuality is traumatically implanted by the parent into the child. I am led to wonder whether intergenerational (and other) transfers of traumatic war experiences might be understood on the model of the enigmatic message as theorized by Laplanche, perhaps offering new ways to think about the murky issue of mechanism in the literature on intergenerational transmission. Might we think of the intergenerational transmission of trauma as a variety of enigmatic message?

In theorizing about the frequently disturbing material I am about to present, I also am addressing a matter of urgent practical concern. Tens of thousands of physically and psychically maimed soldiers have been returning from Iraq and Afghanistan. What can be done to assist them in their healing, and (as we now know to be a regular occurrence) to prevent them from inflicting the sequela of their traumas onto the people in their families and communities (and themselves, for that matter)? While my explorations here may not lend themselves to direct clinical application, I hope they might contribute to our ability to consider the treatment of traumatized soldiers within a larger frame.

In engaging this theoretical effort I follow writers like Leo Bersani, who insisted on the importance of theory, even as, maybe, especially as, matters of life and death were at stake. His seminal essay "Is the Rectum a Grave?" (1987), written at the height of the AIDS crisis in the US, has been an important resource for me in developing my idea of the homosexual imaginary.

Three Scenes: The Curious Appearance of Homosexuality in Cases of War Trauma[1]

1 During lunch David felt that he had perhaps pushed his disdain for middle-class prudery a little too far. Even at the bar of the Cavalry and Guards Club one couldn't boast about homosexual, paedophiliac incest with any confidence of a favorable reception. Who could he tell that he had raped his five-year-old son? He could not think of a single person who would not prefer to change the subject – and some would behave far worse than that. The experience itself had been short and brutish, but not altogether nasty. He smiled at Yvette, said how ravenous he was, and helped himself to the brochette of lamb and flageolets.

(St. Aubyn, 1991, p. 71)

By turns horrifying and hilarious, Edward St. Aubyn's masterfully stylish novel *Never Mind* presents us with the sadistic, alcoholic figure of David Melrose, father of Patrick, whose development will be limned through a succession of novels to follow. Heavily autobiographical and closely observed, *Never Mind* is nevertheless not a psychological novel, and there is little to help us understand David's brutality. We are presented however, with some possible clues. Several pages before the rape that is referred to in the passage above, we see David reflecting on "how much of his father's life had been spent in a trench of one sort or another" (p. 61). We are not told more about the nature of David's father's war service, except for suggestions of the enduring impact it has had on him. Nearing death from emphysema, David's father languishes. "Wearing the oxygen mask which he humorously called his 'gas mask', and unable to negotiate the 'stair drill', he slept in his study, which he renamed the 'departure lounge', on an old Crimean campaign bed left to him by his uncle" (p. 61). A page earlier, there is an intimation of the influence David's father's soldiering may have had on David, who "could turn the piano on [his guests] like a machine gun and concentrate a hostility into his music that made them long for the more conventional unkindness of his conversation" (p. 60).

The novel's title suggests how thoroughly unmentalized Patrick is by either of his parents or by anyone else. It also evokes the incomprehension the reader feels in trying to understand David's sadism. We are left to try to fathom the mind of the father who could inflict such a brutal sexual assault on his son, perhaps wondering how it may have been shaped by his own father's combat experience in World War I.

> 2) ...The father's tellings are injected ... they slide in through an opening that can't be seen. They slide in at a point of attachment, a kind of umbilical attachment, binding father to son. The opening changes character when these stories flow through. The opening takes on muscle and force ... male bodies, hard, muscular, forceful, binding.... The point of attachment, the place where the stories come in, then, is behind you, behind what you can be conscious of. You can only be conscious of the tellings once they have arrived inside you.
>
> (Moss, 2010, p. 249).

Though rendered in visceral, sexually textured terms, Donald Moss's telling of his father's shameful, excited (shameful because excited; exciting because shameful?) recounting of his war stories, to his boyhood self, is a fatherly penetration of a merely metaphoric sort – though, as we will learn, no less penetrating. In "War Stories" he offers us an account of the intergenerational transmission of trauma as it occurred in real time. Prefacing each telling with "And I'll say this only once," the father cannot stop himself from telling, and telling again, what he did in the war (World War II): throwing a couple grenades into a building he later discovered was a nursery, "babies in bassinets [blown] all over the room"; observing a "Polack" soldier (Polish-American or Polish, we're not told) "kneeing" a German POW with his gun, knocking him to the floor, then threatening to kill anyone else who would touch him (it's not clear whether this account suggests some sexual overtone, as in "He's my bitch, I'll have my way with him but everyone else leave him alone"); sniping ("a sneaky way of doing anything") an enemy soldier on his way "to the can to take a shit ... a guy might be thinking of his Fraulein ... I'd kill that poor fucker, or at least I'd hit him, and enjoy it, Jesus, Donald, I enjoyed it" (p. 246).

Moss's descriptions tap into something fundamental, elemental, that links (homo)sexuality with trauma, and both of them – perhaps, as I will go on to speculate – with the very origins of personhood. There's the breaking of a taboo, the indulgence of a forbidden pleasure. Moss: "...[O]nly because it happened can you enjoy the intimacy that all of civilization aims to forbid: the pleasures and excitements of telling it" (p. 247). Two things men are not supposed to do: to kill, and to fuck (each other). And maybe one more taboo: fathers are not supposed to tell such stories to their sons. But here they are, doing it together:

> [Y]ou play the soldier, I'll play the babies. Let's do it again and again.... But, let's really be in on it together, each of us the soldier, each of us the babies, each of us telling each of us, without it mattering really who appears to be telling, who listening. Let's go beneath differences like that. Let's tap into force, into the joy, power and energy pulsing through and destroying all those arbitrary differences.
>
> (p. 247–48)

For Chasseguet-Smirgel (1984), French analyst in the classical tradition, homosexuality is marked as a perversion based on its supposed denial of difference, specifically the denial of the difference between the sexes and the generations. (I cite Chasseguet-Smirgel's homophobic formulation here not to endorse it but because it forms part of the homosexual imaginary, towards which psychoanalytic theorizing has made a substantial contribution.)

Moss again:

> 'I cannot distinguish pleasure from harm. I know ... that he told me too much, that I, like any child, was, in some sense, harmed by hearing what I heard, by knowing what I knew. But only in some sense. I also feel that the stories were a gift, providing pleasures unrivalled to this day.'
>
> (p. 247–48)

The irresistible urge to indulge in the forbidden pleasure (not that Moss's boyhood self had a choice in the matter), in spite of awareness of the damage that would ensue – compare Leo Bersani's description of passive anal sex, within the cultural imaginary: ... "the seductive and intolerable image of a grown man, legs high in the air, unable to refuse the suicidal ecstasy of being a woman" (1987, p. 212). Riffing further on this association, I am reminded that men looking to contract HIV (about whom Bersani (2008) has recently written) refer to the virus as "the gift." Coming in from behind you, indeed.

Moss:

> 'The stories [represent] ... such an overflow, of all the constraints and limits established by the mere demands of being decent. The babies are blown apart and so is the mind of the child who hears of it.'
>
> (p. 248)

The excess ("overflow") that shatters the mind: writers as different as Leo Bersani (1987) and Ruth Stein (1998), following Bataille, invoke this excess as in the very nature of sexuality. In a creative subtextual reading of *The Three Essays on Sexuality*, Bersani understands Freud there to be defining the sexual as "the jouissance of exploded limits, as the ecstatic suffering into which the human organism momentarily plunges when it is "pressed" beyond a certain threshold of endurance" (p. 217). He speculates that there is an essentially masochistic basis to all sexuality, rooted in the infant's need to learn to tolerate – in fact enjoy – the bombardment of stimuli directed at it prior to the development of an ego that will eventually allow this stimulation to be processed and integrated. For Bersani, "the mystery of sexuality is that we seek not only to get rid of this shattering tension but also to repeat, even to increase, it" (1986, p. 38). From his description Moss's childhood self seems to have been thrown back into this primordial mind-blowing state where self and sexuality, together, came into being.

One might imagine Moss's father to have been motivated, in his tellings, by his need to come to terms with his experience of having, on some level, enjoyed being penetrated – traumatically, I think we have to imagine – by the tabooed, limit-exploding, excessive, difference-obliterating killing he did ["...the delight I felt ... in killing things, now not those babies, that was, Jesus Christ" (Moss, 2010, p. 246)]. Literal bombardments recapitulate psychic bombardments for the traumatized soldier, inducing an experience of pleasure-in-pain by evoking "the strong appeal of powerlessness, of the loss of control" (Bersani, 1987, p. 217). Yes, he has enjoyed the killing but in the process he has also undergone something, been given over to a force that has altered him in some manner. Part of his self has unraveled in a way he cannot formulate but which self he struggles to reassemble through his tellings to his son, even if he can never quite manage to do so. He repeatedly if implicitly tries to establish with Don that he is the one who penetrates, the "impenetrable penetrator" (Butler, 1993, p. 50) only to be undone by this effort, again and again. His tellings have the quality of the sexual in their pleasurable repetition, in their discharge of a recurring tension.

In an intriguing coda, Moss traces the line of transmission through to the next generation. On the eve of Barack Obama's inauguration, Moss finds his son preoccupied with the odds of Obama's being assassinated the next day. "All you need to do, he said, is to sit two miles away with a high-powered sniper rifle and have a clear line of sight. Do that, he said, and Obama's dead" (p. 250). Moss reflects:

> My father's story is about being a sniper, about how he liked it, and I wondered how that story is filtering through me to my 12-year-old.... My father's sniper bullet goes through that guy on the can and then continues through the assassinations of the '60s and '70s until it comes to a moment's rest in my son's question about the odds of Obama's being killed today.
>
> (p. 250)

Don's exchange with his son takes place in the context of their anticipatory grief for the family dog, which that very day received a terminal diagnosis. Don wants to console his son, but cannot find the words. "He wouldn't let me touch him" (p. 249).

> 3 ..."I'm not gay you know, Jesus. This therapy shit." I ask him what he is dreaming, and he tells me that sometimes it's a man, sometimes it's a woman sucking his penis. "Jesus. I'm not gay am I? How could I be gay?"
>
> (Grand, 2010, p. 231)

Sue Grand's treatment of a Vietnam war veteran who was responsible for firebombing a Vietnamese village, killing women and children, begins in a countertransferential standoff as her pacifist revulsion prevents her from making any identification, any empathic entry into his world. The relationship shifts after he comes to her aid when he sees her confronting the unhinged estranged husband of another patient in her driveway. She is touched by his protectiveness and caught up by his perception of the toughness she showed in this dangerous situation: "He could not have given me a better gift ... Right now, I need my toughness to be real" (p. 229). More than caught up, Grand is transformed: "Together, we make that toughness real. I am becoming hard-bodied, because a hard-bodied old soldier sees and admires my prowess" (p. 229). Breaking free of the heterosexual binarism that dictates that one not want that which one is, Grand finds that "Now, I want to be him, and to have him" (p. 229). Their sessions take on an air of masculine bonhomie as the therapeutic scene transforms into an encounter between two men bonded in "phallic solidarity" (p. 230). Within this homosexualized transference-countertransference matrix, Grand imagines that the treatment will make her patient feel "that he could be loved by a man, and love a man, without ever having his sexual identity unravel" (p. 230).

This turns out to not quite be the case, as the patient moves into a homosexual panic, as quoted above, as he experiences the terror and desire – terror of the desire – to be passive. I think this may be the moment that occasions traumatic transfer, when it emerges outside a therapeutic context: the moment when David, the father of St. Aubyn's Patrick is moved to rape him; the moment Moss's father begins to tell Don his war stories again. Grand shows us how, within a therapeutic context, such feelings can be worked through. "Maybe passivity has something exciting to it" (p. 231), Grand suggests to her patient. Together they come to understand the patient's wishes to "lay back" (p. 231), be taken care of, by someone the patient believed tough enough to allow him to do so. "[I]n your mind, they would have to be sort of a man and sort of a woman" (p. 231). Grand does not relationalize away the sexuality of the wish, or the fear, as she speaks to him of his worry that "some jerk might fuck with him or fuck him up" (p. 231). Following her patient's associations, as well as her own developing ideas about the possible linkage between the atrocities he has committed and his emerging fantasies, Grand tells him that "the desire that would fulfill him is associated with violence" (p. 231). Having become enthralled herself in their "shared seduction" (p. 232), Grand has come to understand that for both herself and her patient "desire had become more elastic; but it had an affinity with killing, with that 'awe, fascination with power, and feelings of violence and boundlessness that transgression arouses'" (Stein, 1998, as quoted in Grand, 2010, p. 232).

The patient's grief and guilt come unblocked. Moving through her identification/love affair with him, Grand mourns as well, for her heretofore strenuously self-avowed pacifism. "Together, we evolved a more tragic world view" (p. 239). Peter's sons, 30-something men who have been floundering in their lives, enter the narrative here. Grand asks Peter whether they know about the atrocities he committed. "He thinks so, he is sobbing, 'How can they touch me?'" (p. 239).

Male-on-Male Rape: Underreported Scourge of the American Military

I am aware of the constraints on my ability based on these three examples, one of them fictional, to advance a strong thesis about the relationship between war trauma and (homo)sexual abuse, expressed intergenerationally or otherwise, in fantasies that emerge in the context of therapeutic conversation, in the texture of tabooed talk between a father and son, or in brute physical assault. For one thing, even though the Department of Defense's Military Sexual Assault Report for 2012 revealed an epidemic of sexual abuse in the US military estimating that 26,000 members of the US military had been sexually assaulted that year (Matthews, 2013), it is not clear how many of the perpetrators of these assaults had themselves been traumatized. (Estimates of the proportion of soldiers and veterans meeting criteria for PTSD are highly variable and contested, given the politicized nature of the diagnosis due to its implications for disability benefit determinations. A case could be made however that the circumstances of military service in a war zone could be considered to some degree traumatic, in all instances.) We simply do not know what features of military life contribute to the very high rates of sexual abuse that occur there, including how large a role trauma among perpetrators may play. Second, as we recognize Don's father and Peter as having been traumatized by violent acts they committed, as perpetrator trauma, we are left unclear about whether the sexual sequela in those cases would follow in a similar manner for soldiers who were (instead, or only) victims of violence.

Nevertheless with these qualifications in mind I will persist, if only because the issues involved are so little recognized or explored. For instance, while the figure of 26,000 sexual assaults in the American military in 2012 was widely reported in the media, there was little mention of the fact that an astounding (compared with public perceptions) 53% of these involved male victims (Matthews, 2013). Even as homosexuality has become a familiar topic in public discourse, including in the longstanding national debate about "gays in the military," the fact of male-on-male rape in the armed services (overwhelmingly committed by men who self-identify as heterosexual) remains largely unpublicized. Many such assaults go literally unreported due to the shame experienced by victims, but beyond this popular media are often reluctant to address the issue. For instance, a movie about sexual assault in the military, The

Invisible War, has been criticized by male rape survivors' groups for the scant attention it paid to male victims. Discussing the film, Michael Matthews, a 20-year Air Force veteran who was gang raped in 1973 by three other airmen, complained that he and his fellow survivors "feel ostracized in our society. Nobody wants to talk about the truth – that most of the rapes in the military (victimize) men" (Briggs, 2013).

Thesis: Male-on-Male Rape as Sequela of Unraveled Enigmatic Messages

Violence begets violence, this is a commonplace; but why would the violence undergone or inflicted in the context of war instigate this particular form of violence, a sexual assault on another man? How might we try to understand the psychic linkages that are operating in these cases? Most generally, as Ruth Stein (1998) reminds us, "sexuality and sexualization are poignantly suitable to displace and express other, non-sexual, self- and object-related psychic conflicts and concerns" (p. 254). Joyce McDougall (1989, 1996) has written of how sexuality can be recruited to express traumatic pain. Perhaps male-on-male sexual violence represents a distortion, a defensive transformation, of the male bonding that is fostered within the culture of military life. Male camaraderie may unravel under the stressful, sometimes traumatic conditions of war service. Unusual compromise formations may result. Sebastian Junger writes of a soldier serving in Afghanistan who was asked whether he would consider having sex with another man. In a moment at once homophobic and homophilic, the soldier answers, "Of course – it would be gay not to" (quoted in Moss, 2012, p. 2).

Going further, I propose that the project of thinking about the specific association of violence and sexuality we observe in these cases can be advanced through a consideration of Jean Laplanche's conception of the enigmatic message. Laplanche theorizes at a deep level the connection between sexuality and violence. For him, sexuality comes to us through the (m)other. Words, gestures directed at the child, no matter how innocently intended, contain the mothering figure's knowledge of sexuality. Registering this excess of meaning, but unable to make psychic sense of it, the child feels assaulted. Laplanche's theory is itself one of intergenerational transmission of trauma, a normative developmental trauma that inaugurates sexuality, the unconscious, and as development proceeds the ego itself, which comes into being through the child's need to make sense of the psychic bombardments directed at him by caretakers. To be very clear: This is not 'big T' trauma, but something undergone by every human child as an ordinary – if ineffable and enigmatic – aspect of being raised by adult persons who "know" sexuality.

Laplanche's theorizing further recommends itself to us here in its recognition of the "priority of the other" (1997, p. 662). For Laplanche sexuality originates through the interventions (however unconscious and unintended) of the real other, rather than (as Freud would have it) endogenously-based fantasy. In this way his conception is consilient with current work in psychoanalytic trauma studies, which emphasizes the role of actual experience in pathogenesis (e.g., Boulanger, 2007).

Laplanche insists on the traumatic nature of the way in which sexuality comes to us. "[T]he necessarily traumatic intervention of the other must entail – most often in a minor way but sometimes in a major one – the effraction or breaking in characteristic of pain," he writes (1999, p. 123). While some part of what is received through this intervention can be "translated," metabolized into a developing ego (developed precisely in order to effect this work of translation) and made sense of, other parts remain beyond the child's ken, are repressed and come to constitute the unconscious. Under certain conditions, including circumstances that in some ways may re-evoke the scene of the original transmission ("implantation" or "intromission" in Laplanche's language), this untranslated part is reactivated and becomes available once again for the subject to attempt to make sense of. In John Fletcher's (2007) words, "the primary traumatic inscription, one that is excessive and remains unassimilated in a first moment, is reactivated in a second ... moment and its enigmatic sexual meaning is precipitated out and becomes subject to reinscription and/or repression" (p. 1254). Violence undergone or inflicted in war could be one such set of circumstances, a later trauma evoking an earlier one along the classic lines of Nachtraeglichkeit. This violence, in its too-muchness, may unleash the enigmatic implants that had remained untranslated, perhaps creating (under auspicious circumstances) a new opportunity for translation to take place. Alternatively, or in addition, such violence may have the effect of destabilizing the self and mobilizing efforts to reestablish psychic equilibrium.

War Trauma as Assault on Male Gender

One could speculate on the nature of the untranslated messages freshly thrown up for deencryption (Saketopoulou's term, 2014), reinscription and/or repression by war trauma. While of course variable across individuals, the untranslated messages unleashed in these instances might be expected to have some common features due to the cultural symbolic that is activated when men go to war. As Don Moss has written, "The relation between masculinity and war cannot be ignored ... The warrior is the realization of the masculine" (2012, p. 128), and the injury to male gender must be figured among the psychological sequela of violence experienced in war. Such injury may occur in the quotidian aspects of military life as much as in the throes of combat and active (sometimes not so active) fighting. In her 1991 novel *Regeneration*, Pat Barker captured some of the gender-threatening conditions that were imposed on men who served in World War I:

> One of the paradoxes of the war – one of the many – was that this most brutal of conflicts should set up a relationship between officers and men that was ... domestic. Caring ... maternal.... [T]he Great Adventure – the real life equivalent of all the adventure stories they'd devoured as boys – consisted of crouching in a dugout, waiting to be killed. The war that had promised so much in the way of 'manly' activity had actually delivered 'feminine' passivity, and on a scale that their mothers and sisters had hardly known. No wonder they broke down.
>
> (pp. 107–8)

Military training sometimes proceeds through the deliberate breaking down of recruits' masculine self-esteem. Chaim Shatan (1977), an analyst who learned from members of the U.S. Marine Corps about the training practices they had undergone, described the systematic process by which recruits are "robbed of their masculinity, pillaged of their individuality, and forced into humiliating submission" (p. 587). Such practices aim to inculcate subservience to commanders, whose sense of masculinity is enhanced through recruits' obedience to their orders, as well as to stoke recruits' narcissistic rage, which they will later be encouraged to direct against "the enemy."

While it was generally considered a conceptual advance when psychologists separated out gender as a distinct category from sexuality and sexual orientation (in contrast to Freud, who tended to conflate them), recent theorizing has emphasized their interimplication. Diane Elise (2001), for example, has written of how normative male gender is grounded in the ability to penetrate and a corresponding renunciation of early childhood experiences of excitement and pleasure in the mode of being penetrated (e.g., by the breast). Psychic or bodily penetration poses a threat to men's sense of gender as it rouses the fear that "if they are penetrated, they will then be unable to penetrate" (2001, p. 505). Within the homosexual imaginary, gay men are considered to have lost their grip on their gender by virtue of their willingness, if not enthusiasm, to be penetrated.

Laplanche has only recently (2007) introduced gender into his thinking about the enigmatic message and his ideas have a provisional quality. In a thoughtful exegesis of this work, Ruth Stein notes his affinity with Butler, who like Laplanche is interested in "the inarticulate, impermissible, repudiated dimensions of sexuality" (2007, p. 195). For Butler (1995) male gender is secreted out of a double disavowal: never having loved a man, I never lost a man. Sharing the fate of all refused or abandoned identifications, this never-loved never-lost object is installed as part of the ego. The identification contains within it both the prohibition on same sex love, and the desire for it. Butler speculates further that more exaggerated forms of masculine identification, as might be found among – are certainly cultivated among – men in the military, betray the existence of an especially "fierce ... ungrieved homosexual cathexis" (1995, p. 171).

Butler's (1995) conception of gender as that which "remains inarticulate in sexuality" (p. 172) could equate to an untranslated piece of some enigmatic message, in Laplanche's terms. Saketopoulou (2014) provides us with an evocative example of what might have taken place at one scene of the original implantation when she imagines "a father who applies slightly yet identifiably less pressure on his infant's genitals as he cleans his anus after a diaper change" (p. 17). Therein may lie for the infant boy the germ of his sense of what forms of touch, of pleasure are allowable to (what he will only later come to understand as) his male category of person.

War trauma, I speculate, reactivates the trauma of the primal seduction by early caretakers, unraveling untranslated messages. The ego "come(s) undone along the fault lines of its own formation" (Fletcher, 2007, p. 1251), creating new opportunities for translation. Trauma, in its excess, its unrepresentability, in its aspect of passive subjection, blasts into the place in the self where the possibility of homosexual love lived (still lives) before it was renounced in the consolidation of normative heterosexual gender identity. In some cases sexual assault against another man (here we might consider Don's father's storytelling as a kind of verbal sexual assault) may be an effort to deny the psychic reverberations of the trauma, of stuffing the enigmatic messages that have been released back into the box, as it were, by imposing a psychically analogous experience onto the body (or mind) of another man: "This hasn't happened to me; I am doing this to you." Psychically structuring disavowals must be reinstalled: "It is not I who desires, who has been passive in relation to another man – it is the man/boy I am violating." The reader of "War Stories" feels the importance to Don's father of his sense of Don's excitement in listening to and eventually participating in his stories. Michael Matthews, the Vietnam vet who wrote of his rape in a recent NY Times Op-Ed, said that before raping him another soldier told him "I bet you're going to like this" (2013, p. A23).

These examples and this analysis highlight the role that touch may play as a medium of traumatic transfer. For Butler, that we as humans are "given over to the touch of the other" (2003, p. 20) is the condition of our primary vulnerability. Touch is one medium of the ordinary care of the infant through which enigmatic messages are implanted. Touch is violence, the sniper's bullet directed at the German soldier, the firebomb thrown into the Vietnamese village. Touch is sexualized violence, the rape of so many men and women at the hands of soldiers inside and outside of war zones. Touch is the means by which intergenerational transmission may take place, or in some instances be fearfully held off: When Don Moss tries to comfort his son, "[h]e wouldn't let me touch him" (2010, p. 249). Near the end of his therapy Sue Grand's patient Peter sobs over his sons, "How can they touch me?" (2010, p. 239).

Repetition, or Healing?

What are the possibilities for interrupting traumatic transfer? Grand, in the careful intersubjective excavation she undertakes with Peter, shows how psychotherapy may "open fissures in the seamless wall of repetition" (Benjamin, 2004, p. 55), replacing the need for traumatic transmissions by allowing grief that opens onto deep self-understanding and acceptance. Her description of the therapeutic process with Peter traces a mutual unraveling that allows him to make contact with parts of his self that had been released by his trauma, now reactivated in the transference, in a manner safe enough for him to grieve both his war comrades and the never-loved, never-lost man that constituted that self at its origin. Telling us of the denouement of their work together, Grand links these two elements, precisely: "Grief emerges about all of his lost men ... he is less shy about wanting male love" (p. 231). Peter relinquishes "his fixed vision of a man;" he no longer needs "to be the man whom he could not want to love" (p. 230).

Grand's work with Peter demonstrates the manner in which trauma may create an opening to alterity (cf. Dean, 2009) – the 'otherness' within the self – that one might otherwise live a lifetime without accessing or becoming aware of. Without therapeutic assistance (or perhaps improbable capacities for self-analysis and self acceptance), the otherness released by trauma is likely to be refused, perhaps by attempting to force it into an actual "other" in the service of reestablishing and reasserting one's male selfhood. That would be a selfhood grounded – if we are to take Bersani, Butler and Laplanche seriously – in the disavowal of the pleasure-in-pain, pleasure-in-passivity, pleasure in the possibility of same-sex love that has formed that very self. A selfhood that, according to Bersani, "accounts for human beings' extraordinary willingness to kill in order to protect the seriousness of their statements" (1987, p. 222). A selfhood that, "promoted to the status of an ethical ideal, is a sanction for violence" (Bersani, 1987, p. 222).

Trauma goes deep. Psychoanalytic thinking, as I have deployed it here, helps us appreciate just how deep. While Grand's work with Peter demonstrates the possibility for repair, the availability of the deep, sensitive psychotherapeutic work necessary for healing from war trauma is likely to remain scarce. We must put more of our energies into the prevention of war.

Note

1 Quoted excerpts from "Never Mind" from THE PATRICK MELROSE NOVELS by Edward St. Aubyn (2012) reprinted with kind permission of Farrar, Straus and Giroux, LLC.

References

Barker, P. (1991), *Regeneration*. New York: Penguin.
Benjamin, J. (2004), Deconstructing femininity: Understanding "passivity" and the daughter position. *Annu. Psychoanal.*, 32: 45–57.
Bersani, L. (1986), *The Freudian Body: Psychoanalysis and Art*. New York: Columbia University Press.
Bersani, L. (1987), Is the rectum a grave? In *AIDS: Cultural Analysis, Cultural Activism* ed. by D. Crimp. Cambridge, MA: MIT Press. Pp 197–222.

Boulanger, G. (2007), *Wounded by Reality: Understanding and Treating Adult Onset Trauma*. Mahwah, NJ: The Analytic Press.

Briggs, B. (2013), Male rape victims slam Oscar-nominated filmmakers over focus on women. Retrieved from http://usnews.nbcnews.com/_news/2013/02/08/1689067.

Butler, J. (1993), *Bodies That Matter: On the Discursive Limits of Sex*. New York: Routledge.

Butler, J. (1995), Melancholy gender: Refused identification. *Psychoanal. Dial.*, 5: 165–180.

Butler, J. (2003), Violence, mourning, politics. *Studies in Gender and Sexuality*, 4(1): 9–37.

Chasseguet-Smirgel, J. (1984), *Creativity and Perversion*. New York: Norton.

Dean, T. (2009), *Unlimited Intimacy: Reflections on the Subculture of Barebacking*. Chicago, IL: University of Chicago Press.

Elise, D. (2001), Unlawful entry: Male fears of psychic penetration. *Psychoanal. Dial.*, 11: 499–531.

Fletcher, J. (2007), Seduction and the vicissitudes of translation: The work of Jean Laplanche. *Psychoanal. Q.*, 76: 1241–1291.

Grand, S. (2010), Combat speaks: Grief and tragic memory. In *First Do No Harm: The Paradoxical Encounters of Psychoanalysis, Warmaking and Resistance*, ed. by A. Harris and S. Botticelli. New York: Routledge. Pp 223–242.

Green, A. (1995), Has sexuality anything to do with psychoanalysis?. *Int. J. Psycho-Anal.*, 76: 871–883.

Laplanche, J. (1997), The theory of seduction and the problem of the other. *Int. J. Psycho-Anal.*, 78:653–666.

Laplanche, J. (1999), *Essays on Otherness*. trans J. Fletcher. London: Routledge.

Laplanche, J. (2007), Gender, sex, and the sexual. *Studies in Gender and Sexuality*, 8: 201–219.

McDougall, J. (1989), *Theaters of the Body*. New York: W. W. Norton.

McDougall, J. (1996), *The Many Faces of Eros: A Psychoanalytic Study of Human Sexuality*. New York: W. W. Norton.

Matthews, M. (2013), The untold story of military sexual assault. *New York Times*. Nov. 25, p. A23.

Moss, D. (2010), War stories. In *First Do No Harm: The Paradoxical Encounters of Psychoanalysis, Warmaking and Resistance*, ed. by A. Harris and S. Botticelli. New York: Routledge. Pp 243–250.

Moss, D. (2012), *Thirteen Ways of Looking at a Man: Psychoanalysis and Masculinity*. New York: Routledge.

Saketopoulou, A. (2014), To suffer pleasure: The shattering of the ego as psychic labor of perverse sexuality. *Studies in Gender and Sexuality*, 15: 254–268.

Shatan, C. F. (1977), Bogus manhood, bogus honor: Surrender and transfiguration in the US Marine Corps. *Psychoanal. Review*, 64: 585–610.

St. Aubyn, E. (1991), *Never Mind*. New York: Picador.

Stein, R. (1998), The poignant, the excessive and the enigmatic in sexuality. *Int. J. Psychoanal.*, 79: 253–268.

Stein, R. (2007), Moments in Laplanche's theory of sexuality. *Studies in Gender and Sexuality*, 8: 177–200.

Chapter 6

Repairing an Immigrant Chinese Family's "Box of Terrible Things"

Amy Klatzkin, Alicia F. Lieberman, and
Patricia Van Horn

Historical trauma has a profound impact on the psychological functioning of individuals and, like interpersonal trauma, gets transmitted from generation to generation. Maria Yellow Horse Brave Heart (2010) defines historical trauma as "cumulative emotional and psychological wounding over the lifespan and across generations, emanating from massive group trauma" (p. 2). Traumatic historical events with long-term psychological consequences include collective catastrophes such as war, famine, and forced colonization as well as intracountry genocide in the absence of war (e.g., Cambodia in the 1970s, Rwanda in the 1990s). Racial, gender, and religious oppression may also lead to historical trauma, as evidenced, for example, by the legacies of slavery, the Holocaust, massacres of Native Americans, the removal of Native American children from their families and communities for placement in boarding schools, and culturally or politically sanctioned discriminatory practices such as female infant abandonment (Brave Heart, 1999, 2010; Johnson, 1996). Tracing current individual and interpersonal conflicts to their possible roots in historical trauma can have significant beneficial effects, creating understanding and compassion in the parent generation for the grandparent generation and freeing the parent generation from the mindless repetition of the past in the present with the child.

The impact of historical trauma across generations is particularly relevant when its effects filter down from the broader social-cultural-political arena into the lives of young children and their parents. In early childhood, a traumatic stressor can be defined as an unpredictable, uncontrollable external event that threatens the physical or psychological

This paper is a revised reprint of "Child-Parent Psychotherapy and the Intergenerational Transmission of Historical Trauma" by Klatzkin, Lieberman and Van Horn originally published in *Treating Complex Traumatic Stress Disorders in Children and Adolescents*, edited by Ford, J.D. & Courtois, C.A., New York: Guilford Press.

integrity of the child and induces overwhelming fear, horror, or helplessness (Zero to Three, 2005). Exposure to a traumatic event, whether direct (as in physical or sexual abuse) or indirect (as a witness to violence, war, or natural disaster), puts a young child at risk of serious mental health problems, such as posttraumatic stress disorder (PTSD), conduct disorder, anxiety, and depression, and may disrupt not only the child's developmental momentum but also the safety and security of the child-parent relationship (Lieberman & Van Horn, 2005). In the moment of trauma, children are flooded with negative affect so intense that it often exceeds their developmental capacity to self-regulate (Schore, 2013). If the parent is unable to protect the child from this overwhelming distress, the traumatic event shatters the child's internal working model of the parent as a secure base and protective shield (Bowlby, 1969/1982; Freud, 1920/1959). It also changes the child's worldview. Before the trauma, the child may view the world as a sufficiently predictable, sufficiently benevolent place and people as generally trustworthy. Afterward, negative attributions and mental representations may consistently displace the child's previous expectations of care and safety (Janoff-Bulmann, 1992).

Although any trauma in early childhood may interfere with normal biopsychosocial development, complex forms such as historical trauma and other chronic types of victimization disrupt development more than an isolated traumatic event (Lieberman, Chu, Van Horn, & Harris, 2011). The child's functioning may be impaired across multiple domains, affecting attachment, self-concept, cognition, and regulation of affect and behavior (Cook et al., 2005). Because infants and young children depend on their primary caregivers for safety and co-regulation of physical and emotional states, the risk of developmental disturbances increases when a caregiver is also the source of danger (Freud, 1926/1959; Main & Hesse, 1990).

Trauma in early childhood not only may alter the child's general beliefs about self and the world, but more specifically may damage the relationship between a securely attached child and an attuned parent. The parent may form distorted negative attributions of the child, and the child and parent may develop mutual adverse expectations of each other (Pynoos, 1997). If before the trauma the quality of attachment was insecure and parental attunement intermittent, the relationship may deteriorate further under the stress of the traumatic event, leading to internalizing problems such as anxiety, depression, avoidance, somatization, and emotional withdrawal and/or to externalizing problems in the form of aggressive or self-endangering behaviors. The child may also lose trust in bodily sensations, leading to increased arousal in the form of sleep problems, nightmares, hypervigilance, and distractibility. He or she may regress to an earlier stage of development, losing skills that had been mastered. When the parent has also experienced trauma – as is often the case with historical trauma, which affects entire communities and societies – the child's problems are compounded by the parent's impaired affect regulation, negative attributions, and confusion about what is safe and what is dangerous. These effects may persist long after the traumatic event ends, particularly when either member of the dyad is triggered by a traumatic reminder or secondary adversity. Often parent and child become traumatic reminders for each other (Pynoos, 1997). Therefore, in addition to broad-based interventions designed to help entire societies recover from traumatic historical events, it is crucial to provide therapeutic assistance to the individual children and families whose most basic relationships (e.g., the parent-child dyad) have been altered by historical trauma.

Child-Parent Psychotherapy for Traumatized Children

This chapter describes child-parent psychotherapy (CPP) as a treatment model for traumatized children and presents a case in which the exploration of interpersonal trauma opened the door to understanding the impact of historical trauma on four generations of an immigrant family. CPP is an evidence-based, manualized dyadic treatment model for children in the first 6 years of life who have experienced, or are at risk of, mental health problems because of adverse life circumstances or traumatic events (Lieberman & Van Horn, 2009). With its foundations in psychoanalysis and attachment theory (Fraiberg, Adelson, & Shapiro, 1975; Bowlby, 1969/1982), CPP uses a multitheoretical approach – developmentally informed, culturally attuned, and trauma focused – to change maladaptive interactions and distorted perceptions with the goal of promoting safety and trust in the child-parent relationship. CPP provides a clinical model for treating trauma-related disturbances in the child's developmental course and mental health and in the quality of the parent-child relationship (Lieberman & Van Horn, 2008).

The process of CPP involves helping the parent and child learn to play together and supporting the parent in witnessing the child's play, particularly when the child reenacts violent events or engages in disturbing, repetitive symbolic play. At times the therapist takes the stance of an observer to "watch, wait, and wonder" with the parent about the child's play (Johnson, Dowling, & Wesner, 1980; Wesner, Johnson, & Dowling, 1962). At other times the therapist becomes the translator of experience and feelings or thinks together with the parent about the meaning of the child's behavior. If deemed appropriate, the therapist may suggest cognitive-behavioral strategies, mindfulness practices, or other interventions to help the dyad regulate affect and behavior while continuing to explore the subjective meaning for the child and the parent of thoughts, feelings, and maladaptive responses associated with the trauma. Knowing that parent and child may experience the same event differently and have different emotional responses, the child-parent psychotherapist endeavors to hold the perspectives of both members of the dyad, helping the parent understand the child's internal world and helping both child and parent understand each other's perspectives, motivations, behaviors, and emotional states.

Restoring safety in the environment and in the parent-child relationship is the first goal of treatment and the cornerstone of all other therapeutic goals. If necessary, the child-parent psychotherapist assists the parent in securing basic needs, such as safe living conditions and adequate clothing, household supplies, and nourishment. Within the framework of increased environmental safety, the clinician then works with the dyad to promote affect regulation, restore trust in bodily sensations, and foster reciprocity in the parent-child relationship. By providing developmental guidance to explain and normalize the traumatic response, the therapist helps the parent understand the child's behavior as an effort to self-protect and works with the parent to promote more accurate reality testing and more realistic responses to threat. These skills in turn increase the parent's capacity to provide a secure base and reengage the child in learning in order to restore developmental progress. Ultimately the therapist and parent co-create a narrative with the child that places the traumatic event firmly in the past so that parent and child can dependably distinguish between remembering the trauma and reliving it (Lieberman & Van Horn, 2005).

Because the locus of healing in CPP is the child-parent relationship, whatever the therapist can do to support the parent is intended as a means to support the child as well. If the situation warrants, the child-parent psychotherapist provides crisis intervention and concrete assistance with problems of daily living. Often the most pressing need at the outset of treatment is to establish physical safety by helping the parent create a safety plan and by promoting the parent's ability to act as a protective shield (Lieberman & Van Horn, 2005, 2008).

Key forces that shape the parent's perspective include cultural background, attachment status, and trauma history (Ghosh Ippen, 2009). For this reason CPP assesses the parent's as well as the child's history and current functioning. The child-parent psychotherapist needs to understand the complexity of the traumatic experience for child and parent (single or recurrent events, range of events), its context (familial, societal, historical, and cultural), and its repercussions in the present and in the past. The initial assessment aims to identify traumatic reminders and secondary adversities, such as increased susceptibility to dysregulation of thoughts, feelings, or behavior and decreased capacity to cope and problem solve. The comprehensive assessment of the parent's trauma history enables the therapist to help the parent anticipate and cope with traumatic reminders that may arise from the child's play – reminders that may trigger the parent's response to traumas experienced in his or her childhood as well as in adulthood and that may then be projected onto, and enacted with, the child.

Drawing on its foundation in infant-parent psychotherapy, CPP looks for "ghosts in the nursery" to understand how the past influences the present (Fraiberg et al., 1975). Ghosts are said to arise when parents unconsciously reenact the maladaptive parenting behaviors they experienced as children. Unresolved conflicts, losses, trauma, and negative parenting styles can be transmitted from generation to generation, as when an abused child becomes an abusive parent, the child of an alcoholic becomes or marries an alcoholic, or the daughter of a violent father marries a violent man. Yet ghosts do not always commandeer the infant-parent relationship. They may be transient, arising only under certain stressful circumstances, or banished altogether when the compelling reality of the baby makes an emotional claim on the mother that helps her keep unresolved early conflicts from contaminating their relationship (Fraiberg, 1980). A history of abuse in the parents' past does not doom them to repeat it. For some parents, the memory of childhood fear and pain allows them to see their own child as a new beginning, a chance to set things right. For others, helping them remember how it felt to be the helpless and terrified child – in other words, reconnecting narrative memory to affect – may empower them to parent their own children differently.

In a parallel exploration of protective factors, strengths, and wellness, CPP also looks for "angels in the nursery" by facilitating the retrieval of loving and supportive memories, recognizing the positive influences of benevolent relationships, and promoting identification with the protector (Lieberman, Padrón, Van Horn, & Harris, 2005, p. 507). Just as ghosts can hide from conscious awareness, so too can angels. A skilled therapist can support parents as they search for angels even in dark places. For example, a parent who did not experience her own mother as protective may come to understand her mother's behavior as an attempt to protect her and benefit in the present from recognizing that previously misunderstood intent. When a parent cannot retrieve any benevolent memories, therapy can provide a corrective experience that serves to create new experiences of safety, love, and support in both the parent-child relationship and the therapeutic relationship.

Drawing on the Client's Sociocultural and Historical Context in CPP

Although trauma affects people of all races, ethnicities, and cultures, of all sexual orientations, and at all socioeconomic levels, the way people typically respond to and understand traumatic experiences may vary widely among different groups and subgroups. Cultural competency and "contextually congruent interventions" are therefore critical to working with diverse populations (Brown, 2008; Ghosh Ippen, 2009). Yet therapists cannot be competent in all the cultures their clients represent or accurately predict a particular family's variations from cultural norms. While it is the therapist's responsibility to develop cross-cultural competence and seek consultation as needed, the parent may be the best guide to how the family actually lives the culture.

Using CPP as a conceptual clinical framework, Ghosh Ippen (2009) encourages clinicians to "focus not only on culture but also on the family's history, current situation, and future goals" (p. 107). With immigrant parents, clinicians tend to look at the family's history of immigration and adaptation to the new country and at the events in the country of origin that led directly to the decision to emigrate. It is possible, however, to gain greater insight by widening the focus beyond the family to include external historical events and indirect experiences that act as traumatic stressors on individuals. In addition, extending the time line back several generations before immigration may reveal cumulative communal trauma – such as a history of gender, racial, religious, or political oppression in the family's country of origin – that continues to affect family members in the present. The following case study shows how opening a dialogue about historical trauma can lead to contextually congruent interventions and the co-creation of a multigenerational trauma narrative that assists the healing process.

A CPP Case Involving the Intergenerational Transmission of Traumatic Stress

A Mother and Daughter Begin Therapy

When Rose Liu and her 4-year-old daughter, Sophia Zhang, were referred to a clinic for CPP, Sophia's symptoms were typical for a young child who had witnessed domestic violence: separation anxiety, explosive anger, aggression, oppositional behavior, withdrawal, sleep problems, and somatic complaints. Sophia's externalizing behaviors clashed with the cultural expectations of her immigrant Chinese parents and grandparents, increasing intrafamilial conflict. The therapist assigned to the case, a European American woman about 10 years younger than Rose, knew she would need to understand the family's response to Sophia's behavior in order to identify culturally competent interventions.

In the intake assessment, Rose told the therapist that she was having a hard time coping with Sophia's outbursts. "We used to be so close," Rose said, "but now she's always angry, and she even hits me. Chinese children do not hit their parents. My parents criticize me for her behavior, but I don't know how to stop it." The therapist empathized with Rose's pain and frustration and reassured her that CPP focuses on healing the parent-child relationship as well as improving behavior. Restoring safety and security in the relationship would be the first goal of treatment.

In addition to exploring Rose's concerns about her daughter, the therapist assessed for trauma in the recent and more distant past. Rose disclosed a history of domestic violence that began when Sophia was about 2 years old. On multiple occasions Sophia's father, Ming Zhang, had abused Rose emotionally and physically (choking, pushing, slapping, hitting) in front of Sophia and her 7-year-old brother, Brandon. Eighteen months earlier Sophia and Brandon were in their father's car when the police pulled them over and arrested Ming for driving under the influence of alcohol and child endangerment. The children saw policemen handcuff their father and take him away in a police car. They were then driven in a separate patrol car to a police station, where Rose picked them up.

Although the parents had joint legal custody, Rose had had sole physical custody since Ming's arrest. Rose, who worked full time as a pharmacist, moved to a new apartment and filed for divorce. Ming spent 3 months in jail and lived in a residential treatment center after his release. Rose reported that he had lost his job with the US Postal Service and was currently unemployed, depressed, and anxious. The paternal grandparents supervised the children's Sunday visits with their father. When interviewed about her own history, Rose reported that she too had witnessed domestic violence as a child, and her parents continued to have violent arguments. Rose believed that her grandparents on both sides also had a history of DV, and there was a family history of anxiety as well.

Both Rose and Ming were born in 1967 and grew up in Taiyuan, the capital of Shanxi province in northern China. They married in their hometown in 1991 and two years later emigrated to the United States, together with both sets of parents. Brandon and Sophia were born in the United States. Rose, Ming, and the children spoke Mandarin and English at home; the grandparents spoke only Mandarin. Despite frequent loud arguments among the adults, the extended family members remained close, lived in the same neighborhood, and often shared meals. Before the children started preschool, Rose's parents took care of them during the week, and they continued to provide childcare as needed. Rose believed that the children had witnessed violent arguments between the maternal grandparents while in their care, though they did not speak about that.

After assessing for trauma, the therapist used a structured interview to discover "angels in the nursery" and other protective factors in Rose's past to reinforce their positive influence and provide a source of internalized support. Rose's most important angel was her maternal grandmother, with whom she lived for 3 years in the early 1970s. Rose started university in her hometown in 1984 and developed a close relationship with one of her professors, who encouraged Rose's interest in biochemistry and became a life-long mentor and friend. Although Rose's grandmother died before the family emigrated and her professor still lived in Taiyuan, Rose felt that both were still present in her life. She hoped she could raise her daughter to be kind, loving, and funny like her grandmother and as smart and academically successful as her professor.

Rose and Sophia attended 19 sessions of CPP over a period of 6 months, during which time many of Sophia's problematic behaviors subsided. She no longer behaved aggressively at home or at preschool. She developed an extensive emotional vocabulary and could usually use it to tell her mother how she was feeling before she became dysregulated. She daydreamed much less at school. At home she was generally compliant, and Rose felt that their close relationship had been restored. Although playing together had initially been difficult for this dyad, they now looked forward to playing with dolls, working on puzzles, and drawing together during sessions.

As they approached the end of their work together, Rose, Sophia, and the therapist co-created a narrative that recapitulated, acknowledged, and made sense of the frightening events Sophia had witnessed, from her repeated exposure to DV to the terrifying day her father was arrested, her separation from him while he was in jail, and her continuing wish that her parents would get back together. Sophia could now express "two different feelings at the very same time," as one of her favorite books put it. She loved and missed her dad while also fearing that he might become violent again.

Sophia still sometimes had unexplained stomachaches, and once in a while she resisted going to preschool, saying that she'd rather stay home and play with Mama. Rose considered these to be small issues compared with the long list of behavioral symptoms with which they began. In a collateral session, Rose and the therapist agreed that it was time to begin termination. Posttreatment assessment measures, however, indicated that both Sophia and Rose still had high levels of anxiety consistent with PTSD. The therapist discussed the problem with her supervisor; both were surprised by the results. They agreed that the dyad would benefit from continuing treatment focused specifically on the anxiety. Rose concurred.

Treatment Resumes with a New Therapist

At this point the original therapist's internship came to an end, and the case was transferred to another clinician (AK), a European American woman about 10 years older than Rose. On meeting Rose and Sophia, the new therapist immediately noticed the anxious quality of their speech. Both spoke with rapid-fire intensity, and Sophia interspersed her words with frequent gasping breaths. If Rose's affect intensified, Sophia's would quickly match it. Mother and daughter were clearly attuned to each other, but that connection appeared to reinforce and amplify the dyad's anxiety. The new therapist hypothesized that lowering the mother's anxiety would also lower the daughter's.

Like many preschoolers, Sophia was afraid of monsters and of the dark, but she had other fears as well. For example, she was afraid of hotel rooms, especially in the mountains. "And the chair," Sophia said, "the chair that moves by itself! You have to get on and shut the door." Rose explained that she meant pulling down the bar on the ski lift. The therapist assured Sophia that lots of people are scared of those moving chairs. "She doesn't want to go anywhere," Rose said. "She's afraid of everywhere but home, and even at home she still sleeps with me and touches me all night. If I move away from her when I'm sleeping, she wakes up." The therapist said it sounded like Sophia's fears were getting in the way of enjoying life and trying new things, and they were also interfering with both Rose's and Sophia's well-being. Rose agreed.

In a collateral session, Rose confided that she herself had always been anxious, even as a child, and she worried that she had passed this trait along to her daughter. "My brother and my parents are even more anxious than I am," she reported. "It must be genetic. My brother has four deadbolts on his front door and heavy curtains on the windows. He doesn't even live in a dangerous neighborhood." The therapist assured Rose that even if there was a genetic component to Sophia's anxiety, there was much they could do to reduce its impact on her life at home and at school. She described how Rose and Sophia mirrored each other's emotional states, so that when one began to worry, the other would quickly join in, setting off a negative feedback loop. If Rose got individual or group therapy for her anxiety, the therapist suggested, Sophia would likely benefit as well. Rose never rejected the suggestion outright, but she also didn't act on it, so the therapist revised her approach. Instead of targeting the mother's anxiety so the mother could lower the daughter's, the therapist could address the child's anxiety directly, and perhaps the mother would benefit too. It was worth a shot.

At this point the therapist hypothesized that the dyad's anxiety persisted because of a combination of genetic predisposition ("generations of anxious ancestors," as Rose put it) and residual traumatic stress from the events Rose and Sophia had each lived through and recounted in the original trauma narrative. The therapist decided to introduce some mindfulness and body-based interventions, which had not been used previously in the therapy.

Learning to Slow Down and Breathe

At the next session, the therapist introduced a new game, the slow race, which they could play on their way to the toy cabinet. "You're really good at being fast," she told Sophia, "so we don't need to practice that. In the slow race the slowest person wins. Who can be slowest to walk around the carpet?" Sophia tried a few slow steps but couldn't tolerate it long and broke into a run. Rose stood up and said she wanted to do the slow race with Sophia. This time Sophia made it all the way around the carpet moving slowly. She then selected a puzzle from the toy cabinet and began talking about it in her breathless, pressured way. The therapist brought Sophia's attention to the gasping breathing and said gently, "You have time to say what you want and then breathe." Sophia thought for a moment and then replied, "I feel like I *can't* breathe." "Is that why you stop in the middle of what you're saying, to take another breath?" the therapist asked. Sophia nodded. The therapist said, "I'm guessing that if you slow down, your breath will last longer. You're very good at breathing. You can trust your breath." Sophia tried speaking a little more slowly and said a whole sentence without gasping. Then she invited her mother to join her on the floor with the puzzle.

From this point on, the therapist began incorporating simple body awareness and breathing exercises from *The Mindful Child* (Greenland, 2010) as well as suggestions from participants in Susan Kaiser Greenland's online community, Mindfulness Together (http://innerkids.ning.com). At the beginning of each child-parent therapy session they would all do a starfish stretch (Greenland, 2010), 10 jumping jacks moving and breathing in sync, pinwheel breathing, or the slow race. The therapist used a glitter ball as a metaphor for a mind swirling with worries compared with a quiet mind (with the glitter settled on the bottom). She introduced the idea that people are much more than their thoughts and that they can learn to observe their thoughts without necessarily reacting to them or acting on them. She also explained to Sophia that minds and bodies are linked: "If your breathing is anxious, it can make you feel anxious, and if you feel anxious, you start breathing that way."

After practicing the mindfulness activities for about a month, Rose observed that Sophia was moving more calmly and speaking more fluidly at home as well as in sessions. Her comment opened a port of entry to talk about what the therapist was seeing in Rose – how much calmer she seemed, how her shoulders were relaxed, her speech was slower, and her affect less intense. "I'm learning," she said. "The exercises have been good for me. I can see that when I'm calm, it's easier for Sophia to be calm. It's really working." Now that Sophia was less anxious, she became more spontaneous and joyful in both her play and her interactions with Rose and the therapist. Rose in turn worried less and enjoyed her daughter more. A new openness and playfulness infused the therapy sessions.

A Port of Entry to the Past

Like many Chinese American children, Sophia attended Chinese School in the afternoons. Lunar New Year was fast approaching, and Sophia's class was going to sing and dance at the school's celebration. After performing one of the songs in session, Sophia asked the therapist, "Have you ever been to China?" As it happened, the therapist had taught at a university in north China for two years during the 1980s, but she had not disclosed that. Out of respect for the child, however, she answered the question honestly. Rose and Sophia asked many questions, and when the therapist told them where she had lived and when, Rose exclaimed, "I started university in Taiyuan in 1984!" The therapist had lived in the capital city of a neighboring province and had taught students the same age as Rose.

The therapist's disclosure of her years in China opened the first historical port of entry in large part because the timing was right. Had she disclosed sooner, when the dyad's anxiety was higher, it likely would have led to a brief and superficial conversation about the therapist's experiences in China. Instead, the disclosure prompted Rose to describe experiences from her youth that hadn't seemed relevant before, starting with the months leading up to her college graduation in 1989. On the national stage that spring, student activists across China launched a pro-democracy movement that ultimately attracted more than a million protesters from all walks of life, triggering a power struggle in the Communist Party leadership at the highest levels (Richelson & Evans, 1999). The largest demonstrations took place in the heart of the nation's capital, Tiananmen Square in Beijing, the site of a brutal crackdown on June 4, 1989, when the army entered the city and attacked protesters (Richelson & Evans, 1999).

In the provincial capital of Taiyuan, Rose knew little about the democracy movement. Her parents made sure of that. During the spring of 1989 they repeatedly took her to the hospital. Rose couldn't figure out why her parents thought she was sick; she began to wonder if there wasn't something terribly wrong with her – so terrible that no one would name it. Suddenly in the middle of June the trips to the hospital ceased. No one told her why, and she did not ask. No one ever mentioned her "illness" again. Rose was hugely disappointed when college graduation ceremonies were canceled – in fact all large public gatherings were forbidden at that time – and baffled when she heard that graduating seniors would have to sign a statement attesting that they had not participated in demonstrations.

Looking back, Rose now realized how worried her parents must have been. They had lived through the Cultural Revolution (1966–1976) – a decade of chaos, repression, and violence (Lü, 1994–1995) – and were terrified of getting in trouble. During the Cultural Revolution children were encouraged to listen in on their parents' conversations and report any "counterrevolutionary" content. Such reports, even from a young child, could lead to public "struggle sessions," brutal punishments, and even expulsion to reform-through-labor camps (Kleinman & Kleinman, 1994). Rose's parents learned to keep silent about anything even remotely related to politics. When they heard about the demonstrations in 1989, they decided it would be safer for Rose to be in the hospital with an imaginary ailment than to risk her involvement in the democracy movement. They never explained what they were doing, and that too paralleled the past. "I was just a little girl during the Cultural Revolution," Rose explained. "I don't remember much about it except that everyone was anxious and scared all the time – for years. But no one ever explained what they were scared of."

"When you think about the Cultural Revolution and 1989," the therapist said, "both were traumatic events on many levels, from the personal to the political." Rose agreed that during the Cultural Revolution the whole country was traumatized for a decade. They talked about the intergenerational transmission of trauma, how traumatized parents implant their own emotional responses and any resultant instability in their children, and how children internalize the parents' stress and social mistrust. "Yes!" Rose said excitedly. "My brother won't open his curtains. He never wants anyone to see inside. During the Cultural Revolution, it was dangerous. But he was just a kid then too. He must have gotten that fear from my parents." "Grandma told us not to open the curtains this morning," Sophia added. Rose replied, "They're still scared, Sophia, even though the things that made them afraid happened a long time ago back in China." Rose said she remembered after June 4, 1989, seeing people who had been arrested for participating in the demonstrations paraded through town on open-backed trucks, crackling loudspeakers broadcasting their crimes. "Half of everyone's head was shaved," she said, "and they had big signs around their necks. They looked so scared."

"You can see how your brother inherited your parents' trauma," said the therapist, "and you've experienced your own too – the aftermath of 1989, the domestic violence between your parents and with your husband. I think in coming here you are trying to prevent the transmission of your and your parents' trauma to Sophia. And it's working. As you lower your anxiety, hers lowers too." The therapist recounted ways in which Rose was selecting what of her history and culture she wanted to pass on to Sophia and what she wanted to change for her – how she was taking steps to ensure that her daughter inherited the best of both cultures and to give her daughter the secure and carefree childhood she wished she had had.

Sophia had always enjoyed her mother's stories of her childhood in China, although she had never heard stories like these. Periodically the therapist would rephrase Rose's comments for Sophia – for example, "Mama is telling me that things were very scary in China when she was a little girl." Because the therapist was familiar with modern Chinese history, Rose did not need to explain the Cultural Revolution or the pro-democracy movement of 1989; she talked only about her personal experiences during those times, and she did so with remarkable equilibrium. In fact, she modeled what Siegel (2007) calls a FACES state: "flexible, adaptive, coherent, energized, and stable" (p. 78). Sophia, who worked on art projects during those sessions, mirrored her mother's affect. The therapist felt optimistic about this dyad's ability to reduce their anxiety to within the normal range.

One Port of Entry Opens Another: Tracking Trauma through Four Generations

In a collateral meeting with Rose a week before Sophia's fifth birthday, the therapist explored the impact of historical trauma on Rose's family as a way to understand and normalize the high level of anxiety afflicting generation after generation. Twentieth-century Chinese history comprised decades of traumatic political events that could easily have exacerbated a genetic predisposition to anxiety disorders. The therapist began by drawing out more of Rose's memories of early childhood. Born in December 1967, she was nearly 9 by the time the Cultural Revolution finally ended. In an article titled "How Bodies Remember," Arthur Kleinman and Joan Kleinman (1994) describe the traumatic social upheaval of that period:

> Between 1966 and 1976 China experienced a decade of brutal political turmoil.... Tens of millions of people were affected by criticism, physical assault, suicide, and murder.... Literally hundreds of millions were caught up in the whirlwind of accusation, counteraccusation, self-criticism, and criticism of others. The ancient spine of Chinese society, the bureaucratic order, dislocated; factions fought each other...; families were broken; systems of communication, transportation, justice, public safety, health, and welfare fragmented. Parents were attacked by children; teachers were assaulted by students; Red Guards – adolescent and young adult revolutionaries – broke into homes, looted their contents, beat their occupants, and destroyed precious objects such as ancestral tablets, heirlooms, and books (p. 713).

Rose's mother was pregnant with Rose for most of 1967 (see Table 6.1), one of the most violent and chaotic years of the Cultural Revolution (MacFarquhar & Schoenhals, 2006). Rose and the therapist discussed the events of that year and thought together about the potential impact of the sociopolitical environment of fear and violence on her mother and the developing fetus. The therapist guessed that Rose had been "bathed in cortisol" in utero. Rose stated that her brother, who was 5 when Rose was born, had terrifying memories from that time. The family lived in a work unit between two munitions factories allied

Table 6.1 The Sociopolitical Context of Rose's Life in China: From Cultural Revolution to Emigration

1966	*From 1966 to 1969 tens of millions of Chinese suffer violent persecution; more than half a million die.*
May–August	In a bid to regain control of the Communist Party, Mao Zedong launches the Great Proletarian Cultural Revolution. Student insurrection begins at Beijing University and quickly spreads across the country.
August–November	With Mao's approval, radical students become Red Guards, the new vanguard of the revolution. They quickly gain power and split into factions, terrorizing ordinary citizens. For 2 years they rampage out of control. Mao closes universities and schools and condemns all forms of religion.
1967	
January	Red Guards overthrow provincial leaders.
March	*Rose's mother becomes pregnant.*
July–August	Insurrections erupt across the country. Red Guards rule through violence, intimidation, and chaos. Millions of innocent people are "struggled against" because of their class background, publicly humiliated in mass rallies, and shipped off to remote work camps for "reeducation." Executions and suicides abound. Mass purges continue for years. Rival factions of Red Guards fight each other. Tens of thousands of people take part in pitched battles in the streets. Mao enlists the People's Liberation Army (PLA) to bring order. There are numerous bloody clashes between the PLA and Red Guard factions.
December	*Rose is born. Her parents give her a revolutionary name, Hong (Red).*
1968	
July	The PLA takes control of government offices, schools, and factories, breaking the power of the Red Guards.
December	Mao dismantles the Red Guards by sending millions of young people to the countryside "to learn from the peasants." Urban youth continue to be sent off to the countryside for a decade, finally being permitted to return to the cities in the late 1970s.
1969–1975	Although the Cultural Revolution continues under Mao's leadership, political stability is gradually restored. Universities begin to reopen (1970–1974).

1976	
July	A 7.8 earthquake devastates North China, killing a quarter of a million people. The epicenter is in the province directly east of Rose's. Millions sleep outside for months in fear of aftershocks and collapsing buildings.
September	Mao Zedong dies.
October	Armed forces arrest Mao's wife and her radical associates. The Cultural Revolution finally ends, but in interior provinces such as Rose's, the aftermath of fear and political uncertainty lasts well into the 1980s.
1980–1981	China begins "opening to the outside world."
1983	Anti-Spiritual Pollution Campaign: Many fear that the Cultural Revolution might return, but the campaign fizzles out, economic liberalization picks up, and opening accelerates.
1984	*Rose begins university.*
1987	Anti-Bourgeois Liberalization Campaign: Despite some purges, the campaign is widely disregarded, prompting the "bourgeois liberal" astrophysicist Fang Lizhi to state, "No one is afraid of anyone anymore."
1989	Democracy Movement begins at Beijing University and quickly spreads. By late spring mass demonstrations take place all over the country.
April–May	Students take over Tiananmen Square in Beijing, call for a general strike, demand democratic reform. More than 1,000 students begin a hunger strike in Tiananmen Square. Protests are televised nationwide. The PLA enters Beijing and then withdraws.
June 4–5	Troops approach Tiananmen Square in tanks and open fire. Estimates of deaths range from the official 241 to 1,000 or more.
July	*Rose graduates university.* University graduation ceremonies canceled nationwide to prevent large gatherings of students.
1991	*Rose Liu marries Ming Zhang.*
1993	*Rose and family emigrate to the United States.*

Sources of data: FitzGerald (1968); Gold (1984); Kleinman and Kleinman (1994); Lü (1994–1995); MacFarquhar (n.d.); MacFarquhar and Schoenhals (2006); Nathan (1989); and Richelson and Evans (1999).

with different factions of Red Guards that fought pitched battles in the street. He still remembered the family escaping in the back of a truck as bullets flew around them.

When Rose was 5 all the schools near her home were still closed, so her mother enrolled her in a school in the rural village where her maternal grandmother lived. Although life in the impoverished Shanxi countryside was harsh, under her grandmother's roof Rose felt especially loved, understood, and safe. Walking through the fields from her grandmother's house to the school felt almost magical, especially in the springtime when the fruit trees blossomed. Rose lived with her grandmother for 3 years and to this day can recall in vivid detail the sights, sounds, and smells of village life. Her grandmother was her "angel in the nursery," and the 3 years she lived with her in the midst of the Cultural Revolution were Rose's angel years.

Winding back the clock another generation, Rose and the therapist created a time line of historical events experienced by four generations of her family over 100 years (see Table 6.2). They did not discuss family history per se; indeed, Rose knew little about her family's experience of the political upheavals of the twentieth century. People in China were still cautious about discussing Mao Zedong's disastrous political campaigns, such as the Great Leap Forward, long after his death, and Rose's parents continued their silence about the dark parts of the past even after immigration. What shifted Rose's perspective was talking about her memories of 1989, connecting her parents' behavior in 1989 to their experience of the Cultural Revolution, and then looking back farther on the time line at the sweep of twentieth-century Chinese history and naming it for what it was: trauma after trauma after trauma that was both deeply personal and nationwide in its impact. The time line showed something else as well: visual evidence of decreasing historical trauma, despite the DV in Rose's marriage. In creating this visual presentation of traumatic historical events, the therapist intended to instill hope that the family history of high anxiety was not just a genetic predisposition about which they could do nothing. Given decade upon decade of historical trauma, it made sense that any family propensity toward anxiety might be exacerbated by external events such as those noted in Table 6.2. Seeing that Sophia had not experienced any political or social trauma, Rose began to feel hopeful that she could change the family pattern. She was able to

Table 6.2 Four Generations of Historical Trauma and Domestic Violence

Historical events		Rose's grand-parents	Rose's parents	Rose	Sophia
1900s	Qing dynasty on its knees, dominated and humiliated by Western powers; Boxer Rebellion leads to armed conflict between rebels and Western forces				
1910s	Collapse of Qing dynasty, Republican Revolution, warlord era begins, World War I, May 4th Movement				
1920s	Warlord era, 1925–1927 Revolution, Civil War				
1930s	Civil War, depression, Japanese invasion (20 million Chinese die)				
1937–1945	Japanese occupation, Anti-Japanese War/World War II, Civil War				
1945–1949	Civil War				
1949	Communist triumph (positive or negative depending on family's class status)				
1958–1961	Great Leap Forward: massive famine, 30 million die				
1966–1976	Cultural Revolution: more than half a million die, millions more forcibly displaced				
1976	Tangshan earthquake (7.8): a quarter of a million die				
1989	Students launch Democracy Movement, leading to nationwide mass demonstrations; Beijing massacre of June 4: hundreds, possibly thousands, die				
Intrafamilial stressors					
1993	Emigration to the United States Domestic violence				

Sources of data: Bowblis (2000); MacFarquhar (n.d.); MacFarquhar and Schoenhals (2006); and Spence and Chin (1996).

imagine a brighter future for her daughter, one that left the past (including DV) in the past. That hope further reduced Rose's anxiety – and in turn, Sophia's as well.

Connecting Past and Present: Co-Constructing an Intergenerational Trauma Narrative with a 5-Year-Old

It was now time to revise and expand the trauma narrative that Rose and the first CPP therapist had co-created with Sophia to make sense of the frightening and confusing experiences she had endured, from the DV to her father's arrest and imprisonment to her unrealizable dream that the family would all live together again. Whereas Rose's narrative, developed in collaterals with the therapist, itemized a century of historical trauma and mapped the events of Rose's life alongside those of the Cultural Revolution and later political movements in China, the historical trauma narrative for Sophia was short and simple. Rose explained that the family had lived through many scary times long before Sophia was born – times when there was a lot of fighting and fear in China. That history was part of the reason some family members worried so much and did peculiar things like keeping the curtains closed all the time. Sophia's narrative also addressed the family history of domestic violence not only between her parents, but also between her maternal grandparents and great-grandparents. When Sophia asked why people in her family had hurt each other, Rose connected the violence in the family to the violence in China: When fighting is normal outside, it can become normal at home too. But Rose had made changes to protect them both because she didn't want Sophia to grow up worried and scared. Now they were safe: no more hitting and much less worrying.

As a metaphor for the intergenerational transmission of trauma, they imagined all those scary experiences crammed into a "box of terrible things" that is passed from parent to child, child to grandchild, and gets bigger and heavier if you don't open it up and talk about what's inside. Because Rose and Sophia could talk about their extended family's box of terrible things without getting triggered, they were now able to remember bad experiences from the past without feeling as if they were reliving them. In addition, they could identify some of the good things – the "angels in the nursery," such as Rose's sweet memories of her grandmother – that had helped each generation maintain hope and connection.

The summer before Sophia started kindergarten, Rose and the therapist agreed on a schedule for termination and began the posttreatment assessment. Although the Child Behavior Checklist (CBCL) still indicated elevated anxiety, the levels were significantly lower than in the original assessment, and the Trauma Symptom Checklist for Young Children (TSCYC) – designed specifically to assess trauma-related symptoms in children ages 3–12 – showed no elevations at all. In other words, Sophia's PTSD was itself a thing of the past. Most strikingly, her scores on the Wechsler Preschool and Primary Scale of Intelligence (WPPSI II) showed remarkable improvements – verbal and global language scores increased from average to high average, full scale from average to superior, and performance from average to very superior – suggesting that trauma symptoms had interfered with cognitive functioning at intake (Gil, Calev, Greenberg, Kugelmass, & Lerer, 1990; Samuelson & Cashman, 2009; Mueller-Pfeiffer et al., 2010).

Conclusion

To support families struggling with the intergenerational transmission of historical trauma, the clinician needs both to assess for it and to address it in treatment planning. Although the therapists treating Rose and Sophia followed an extensive assessment protocol at intake that inquired about parents' life stressors, including exposure to war and terrorism, there was no systematic assessment for other types of cumulative historical trauma. Political trauma such as the decade-long Cultural Revolution would have gone unmentioned had the second therapist not been familiar with twentieth-century Chinese history and explored with Rose how those events had affected her and her family. Cultural competence alone does not open that dialogue.

A clinician can become sufficiently conversant with historical trauma that may have affected a client or his or her family in past generations if the clinical history taking includes a careful review of the sociopolitical as well as cultural history of the client's family in past generations, along with more traditional assessment foci such as the family's history of medical and mental health problems. Often a simple Internet search can locate a summary of major historical events anywhere in the world. If a client's family had emigrated from Iran, for example, the therapist could find a link to the BBC's "chronology of key events" in Iranian history from 550 B.C. in less than a minute (www.bbc.com/news/world-middle-east-14542438). The therapist might then inquire whether family members were affected by or involved in the pro-democracy protests of 1999, the Iran-Iraq War of 1980–1988, the overthrow of the Shah in 1979, or repression by the secret police before or after the emergence of the Islamic state. Sometimes an online search retrieves an extensive literature on survivors and descendants of historical trauma. The requisite clinical skill here is not knowing the history per se, but rather figuring out what questions to ask.

Carol Kidron (2003) proposed that if PTSD "allows the invasive past of the trauma survivor to be perpetually present, then the more recent construct of intergenerationally transmitted PTSD has extended the temporal range between the traumatic founding event and its sequelae. It is this temporal extension, which enables descendants to embody and commemorate a distant traumatic past" (p. 538).

With historical trauma that afflicted entire nations, races, genders, or peoples, the therapist needs both cultural competence and an awareness of history in order to develop what Ghosh Ippen (2009) describes as "contextually congruent interventions ... that guide family members in a way that is responsive to where they are, where they've come from, and where they hope to go" (p. 116). Ultimately, the parent holds the key to understanding how historical trauma plays out in the present for the dyad in the therapy room. The onus is on the therapist to open the dialogue and help the parent find that key.

References

Bowblis, J. (2000). China in the 20th century. In *King's College History Department*. Retrieved from http://departments.kings.edu/history/20c/china.html.

Bowlby, J. (1982). *Attachment and loss: Vol. 1. Attachment* (2nd ed.). New York: Basic Books. (Original work published 1969).

Brave Heart, M. Y. H. (1999). *Oyate ptayela:* Rebuilding the Lakota Nation through addressing historical trauma among Lakota parents. *Journal of Human Behavior in the Social Environment, 2*(1–2), 109–126.

Brave Heart, M. Y. H. (2010). *Culturally congruent assessment and intervention with indigenous peoples of the Americas* [pdf document]. Retrieved from http://hsc.unm.edu/som/psychiatry/crcbh/docs/Archive/11-09-10.CulturallyCongruentAssessment.pdf.

Brown, L. S. (2008). *Cultural competence in trauma practice: Beyond the flashback.* Washington, DC: American Psychological Association.

Cook, A., Spinazzola, J., Ford, J. D., Lanktree, C., Blaustein, M., Cloitre, M., et al. (2005). Complex trauma in children and adolescents. *Psychiatric Annals, 35*(5), 390–398.

FitzGerald, C. P. (1968). Reflections on the Cultural Revolution in China. *Pacific Affairs, 41*(1), 51–59.

Fraiberg, S. (1980). *Clinical studies in infant mental health.* New York: Basic Books.

Fraiberg, S., Adelson, E., & Shapiro, V. (1975). Ghosts in the nursery: A psychoanalytic approach to the problems of impaired infant-mother relationships. *Journal of the American Academy of Child Psychiatry, 14,* 387–421.

Freud, S. (1959). Beyond the pleasure principle. In J. Strachey (Ed. & Trans.), *The standard edition of the complete psychological works of Sigmund Freud* (Vol. 19, pp. 1–30). London: Hogarth Press. (Original work published 1920).

Freud, S. (1959). Inhibitions, symptoms and anxiety. In J. Strachey (Ed. & Trans.), *The standard edition of the complete psychological works of Sigmund Freud* (Vol. 20, pp. 75–175). London: Hogarth Press. (Original work published 1926).

Ghosh Ippen, C. M. (2009). The sociocultural context of infant mental health: Toward contextually congruent interventions. In C. H. Zeanah, Jr. (Ed.), *Handbook of infant mental health* (3rd ed., pp. 104–119). New York: Guilford Press.

Gil, T., Calev, A., Greenberg, D., Kugelmass, S., & Lerer, B. (1990). Cognitive functioning in Post Traumatic Stress Disorder. *Journal of Traumatic Stress, 3*(1), 29–45.

Gold, T. B. (1984). "Just in time!": China battles spiritual pollution on the eve of 1984. *Asian Survey, 24*(9), 947–974.

Greenland, S. K. (2010). *The mindful child: How to help your kid manage stress and become happier, kinder, and more compassionate.* New York: Free Press.

Janoff-Bulmann, R. (1992). *Shattered assumptions: Towards a new psychology of trauma.* New York: Free Press.

Johnson, F. K., Dowling, J., & Wesner, D. (1980). Notes on infant psychotherapy. *Infant Mental Health Journal, 1,* 19–33.

Johnson, K. (1996). The politics of the revival of female infant abandonment in China, with special reference to Hunan. *Population and Development Review, 22*(1), 77–98.

Kidron, C. A. (2003). Surviving a distant past: A case study of the cultural construction of trauma descendant identity. *Ethos, 31*(4), 513–544.

Kleinman, A., & Kleinman, J. (1994). How bodies remember: Social memory and bodily experience of criticism, resistance, and delegitimation following China's Cultural Revolution. *New Literary History, 25,* 708–723.

Lieberman, A. F., Chu, A., Van Horn, P., & Harris, W. W. (2011). Trauma in early childhood: Empirical evidence and clinical implications. *Development and Psychopathology, 23,* 397–410.

Lieberman, A. F., Padrón, E., Van Horn, P., & Harris, W. W. (2005). Angels in the nursery: The intergenerational transmission of benevolent parental influences. *Infant Mental Health Journal, 26*(6), 504–520.

Lieberman, A. F., & Van Horn, P. (2005). *"Don't hit my mommy!": A manual for child-parent psychotherapy with young witnesses of family violence.* Washington, DC: Zero to Three: National Center for Infants, Toddlers and Families.

Lieberman, A. F., & Van Horn, P. (2008). *Psychotherapy with infants and young children: Repairing the effects of stress and trauma on early attachment.* New York: Guilford Press.

Lieberman, A. F., & Van Horn, P. (2009). Child-parent psychotherapy: A developmental approach in infancy and early childhood. In C. H. Zeanah, Jr. (Ed.), *Handbook of infant mental health* (3rd ed., pp. 439–449). New York: Guilford Press.

Lü, X. (1994–1995). A step toward understanding popular violence in China's Cultural Revolution. *Pacific Affairs, 67*(4), 533–563.

MacFarquhar, R. (n.d.). 20th century Chinese timeline. In *Perspectives on China with Harvard Professor Roderick MacFarquhar*. Retrieved from http://athome.harvard.edu/programs/macfarquhar/macfarquhar_timelineset.html.

MacFarquhar, R., & Schoenhals, M. (2006). *Mao's last revolution*. Cambridge, MA: Belknap Press.

Main, M., & Hesse, E. (1990). Parents' unresolved traumatic experiences are related to infant disorganized attachment status: Is frightened and/or frightening parental behavior the linking mechanism? In M. T. Greenberg, D. Cicchetti, & E. M. Cummings (Eds.), *Attachment in the preschool years: Theory, research, and interventions* (pp. 161–182). Chicago: University of Chicago Press.

Mueller-Pfeiffer, C., Martin-Soelch, C., Blair, J. R., Carnier, A., Kaiser, N., Rufer, M., Schnyder, U., & Hasler, G. (2010). Impact of emotion on cognition in trauma survivors: What is the role of posttraumatic stress disorder? *Journal of Affective Disorders, 123*(1–2), 287–292.

Nathan, A. J. (1989). Chinese democracy in 1989: Continuity and change. *Problems of Communism, 38*, 16.

Pynoos, R. S. (1997, February). The transgenerational repercussions of traumatic expectations. Paper presented at the Southern Florida Psychiatric Society/University of Miami School of Medicine, Miami, FL.

Richelson, J. T., & Evans, M. L. (1999). *Tiananmen Square, 1989: The declassified history*. National Security Archive electronic briefing book 16. Retrieved from www.gwu.edu/~nsarchiv/NSAEBB/NSAEBB16/documents/index.html.

Samuelson, K., & Cashman, C. (2009). Effects of intimate partner violence and maternal posttraumatic stress symptoms on children's emotional and behavioral functioning. In R. Geffner, D. Griffin, & J. Lewis (Eds.), *Children exposed to violence: Current issues, interventions and research* (pp. 132–146). New York: Routledge.

Schore, Allan N. (2013). Relational trauma, brain development, and dissociation. In J. D. Ford & C. A. Courtois (Eds.), *Treating complex traumatic stress disorders in children and adolescents: Scientific foundations and therapeutic models* (pp. 3–23). New York: Guilford Press.

Siegel, D. J. (2007). *The mindful brain: Reflection and attunement in the cultivation of well-being*. New York: Norton.

Spence, J. D., & Chin, A. (1996). *The Chinese century: A photographic history of the last hundred years*. New York: Random House.

Wesner, D., Johnson F., & Dowling, J. (1962). What is maternal-infant intervention? The role of infant psychotherapy. *Psychiatry, 45*, 307–315.

Zero to Three. (2005). *Diagnostic classification of mental health and developmental disorders of infancy and early childhood, revised (DC:0–3R)*. Washington, DC.

Chapter 7

Enduring Mothers, Enduring Knowledge
On Rape and History

Judith L. Alpert

The Shaping of Internal Representations of Reality

I always knew that something terrible had happened to my mother. She was afraid of everything. She was afraid of dogs. She was afraid to stay alone. Lights had to be on at night, even when we were sleeping. Lurking strangers must be seen or frightened away. She was afraid of men she did not know. When there was a delivery, she would tell me to hide under the bed until *he* was gone. And when she opened the door to these unfamiliar men who delivered our groceries, she concealed a knife in her pocket, "just in case". There wasn't much she wasn't afraid of and there weren't many possibilities of wickedness she didn't prepare for.

Before she married, she lived with my grandmother and an aunt and uncle who had a child. I have been told that there was a time when my mother participated in the family Sundays. At ten o'clock in the morning, all those who lived with grandma would lay out tables in the foyer of grandma's apartment and all the other family members would arrive. Everyone would bring food. After eating, the work for the day began. The agenda was always the same. Every problem that arose over the week for each person was presented and discussed and some resolution or reassuring words followed. Everyone talked. Everyone helped. Decisions were not made and big items were not purchased without being evaluated by this powerful counsel. This was a strong family unit and the members were involved in each other's lives.

I am told that my mother would participate at these events. At some point, though, she stopped participating. It was around the time that she

---

Reprinted with kind permission:
Alpert, J. (2015). Enduring Mothers, Enduring Knowledge: On Rape and History. *Contemporary Psychoanalysis*, 51 (2): 296–311.

became afraid of everything. People let my mother be quiet. Perhaps they didn't even notice the change, her unusual silence. Perhaps they didn't know what to do about the sudden shift. Perhaps they knew and didn't know and, at the same time, didn't want to know. Only later did I discover how much trans-generational history was distilled into my mother's silence and into my family's inability to ask, to comment, to inquire. This silence referred back to my mother's trauma and to the history of my grandmother in the pogroms about which no one spoke.

The family may have pushed my mother to marry because they thought that marriage was the solution. She was 28. That was approaching old for singledom in the 1930s. She was fixed up with a man. Everyone at the family table said that he was a good catch. He was sweet and calm, and was described as the kind of person who wouldn't hurt a fly, the kind of person whose cheeks one would love to pinch.

Marriage was not about love in my extended family. All agreed that he was perfect for my mother. He was not scary. He would be patient. He would be a good provider and, besides, it was time for my mom to be on her own. The family grouping all agreed on this one Sunday afternoon. One thing the family tribunal hadn't counted on: my mother did not like to be home alone at night and this man would be working many nights. The solution: grandma moved in with them. Mom and dad and grandma lived at 109 Elm Hill Avenue while some other family members continued to live at 57 Elm Hill Avenue.

Somehow life moved on. I was born. Then I caught "it". It was as if I was invaded by her emotional state. "It", the fear that is, was transmitted to me. Within five years I managed to accrue a mountain of them. I had a lot of my mother's terrors. I was afraid of dogs. I was afraid of men, and I was sometimes even afraid of my father. I would cry a lot. My mother did for me what all the wise family members who made wise decisions never did for her: she put me in therapy and she got a therapist for herself. This was 1949.

My therapist and I had an invisible war to engage in which appeared to be linked to my mother's trauma and my grandmother's trauma. My internal house was haunted, and my five year old fears were linked to their unresolved emotional shocks and loss.

I remember my therapist. She was young and pretty and calm, and she didn't seem to be afraid. We met in a room full of colorful toys. There was a one-way mirror and my mother told me that she and her therapist would sometimes watch me play. While there were many play options, I always engaged in one of two activities. I hammered fat wooden round pegs into a piece of wood with round holes. Over and over again I did this. What was my play about? Was I announcing that I knew some secret about forbidden entry of some fat round thing being hammered into a hole? Did I repeat the hammering in an effort to have control of this forbidden entry, this violation, that never should have happened? I wonder now. But then I played.

Also I played with the two story dollhouse which was opened on one side. I moved the mother in it. I kept putting her in different places until she was in just the right situation. And I moved the doll-house furniture. I changed which rooms would be near the front door. I made the house safe. And then I made the house even safer. No one was going to enter who didn't belong. I was making sure of that.

I don't remember talking in my childhood therapy, but I probably did. And, for sure, I got better and I felt understood. I didn't cry as much. I wasn't as scared. In time, my tears and my fears were like those of others my age. "It", the thing I caught, got hammered away. "It", the thing I caught, moved into nonexistence like some of the dollhouse furniture. Safety and security had been established. I had found a way to tell my story. My mother got better too. Over time her mind was freer. She was *there*. She, too, had an opportunity to re-arrange, to re-experience, to grieve, and to re-represent. She, too, found free-flowing psychic circulation. And I believe that she faced her trauma in order to release me from permanently inheriting it.

What happened to my mother? What made her so fearful? She was 87 years old when she finally told me, and it was many years after I had completed my own adult analysis. She was in hospice at the time of telling. I had been with her by her bedside for about five days. She was too tired to talk and I had talked so much. I had told her everything that I wanted to tell her. I acknowledged what a good mother she had been and how much I loved her and how much I knew she loved me. I acknowledged how much she had given me. There were only truths and tears and deep love in that room. Finally it seemed that there was little else to say. I filled the space by singing songs that I used to sing as a child and she used to sing to me. Mom listened, too weak to do anything else. Although dying, she seemed content.

Right before she died, she asked for some chocolate. I had a piece in my pocketbook that was left on my hotel pillow the night before. I melted it in my hand and then I took a q-tip and scraped it in the chocolate. I put the chocolate covered q-tip in her mouth, her first food in five days. Her eyes opened wide. She told me it was delicious. I offered more. She said she was full. She smiled and then she died.

But something happened right before she asked for the chocolate. Before I gave her the treasured sweet, she gave me something. She gave me structure and representation or the gift of her trauma story. It was a one-liner: "I was raped by the dress shop owner when I was 15." While she had never told me this before, once she told me I knew that she had told me what I had always known. I knew why I had been hammering fat wooden round pegs into a piece of wood with round holes. I knew why I had to make the house safe.

Intergenerational Transmission of Trauma: How There is Knowledge and Transmission

As a child, I felt the intergenerational force of her trauma. The transmission of her unresolved trauma was silent and the cargo was toxic and, had it not been treated as it was, it might have been passed on to more generations. It occurred because my mother could not speak the unspeakable and the unimaginable but, nevertheless, it was revealed. There is no such thing as silence. The passing from one generation to the next can be delicate or obvious. Once passed, they can even form life themes where they comprise a core of one's identity.

In a discussion of the role of the other in the development of the capacity to mentalize, Fonagy and Target (1996) states (p. 231): "– when a parent is unable to incorporate and think about a piece of reality, and cannot then enable the child to do so safely through playing with the frightening ideas, this reality remains to be experienced in the mode of psychic equivalence. Neither child nor parent can "metabolize" the thoughts, and the "unthinkable" thoughts are passed from one generation to the next."

It appears that unconscious phantasies can evolve from events that were never experienced by the child. The child doesn't have to experience the parent's trauma for the child to imagine how these events happened and for these imaginings to become the content of unconscious phantasy. The child takes in what is ongoing in the present that truly belongs in the past. The child observes the mother's triggers and its effects on mother. The child just may need to experience the absence that trauma created in the parent in order for the child to come to know the antiquated misdeeds.

Different terms are used to describe the intergenerational transmission of trauma. Faimberg (1988) speaks of *telescoping of generations* to explain an unconscious identification process occurring across generations and thickening a history that at least, in part, does not belong to the patient's generation. Kestenberg (1988) speaks of *transposition* to describe the situation in which there is reliving, without conscious awareness, of the experience of another generation as though it was their very own experience. What is clear is that when there is silence and absence, there is a repetition of the past in the present and the victim as well as future generations are burdened. Grief and intolerable pain cannot be hidden, not from the victim or from the generations which follow.

Scientific data confirms the transfer from generation to generation of massive psychic trauma (Laub and Lee, 2003) and solid epidemiological evidence supports clinical observations of its existence. Some research stands out. Yehuda, Schmeidler, Giller, Siever, and Binder-Brynes (1998), for example, found lasting hormonal changes in the adult children of parents suffering PTSD and found that they, too, were more likely to develop PTSD themselves. Van der Kolk's (1994, p. 253) much quoted statement that "The body keeps the score" is apparently true as well for the experience of traumatic events across generations.

While she did not tell me in words, my mother was not silenced. Her behavior spoke. She was responding to things I couldn't see or make sense of. She managed her flooding by means of dissociative mechanisms. I saw this and couldn't make sense of what I saw. I wanted to know. She needed *not* to know. She spoke but not with the language of conscious, coherent speech. Painful aspects of her past were living in the present. Her mind was not hers, not really. Of course I knew. And of course she knew. It is my impression that she always had conscious memory and that she used dissociation to manage the flooding of affect and the overwhelming flashbacks that she experienced. When she saw fears being played out in me, she took action. She put us both in treatment. She stopped the intergenerational transmission of trauma.

Unresolved traumas get handed down to children, and these hand-me-downs are too massive for them. It is confusing and scary. There are strong reactions to things that cannot be seen or understood. The child needs to know. At the same time, mother needs to *not* know. The mother does not fully own her own mind. That is what happens when there is dissociated trauma. It takes up space and leaves her less free to imagine, to delight, and to be open to what emerges in her life and in the life of her family. Dissociated affect and ideas may leave a parent more easily affected by triggers aroused by their child (Moldawsky Silber, 2012). Seligman (1999) noted that procedural and pre-reflective experiences which are located around physical and affective registers are susceptible to transfer.

I have often wondered what my normal baby and early childhood screams, demands, cries, helplessness, tantrums, and terrors triggered in my mother. How did she respond to them? What did they release in her? Did they serve to put in motion her dissociated affects? Did I, in turn, co-regulate? Is this, in part how there was transfer of her dissociated affect? I wonder too what my mother's normal baby and early childhood behavior triggered in my grandmother. "Stuff" was free floating and unlinked to the traumatic experience and triggers had to be widely distributed. And we know that there is transmission of trauma from generation to generation when the survivor of trauma cannot enact representation or symbolization to know "it" and to mourn "it". When this occurs, then the trauma back-pack is transmitted and the haunting to future generations has begun.

This Explains (Partially, at Least) My Interest in Trauma

While I knew something terrible had happened to my mother, I wanted to understand her experience more deeply. I specialize in trauma. I teach courses in trauma. I supervise psychoanalysts who work with traumatized patients. And I work with trauma survivors. Rape. Incest. Sexual harassment. Forensic cases involving kids who were sexually abused on a school bus by a school bus driver or teenagers who were victims of inappropriate teacher behavior are part of my professional life. I have always been interested in the issue of recovered memories. Along with others, I work with patients who want to know what happened to them, who want to remember. There were secrets in their families. Or there were secrets which lived within their dissociated selves which were known and unknown to them and which would make their appearance in intrusive, disguised, and unwanted ways. Vacant spaces of discourse. The unknown. Silence. These were some of the areas I inhabited and continue to inhabit in my professional world. I think part of my interest has always been to visit my mother's world, to understand her strange and frightening and disconnected behavior, and to define her trauma. I think some of my interest was to *really* know her and my grandma's trauma.

Professionals in the trauma world often ask how they came to reside in the professional world of ghosts and unknowns and vacant spaces. We know that when there is a positive outcome, traumatized children become caretakers and psychoanalysts (Garon, 2004). And sometimes they become historians. This seems to be true in the case of intergenerational transmission of trauma as well. Perhaps it is even truer for those of us who are second and third generation as there may be more absence, more interior spaces, and more haunting ghosts. While your internal house, like mine, may be big and fully populated with wonder and delight, nevertheless the ghosts from the past may have provided, and may even continue to provide, a bit of Halloween. They may extend this Halloween to the next generation. And you may want to know and to understand.

Widespread Force of Intergenerational Trauma

While I consider how the ghosts from the past and my transgenerational legacy may have provided a bit of Halloween in my childhood, the focus of the present paper is on the widespread force of intergenerational trauma on the others who somehow participated, whether through fellowship, witnessing, or transmission of traumas from antecedent generations. My mother, too, carried memories of massive psychic trauma from previous generations. Of this I am sure. Her presentation indicated that trauma had become an unconscious organizing theme which was passed on from previous generations and became internalized. While hers was eventually treated, when left untreated, it compromises the well-being of generations to come. Accumulated trauma makes new trauma more traumatizing. It is like compounded interest. The trauma is added to the existing principal so that, from that trauma moment on, the trauma that had been added also earns more trauma. My mother had compounded-trauma-interest. She had a transgenerational legacy of trauma at the time of her rape. That is clear because she was Jewish and a woman, and trauma is endemic to both groups.

Pogroms Against the Jews

It wasn't just the rape that became an unconscious organizing principle for my mother. I think of the pogroms. While I am writing about my mother, because that is the story I am coming to know, I hope it is clear that my mother's story is that of many women who have legacies of pogroms – Armenians, Greeks, Turks, and Palestinian Arabs, for example – as well as Jews. In the early 1900s, shortly after the tsar granted fundamental civil rights and political liberties, pogroms directly mainly at Jews broke out in hundreds of cities, towns, and villages, resulting in deaths and injuries to thousands of people and damage and ruin to thousands of Jewish owned homes and businesses. While non-Jews maintained most of the wealth in Odessa, where grandma lived at this time, Jews were seen as an economic threat and their growing visibility enhanced the predisposition of Russians to blame Jews for their difficulties. Clashes turned into pogroms and Russians indiscriminately attacked Jews and vandalized and looted their homes and stores. Weinberg (1987, pp. 63–64) writes: "A list of atrocities perpetrated against the Jews is too long to recount here, but suffice it to say that pogromists brutally and indiscriminately beat, mutilated, and murdered defenseless Jewish men, women, and children. They hurled Jews out of windows, raped and cut open the stomachs of pregnant women, and slaughtered infants in front of their parents. In one particularly gruesome incident, pogromists hung a woman upside down by her legs and arranged the bodies of her six dead children on the floor below her."

Where were the police, you may wonder. The literature is pretty consistent on this point. In order to facilitate attacks against Jews, policemen compiled lists of Jewish-owned stores and apartments. They participated in the looting and killing. They directed pogromists to Jewish-owned stores or apartments and prevented them from damaging the property of non-Jews. Protection for Jews was non-existent.

Like most Jews living in Russia in the late 1800s and early 1900s, my grandmother experienced anti-Jewish legislation and pogroms. My grandmother was beautiful and strong. She had long white hair down to her knees which she would wash, brush, make snarl-free, and put into a bun of sorts. She spent most of the day sitting on a big gray armchair in the second floor living room seeming to look out the window of our quiet suburban neighborhood. When I would speak to her in the midst of her vigilant watch, she would jump up, as if I had scared her. It would take a few seconds, too many seconds I always thought, before she responded. There wasn't much to see out the window. One neighbor would walk his dog. Another would leave her house in her slippers to get mail. Occasionally cars would drive by. It was a sleepy street that didn't seem to warrant grandma's alert stare.

I often wondered why she looked at sameness and stillness for so long and why she kept her hair so very, very long. I used to think about the German fairy tale Rapunzel and how the enchantress would say "Rapunzel, Rapunzel, let down your golden hair". Like Rapunzel in the fairy tale, my grandma was the most beautiful woman in the world. And as Rapunzel would drop her hair down to the enchantress who would then climb up Rapunzel's hair to her tower room, I thought about my grandma dropping her hair out the window so that we could climb down to safety. I knew we might need to vacate in a hurry and that the stairs would not serve us well.

I had many reasons to explain grandma's need for a "long-hair-escape-rope". A delivery man would say that he was from Filene's department store and mom would let him in even though she was not expecting a delivery. The non-delivery, delivery-man would deliver trouble. Or a man would arrive in a policeman's or a fireman's uniform and he would try to kill all of us. Only he was not a policeman or a fireman. What appeared to be a good, protective man (a policeman or a fireman) was really a bad, dangerous man in uniform-disguise. The theme of my explanations was consistent: Some bad man would present as something other than who he was and would try to do something bad to us.

Yes. I think I had some knowledge about my mother's rape and the fire in the pogroms and the police who did not protect the Jews as they were supposed to but, instead, rounded up Jews and stripped them naked and beat them mercilessly. And while I may not have known the specifics, such as the details of the female rape in the family and the burning alive of grandma's three children in a pogrom fire in Odessa, I knew enough. I knew that men who were supposed to be good and protective were bad and caused harm. I knew that we needed to be able to escape, and grandma, by her alert stare from the second floor living room was watching out for us, and by her long hair that touched her knees was providing an exit. And maybe my mother knew about the fires and the killing in Odessa too. That, along with the rape, would explain her wielding a knife and telling me to hide under the bed when the doorbell rang.

My grandma was alive for all three large-scale waves of pogroms directed at the Jews of Russia (1881–1884, 1903–1906, and 1917–1921). This too is mine and my mother's legacy. Grandma lived with us until I was 13. She arrived in Boston from Odessa around 1906. While initially poor upon coming to this country, life hadn't always been like that for grandma. In Odessa, my great-grandfather owned clothing stores and she lived a relatively privileged life until the family was targeted by the pogromist mobs. Many women were violated in these pogroms. I don't know for sure if my beautiful grandmother was. She escaped from Odessa after three of her children died in a fire in the 1905 anti-Jewish pogrom. While there were other pogroms before and after this one, the 1905 Odessa Pogrom is recorded as one of the most severe both in Odessa's history and across the Russian empire (Jewish Virtual Library, A division of the American-Israeli Cooperative Enterprise).

I want to know more about my grandmother's experience. I wasn't curious as a child. Only now am I. I think about the Jews who were killed and wounded, about their homes and businesses which were damaged, and, mostly, I think about violations that were inflicted on women. Had the family counsel that was part of my mother's childhood and adult life not been able to help my mother because grandma and some of the other elders were dealing with their own past witnessings and violations? Was my mother's rape somehow known to grandma and was grandma's trauma from the pogroms somehow transmitted to my mother? I think so.

So I read more about pogroms. I read about the homes and businesses which were destroyed and looted; about men, women, and children being beaten, mutilated, and murdered; and I read about women being gang-raped. I read about how the Russian police stood by, how local government officials ignored pleas for help, and I read about how the postal service refused to deliver telegrams requesting that the central government intervene. Basically I read about how people who were supposed to be good and protective were neither. I read about how this goes on for days and days and I know my grandmother was there. I wonder what she witnessed and I wonder what happened to her. And I read about the rape of women in the pogroms.

The 1903 Kishinev pogrom was one of the most ruthless and brutal. Generations of Jews learned about it from reading Hayyim Nahman Bialik's 1904 (reprinted in Hadari, 2000) poem, "In the City of Killing". How he came to write this poem is significant. In order to gather survivor testimonies and to publish them in a book, Bialik was sent to Kishinev. While there he interviewed people and gathered eyewitness accounts and corroborated them with other testimonies from other witnesses. In all he collected 150 testimonies, some as short as a paragraph and some as long as eight pages. While he was commissioned to write a book of survivor testimony, for reason he did not disclose he abandoned the project. Instead, he wrote an indirect testimony, the poem.

There was much speculation (as cited by Dekel, 2008) as to why he wrote the poem rather than a book of survivor testimonies. Was it because the image of pure Jewish maidens attacked by "raping paddock of centaurs", his word from the poem, was more powerful than the narrative of a rape by an acquaintance and his drunken friends? Was it because the treacheries of witnessing was too much? Was it because the testimonies reactivated his own early sexual trauma? Was it because his exposure to the exposed resulted in vicarious traumatization? The poem he eventually wrote is about male witnessing. It begins with God's command to the male poet to "rise and go to the town of killing", to see with his own eyes and feel with his own hand "the congealed blood and hardened brains of the dead". Then there is a cataloguing, a shocking cataloguing: "a disemboweled chest filled with feathers", "a case of nostrils and nine inch nails", "a baby found by the side of his stabbed mother/still dozing with her cold nipple in his sucking mouth".

The second stanza was based on the testimony of Rivka Schiff, who was gang-raped by a business acquaintance and his drunken friends in front of everyone in the attic. After Rivka's gang-rape, the other females in the attic were raped. I think about this. Then I remember my father telling me how groups of anti-Semitic youth would chase him and other Jewish boys on their way home from school. The bullies would throw rocks at them and scream anti-Semitic epithets at them, and, if caught, would beat them. This was in Boston in the 1920s. My Dad was able to talk about this brutality. Why was the family able to listen? Why could he tell? Why did my mother remain silent? Why did my grandmother remain silent? I came to know that *what* wasn't spoken was *much worse* than what was spoken. I came to know that silence is a euphemism for a too-horrific story.

Conclusion

It is not simply the victims or the witnesses who are impacted by the trauma. It is also the perpetrator. And it may also be the children and the grandchildren of all of these. The net is broad and expansive and can extend through culture and society as well. Consider my courses on trauma. Over the years, for example, my trauma courses have been heavily represented with students with German nationality, and many of these have parents who were somehow involved in the Holocaust. These students take trauma courses in an effort to know. The children and grandchildren inherit the damage and the ghosts from the past because they are deprived of the memory.

The book *Collective Silence: German Identity and the Legacy of Shame* (Heimannsberg and Schmidt, 1993) comprises accounts, histories, and experiences of psychotherapists who practice in Germany. The therapists tell of their work with German patients who continue to struggle with the Holocaust. The patients are grandparents, children, grandchildren, perpetrators (or Nazis), resisters, and victims from the Holocaust, and their stories are replete with denial in the older generations and anger and confusion in the younger generation. Still coping with pain, for example, are the daughter of a high ranking Nazi official, children of Jewish emigres, children raised in the Hitler Youth Movement, and those born after the war. This book makes vividly clear that trauma is transmitted to the next generation.

Space, time, or agency are not limits for massive psychic trauma. It transmits through the memories of generations and shapes internal representations of reality. It becomes an unconscious organizing principle and may even become a life theme for its victims. It gets passed on like the flu and, at the same time, like a genetic disease in that it spreads vertically and horizontally. It is like the flu in that many of those around it at the time – victim, perpetrator, or even witness – may be affected. And it is like a genetic disease in that those victims, perpetrators, or even witnesses who are distant in future time may be affected. It can be a broad and long distance traveler in that it can extend into culture and society. The welfare of generations can be reduced by this powerful transmitter. So, what we must do is clear. We have no choice. The stories must be told.

A young man told me that I should not tell my mother's story. He said that it died with her. I see it differently. It is *my* story. And it didn't die. It lives in me. It influenced me, and continues to do so. In fact, it is my story-truth (Alpert, 1997 in Gartner), which is my present understanding of my real past and it comprises my psychic reality. While historical truth cannot be fully known, the reality of suffering, fear, anxiety, and internal limitations can be. The events that I report here may not have occurred exactly as I have reconstructed them. What I have done is taken the pieces of what Andre Green (1999) calls my "interior souvenirs" and given them conscious shape.

I conclude by referring back to my mother. My mother did one of the noblest and bravest things. It was a tender and loving gift to me. This very frightened woman became a very brave, frightened woman. She dealt with her trauma on my behalf and put us both into treatment. She stopped the intergenerational transmission of trauma.

Notes

The author gratefully acknowledges the careful reading and insightful comments of Dr. Sue Grand and the library assistance of Ms. Natalie Ann Schaad.

References

Alpert, J. L. (1997). Story truth and happening truth. In R. B. Gartner (Ed.), *Memories of Sexual Betrayal: Truth, Fantasy, Repression and Dissociation.* Northvale, NJ: Aronson, pp. 237–252.

Dekel, M. (2008). "From the mouth of the raped woman Rivka Schiff," Kishinev, 1903. *Women's Studies Quarterly*, 36 (1 & 2):199–207.

Faimberg, H. (1988). The telescoping of generations. *Contemporary Psychoanalysis*, 24:99–118.

Fonagy, P. and Target, M. (1996). Playing with reality: I. Theory of mind and the normal development of psychic reality. *International Journal of Psychoanalysis*, 77:217–233.

Garon, J. (2004). Skeletons in the closet. *International Forum of Psychoanalysis*, 13:84–92.

Grand, S. (2000). *The Reproduction of Evil: A Clinical and Cultural Perspective.* Hillsdale, NJ: Analytic Press.

Green, A. (1999) *The Work of the Negative.* London, UK: Free Association Books.

Hadari, A., trans. and ed. (2000). *Songs from Bialik.* Syracuse, NY: Syracuse University Press.

Heimannsberg, B. and Schmidt, C. J. (1993) *Collective Silence: German Identity and the Legacy of Shame.* Jewish Virtual Library, A Division of the American-Israeli Cooperative Enterprise.

Kestenberg, J. (1998). *Child Survivors of the Holocaust.* New York: Guilford.

Laub, D. and Lee, S. (2003). Thanatos and massive psychic trauma: The impact of the death instinct on knowing, remembering and forgetting. *Journal of the American Psychoanalytic Association*, 51(2):433–464.

Moldawsky Silber, L. (2012) Ghostbusting transgenerational processes. *Psychoanalytic Dialogues*, 22:106–122.

Seligman, S. (1999). Integrating Kleinian theory and intersubjective infant research: Observing projective identification. *Psychoanalytic Dialogues*, 9:120–159.

van der Kolk, B. (1994). The body keeps score: Memory and the evolving psychobiology of posttraumatic stress. *Harvard Review of Psychiatry*, 1:253–265.

Weinberg, R. (1987). Workers, Pogroms, and the 1905 Revolution in Odessa. *Russian Review*, 46(1):53–75.

Yehuda, R., Schmeidler, J., Giller Jr., E., Siever, L., & Binder-Brynes, K. (1998). Relationship between post-traumatic stress disorder characteristics of Holocaust survivors and their adult offspring. *American Journal of Psychiatry*, 155:841–843.

Part III
Persecution and Otherness
Different Subjectivities and the Restoration of Trust

Introduction
Samuel C. Gable and David M. Goodman

In the final book written before her death, Jane Jacobs (2004), a progenitor of modern urban planning and the author of the defining *Death and Life of Great American Cities*, wrote about a phenomenon of denial and fantasy that occurs in the dark age after civilizations collapse. "Mass amnesia" was the term coined for an intriguing co-occurrence of denial regarding a society's destruction by self or other, alongside the misplaced fantasy that once the collapse occurs there will be some meaningful remnant of what *was* that will carry their song through the night. More often, the remaining communities, if they remain, eventually forget what has been lost as well as forget that they have forgotten. Jacobs summarizes the example of Mesopotamia, whose trade and technological ingenuity allowed the region of modern Iraq, Syria, and Kuwait to become a locus of agricultural activity and site of some of our earliest cities. Mesopotamia's long and frustrating decline was brought by compounding problems of deforestation and accelerated irrigation, leading to the increased salinization of once fertile soil, as well as sieges and the political misestimations of various eras. What may be lost in the copious histories of the fertile crescent is that what remains is a discontinuous lineage, with many linkages retrieved only fantastically through archeological reconstructions and having no thread to the present day. Indeed, uncountable societies have been genuinely lost, and some are recalled after a painful erosion of memory such as occurred in aboriginal societies and empires of the Americas after European-borne disease, displacement, and genocide.

The chapters in this collection have in common with Jacobs (2004) the themes of loss and excavation. These chapters speak of the spaces across time and between people, spaces of nothing through which legacies are nonetheless transmitted. Shared with these themes is the ambivalent promise of "crossing the divide" (Gump, 2015). As the reader will see, the touching that may occur across interpersonal and temporal divides can be both a necessary and healing attempt at unison, in some contexts, and, in others, a bruising or even terrorizing collapse of space and re-enacted trauma. Like the archeological past, though, the need to fill gaps in traumatized history may be powerful and even glorious as any renaissance brings light and activity. We may never know what life was like in those early cities, but the parameters of our own urban spaces and lives are certainly defined by them. Likewise, the authors in this collection have detailed excavations precisely to speak to those absolute silences that fill post-traumatic divides and reproduce social and interpersonal dynamics, in order to exorcise and honor, so that movement may finally occur.

In "Collectively Creating Conditions for Emergence," Katie Gentile describes a powerful analysis within which trauma was expressed in the bodies of both analyst and patient throughout their years of work together. Gentile focuses on the intersections of trauma, specifically violence against women that often times is coded and split as either racially based or gendered. Utilizing her own embodied experience within sessions, Gentile finds deep empathic resonance which enabled her to identify and assist in mourning the sexual and gendered violence experienced by her patient, a second generation Puerto Rican-American young woman. Gentile acknowledges the risk of colonization and the need for it to become mutual, representing an opening – multitemporal and consummating multiple identities – such that the patient could orient the other to ideally share experience and dispel a mutual "haunting" of futures lost.

Judith Lewis Herman's "Trauma and Recovery: A Legacy of Political Persecution and Activism Across Three Generations" takes as its beginning the year 1953 and the United States government's persecutory efforts to end the progressive movements of the early and mid-twentieth century. As with all the chapters in this collection, Lewis does not consider individual narratives alone but enjoins them with a generational constellation. The protagonist in Lewis' chapter is her mother, the psychologist and analyst Helen Block Lewis, who, in 1953, was being interrogated by the McCarthy committee accused of Communist Party membership. Lewis describes an ideological tension with Helen – a divide of generations – that parallels disconnections in progressive movements that upheld sexism in obvious contradiction to liberationalist ideals. For Lewis these are not despairing observations, as she speaks of life as opened in political mobilization and contact with others, including the political act of psychoanalysis.

In "Shadows of Terror: An Intergenerational Tale of Growing Up in the Old Left," Lisa S. Lyons considers the influence of state power in her family's life. Lyons puts forth a clear and sophisticated message that when considering trauma the goal is not always to close space through contact – touching across the divide. Rather, there can be safety in distance from both powerful *and* close others. Lyons offers an open question regarding the decisions of leftist parents who devote their lives to activism while risking exposure of their children to terrifying potentialities. By the chapter's conclusion, Lyons takes the reader outside of the family to a case study that details a mutual movement through trauma. In a compelling manner, Lyons shows how the present is informed, even if only vaguely, from the distal immanence of generational transmission.

In "To Unchain Haunting Blood Memories," Kirkland C. Vaughans explicates the massive failure and consequence of banishing slavery to the neglected corridors of American remembrance. This "secret," terribly concealed since Reconstruction, succeeds in expanding the traumatic sequelae of slavery in African American lives as a denial of memory and obstruction to flourishing in hostile social structures. The memories are denied, not lost. Although slavery may haunt, its artifact is alive and embedded in American institutions and decried by the activists and resisters of subsequent generations. Vaughans locates healing in the psychoanalytic closure of neglected space, allowing voices their truth and speaking of a psychic and political dimensionality that is often felt but unacknowledged.

These chapters are meditations on space and its closure in trauma and across generations. Yet this may not be an empty space after all. Instead, lives travel through the radiation of histories, ever exquisite in their non-linearity. The excavations of the past are not irretrievable, only inchoate; an inheritance that fascinates but cannot be revealed outside of its embodied, creative reconstruction. As these authors demonstrate, contact across distance brings ambiguous outcomes. Humans have mass and move heavily through space. We may join or colonize with our reach. The closing of space can be touch and holding and/or the oppressing impingement of repetition. We cannot help but bring our histories – in their full constellation – into our spaces. Excavation is the work of justice. It takes the courage of authors like these to begin the re-tellings that are necessary to invite us more ethically into our past and our futures.

References

Gump, J. (2015, October). *The transmission of slavery's traumas: Past is present*, presented at the Psychology and the Other Conference, Cambridge, MA.

Jacobs, J. (2004). *Dark age ahead*. New York: Random House.

Chapter 8

Collectively Creating Conditions for Emergence

Katie Gentile

In many case studies in the literature, the focus is on what occurs in the clinical space with little description of the patient's outside life that contributes to the therapeutic work. Ettinger (2006) describes the "traumatic thing" being located within her "other's other." "Aching" inside of her is this unknown that is awaiting a memory for signification. As she writes, "[s]uch are the traumatic" (p. 166). In this chapter I want to revisit a case I had already written about (Gentile, 2013), in order to add a form of engagement I did not describe in my previous work. This case directly speaks to trans-generational trauma that happened not only within the patients' family but I feel reproduces trauma transmitted within cultural domains as carried by race, class, and gender. This chapter functions as a part two to that earlier case study. In many ways I have come to feel that this case illustrates one of the common forms of violence against women that is embedded within the white supremest patriarchal culture and that oftentimes get coded as either only racial or gender based violence. I hope to focus on the intersections (Collins, 1990; Crenshaw, 1991).

Freire (1972) claimed transformation only occurs through a deep engagement with the world. I am using this chapter as a special opportunity to complicate a story of transformation that, like all such stories, was kaleidoscopic and included other spaces of engagement, namely community-based activism. This activism took place side by side to the clinical work. While there is no doubt our clinical work enabled my patient, Vasialys, to volunteer and participate in community activism, the activism fed back into the clinical work, deepening our engagement. This chapter reviews the case, focusing more on the trans-generational enactments of violence and the role of activism in disrupting these repetitions.

Vasialys, a young Puerto Rican-American college student, grew up witnessing her father's frequent physical and verbal abuse of her mother.

The clinical work with her stood out to me because whenever I saw her it seemed as if there were two parallel sessions occurring: one verbal that had the affectless rhythm of a drone, and a physical session. The physical session involved her sitting on the couch completely still, intensely staring at me with huge eyes, while I felt evacuated of all energy. I was not just listless but almost paralyzed with hopelessness. It was too much work to pick up my hand to gesticulate when I could manage to utter a word and I felt a weight on my chest and lap that made breathing a chore.

To better understand this clinical experience I reviewed psychoanalytic theories of witnessing and trauma. As I observed (Gentile, 2013), much of the literature on witnessing has evolved from certain examples of trans-generational trauma that did not exactly fit with Vasialys' particular history. First of all, much psychoanalytic thinking about trans-generational trauma comes from the Holocaust primarily, and secondarily from other forms of mass genocide. This means the identified originary trauma is understood to be discrete in time and space, for instance, the Holocaust and other genocides have temporal beginnings and endings, although many identified beginnings can be gradual and the "endings" may be more equivalent to transitions. U.S. slavery transitioned into different forms of institutionalized genocide such as Jim Crow laws, rampant lynching, and now the prison industrial complex and criminal justice system (Alexander, 2010). Additionally some might understand the impact of the Holocaust also having roots in histories of displacement and religious-based violence. In contrast to this model of genocidal violence, the cases of trans-generational trauma I see most often have less discrete, more diffuse temporal boundaries. They involve generations of domestic violence, sexual violence, and profound child neglect. These forms of violence, in my cases violence against women, reproduce misogynous values that are so endemic and central to our culture that we may not even consider their transmissions a manifestation of trans-generational trauma. Indeed in a search of PEP and Psychinfo databases there were only a handful of articles that described sexual violence through the lens of trans-generational trauma. And certainly because violence against women is so endemic and enduring within most cultures it can be hard to consider it akin to or a form of genocidal violence. I am just making a point here, not necessarily saying violence against women is a form of genocide. Obviously it is complex as women do not constitute a universal or unitary racial or ethnic group. However the practices of genocide – to cause serious bodily or mental harm to members of a specific identified group, to deliberately inflict certain conditions to their lives, to impose some measures to restrict births (here I cannot help but include not only female infanticide and gender-selective abortions, but also lack of access to abortion and criminalization of pregnancies through personhood amendments that target poor women and women of color, see Gentile, 2014), forcibly transferring children of one group to another (the continual naming of children primarily for the father) – carry many similarities to practices of patriarchy. The slipperiness of patriarchal violence, the way it is central to formations of identity, gender, and sexuality, make it difficult to recognize and name. Until 1994, sexual violence against women was not even considered a human rights violation. All this is to say that the forms of traumatic violence that women in particular tend to experience has been left out of most theories and models of transgenerational trauma. As Apprey (2003) has urged in relation to transmissions of racial trauma, violence against women should also be seen as a manifestation of social systems in order to help widen the frame of our analysis and deepen engagement and processes of healing.

Some Complexities of Translating Trauma

We know well that trauma can obliterate linear narrative, chronological time, and capacities for reflection (Feldman & Laub, 1992; Laub & Auerhahn, 1993; van der Kolk, 1994; Grand, 2002, 2003; Gentile, 2007, 2013, 2015). Experiences of violence can jeopardize capacities to create the time and space necessary for reflection and representation of experience (Gentile, 2007, 2013, 2015). Affects produced within traumatic circumstances place extra "pressure on conventional forms of documentation, representation and commemoration" (Cvetkovich, 2003, p. 7). Trauma can render the precariousness of subjectivity that ideally presents opportunities for innovative re-creation, persecutory and re-traumatizing. Space for reflection can feel intolerable. In the face of dealing with patients who have profound histories of trauma, psychoanalysts have developed theories of witnessing as a way of describing therapeutic engagement and action. Witnessing implies the existence of space, and this space has been described as creating the conditions for a "live" or "moral third" (Feldman & Laub, 1992; Benjamin, 2009; Boulanger, 2012) and recognition (Benjamin, 1995, 2009). Gerson (2009) describes his third as a occurring between experience and meaning. This space between creates the conditions for an emergent future that can be bridged by what Boulanger (2012) calls "an act of imagination" that can function to move the analyst closer to the patient. This location of witnessing and thirdness, then, is in the space between meaning and experience. Thus much of the focus has been on the analyst translating affective and bodily experiences into symbolic language (Reis, 2009), for instance, working collaboratively to construct a "missing story" (Ullman, 2006, p. 183). This privileging of words to hold vs. interpret is a central focus of the literature on witnessing. Just consider Bernstein's (2003) notion of the analyst being a substitute signifier toward the goal of linguistic translation.

Certainly this is one way of looking at the embodied experience of paralysis in the session. Perhaps my body was translating affective experience for Vasialys, as a step toward signification, a goal. But this interpretation sends complex messages. Describing embodied experience as a step toward linguistic representation privileges the symbolic beyond other forms of expression and communication, thus re-creating the artificial and harmful split between body and mind. But it also reifies embodied experience, including embodied countertransference, casting it as somehow pure, and truthful, as if my embodied experiences of Vasialys were somehow more valid than her words, that might have functioned as distractions. Embodied experience is also described as if it is outside the bounds of cultural signification (Gentile, 2013). Yet the rhythm of bodies is shaped through cultural engagement (Bourdieu, 1977). Bodies are not neutral entities and embodied communications emerge only through cultural systems of power (Bourdieu), where even unconscious and neurological embodied experiences are shaped by cultural/relational experiences (Wilson, 2004). Just the process of hearing a sound involves unconscious forms of perception that function to simplify and chunk information (Terranova, cited in Diamond, 2013).

Symbolic and representational forms are also anything but neutral. They function to distort and produce experience, limiting what can be communicated and contained, while creating new experiences through the representative forms. But these forms emerge within cultural spaces, thus they function to re-inscribe cultural oppressions and privileges. Linguistic forms of meaning making themselves can function to victim-blame and re-traumatize, especially in the areas of violence against women and intimate partner violence where the first question most people ask is "what were you wearing?" "why were you out so late?" "why didn't you leave him/her?" erasing the accountability of the perpetrator and maintaining the violence as an individual, not a social problem.

Given the limited nature of the symbolic, much of trauma, especially "unspeakable" forms of sexual trauma against women and children, may remain in non-representational spaces. These can then be multiply disruptive, as traumatic memory can function like a "charismatic wound," attracting and organizing other experiences around or/and within it, all the while resisting representation, "defy[ing] the meaning-making activity" (Roth, 2012, p. xviii). As trauma remains "immune from use" (Roth, 2012, p. 92), or at least conscious use, it organizes ongoing past, present, and future relational experiences. And when trauma is culturally sanctioned and condoned, and representations of similar instances are part of our surroundings (rape, sexual dominance over women, racism), this traumatic organizing is reaffirmed constantly. These interpersonal, familial, cultural, and linguistic repetitions of oppression underlie Apprey's (2003) plea that at the very least, therapeutic repair requires that analysts honestly interrogate their own assumptions, attempt to engage in an "ethic of translation" (p. 3), understanding the dynamics of oppression differ so our theories must be alive and shifting. Lastly, the resulting interventions must weigh the impact of the psychosocial.

Psychoanalytic descriptions of witnessing and thirds commonly fail to consider the psychosocial and do not link to cultural systems of power (Gentile, 2013). If traumatic response is the "hinge" between the cultural and psyche (Cvetkovich, 2003), then intervening in trauma provides not only a unique opportunity but an ethical mandate to develop a social/psychoanalytic response. Without this integration, psychoanalysis continues to conceptualize individualized solutions to structural, political, and social problems. Indeed psychoanalytic notions of witnessing have so far failed to capture and articulate these and other complexities of power, which, being central to trauma and violence, are also key to witnessing.

In the original paper (Gentile, 2013), I wove in and out of a clinical case to present a process of witnessing that sought to link culture to psychoanalytic engagement, and to highlight ways this linking would impact our tools of analysis as well as our forms of engagement and our production of subjectivities. Central to this paper was the idea that witnessing must re-make the analyst as well, and do so through ideas of accountability for racial, ethnic, and/or economic privilege. This approach mirrors the fact that categories of race, class, gender, and sexualities are encounters, not entities or attributes of people or populations (Puar, 2009, p. 168), and as encounters their continual emergence repositions ourselves and our worlds. Thus, to paraphrase Cvetkovich (2012), in order to create a truly multicultural intervention the psychoanalyst must re-conceptualize ideas of selfhood. Central to this is embodying the culpability of the analyst witness and attendant dynamics of power. Without doing this, psychoanalysis will not just continue to find affective, temporary solutions for structural inequities, as Cvetkovich has critiqued, it will re-inscribe these structural inequities.

Vasialys

As described (Gentile 2013), I saw Vasialys weekly for four years. She came to me initially because her father was about to be released from jail. Her father regularly attacked her mother so violently that the older brother had to intercede, sometimes calling 911.

Vasialys' father was born in Puerto Rico to a violent family. He was physically beaten up by his own father, the grandfather, and he grew up watching his own father psychologically and physically terrorize his mother. The family was economically disadvantaged and the grandfather, who Vasialys described as an alcoholic, often could not find work. The grandmother was a domestic worker and was often the sole breadwinner. This was experienced by the grandfather as a blow to his masculinity. The family story was that the grandfather beat the grandmother when she lorded her economic power. Here gender, class, and ethnicity merge to create a specific experience of patriarchal shame for the grandmother, grandfather, son, and, in telling the story, Vasialys. Vasialys added that her grandfather's violence was also linked to his drinking and his wife's anger about it, i.e., not necessarily about his increased violent response when drinking. Thus the family story identifies the grandfather as violent while exonerating him by blaming the grandmother for "nagging" him about it and his drinking.

When Vasialys' father turned 16 he stood up to his father during a violent episode. Both of his parents then threw him out of the family home. The father made his way to New York City on his own, knowing no one. He cobbled together odd jobs and was still doing so when I met Vasialys. In perfect repetition, her mother was the one with the steady income, working in an office. And like his own father, he resented his wife's earning power and had a history of alcoholism.

While the father was in jail, however, the family was quiet. The apartment became a nice place to be. Vasialys and her two brothers and younger sister did not fight. Her mother seemed happy. As we spoke it became clear she also came because she was experiencing difficulty in a psychology class that focused on the sexual crimes against children. Although she did not identify them as such, she described experiencing flashbacks to previous incidents of abuse. She did not provide details and it was unclear whether she was describing sexual or physical abuse. Although the father was violent toward the mother, Vasialys described him being one of her primary cheerleaders. He, not her mother, was proud of her. He asked about her day, wanted details about school, took an interest in her life and bragged about her academic accomplishments to his friends. Vasialys' mother, on the other hand, competed and treated her as a friend, telling Vasialys about her day and her problems.

As the work progressed I found myself experiencing profound moments of fatigue that could be so intense I had difficulty moving. I almost felt I was in a trance or a tractor beam. It felt to be an act of violence to shift my focus away from Vasialys as she spoke, but I also felt like when I was looking at her she was sucking out my energy. Despite this vampiric relational experience, I enjoyed seeing her.

Three-and-a-half years into our work she arrived to a session quite anxious and upset. She was about to leave to visit her boyfriend who lived elsewhere but his apartment building had had a serial peeping tom. Vasialys was terrified of being watched while she was asleep. I asked if this scenario was familiar at all to her and she began to detail her repeated rape by her father from the time she was 6 to 10 years old. As she narrated her experience of abuse, I could feel myself again being subdued by a force, just like usual, but this time I realized I was experiencing a version of her abuse. Her father, much larger than her, had been on top of her, inhibiting her breath and motion. In response, she was terrified of dying and played dead, keeping her eyes closed, pretending she was asleep, just hoping he would stop.

The spell of our sessions was broken when I suddenly felt an overwhelming wave of sadness so visceral that I could not stop myself from crying. I felt like my body was leaking sadness all over my chair (Gentile 2013). I blurted out to her that I felt so sad for her. She looked stunned at my tears and verbal admission of sadness. She told me no one had ever felt sad for her. Vasialys experienced me as crying "for her." This understanding was important to her. When she was six, she told her mother what her father had done. Her mother not only did not feel sad for her, she did not believe her, even though her mother's much younger sister had also claimed she was sexually abused by Vasialys' father, when the mother was first married to him. Vasialys had nowhere to go for safety, no way out. I was witnessing her experience but doing so in a deeply embodied way by "allowing" myself to be immobilized for years and then actively crying. It was not just that I did believe her, but that my body was open to be colonized by her experience. Her mother's body was closed to it. When Vasialys first told her, she must have registered it with an echo to the past when her own younger sister told her. This embodied echo had to be shut down, stopped from reverberating into the present, leaving Vasialys holding all the shame, guilt, terror, and confusion in the present, as well as that which she was forced to embody from her father's past.

Certainly Vasialys' father re-enacted his own childhood. He placed his own son in the role of the protector for the mother while he now moved "up" in familial status to be the angry and violent patriarch, disenfranchised by his economically successful wife. The son complied by being the one to intercede to save his mother by calling 911. This time neither of the parents responded by excising the son. Usually the police would appear, the father would calm down and no one would mention the incident.[1] It may be that for the father, the involvement of the police changed the dynamics of repetition in such a way that altered the need to re-establish dominion by kicking out the son. Instead the police can become the target of aggression, and given the colonializing dynamics that can be common in policing practices in low-income communities of color, such displacement could function to pull the father close to the son.

The father also strays from the repetition by breaking the incest taboo and having sex with his very young daughter. Here recent generations of patriarchal disenfranchisement through colonization may have been buffered and momentarily undone by his vampiric usurpation of Vasialys' childhood and her young body. He takes both as he re-establishes himself as the patriarch of the house, entitled to unfettered access to all female bodies. While Vasialys was the good daughter during the day, the child that provided the father with great pride, at night she became an objectified female to be invaded and colonized. As he turns to/on the daughter he humiliates the mother, the woman who has out-shone him. Vasialys becomes a pawn between her parents, and between her father and his history, at a very high cost to her.

So it is not surprising our transference expresses these experiences, contradictions, and dissociations. As I am rendered physically inert in our sessions, Vasialys "convert[s] torment to mastery," "absence to presence" (Grand, 2000, p. 31). In so doing, we both begin to "know" the father's (and Vasialys') pain(s) – Vasialys by reliving both roles of perpetrator and silenced victim, and myself by being colonized by Vasialys and her experiences.

Creating Spaces for Consciously Integrating Colonizing Subjectivities

> We are all living in an environment steeped with racialized violence; the land we walk on is stolen, the labor that produced the things we use is underpaid and exploited, the neighborhoods we live in are either segregated or gentrifying.
>
> (Cvetkovich, 2003, p. 125)

As is evident, working with Vasialys meant attempting to organize traumatic fallout not just of sexual abuse but also of current and past colonialism (Gentile, 2013). While exploring her and my experiences in the moment, I struggled to hold cultural forms of subjectification, to create space for both the gender-based violence she experienced and the culture-based violence she experienced from people who looked like me. This culpability took the forms of opening up the psychoanalytic space to acknowledge some ways the privilege of my whiteness was founded upon her position as a Latina. We had to discuss her fears of identifying her father as an abuser. These fears were not just about losing her connection to her father, but also about her ambivalences around identifying her father, a Latino who had a criminal record, as a criminal in front of me. Here white privilege had to be actively spoken repeatedly as well as consciously held internally (Gentile, 2013). After all, a central network of racism is the unconscious fantasies of the racist (Bass, 2003). Clough (2013) quotes Stoler saying that "intimate relationships 'serve as transfer points of power' not as a microcosm of power but as its marrow"

(p. 166). In psychoanalysis, "[t]he clinical relationship provides the relational framework that regulates the contours of the subjectivity it produces" (Brickman, quoted in Heyer, 2012, p. 631). This means the main instrument of psychoanalysis – unconscious reveries, fantasies, and conscious and unconscious affective exchanges – are not just central to re-traumatization, as Bass (2003) has written, in fact they are tools of re-traumatization.

Sexual violence against all women cannot be separated from racism and ethnic violence (Crenshaw, 1991) Indeed, the status and meaning of my white femininity rests entirely upon the denigrated status of women of color, and in relation to Vasialys, this meant Latinas. Thus my response of empathy around the experience of sexual trauma could also function to "incorporate the other," negate Vasialys' ethnic alterity or otherness (Freccero, 2006, pp. 87–88). This collapse of alterity is then fatal to recognition and equality. But recognition is tricky. If recognition is conveyed by the dominant group onto the oppressed it becomes another form of oppression (Oliver, 2001). "It is precisely the sense of arriving too late to create one's own meaning that makes the colonization of psychic space so effective" (Oliver, quoted in Ingram, 2008, p. 47). In other words, it is very difficult to recognize or create liberating or healing symbolic meaning through cultural systems that are designed to deny agency, subjectivity, and humanity to certain people. Instead, the oppressed are expected to carry the "affective burdens of the culture. They are not only made ashamed of their very being but also forced to carry the shame of the culture" (Oliver, 2004, p. 93). Thus Vasialys' and my interactions came well-scripted by a history of colonization.

So my empathy with Vasialys, crying "for her" functioned both to bring us close and to recolonize (Gentile, 2013). We could feel close as two female identified bodies marked by male sexual violence. She could feel I "knew" her experience on some level. She could feel a safety in being "held" by another female body. Indeed, she described these feelings as we worked. She described how remarkable it was to have a woman listen to her, to pay attention and to cry for her, and to label her experiences abuse and even, at times, rape. However, she was also being "held" by a white female body. She also could bristle at my shining a light on her father as the perpetrator, preferring instead to imagine her experiences as occurring at the hands of someone anonymous, someone without a particular cultural or ethnic heritage, thus someone in relation to whom I would not have privilege. She said she did not want me to hate him, or see him as a criminal. While it is common for daughters to feel this kind of ambivalence with therapists about their paternal perpetrators, by adding that she feared I would see her father as a criminal, she adds an additional dimension to the mix. She elaborated on this, remarking on my status as an "educated person" who might look down on him for his criminal record. Thus to experience my holding was complicated and required her to selectively forget her identification as a Latina and to put her experiences of oppression in a hierarchy – gender violence before racial or/and class violence, as if these could be identified, separated, and bracketed. After all, the history of feminism in the U.S. is one where heterosexual white women defined the discourse, and the issues they sought to address seldomly involved racial, class, or heterocentric-based oppression. So in the case I attempted to hold clinical space for all of our intersecting (see Crenshaw, 1991 and Collins, 1990) identities, attempting to create the potential to explore the simultaneous comforts and colonizing invasions of interactions. Integral to this was sustaining a vigilant awareness of how, when, where I deployed empathy, the power-based roots of it and to what ends.

Oliver (2004) offers a process of "bearing witness" to something that cannot be seen. It's not just about remastery of the situation through the telling or being recognized within the objectification or having the objectification of the trauma or history of traumas validated. It is a process of transformational time travel for both parties. It alters the very process of objectification by bringing someone back there with you in the telling, and transforming them into response-able witnesses – witnesses who can help re-shape systems of representation. This way the relationship and the various currencies of affective exchange – embodied and spoken – are responsive, response-able. For instance, as we discussed her father and his behavior, I would attempt to hold contradictions, letting Vasialys know that I did not know how to feel about him. I knew he was so important to her, but I could not let him off the hook for abusing her, but I also needed to understand his history and how people who looked like me might have contributed to his feeling so disempowered. I opened up the clinical space as best I could by engaging her to work with me to help me figure out how to feel about him. In so doing, we created a therapeutic space for her to more safely experience the contradictions she felt about him, and by talking about cultural oppression and privilege and colonization in relation to her father, we were able to talk about it as it shifted between us.

Hauntings as "Something-To-Be-Done"

Gordon (2011) builds on Derrida's (1993/2006) hauntology by describing haunting not as a psychic or interpersonal phenomena but as a cultural and political one. Hauntings are hidden from view but capture and communicate histories, memories, and the day-to-day organizations and systems of lives. The spectral does not render a discrete moment so much as a system of interactions. Haunting is a "repression that is no longer working" (p. 3), when going on being as we know it becomes impossible because temporal motion seems to cease (Gentile, 2015). But dealing with haunting is complicated. These ghosts must speak for themselves but although this speech is affective, it is conjured into being only in the form of a responsibility on the part of the recipient – a "something-to-be-done" (p. 2). In this sense the haunting is not merely an experience or communication of trauma, oppression, or violence, but the shadow of a lost future, a future without such a history. If the haunting is compelled by the foreclosure of the future, it necessarily impacts the present pressing it for action, action that addresses political and social inequities. Haunting resides in the dense spaces where "history and subjectivity make social life" (Gordon, 1997, p. 8, cited in Ferreday & Kuntsman, 2011), where our response-abilities for creating a future emerge.

So in this case I may have been experiencing Vasialys' abuse but we both were haunted by colonization, oppression, and interpersonal familial violence, all of which foreclosed the potentialities for a better future. It was these hauntings that also needed to be addressed, but addressed with action, something-to-be-done, on both our parts. For Vasialys this additional component of her transformation occurred not only in the clinical space. It also required a larger collective of response-able witnesses.

Expanding Conditions for Recognition and Doing Something

Traditionally, witnessing does reflect the impact of hauntings. Having its origins in women of color's ideas of testimony, witnessing is a collective (not just dyadic) action, that functions to (re)unite the cultural, political, and personal/psychology (Beverley, 1992; Smith & Watson, 1998). Oliver (2004) writes that a theory of witnessing has to operate "between the psyche and the social" (p. xiv), transforming the psychological into social concepts and actions. Witnessing then takes as given that knowledge and transformation are produced through forms of collaborative, reflective action. Again, this active aspect of reflection is central. As described earlier in terms of the oppressive and traumatic limits of the symbolic, when one speaks as a marginalized subject within the culture, the act of speech can disrupt the center of dominance, but it will do so while re-inscribing the marginalized identity and position of the speaker (Bhabha, 1994; Kaplan et al., 1999). Speaking is a form of relationally enacting one's experience. It is a condition of emergence, becoming, and recognition as well as of marginalization. Here is where a participatory action methodology of community-based activism comes into the picture, becoming a collective response to the hauntings of something-to-be-done.

Participatory action methods of engagement emerge from Freire's (1972) ideas of liberation and Kurt Lewin's ideas of psychological group theory. The goals of these approaches are "recovering oppressed voices through the agency of non-Western people to reconstruct both history and knowledge production ... while raising serious questions about the politics of speaking for and writing about others" (Frisby et al., 2009, p. 19). Action methods attempt to address historical and structural inequities through a specific form of engagement and participation that includes consistent reflective analysis of power as it operates at micro and macro levels (Fine & Torre, 2004; Stoudt, 2009).

The assumption grounding participatory action methods of engagement is that when enactments of cultural and social privilege can be experienced, identified, reflected upon, and addressed as such, new ways of relating can emerge that challenge and ideally displace hierarchical structures (Torre & Ayala, 2009, p. 389). As these established structures are displaced, historical memory can be recovered, shifting one's relationship to the dominant culture and traumatic pasts. Here histories and systems of oppression and privilege are not just acknowledged but lived with each other and deconstructed in the moment.

The goals of participatory action methods of engagement are to build complex bridges of witnessing by doing something. These notions of bridges are based on Gloria Anzaldúa's notion of borderlands hybridity

(Anzaldúa, 1987, 2002). This describes the location of women from mixed ethnic backgrounds who are situated in multiple liminal spaces between. This in-betweenness can result in what Anzaldúa describes as the creation of an embodied *mestiza consciousness*. Here instead of pathologizing the marginalized experience of women of color, letting it sit as a victimizing label, Anzaldúa claims it as potentially creating the transformative capacity to bridge differences, based on the physical, psychological, and cultural bridging such women are forced to do every day. This is one way of responding to the call of the haunting for something-to-be-done. This narration of ambivalence and cultural collision (*choque*) results in a more nuanced, complicated capacity to hold multiple perspectives and identities as one realizes one cannot hold the world in rigid categories and must instead have a flexibility to "stretch the psyche horizontally and vertically" (Anzaldúa, 1987, p. 101). As Anzaldúa (2002) observes, bridges are special because they embody in-between spaces and are situated "in a constant state of displacement" (p. xv). But according to Anzaldúa (2002) multiplicity itself becomes transformational only when resolution emerges through embodied action that uses new forms of symbolizations, in other words, the creation of presents that are not built upon the haunting of the pasts, but instead build upon the potentials for different futures.

Activism Creating Conditions for New Emergence

So returning to Vasialys. Certainly my crying "for her" could be seen as a form of Anzaldúa's (2002) new symbolization. I responded with my body in a way that bridged cultures. As I responded from my own experiences of sadness she experienced my crying as a (Latina/white) maternal sadness for her. One could say it was a dyadic collaborative action as she helped me feel some of the violence that she (and her father) experienced by taking me over. But there was an additional space of healing outside of, or to the side of, or perhaps on top of, our clinical dyad.

In our third year of work Vasialys had to have an externship experience for her academic major. She chose to work with an organization that focused on ending teen dating violence. The group embodied the ideals of participatory action methods of engagement. The group organized students from local colleges and worked with them to collectively develop curriculum for high school outreach programs. While the group had some key components to teach (e.g., that abuse is a form of power and control, that love and affection can co-occur with abuse, that gender-based violence hurts women and men), they engaged the college students to shape the messages, to incorporate cultural diversities like sexualities, gender conformity, ethnicity, race, class, and religion and present the material in a way young people might recognize. Many of the volunteers for the group had their own experiences of violence.

The group had a chapter on campus that was housed in the Women's Center – my doing something. This was important because at that point I was the director of the Center. So Vasialys' interest in the group was complicated. Throughout the first two years I worked with her, she did not discuss having many friends. She was quiet and shy and unassuming. She went to school and went home. She did not speak up in class. Due to space issues, when students came to see me clinically, they could either wait in a busy hall or wait in the Women's Center. After about a year of sessions, Vasialys began waiting in the Center. She began talking to women there. After a few weeks, I found when I went to get her for sessions, she was engaged in conversation with other women in the Center. She described her interest in working with the group as being to help protect young women like herself from being in violent relationships, but knowing it was attached to the Center, and thus also to me, and that a couple of the women she had been speaking to were also in the group, made it safe to take the leap of volunteering there.

This choice of externship was also interesting because of the ways in which Vasialys had made meaning of her history up until that point. Although she had been sexually abused by her father for years and had watched him almost kill her mother a number of times, as mentioned he was the only person in the family who took a real interest in her as a separate and valuable person. Her mother competed and merged with her. While we negotiated the creation of new forms of symbolization for her to understand and re-experience her father as an abuser and supporter, Vasialys struggled to make sense of his history and its impact on his behavior. Oftentimes Vasialys would say that given the violence her father saw in his own family, he could not help being violent and she and her mother were at least partially culpable for their own victimizations. For Vasialys, her responsibility for her repeated victimization took the form of her lack of voice: she didn't scream or speak when it happened. Doing so, as the narrative went, would have woken up her brothers who shared her bedroom with her. They would have acted as the father had earlier in his life, and stopped the violence (perhaps then, getting kicked out of the house). If she had just said something she could have stopped her father from being an abuser. Thus, she was somewhat responsible for him being an abuser. So for Vasialys to "speak out" was not only culturally treacherous, as described earlier in terms of symbolizations and repetitions of oppression, it carried great dangers for the integrity of her family structure, her own sense of home, and for the humiliation she might pile on to her fragile and violent father.

Haunting repetitions are important in order to act out not only trauma but ambivalence. As Vasialys took me over, during our sessions she acted out the positions of abuser and colonizer simultaneously, and the traumatic past of oppression "place[d] a demand upon the present" (Freccero, 2006, p. 85) shaping the future. This encounter between us recalls Apprey's (2003) notion of an errand, where succeeding generations can be moved to action by "ghosts" that "figure the impossibility of mastering, through either knowledge or action the past or the present" (Freccero's quote of Brown (2001), p. 86). But errands come in different forms. Vasialys was telling me for years about the action-oriented errand on which she was intent. Her embodied actions toward me recreated history. Action and temporality figures prominently in trauma and oppression. But I had to hold a clinical present that could be produced by multiple pasts, presents, and potential futures (Gentile, 2015). Creating the spaces that enable the negotiation of the representation of one's experiences of trauma and oppression requires calling up multiple temporal spaces into the present. Cvetkovich (2003) observes that feelings are encoded not only for the content of the particular affect but based on the practices that surrounded the production of these affects and their reception, i.e., affective experience is temporal, and continually reproduced with the wash of relational interaction, as the Ettinger quote in the beginning of the chapter says, it is the traumas of my others' others. Thus speaking about incest does not just conjure the affective experience of incest, it is a (re)production of those times, including those times Vasialys was told by her mother that it was not happening, and those times her mother was told by her own sister that it was happening (not to mention whatever family violence the father was acting out from his pasts). So speaking one's experience even under carefully managed, culturally engaged clinical spaces may be insufficient in terms of the necessary flexibility in negotiating temporality and representative spaces, creating new forms of symbolization (Anzaldúa, 2002). In other words, the something-to-be-done requires us to move beyond the clinical space.

Within a few weeks at her externship Vasialys was visibly animated. A stream of life was infused into our sessions. She developed a social network of friends. But not just any friends. She suddenly had friends who, along with her, were all being trained to speak about dating violence. And their speaking, their positions were not just based in male accountability. They deconstructed cultural expectations about masculinity that might lead to and actually value and reward male violence against both men and women. They discussed race, class, and different religious and ethnic gender roles. With their African American female mentor from the organization, they developed outreach activities aimed at creating spaces for others to hold complex accountability and victimization. Vasialys found an organization that trained her to use her ambivalence, her experiences of cultural collisions, *choque*, as strengthening and resilient. For the first time she was surrounded by ethnically diverse peers who identified domestic violence and men's violence against women as a complicated crime. Although it could be deconstructed, it was not to be condoned, it was not about losing one's temper, drinking too much, or being provoked by her mother. It was not because a daughter failed to say "no." And this social network of hers developed around reflective, collaborative, and collective embodied action organized around the goal ending male violence against women. Her relationships with her father could be "detoxified" (Apprey, 2003, p. 16), such that he could be seen as a victim and perpetrator, a supportive and negligent father.

During the semester the student group traveled to the state capital to lobby lawmakers to expand access to Family Court for non-married couples, including dating adults and teens, and same sex couples. Shortly after Vasialys and her friends testified together, the state legislature voted to support expanded family court access. Vasialys had spoken out about the damaging impact of domestic violence and the state legislature responded, symbolically recognizing "her" experience, validating it, and changing the law (of the father). Indeed as Freccero (2006) writes, part of working through trans-generational trauma is helping the ghosts recognize themselves as ghosts. Vasialys had to recognize the errands of re-enactment (Apprey, 2003) as not hers but her father's (and her father's father's), thus, as ghosts that need not continue to live within her embodied relational spaces. Multiplicity itself becomes transformational only when resolution emerges through embodied action that uses new forms of symbolizations (Anzaldúa, 2002). Here our clinical form of reflective witnessing had a collective echo in her activism, and through this interaction of clinical work and community-based activism, Vasialys came to life as an agent of social and interpersonal change.

Note

1 It is important to note that this response, or lack thereof, by the police indicates that by the time they arrived there was either no physical evidence of the father having beaten, threatened, or injured the mother, the mother and family excused the evidence in some way (i.e., "she walked into a door"), or/and the officers ignored the state-wide "mandatory arrest" policy around domestic violence.

References

Alexander, M. (2010). *The new Jim Crow: Mass incarceration in the age of colorblindness*. New York: New Press.

Aprey, M. (2003). Repairing history: Reworking transgenerational trauma. In D. Moss (ed.) *Hating in the first person plural: Psychoanalytic essays on racism, homophobia, misogyny and terror*, pp. 3–28. New York: Other Press.

Anzaldúa, G. (1987). *Borderlands/la frontera: The new mestiza*. San Francisco: Aunt Lute Books.

Anzaldúa, G. (2002). (Un)natural bridges, (Un)safe spaces. In G. Anzaldúa & A.L. Keating (eds), *This bridge called out home: Radical visions for transformation*, pp. 1–5. New York: Routledge.

Bass, A. (2003). Historical and unconscious trauma: Racism and psychoanalysis. In D. Moss (ed.) *Hating in the first person plural: Psychoanalytic essays on racism, homophobia, misogyny, and terror*, pp. 29–42. London: Other Press.

Benjamin, J. (1995). *Like subjects, love objects.* New Haven, CT: Yale University Press.

Benjamin, J. (2009). A relational psychoanalysis perspective on the necessity of acknowledging failure in order to restore the facilitating and containing features of the intersubjective relationship (the shared third). *International Journal of Psychoanalysis, 90*: 441–450.

Bernstein, J. W. (2003). Commentary on Sue Grand's paper. *Studies in Gender and Sexuality, 4*(4): 343–351.

Beverley, J. (1992). The margin at the center: On *Testimonio* (testimonial narrative). In S. Smith & J. Watson (eds.) *De/colonizing the subject: The politics of gender in women's autobiography*, pp. 91–114. Minneapolis, MN: University of Minnesota Press.

Bhabha, H. (1994). *The location of culture.* London: Routledge.

Boulanger, G. (2012). Psychoanalytic witnessing: Professional obligation or moral imperative? *Psychoanalytic Psychology, 29*(3): 318–324.

Bourdieu, P. (1977). *Outline of a theory of practice*. Cambridge: Cambridge University Press.

Clough, P. (2013). Intimacy, lateral relationships and biopolitical governance. In A. Frank, P. Clough, & S. Seidman (eds.) *Intimacies: A new world of relational life*, pp. 165–180. New York: Routledge.

Collins, P. H. (1990). *Black feminist thought: Knowledge, consciousness, and the politics of empowerment.* London: Routledge.

Crenshaw, K. (1991). Mapping the margins: Intersectionality, identity politics, and violence against women of color. *Stanford Law Review, 43*(6): 1241.

Cvetkovich, A. (2003). *An archive of feelings: Trauma, sexuality, and lesbian public culture.* Durham, NC: Duke University Press.

Cvetkovich, A. (2012). *Depression: A public feeling.* Durham, NC: Duke University Press.

Derrida, J. (1993/2006). *Specters of Marx: The state of debt, the work of mourning & the new international.* London: Routledge Classics. Trans. Peggy Kamuf.

Diamond, N. (2013). *Between skins: The body in psychoanalysis – contemporary developments.* Chichester, UK: Wiley-Blackwell.

Ettinger, B. L. (2006). *The matrixial borderspace.* Minneapolis, MN: University of Minnesota Press.

Feldmen, S. & Laub, D. (1992). *Testimony: Crises of witnessing in literature, psychoanalysis, and history.* New York: Routledge.

Ferreday, D. & Kuntsman, A. (2011). Haunted futurities. *Borderlands, 10*(2): 1–13.

Fine, M. & Torre, M. E. (2004). Re-membering exclusions: Participatory action research in public institutions. *Qualitative Research in Psychology, 1*(1): 15–37.

Freccero, C. (2006). *Queer/early/modern.* Durham, NC: Duke University Press.

Freire, P. (1972). *Pedagogy of the oppressed*, trans. M. B. Ramos. New York: Herder & Herder.

Frisby, W., Maguire, P., & Reid, C. (2009). The "f" word has everything to do with it: How feminist theories inform action research. *Action Research, 7*(1): 13–29.

Gentile, K. (2007). *Creating bodies: Eating disorders as self-destructive survival.* New York: Routledge.

Gentile, K. (2013). Bearing the cultural in order to engage in a process of witnessing. *Psychoanalytic Psychology, 30*(3): 456–470.

Gentile, K. (2014). Exploring the troubling temporalities produced by fetal personhood. *Psychoanalysis, Culture & Society, 19*(2): 1–18.

Gentile, K. (2015). Generating subjectivity through the creation of time. *Psychoanalytic Psychology, 33*(2): 264–283.

Gerson, S. (2009). When the third is dead: Memory, mourning, and witnessing in the aftermath of the Holocaust. *International Journal of Psychoanalysis, 90*(6): 1341–1357.

Gordon, A. F. (1997). *Ghostly matters: Haunting and the sociological imagination.* Minneapolis, MN: University of Minnesota Press.

Gordon, A. F. (2011). Some those on haunting and futurity. *Borderlands, 10*(2): 1–21.

Grand, S. (2000). *The reproduction of evil: A clinical and cultural perspective.* Hillsdale, NJ: Analytic Press.

Grand, S. (2002). Between the reader and the read: Commentary on paper by Elizabeth F. Howell. *Psychoanalytic Dialogues, 12*(6): 959–970.

Grand, S. (2003). Unsexed and ungendered bodies: The violated self. *Studies in Gender and Sexuality, 4*(4): 313–341.

Heyer, G. (2012). Caught between cultures: Cultural norms in Jungian psychodynamic process. *Journal of Analytical Psychology, 57*: 629–644.

Ingram, P. (2008). *The signifying body: Toward an ethics of sexual and racial difference.* Albany, NY: SUNY Press.

Kaplan, C., Alarcón, N., & Moallem, M. (1999). Introduction: Between woman and nation. In C. Kaplan, N. Alarcón, & M. Moallem (eds.) *Between woman and nation: Nationalisms, transnational feminisms, and the state,* pp. 1–18. Durham, NC: Duke University Press.

Laub, D. & Auerhahn, N. C. (1993). Knowing and not knowing massive psychic trauma: Forms of traumatic memory. *International Journal of Psycho-Analysis, 74*: 287–302.

Moss, D. (ed.). (2003). *Hating in the first person plural.* London: Other Press.

Oliver, K. (2001). *Witnessing: Beyond recognition.* Minneapolis, MN: University of Minnesota Press.

Oliver, K. (2004). *The colonization of psychic space: A psychoanalytic social theory of oppression.* Minneapolis, MN: University of Minnesota Press.

Puar, J. (2009). Prognosis time: Towards a geopolitics of affect, debility and capacity. *Women and Performance: A Journal of Feminist Theory, 19*(2): 161–172.

Reis, B. (2009). Performative and enactive features of psychoanalytic witnessing: The transference as the scene of address. *International Journal of Psychoanalysis, 90*: 1359–1372.

Roth, M. S. (2012). *Memory, trauma, and history: Essays on living with the past.* New York: Columbia University Press.

Smith, S. & Watson, J. (1998). *Women, autobiography theory: A reader.* Madison, WI: University of Wisconsin Press.

Stoudt, B. (2009). The role of language and discourse in the investigation of privilege: Using participatory action research to discuss theory, develop methodology, and interrupt power. *Urban Review, 41*(1): 7–28.

Torre, M. E. & Ayala, J. (2009). Envisioning participatory action research *entremundos. Feminism and Psychology, 19*(3): 387–393.

Ullman, C. (2006). Bearing witness: Across the barriers in society and in the clinic. *Psychoanalytic Dialogues, 16*(2): 181–198.

van der Kolk, B. A. (1994). The body keeps the score: Memory and the evolving psychobiology of posttraumatic stress. *Harvard Review of Psychiatry, 1*: 253–265.

Wilson, E. (2004). *Psychosomatic: Feminism and the neurological body.* Durham, NC: Duke University Press.

Chapter 9

Trauma and Recovery
A Legacy of Political Persecution and Activism Across Three Generations

Judith Lewis Herman

August, 2014

In 2013, I was invited to contribute a memoir of my mother, the psychologist Helen Block Lewis (1913–1987), to a 30th anniversary edition of *Psychoanalytic Psychology*, the journal of Division 39 (Psychoanalysis) of the American Psychological Association. My mother was one of the founders of Division 39 and the first editor of the journal. The assignment started me on a process of reflection of my own intergenerational heritage; this chapter is an expanded version of the commemorative article that I wrote.

My mother was a complicated person. Brilliant, original, and ahead of her time as a professional woman, she was personally rather shy and restrained. Anxious and conflict-avoidant in her private life, she was, nevertheless, intellectually fearless, and she did not suffer fools gladly. One anecdote might serve to introduce her: When, in 1953, she was called before a US Senate investigating committee, she denied being a current member of the Communist Party, but refused to answer questions regarding her past membership, repeatedly citing her privilege under the Fifth Amendment of the Constitution. Dismissing her, the committee Chairman, Senator Joseph McCarthy, warned:

> "I doubt very much that [the State Department] will give you a passport, unless you come in and tell us about your activity in the party – if and when and why you left the party."

At the time, to be denied a passport was particularly frightening to American Jews, who had so recently witnessed the desperate flight of refugees from Nazi Germany, and who saw in McCarthyism the threat of incipient Fascism in the US.

JL Herman: Helen Block Lewis: A memoir of three generations. *Psychoanalytic Psychology* 2013; 30:528–534.

Following on the Chairman, Senator Stuart Symington offered this advice:

> "It would be far better for you if you said you had been a member and felt it was wrong ... and inasmuch as you feel you are a good American ... if I had anything to do with giving you a passport, I would be glad to see you get one. On the other hand, if you come up here and ... take refuge through a lot of legal 'claptrap' behind the Fifth Amendment, do you think people of this committee will approve of your getting a passport?... I think you are making a mistake. I think you are doing yourself an injustice."

My mother answered him with her best Jane Austen diction (she was a fervent Janeite):

> "I thank you for your interest in my welfare, but I, myself, do not agree with all the interpretations that you put on my testimony and my exercise of the Fifth Amendment, as this is something that I have thought about and do intend to do."[1]

I can still imagine her voice, proud and dripping with scorn.

I was eleven years old when my parents were called before the Committee. I remember the fearfulness of that time. My father, who had never been a member of the CP, kept his academic job; he was a professor of Classics at Brooklyn College, part of the City University of New York (CUNY). But my mother, it turned out, had already been blacklisted some years previously. Though she had started her career in psychology, also at Brooklyn College, expecting to be an academic researcher and, in time, a professor, once she realized that path would be closed to her, she changed course and became a clinician.

Here she encountered another obstacle: at that time, membership in the American Psychoanalytic Association was restricted to physicians. New York, however, was filled with European analysts, recent refugees from Hitler. Many of them had little patience with the guild policies of the American Psychoanalytic and were quite willing to provide "bootlegged" analytic training to psychologists. (Many years later, Helen would participate in the civil action for restraint of trade against the American Psychoanalytic that opened this organization to other professionals.)

That is how my mother became a psychoanalyst. Though she came to it by a circuitous path, she embraced psychoanalysis both as a caretaking profession – she soon had a thriving private practice – and as a method of empirical investigation. Though she no longer had a regular faculty position, she kept up an active collaboration with colleagues who were conducting research, and used the insights developed in her clinical work to frame profound revisions in psychoanalytic thought.

As I have come to understand Helen, her story really begins a generation earlier, with the story of her father. John (Yehuda) Block, for whom I am named, fled to this country from Riga, Latvia in 1887, at the age of 17, after he was arrested for reading revolutionary literature. He was a part of the first great wave of Jewish immigrants who fled persecution in the "bloodlands"[2] of Eastern Europe at the turn of the 20th century. Though he had studied to become a rabbi like generations of his forefathers, he lost his faith and became a committed atheist. Joining his older brother in New York, he worked in the clothing business while studying English and saving money to go to medical school. Eventually he opened a general practice on the Lower East Side.

John Block prospered, married Rose Boorstein, another immigrant from the Pale of Settlement, and had two children. Helen grew up amidst a large extended family. According to Helen's cousin, Bernice, John Block was "a very formidable person. He had the most prestige of everybody in the family. Others might be richer, but he was the one everybody looked up to and feared ... He always sat at the head of the table and deferred to nobody. He was the patriarch."

To her cousin's recollections, Helen added: "My mother was scared of him. My brother was scared of him. But *I* was not scared of him."[3]

As the chosen daughter, Helen was exempted from the usual lot of women. Unlike her own mother, she was to be educated. Helen thrived in the world of ideas. She entered Barnard at the age of 16, and then went on to get her doctoral degree in psychology at Columbia. According to her cousin: "You got a little stuffy there when you got older and went to Barnard. But it was only for a few years. You changed when you met Toli (Naphtali Lewis, my father)."[4] Like Helen, my father was the American-born child of Jewish immigrants, with modern, American ideas about education and careers for women.

Helen married in 1936, at age 22, then finished her doctorate and got her first job. As a junior faculty member at Brooklyn College, she plunged into the activities of the Teachers' Union. I never learned exactly what happened next; my mother remained secretive about that period of her life. But by 1942, when I was born, she had said goodbye to all that. (Most likely, like many idealistic American Jews who joined the CP in the 30s, she left after the signing of the Hitler-Stalin pact in 1939.) As my father testified before Senator McCarthy:

> "Has she ever been a Communist? Well, let me give you a very precise answer. Eleven years ago, when our first child was born, my wife ceased being a teacher, and since then she has devoted herself and concentrated on bringing up a family. She has been, since we have had a family, I would say, all that any man could want in a devoted wife and a devoted mother of his children."[5]

In this very *im*precise answer, I believe my father was trying to protect my mother, by assuring the men of the Committee (needless to say, there were no women) that whatever the indiscretions of her youth, by 1953 she had become a respectable woman who knew her proper place at home. (The senators apparently understood this quite well, and asked no follow-up questions.)

My own relationship with Helen was conflicted at times. Both she and my father were ambitious for me and placed enormous emphasis on intellectual achievement. In that domain of life, both she and my father were unfailingly supportive. When, as a college student, I confided my wish to follow in her footsteps and become a psychologist, she told me to go to medical school instead. "You'll have more power that way," she said, and of course she was right. And of course, though I didn't realize it then, she also wanted me to follow in the footsteps of her adored father, John Block, who died before I was born.

Helen never renounced her leftist beliefs, so she was also supportive of my participation in the civil rights and anti-war movements of the 1950s and 60s. But when the women's liberation movement came along, in the late 1960s and 70s, that was a different story. Although she fully supported equality for women in the spheres of work and education, on matters of sexuality and gender roles within the family, she was utterly conventional. I, on the other hand, threw myself into the feminist movement, as once my mother had thrown herself into the political movements of her generation. To me, it was a true liberation to call into question all the deep structures of patriarchy. I wanted to be part of the "longest revolution," challenging women's subordination in all its domains: production, reproduction, sex, and child rearing.[6]

Consciousness-raising,[7] the women's movement's initial form of organizing and inquiry, created a safe space where small groups of women could reveal their secrets, free from fear and shame. In this "free space,"[8] with personal testimony, women uncovered the coercive methods by which male dominance is enforced. It soon became apparent that rape and domestic violence were a common part of women's lot. Over the following decades, these initial discoveries led to large-scale epidemiological studies documenting the worldwide pandemic of violence against women. The United Nations now recognizes gender-based violence as the most prevalent human rights violation in the world.[9]

Though I had been raised by loving and protective parents and luckily had been spared the extremes of sexual violence, my family legacy had made me sensitive to the social dynamics of oppression. Though it took me many years to apply these social analyses to the condition of women, I had long been painfully aware of the contradictions in my own life between my identities as a female creature and as a sentient being. I was accustomed to the received opinion that being smart (especially being good at math and science) made me "unfeminine." From adolescence on, I continually sought the company of men and social groups where I might feel accepted and free, both in mind and body. One of the great attractions of the civil rights and anti-war movements was the promise of greater sexual equality and fellowship between men and women, and one of the greatest disappointments for me was the way in reality what we then simply called "The Movement" fell so far short of this ideal.

With a few notable exceptions, leadership in both the civil rights and anti-war movements was reserved for men, and women were relegated to subordinate roles as support staff and casual sex partners. The birth of radical feminism in the civil rights movement has been well chronicled by historians such as Sara Evans.[10] Stokely Carmichael's famous quip that "the position of women in SNCC is prone" is often quoted as evidence of women's inferior status in the Movement. In fact, according to women who were there at the time, the statement was made with intentional irony, at a special moment when men and women, black and white, who together had braved the death squads of the Klan, were feeling great mutual tenderness and camaraderie.[11] Nevertheless, Carmichael's statement gained notoriety because of the larger truth that it expressed.

The contradictions of the Movement, and its failed promise of gender equality, were captured in a satirical pamphlet called "The Politics of Housework," first published in the late 1960s by Pat Mainardi of the radical feminist group New York Redstockings:

> "Liberated women – very different from Women's Liberation! The first signals all kinds of goodies, to warm the hearts (not to mention other parts) of the most radical men. The other signals HOUSEWORK."[12]

While Mainardi's tone was light and witty, her social analysis was quite serious. She called into question the deeply ritualized sexual division of labor that pervaded American society, not excepting the Movement. This was a phenomenon that I had first witnessed in my own family. Though my mother had a full time career, in her free time she always took pains to display her "feminine" side as an excellent cook and hostess for my parents' many friends. My father never lifted a finger in the kitchen. It simply never occurred to either of them that "women's work" might be shared. (Carving a turkey or serving alcoholic drinks were the man's department, and these tasks my father did with a flourish.)

Since my mother's professional life kept her too busy to do the day-to-day "women's work," my parents employed a maid (always an African-American woman). My mother tended to have very warm relationships with the women who served our family; nevertheless, these relationships also were highly ritualized. Their friendly conversations always took place in the kitchen, for example, never sitting in the living room. And though we all ate the same food that the maids prepared, they never ate with us at the same table. The unspoken rules of both gender and racial segregation were observed without question.

Later, as a college student, when I became an "outside agitator" in the Deep South, as part of what was known as "Freedom Summer,"[13] I witnessed far more extreme rituals of racial segregation, enforced by murderous violence. Clearly, the tyrannical oppression of Jim Crow was of another order of magnitude from the genteel conventions I had observed in my privileged upbringing. What these conventions shared, however, was the unconscious acceptance of elaborate social rules dictating that the dominant group was entitled to deference and service, and the intense emotional reactions that seemed to result whenever these entitlements were challenged even in the slightest degree.

My four years in medical school (1964–68) hastened my feminist awakening. Here for the first time I truly experienced what it was like to be in a minority. Women constituted 10% of my medical school class. Lectures often included openly derogatory comments about women; these were considered to be humorous. My female classmates and I learned to ignore these slights or to laugh along with the rest of the class; after all, we were a token presence, often reminded that we should be grateful to be admitted at all.

My first experience of frank discrimination, when I applied for internships, also taught me to know my place in the world. Despite my success in an elite medical school, I was told flatly, on more than one occasion, "We don't take women." After all, it was explained, if hired, I would be taking a coveted position away from a man who, as a breadwinner, deserved it far more than I. And anyway, I'd probably just go and get pregnant and all that medical training would be wasted on me. And anyway, what about "that time of the month?" This was said quite seriously. Though in theory the Civil Rights Act of 1964 had prohibited discrimination based on sex as well as race, in practice the law, as applied to women, was still generally ignored.

By the time I was ready to begin my psychiatric residency training (1970–73). I was also ready to join a consciousness-raising group. My feminist awakening coincided with the beginning of my professional career, and profoundly shaped the path that career would take. The safe space of the psychotherapy office had many similarities with the free space of the movement, and as my women patients revealed their secrets, I listened with a new awareness of woman's condition. My first two patients, admitted to the hospital after suicide attempts, disclosed histories of father-daughter incest. It was not hard to see the connection between their despair and their early initiation into the life of a sexual object. I wrote in my journal: "in patriarchy the father maintains the right to sex with his daughter in the same way that the feudal lord maintains the *jus primae noctis* with his subjects." Incest seemed to me like a paradigm of women's sexual oppression.

After completing my residency, I went to work in a women's "free clinic," one of the many "counter-institutions" like rape crisis centers and battered women's shelters that activists in the women's movement created during the early 1970s. There I saw still more patients who revealed histories of incest. My friend Lisa Hirschman, who had recently completed her doctorate in clinical psychology, was making similar observations in her psychotherapy practice. We began to inquire among other clinicians we knew locally, and very quickly collected 20 cases. At that time, a major psychiatry textbook estimated the prevalence of incest as one case per million.[14] Perhaps we were on to something. We decided to publish our findings.

(In hindsight, I realized that along with the inspiration of the women's movement, it was the example of both my parents that enabled me to venture to write down and publish my observations. Lisa came from a similar, and very distinguished heritage, though I did not know this at the time. But that is another, separate story.)[15]

In 1975, Lisa and I submitted our paper to a new women's studies journal.[16] A year elapsed between the time the paper was accepted and the time it was published. During that year, the paper was copied and passed from hand to hand, and soon we started getting letters from women all over the country, saying: "I thought I was the only one," or "I thought no one would believe me," or "I thought it was my fault." By listening to women, and daring to publish what we found, we had become catalysts for a transformative moment, when crimes long hidden were revealed.

As clinicians, we were also privileged to witness the liberation that comes when the burdens of shame and fear are lifted. As our patients told their stories and were met with compassion rather than scorn, their despair gave way to renewed hope, and their isolation to a renewed sense of community. My work for the next forty years has been built on those initial discoveries of that revolutionary moment.

Encouraged by the response to our article on incest, Lisa and I decided to write a book. Then we each had a baby. A year and a half later, when I emerged from my sleep-deprived haze and felt ready to tackle the writing project, Lisa had had a second child. I said I would get started and write my half. By the time that was done, a year later, Lisa told me it would be best for me to keep going and finish the book myself. So I did. *Father-Daughter Incest* was published by Harvard University Press in 1981, and won the C. Wright Mills Award from the Society for the Study of Social Problems. My mother was particularly pleased about this award, given in the name of a radical sociologist who was a hero to leftist intellectuals.[17]

I believe it was on the strength of this book that I was invited to join the Department of Psychiatry at Cambridge Hospital, one of the teaching hospitals of Harvard Medical School. This public, "safety net" hospital, which served the poor and the downtrodden, tended to attract "bleeding hearts" like myself. The relatively new psychiatry department was also a particularly creative place at the time. There, in 1984, I met the psychologist Mary Harvey, who had recently arrived from National Institute of Mental Health, in Washington, DC, where she had conducted a nationwide study of exemplary rape crisis centers.[18] Mary, like myself, saw the promise of bringing the knowledge developed in feminist grass roots organizations to the largely clueless world of academic psychology and psychiatry. Together, we were given encouragement to develop an exemplary program for psychological trauma. Thus the Victims of Violence Program was born. We are now celebrating our 30th year, providing clinical care to survivors of interpersonal violence and training for residents in psychiatry and fellows in psychology and social work, as well as conducting research to advance the trauma field and participating in antiviolence organizing in our own community.

At Cambridge Hospital, in the mid 1980s I also met the psychiatrist Bessel van der Kolk, who had been working with combat veterans. By this time, the diagnosis of post-traumatic stress disorder had gained official recognition in the diagnostic manual of the American Psychiatric Association, largely thanks to the public testimony and organizing of Vietnam Veterans.[19] Bessel was interested in how post-traumatic stress might appear in different populations, so he invited people working with survivors of combat, political persecution, disaster, child abuse, and gender-based violence to come together in an informal study group. For three or four years, we met one evening a month in people's homes. The study group was a fertile gathering place. As I listened to reports from many different walks of life, it became increasingly clear to me that just as oppression is oppression, trauma is trauma, whether in the political sphere of war and dictatorship, or in the private sphere of sex, intimacy, and family life. This fundamental insight inspired my second book, *Trauma and Recovery*, published in 1992.[20]

I hope this narrative has made abundantly clear my how my heritage as the granddaughter of Jewish immigrants fleeing oppression, and as the daughter of leftist intellectuals who suffered political persecution in this country, influenced my own developmental path. I like to believe that I also had a reciprocal influence on my mother's professional development. While Helen the conventional matron responded with alarm and distress to my passionate embrace of feminism, Helen the intellectual responded with curiosity and a new birth of creativity.

In 1971 she had published her first book, *Shame and Guilt in Neurosis*.[21] In this pioneering study of the "moral emotions," which brought together careful clinical observation and rigorous laboratory research methodology, she had documented significant gender differences: women were far more prone to shame, while men were more prone to guilt. Here was a remarkable phenomenon that called out for an explanation.

In the meantime, feminists like myself were raising more general questions regarding the fundamental causes of gender differences. Challenged to address these questions, Helen embarked upon an exhaustive review of literature in evolutionary biology, anthropology, and infant development. In 1976, she published the result of her researches in her second book: *Psychic War in Men and Women*.[22]

"Anatomy contains no inherent prescription for women's social inferiority,"[23] she declared. And despite the universal finding that warfare is the province of men, she argued that men's nature is not inherently aggressive. She based her conclusions heavily on contemporaneous infant research, which demonstrated the central role of affectionate connection with caregivers in the development of both sexes. The subjection of women and the violence of men could not be explained by innate differences between the sexes, she maintained; rather, she proposed that women's oppression was but one consequence of exploitative and authoritarian societies.

Developing her argument further, she explained how exploitative societies damage men and women differently, creating "expendable warriors" and "inferior child-bearers," and causing equally insoluble psychological conflicts for both sexes. (This was the meaning of her term "Psychic War.") The social context of male dominance and female subordination afforded an explanation for the superego differences between the sexes that she had documented in her earlier work. When women are required to be caring and affectionate, yet these very attributes are considered weak and childish, women suffer from shame. When men are required to be aggressive and domineering, yet these demands violate their own affectionate nature, men suffer from guilt.

In the mid-70s, after more than 30 years as an independent scholar, my mother returned to academia, having been offered a position in the

Department of Psychology at Yale. This was the era when institutions like CUNY were formally apologizing to the professors they had purged in the McCarthy years. The blacklist was history. All was forgiven. Delighted to be teaching again, Helen flourished in this environment. One of her popular courses was a joint offering in Women's Studies and Psychology called "Women, Men and Power." Here she invited students to reflect on topics such as "the origins of women's social inferiority," "theories of the sex differential in power," "power and relations between the sexes," and, finally, ever hopefully, "changing the system."

I believe it was her engagement with feminism that enabled Helen to complete the theoretical leap from a one-person psychology based on instinctual drives to a two-person psychology based on relational connections. In particular, a feminist re-valuation of women's caretaking role allowed her to elevate affectionate relationships, rather than the will to power, to the center of human psychology.

In the late 1970s, she began her most ambitious work of all, a complete re-assessment of Freud's work in light of subsequent scientific discoveries. As she wrote in the preface to the first volume of *Freud and Modern Psychology*, which appeared in 1981: "The tension between Freud's clinical discoveries about the power of human emotions and the theoretical framework in which he embedded these discoveries has been most eloquently detailed by Freud himself ... This book is a small step along the road which should ultimately bring Freud's discoveries into a modern theoretical framework in psychology."[24]

In her revision of psychoanalytic theory, she recognized the central importance of the neo-Darwinian concept of attachment. From contemporaneous studies demonstrating the workings of the human attachment system, she drew the theoretical implication that human nature is inherently social rather than individualistic. "With hindsight today," she wrote, "it is possible to see that the problem with which Freud was struggling required a formulation of a social theory of human nature, and with it, a concept of the biosocial nature of the affects ... This deficiency in theory has been partially redressed by the work of Bowlby and his students, who postulate that the organism has a built-in 'attachment system,' in which anxiety operates as a signal for maintaining or restoring the attachment. Similarly, smiling, pleasure, and joy cement the social bond."[25]

In the second volume, published in 1983, Helen went on to revisit many of Freud's theoretical writings, including *The Interpretation of*

Dreams, Three Essays on the Theory of Sexuality, and *Totem and Taboo.* In her preface, she explained once again: "Freud's theoretical difficulties arose from the absence of a viable theory of human nature as cultural, that is, social by biological origin." She added: "Volume 2 also shows clearly how (still) prevailing androcentric attitudes influenced Freud's neglect of the infant-caretaker affectional system in his theorizing."[26]

It seems to me now that my mother's struggle with, and ultimate embrace of feminism, gave her this fundamental insight that allowed her to undertake a comprehensive re-evaluation of psychoanalytic theory. Her recognition of the central role of attachment in human development presaged contemporary relational theories.

Her reassessment of Freud completed, with her energy unabated, Helen returned to the subject of shame. Over the years, her work had inspired a circle of clinicians and researchers who called themselves "shameniks." Now she decided the time had come to put together a collection of their essays. *The Role of Shame in Symptom Formation* was published in 1987.[27] Leading off with the puzzling question why shame had been so little studied, Helen referenced, once again, "...a prevailing sexist attitude in science, which pays less attention to nurturance than to aggression, [and] thereby depreciates the shame that inheres in 'loss of love.'"[28]

This was to be the last of her writings. She fell ill quite suddenly and died at the height of her powers. Having participated in the founding of Division 39 of the American Psychological Association, she had high hopes that psychologists would bring a much-needed empirical methodology to psychoanalytic practice and foster a rapprochement between the clinical and research traditions. (These hopes, like so many others, remain unrealized.) The significance of her work was just beginning to be recognized. She faced death with resolve but also with anger; there was so much more that she wanted to do. She was not resigned.

Our own rapprochement paralleled her intellectual acceptance of feminism. (A grandchild helped, too.) In those precious last years, we even wrote a paper together. Appropriately enough, it was about anger in relations between mothers and daughters. We agreed that such anger was inevitable under patriarchy.[29] We argued that mothers who care about their daughters are obliged to restrict their daughters' freedom, in order to protect them from very real dangers. Daughters are bound to resent this, and mothers are bound to resent the way their daughters fail to appreciate their efforts. (Sublimation and intellectualization, as I learned from Helen, are useful defenses.)

Also in those last years, as I had continued and developed my own work on incest, she encouraged me, along with my friend and collaborator Emily Schatzow, to submit our latest work to the new journal of which she was the editor. This paper, "Recovery and Verification of Memories of Childhood Sexual Abuse,"[30] described a subgroup of our patients who reported periods of partial or complete amnesia followed by delayed recall, and also documented the ways that these patients were able to obtain independent corroboration of their memories. The paper has been widely cited, especially during a period of strong antifeminist backlash in the 1990s, when the credibility of such memories was challenged in professional journals, in court, and in the popular press. The phenomenon we described, now technically called "dissociative amnesia," and popularly known as "repressed memory," has withstood the backlash effort to stigmatize it as "junk science," and is now well established both in the scientific literature[31] and in law.[32] As a result, many more adult survivors of incest and other forms of abuse are now enabled to seek redress in court.

To me, during her last years, Helen offered two "pearls" that I have never forgotten. One was: "Pick your battles." The other was: "Stay engaged." Activism, she explained, is an antidote to despair. I have tried to follow her advice to the best of my ability.

Over the years, I have wondered at her prescience, as I have found so many ways in which her work anticipated my own. Recently, my work on trauma has brought me back to the subject of shame. At this late date, I, too, have become a "shamenik." Helen formulated shame as the reaction to rejection and unrequited love. It seems to me that shame is also an inherent reaction to social subordination.

The implications of this idea are still unfolding. In general psychology, it suggests that human beings innately desire relationships of equality, or mutuality, along with life and liberty. In the trauma field, it suggests that conceptualizing post-traumatic stress as a disorder of fear is far too limited; shame is so central to the experience of victimization that it might be equally useful to conceptualize the post-traumatic reaction as a disorder of shame.

Quite recently, I published these ideas as a chapter in a book called *Shame in the Therapy Hour*.[33] The editors, Ronda Dearing and June Price

Tangney, dedicated this book to Helen's memory, saying: "her innovative ideas on shame and guilt have provided guidance and inspiration." A fitting tribute, I thought. (They had not known that Helen was my mother.) I was glad to know that her work is still providing guidance and inspiration to others, as it has to me throughout my own life and work.

Notes

1. Senate Permanent Subcommittee on Investigations of the Committee on Government Operations, Transcripts v. 2, p. 1251, May 25, 1953.
2. T Snyder: *Bloodlands: Europe Between Hitler and Stalin.* New York: Basic Books 2013.
3. Unpublished interview, 11/25/1971.
4. Ibid.
5. Senate Permanent Subcommittee on Investigations of the Committee on Government Operations, Transcripts v. 2, p. 1238. May 20, 1953.
6. J Mitchell: Women: The longest revolution. *New Left Review* December, 1966; 40.
7. KA Sarachild: Consciousness raising. In: New York Redstockings; *Notes from the Second Year.* New York: (Self-published) 1968.
8. Pamela Allen: *Free Space: A Perspective on the Small Group in Women's Liberation.* San Francisco: Sudsofloppen (pamphlet), 1970.
9. World Health Organization, London School of Hygiene & Tropical Medicine, and the South African Medical Research Council: *Global and Regional Estimates of Violence against Women: Prevalence and Health Effects of Intimate Partner Violence and Non-partner Sexual Violence.* Geneva: 2013.
10. S Evans: *Personal Politics.* New York: Knopf 1979.
11. C Hayden: Fields of blue. In *Deep in Our Hearts: Nine White Women in the Freedom Movement.* Athens: University of Georgia Press 2002, 335–375. The incident is described on p. 366.
12. P Mainardi: The politics of housework. In New York Radical Feminists: *Notes from the Second Year.* New York: (Self-published) 1968.
13. T Branch: Freedom Summer. Part 3 in *Pillar of Fire: America in the King Years 1963–65.* New York: Simon & Schuster 1998, 343–508.
14. DJ Henderson: Incest. In AM Freedman, HI Kaplan, BJ Sadock (Eds.): *Comprehensive Textbook of Psychiatry*, 2nd Edition, Baltimore, MD: Williams & Wilkins 1975, 1532.
15. J Adelman: *Worldly Philosopher: The Odyssey of Albert O. Hirschman.* Princeton, NJ: Princeton University Press 2013.
16. JL Herman, L Hirschman: Father-daughter incest. *Signs: Journal of Women in Culture and Society* 1977; 2:735–756.
17. See, for example, CW Mills: *The Power Elite.* Oxford: Oxford University Press 1956.
18. MR Harvey: *Exemplary Rape Crisis Programs: A Cross-Site Analysis and Case Studies.* Washington, DC: U.S. Department of Health and Human Services 1980.
19. American Psychiatric Association: *Diagnostic and Statistical Manual of Psychiatric Disorders-III.* Washington DC: American Psychiatric Press 1980.
20. JL Herman: *Trauma and Recovery.* New York: Basic Books 1992.
21. HB Lewis: *Shame and Guilt in Neurosis.* New York: International Universities Press 1971.
22. HB Lewis: *Psychic War in Men and Women.* New York: New York University Press 1976.
23. Ibid., viii.

24 HB Lewis: *Freud and Modern Psychology: vol. 1: The Emotional Basis of Mental Illness*. New York: Plenum Press 1981, vii.
25 Ibid., 79–80.
26 HB Lewis: *Freud and Modern Psychology: vol. 2: The Emotional Basis of Human Behavior*. New York: Plenum Press 1983, v.
27 HB Lewis (Ed.): *The Role of Shame in Symptom Formation*. Hillsdale, NJ: Lawrence Erlbaum Associates 1987.
28 Ibid., p. xi.
29 JL Herman, HB Lewis: Anger in the mother-daughter relationship. In T Bernay, D Cantor (Eds.): *The Psychology of Today's Woman: New Psychoanalytic Visions*. Hillsdale, NJ: The Analytic Press 1986, 139–163.
30 JL Herman, E Schatzow: Recovery and verification of memories of childhood sexual trauma. *Psychoanalytic Psychology* 1987; 4:1–14.
31 D Brown: Neuroimaging of Posttraumatic Stress Disorder and Dissociative Disorders. Boston, MA: Unpublished Ms. 2014.
32 *Judgment on Daubert Challenge*. Civil District Court for the Parish of Orleans, State of Louisiana, #2011–11683, May 17, 2013.
33 JL Herman: PTSD as a shame disorder. In RL Dearing, JP Tangney (Eds.): *Shame in the Therapy Hour*. Washington, DC: American Psychological Association Press 2011, 261–276.

Chapter 10

In Shadows of Terror
An Intergenerational Tale of Growing Up in the Old Left

Lisa S. Lyons

In 2009 I received a long awaited copy of the secret file the FBI had kept on my father and our family in the 1950s, during the McCarthy era (Federal Bureau of Investigation. File #1134958). Having ordered it as part of my ongoing exploration of the secrets and silence that had so marked my childhood, I read it with increasing excitement and shock. Aided by that file, I began to piece together a story about the silence and unexplored grief which permeated my growing up. I learned that stories I had thought were more paranoia than reality contained much that had been real, that there was reason for the secrets I had had to hold and the paralyzing silence that had been imposed on me, and that the terror so elaborated in my fantasy life had been an actual and constant presence.

The fear of speaking can still ambush me. As I begin writing this essay, 50 years after the events I will examine, I have a nightmare in which I reveal deeply felt beliefs to someone who disagrees with them. I wake up in terror. If I express my own ideas I will be thrown out in the cold, alone, unprotected in Siberia, literally and figuratively. Some months after the dream, while delivering an early version of this chapter at a conference, I find myself scanning the audience, looking for undercover FBI agents. An old and familiar paranoia, based, I now know, on real events as well as fantasied elaborations. Half a century has passed, and speaking remains unsafe.

How did that era come to weave its way into my more personal history and fantasy life? As I begin to think about this question, I am alive with memory fragments: stories, images, names. Each element feels compelling and bound to powerful emotions, but still, each piece is a shard, a bit of colored glass washed up on a beach. Starting with these shards, as well as dreams and reverie, I have used a wide range of sources to craft a mosaic. Like any complex family history, mine is multi-dimensional, non-linear. I have attempted to be rigorous and accurate, but in the end it is my narrative, a reconstruction and a re-invention, understood as I look backwards through the lens of the present: *Nachträglichkeit*, a reconfiguration as well as a "remembrance of things past" (Shakespeare, W. Sonnet XXX).

The multilayered understanding offered by psychoanalysis has expanded my remembrance and turned my attention to how state-imposed terror and the demand to keep secrets get inscribed, managed internally, and then transmitted across generations. What is done to us and for us by the state is taken in both directly and in multiple transformations, decoded and interpreted, as well as dissociated and re-enacted by parents and community. The "trans-social" (Puget, 1989), the social background in which we are all embedded, shapes our normative unconscious (Layton, 2004) and becomes an internalized object. This internalized object is elaborated within from our earliest years, kaleidoscopically shaping and shaped both by interpersonal experience and intra-psychic fantasy. In my family, the interweaving of the individual, the state, and the affects linking them offered to each of us multiple roles as doer and done-to (Benjamin, 2012); we each played many parts, in ever-shifting configurations.

Fragment: History

By the 1930s, my father had left the small working-class Jewish community in the New England town where he grew up, gotten an education, including a Ph.D., and become a scientist. Like my mother, he was briefly a Communist Party member. He was drawn to the party, I believe, both by the vision it offered of a world organized around social justice and by his reading of the internal logic and intellectual rigor of party rhetoric; my mother was drawn by a fantasy of humanitarian largesse. In the early 1950s, as I was starting elementary school, Joe McCarthy was whipping up a fear of Communism and of traitors in our midst, and the cold war dominated national and international politics. My father was a left-wing intellectual, a philosophical Marxist, and something of an activist; no longer a card-carrying Communist Party member, his activism was by then limited to writing, to membership in a few left-of-center academic organizations, and to occasional donations to left-wing causes. He was also a dreamer who until his death in the late 1970s remained committed to the belief that someday the working class would rise up and take over the reins of the state. His history makes me what is now called a Red Diaper baby, a term used to describe the children of Communist or left-leaning parents in the period from the 1930s to the 1950s (Kaplan & Shapiro, 1998).

Like many Red Diaper babies, I attended school with children of other left-wing families, including the children of Ethel and Julius Rosenberg, American citizens and New Yorkers like my family, who were arrested in 1950, tried, and convicted of being Soviet spies. In 1953, the Rosenbergs were executed, leaving behind two young children. Growing up, I knew this story well, and knew when my elementary school teachers had been called to testify before the McCarthy committee (the informal term used for the House Un-American Activities Committee, HUAC). I learned early to distrust the media and knew almost nothing of pop-culture. In my small school we sang pro-union songs and studied the history of the American Labor movement, Women's Rights, Black and Jewish history. The messages we received were more humanitarian than political: equal rights, equal opportunity, and peace were the dominant values. We were also imbued with a deep belief in the importance of social engagement and the power of collective action. In the dense web of fear created by the McCarthy-era witch-hunts, by news of my teachers being subpoenaed, by the black-listing of prominent people in the entertainment industry, and by the Rosenbergs' arrest and execution, I learned early to abhor and fear those who "named names" (the term used to describe saving one's own skin by giving the McCarthy committee names of others who might have Communist affiliations).

But most powerfully I learned that survival depended on silence, and that silence was heroic. This was not a simple message. Home and school placed contradictory demands on me for quiet and activism, and transmitted confusing messages about when to speak and when to be mute. It was often unclear to me what constituted protection and what constituted betrayal. Consider this: I had listened with my parents to the radio broadcast of the Rosenberg execution, with its multiple references to the two young children left orphaned. Was I being protected or betrayed? Perhaps my parents were using this event to teach me the importance of silence. Did they not think of the harm such horrific exposure might do to a young child or that in this instance silence (their silence) might have offered me much needed protection and insulation? I learned early on from the story of the Rosenbergs that speaking could turn to betrayal and, most terrifying, that parents could be framed and killed and mothers could subordinate care for their children to devotion to their political ideals. I consider here the dark side of the (often necessary) silence: the confusion; the terror that couldn't be registered; the unexpressed grief; and the multiple contradictions against which silence defended.

Silence, terror, and grief were not new to my family in the 1950s. They are woven through a history that antedates my memories. The little I know about my ancestors' lives in Eastern Europe hints at both hardship and monumental personal loss and trauma. Each of my grandmothers lost family in pogroms in Eastern Europe; my maternal grandmother – the only grandparent I ever knew – saw her little brother murdered in their small shtetl outside of Vilna, Lithuania.

My beloved Grandma spoke little about life in the shtetl, but one tale she did tell me was of her parents watering down the alcohol they served to the Russian soldiers who came to drink at the family-run tavern. As a child I assumed that the alcohol was watered down in a spirit of defiance; an act of civil disobedience and protest. Now, having read about the random, deadly, anti-Jewish violence that could erupt in the shtetls, I wonder if watering down the alcohol was an attempt to prevent a group of jovial drinking buddies from turning into a drunken anti-Semitic lynch mob.

Another story, the one she most often recounted, was about having once been briefly kidnapped by Russian soldiers who had come to drink at the tavern, and then being rescued relatively quickly by her brothers. She would tell me that story as a fairy tale, complete with heroes, villains, and a beautiful princess; a signifier of her great beauty and desirability as a young woman. I wonder though about her need to tell and retell this tale. Had there been terror, never spoken, that filled the space between her kidnapping and rescue? Was it too dangerous afterwards to speak out against the authorities? Perhaps never expressed fear and anger, dissociated and later reconfigured and transformed, pushed her to keep telling the story; an attempt to master a trauma, and to turn a nightmare into a fairy tale.

There are also explicit threads of activism in the family history. My father's great uncle emigrated first to South Africa, where he became a community organizer of black miners and an early voice against racial injustice. I am told he was thrown out of the country for his activism. He re-emerged in America as a union organizer and a friend of Eugene Debs, the labor leader. This relative's grandson – whom I never met – was one of the founders of SANE[1] (Sane, 2014) and an environmental activist who has a hiking trail named after him in the Muir Woods in California.

Both sets of my grandparents traveled to America around the turn of the century; young adults, they left behind parents and siblings. Subsequently, each of my grandmothers endured life-long anxiety and depression. As I learned only when well into adulthood, in 1923 my father's mother killed herself; my father was 22. The initial explanation for this suicide, offered by my mother, referenced my grandmother's long struggle with tuberculosis. As it turned out, this version was another nightmare reconfigured into a fairy tale. The story was revised much later by a relative more willing to challenge silence in the family and confront reality: I learned that my grandmother killed herself in the context of some 20 years of serious and crippling depression and multiple psychiatric hospitalizations, a few years after her oldest son, my father's brother, returned from World War I badly shell-shocked (the term used then for PTSD), a condition from which he never recovered.

Fragment: History Revisited

A few memories:

> It's 1952, I am 5-years-old and Dwight Eisenhower, the much decorated, Republican army General and Adlai Stevenson, a Democrat and an iconic symbol of liberalism, are running for president. My mother is taking me with her to vote. She has told me, over and over, that I must be silent; never ever tell anyone that "we" are going to vote not for Eisenhower or Stevenson, but for the American Labor Party (ALP) (a party founded in the mid-1930s principally to coendorse candidates who were sympathetic to the interests of Labor but which by the 1952 presidential election had been accused of communist affiliations). In the elevator of our building we meet a neighbor, the mother of children I play with, and someone whose Catholic faith, conservative politics, and formal presentation felt, even to my 5-year-old self, to be "other." Embedded as I was in my left wing, Jewish, informal, secular family, I found this neighbor unfathomable and vaguely dangerous. "And where are you going,

little girl?" she asks. Momentarily forgetting, or perhaps defiantly ignoring the injunction to be silent, I say, proudly, so the story goes, "I'm going to vote for the American Labor Party." Stunned silence, horror, a quick exit. The file the FBI kept on my father reports that in 1952, the year this event took place, my parents were registered with the ALP. Although my more rational self knows that the registration rolls of the ALP were public knowledge and easily available to the FBI, my more terrified self wonders if it was I who leaked this information. Was this neighbor one of the many moles whose names are redacted in my father's FBI file? Was I the informer?

It's a few years later, about a year past the Rosenberg execution. I am 8, and taking the city bus by myself to my dance class. A man sits down next to me and exposes himself. The next few Saturdays, when I take the same bus to the same class he is there, exposed. I am terrified, alone, and unprotected, but frozen in silence. I don't scream, move, find a policeman, or tell my parents. My well-learned distrust of anyone who represented the law had taught me to ignore even a predator. And perhaps too I had some unconscious sense of the frightening linkages among the multiple meanings of exposure, danger, and silence.

Feisty and eager to talk at 5; scared and silent at 8. These events, juxtaposed as they are in my memory, and although part of a more complex developmental story, speak of a critical shift in my internal world. I well remember being scared and silent at 8. My memories of 5 are more fragmented. I recall the incident in the elevator, but I have little memory of feeling mischievous or talkative; the more outspoken parts of me were perhaps already disconnected from my lived experience of myself. But in the three years between 5 and 8 my social surround had changed drastically. The Rosenbergs had been arrested, tried, and executed, the FBI had begun investigating my father, and my family's sense of safety had eroded. My parents, and especially my mother, were overwhelmed by anxiety. I had learned not only that the state, in many representations, including policemen, was of no help, but that my parents, immersed in their own silence, political otherness, and overwhelming fear of government terror, had in a certain sense already been taken from me. Their compromised ability to protect a young child from horrors like the Rosenberg execution, a neighbor's searching questions, or a predator on a bus had perhaps further disintegrated, overpowered by currents events and subsumed in re-enactments of their own fear, vulnerability, and rage.

The traumatic fear of exposure in the McCarthy era, and the silence around it in my family froze time. It is now the mid-1970s. I am around 30. The political climate has shifted: the open rebellion of the 1960s has already happened, and officially, McCarthy and HUAC are history. It's Saturday night, the end of a dinner at an aunt's house in New York City; parents, aunts, and uncles, now in their seventies, are there. All are former Communist Party members, long retired (or scared off) from social and political activism, and settled into lives of relative comfort, accomplishment, and security. It's around 10 p.m.; we've eaten, had wine; a relaxed, comfortable family gathering. The doorbell rings. The doorman announces someone would like to come up. The FBI, he says.

Silence.

The air in the room turns still. Everybody freezes. Faces drain, the room enveloped in terror. Panic engulfs me.

My memory stops there.

It turned out that the FBI was doing a routine security clearance on my cousin's partner, a research physicist about to start work at a government-funded lab. This moment, the intrusion of the FBI into a family dinner and the fear I registered, were never discussed. In retrospect, the entire incident seems to have occurred in a space of terror that, like the terror of my grandmother's kidnapping, has gone unnamed in the family, dissociated from the discourse, the political theorizing, and the comfort of everyday experience. The silence went unrecognized as a relational breach among us. But the incident was a moment well known in my fantasies – the ominous knock at the door – someone evil coming to get us. As a child, I had been told, "If men in dark suits and ties [the iconic image of 1950s FBI agents] ever come to visit, tell them that no-body is home." By the 1970s I had read and re-read *The Diary of Anne Frank* (Frank, 1952) with its vividly portrayed fear of a similar knock. And here it was, happening in New York, in the 1970s.

Fragment: Silence Revisited

Wordlessness weaves through my history. And yet, side by side with the imperative to be silent, much was spoken at home that should not have been: I knew, in vague and fearful outline, about the FBI investigation; I knew about family friends in prison for their political views; I had listened with my parents to the broadcast of the Rosenberg execution. I was frightened, and confused about when to speak, when to be silent. I was also trapped in a doubled demand for silence that emerged from the rigid political subculture in which my family was embedded. On the one hand was a demand for public silence to protect us from the terror of the state. On the other hand was an expectation of silent acquiescence within the family. This doubling came from a contradiction: we were revolutionaries, but as disciples of that revolution we were to conform rigidly and to suppress internal dissent. There wasn't space for discussion, examination, or critique of our beliefs; the lively debate and shared joyful, creative imagining of a new world order that others from that period report (e.g., Gornick, 1977) were absent in my home.

Demands for silence in the family emerged not only explicitly, but also subtly, as pressure to create the appearance of conformity. There were admonitions to be unseen and totally unremarkable externally. I have memories of family arguments about what then seemed trivial: the imperative that my brother have a good haircut, my somewhat Bohemian clothes, and the often repeated query, "what will the neighbors say," uttered by my mother whenever I did anything that might draw unwanted attention. Given my non-conformist family and my associations of the left with protest, rebellion, and mass action, that phrase was to me something of an anomaly. I can now understand it not only as an attempt to avoid scrutiny, but also, looking through the lens of normative unconscious process, as the defensive response of an upwardly mobile family to anxiety that they might somehow fall back down the social ladder (Layton, 2014).

There were other secrets and silences. In my post-holocaust childhood my family had a complex relationship to being Jewish. My father rebelled against Judaism even as a young boy. He grew up in an observant Jewish home, but he would earn pennies as a child (unbeknownst to his parents) by lighting lights and performing other tasks dis-allowed on the Sabbath for observant families. After his mother's suicide, when he was beginning to search for a place in academe in the then openly anti-Semitic culture of Columbia University (Schrecker, 1986), he wrote to his own father of his despair and dis-affection with religion. Much later, he told me with no uncertainty that religion was "the opiate of the masses" (Marxism and Religion, 2015); a collection of myths that would slow down the advent of the revolution.

In defiance of, or perhaps oblivious to our Jewishness, and in keeping with other left-wing Jews, we celebrated Christmas. It was a fun, child-friendly holiday, religion absent. However, one familiar Christmas symbol was not allowed: a wreath on the front door. That public exhibition was prohibited, with no explanation offered. Forbidding a wreath was incongruous, but I believe it was not the religious significance of a wreath that troubled my parents. Rather, it was that anything hung on the outside of the door exposed private beliefs to the outside world; in the climate of the McCarthy era, for my parents, exposure evoked fear and invited annihilation. I also believe that such a public display conjured a more distant history: for my forebears in the shtetl, there must have been fear and risk connected to being seen as Jewish (something I imagine was virtually impossible to hide!). In my modern home then, the wreath on the door evoked both extant danger and unsymbolized history.

My left-wing elementary school was a place where the excitement of possibility often came alive, but it too was a place of silence. Politics was implicit in the curriculum and culture but there was an unbreachable wall around speaking about each family's involvement. The true identity of the Meeropols – the children of the Rosenbergs and students at the school – was, understandably, unspoken. I had no idea who they were for the first few years that they attended the school. Some of my friends knew little of the dangers around us or of their parents' political beliefs and activities; these children were well protected from things to which I was over-exposed. The silence at school was protective, but paradoxically deprived us of an opportunity to examine the tension in the very air we breathed. Now, many years later, I have talked with former classmates and made connections between names and family stories: the boy in the class whom I only recently learned was the son of a blacklisted Hollywood screenwriter (Hollywood blacklist, 2015); the many students – mostly the children of teachers – whom I envied for the homes their families had in a small village in Vermont. These homes, some of my former classmates have recently explained, were bought not only for pleasure. They were potential hideouts for the families should the need arise, and were at times used to house strangers who were trying to disappear from the reach of HUAC.

At night, as a child, the unspoken terrors often came alive. "I can't sleep," I would say, "I'm having bad thoughts," but I couldn't give voice to those thoughts. I had nightmares with recurrent themes which persisted way into adulthood: I am being pursued by Nazis, even though the Holocaust was further, much further from my family's experience than the dangers lurking among us; I am on the street where we live and I fall down, voice and body mute, traffic bearing down, unable to speak, to scream for help, to move. In dreams I am unprotected, exposed, and in great danger. Terrors present at night and often unremembered by day.

Fragment: Grief and Loss

Reading the political and social history of the McCarthy era, one might get the idea that, except for a few dramatic cases, the personal losses suffered were relatively mild and the historical impact minimal (Schrecker, 1986, 1998). Nothing could be further from the case. The repression and terror during the McCarthy era were massively destructive to the lives of those who were targeted (Schrecker, 1986, 1998; Holmes, 1989). In the stress of investigations, firings, and the loss of security, lives unraveled, marriages broke up. There were suicides, descents into alcoholism and mental illness, and the emergence of crippling physical illnesses (Schrecker, 1986, 1998). The private destruction persisted long past the end of HUAC, and, as I am arguing, carried into the next generation.

In addition to being a source of catastrophic personal destruction and loss, the McCarthy era lives on in our normative social unconscious (Layton, 2004) and may be understood to be one of many pre-cursers to the fragmentation of democratic process and constitutional rights that has occurred since 9/11. Long after the end of the cold war and the breakup of the Soviet Union, the ghosts of HUAC haunt us: they appear in the United States in the persistent background fear of Communism, Socialism, and political and social "otherness," in the ongoing revelations of official and often undercover violations of human rights, and in the culture of hyper-vigilance perpetuated by our government and pervasive in our lives.

For my father and many of his generation, there was, in addition, a different and less concrete loss, related to the gradual destruction of the ego ideal of the Communist state. This loss of belief and hope couldn't be openly grieved. In the 1950s, as the state continued to use terror tactics, including public black listings, firings, and prolonged investigations that held the potential for financial ruin and social ostracism, many were locked in silence imposed by the impossibility of knowing whom to trust.

Speaking was dangerous. As a "dream deferred" (Hughes, 1951) shriveled and became a dream destroyed, the grief couldn't be spoken.

Nine months after the execution of the Rosenbergs, my father was intercepted and interrogated outside our building by two FBI agents. From the transcript of that conversation in his FBI file, I learned that he was quizzed on his memberships, associates, and political views, and that the agents clearly tried to terrorize him. Although my father refused to name names, in the conversation his terror is palpable, as is his hesitation; the pull of family and safety against the revulsion of betrayal. In his notated responses I can read uncertainty about whether the greater danger lay in speaking or in silence. The FBI reports that from that meeting he went directly upstairs to us – my mother, me, and my brother, aged about 7 and 10. I don't remember that day, but I have many memories from around that time of growing fear and tension at home.

After the visit from the FBI, along with the sense of a disaster barely averted and the frequently re-iterated warnings to maintain silence, in the family an additional story emerged. This was the tale of how my father refused to name names and, more important to me, protected us by not allowing the FBI to come upstairs. That story became part of the spoken, shared family lore, and for me, a child who badly needed protection, assumed legendary proportions. The story filled me with unaccustomed safety, pride in my father, and a sense of superiority over those on the left who had been unable to maintain silence. Again, the family turned a horror story to a fairy tale; my father as epic Hero became an antidote to fear, rage, and silence (Grand, 2010). This legend also took shape in me as part of an internal dyad connecting safety to silence and to exercising the power to say "no" to authority. Paradoxically then, for me silence became a contradictory signifier of safety, pride, terror, and isolation.

The FBI investigation of my father continued into the late 1950s. During that time he slid into a deep depression and left his tenured position at New York University, a job that for him had represented a lifelong dream. His psychic collapse was explained to me then as a response to the bigger responsibilities of his new job, a spin that avoided more painful realities. I know now that my father was struggling with much more than increased responsibilities. His university job had been made untenable, and he was being bombarded with complicated and unexamined losses. Two of his closest friends had been the only two professors fired outright from NYU for their politics (Ellen Schrecker, personal communication), another was in prison for being a member of the Communist Party, and my father himself was the subject of an ongoing investigation (1953–1959) by the FBI. At NYU he was in a department chaired by someone he viewed as a virulent anti-Communist. I heard often his fear of speaking about politics at work; about lunches where he sat tense and silent during political discussions, hoping not to be unveiled. I have wondered if his Chair was one of the informers whose name is redacted in his FBI file. I haven't been able to find out (in a Kafka-esque twist the FBI has informed me that they will provide the redacted names only if I can first provide a death certificate for each name). The file does name another professor who reported my father to the FBI as a possible subversive, based on the professor having found something possibly political in one student's notes from a biology class taught by my father. The file also confirms that my father's Dean denied him promotion to full professor because of his politics (an explanation I had previously dismissed as my father's paranoia).

In response to this top-down spreading of terror and degradation my father eventually became silent and ceased all political involvement. As the world in which he was embedded became unresponsive and treacherous, this man about whom I have many early memories of lively warmth and intellectual excitement went dead. This shift, not unlike my own from feisty to silent, brings to mind Gerson's (2009) elegant discussion of a dead third constituted from an external environment marked by numbness and absence. I imagine my father's unspoken and unattended rage, grief, and loss; the erosion of belief in a world where thoughts and opinions could be spoken, this new silence, absence, and unsafety resonating with the old and cementing internal deadness. Life might have been restored to him and the dead third revived if he had had a place and context to grieve openly for losses that had to be kept secret, to experience speaking to a responsive, empathic other (Davoine & Gaudillière, 2004).

Whatever my father's personal proclivity to silence, openness was precluded by the social surround of danger and secret terror. When it is impossible to speak out and mourn loss, depression and silence defend against longing and rage and maintain the dissociation and paranoia that secret terror creates (Hollander, 2010; Davoine & Gaudillière, 2004; Cairo, 2004). In the silence and fear of speaking, so present in my nightmares, the confusion between genuine threat and fantasy can persist and grow.

It was impossible for my father to grieve the destruction of an ideal that was too dangerous to admit having had, and too dangerous to admit having lost. Rage, anger, and grief over the loss of his academic world and the loss of safety in any world could not be experienced or mourned without jeopardizing both his external and internal safety.

Judith Butler (1995) weaves the social world into Freud's intra-psychic formulation that understands grieving as a melancholic identification with an incorporated object (Freud, 1917, 1923). She highlights the difficulties of grieving with relation to gender, when there are cultural prohibitions related to the object of grief, when there is no "public recognition or discourse" which allows the naming and grieving of the identification and loss. Butler locates melancholy in this absence. Her insight can be extended to other identifications: when the loss of forbidden political, social and intellectual ideals, beliefs, and community has to be kept secret, the possibility of grieving and working through is foreclosed by the dangers of the identification and the prohibition of social discourse. In the imperative to be silent about breaches with the social surround, the transitional space between one's self and society collapses. Without space for open reflection, paranoia about the external world grows (Hollander, 2010), the hated attributes of the socio-cultural environment are internalized (Etchegoyen, 1996), and defensive rigidity can take hold. Unable to talk either about the breakup of his political world, or the collapse of his idealized version of a Communist state, my father defended against disillusionment with both rigid dogmatism and depression.

There were many echoes of the past in my father's depression. In addition to traumas related to the pogroms that had shaped the immigration experience of his own parents and his mother's suicide, in the 1950s my father's oldest brother was still visibly shell-shocked. In my memory my uncle is for ever on a battlefield in Europe; I see his tremors, his almost constant hyper-vigilance and fear; I feel the unspoken horrors he must have seen. Additionally, as the state was closing in on leftists, the world was beginning to learn the details of the Nazi atrocities, and my parents were still reeling from the hardships of the Great Depression. My father's psychic state manifested the anxiety inherent in class mobility (Layton, 2004, 2014), and the annihilation anxiety that can arise when we feel excluded from a large group to which we are connected (Bion, 1992). After two generations of disruption and escape from the repressive power of the state, the place to which he and his family had come for protection was for my father marked by terror and betrayal, the fantasied safety of this new world destroyed.

Caught in a "social catastrophe," as Puget (1989) calls the broken connection between an individual and the social world, and depressed, my father entered therapy. In the 1950s, psychoanalysis had yet to explore the impact of the normative social unconscious. For the most part, consideration of political and social forces was rigidly excluded from psychoanalytic discourse. This theoretical and clinical scotoma perhaps relates to the difficulty for many of the analysts who had recently emigrated to America, of considering the horrors of the Holocaust that had forced them to leave home. In any event, my father's therapist probably would not have had an analytic language for integrating the external social world into the intra-psychic. But whomever he saw, I imagine that he would have been too afraid to talk about the political in his treatment; the rule of silence about politics was sacrosanct, and with good reason. We know now that in the McCarthy era there were analysts who reported their patients' political views and associates to the FBI (e.g., Belafonte, 2012).

I responded to the climate around me with physical representations of the tension, fear, and silence, and was also sent to therapy. In keeping with the 1950s' separation of the intra-psychic from the social surround, my therapist (personal communication) was told nothing by my parents either about my father's depression or the family's politics. I spoke little in therapy; like my father, I kept the silence. Speech, a dangerous act, would have been a signifier of what was most feared: the naming of names, betrayal, and potential loss of family; a summoning of the terror of the state. Silence was an enactment of the dilemmas imposed by the political terror. It was safe and a signifier of heroism, but also a representation of my own loss of agency in the face of a dead third. Locked in a silence that my therapist didn't decode, I too was unable to mourn.

Fragment: Contradictions

As a child, I excitedly anticipated the impending takeover of the state and the means of production by the working class; I imagined it would begin as soon as tomorrow! And in my fantasies I imagined that the takeover would immediately solve all of the economic and humanitarian woes of the world. But my world was also filled with unacknowledged friction from contradictory and irreconcilable desires. There were clashes between elitism and egalitarianism; between speech and silence; between the revolutionary idealism of Marxism and the excitement of material delights.

The contradictions were difficult to process. As my parents were proclaiming their faith in the working class and anticipating the revolution against capitalist entrepreneurs, they were also enjoying the fruits of the world around them. The wish for luxury and an elite position in society was split off from their Marxist ideal of an egalitarian world. I imagine that for them there were secrets hidden in the dissociation of desire; the external dangerous object (material luxury) became the internalized exciting object. Among the first of their families to go to college and to live urban, sophisticated lives, my parents seemed to aspire to become part of a new ruling class (a dream supported by Lenin and Stalin's often expressed disdain of the working class and their directives to elevate scientists and intellectuals to leadership positions (Lenin, 1902)). We were not living according to values I understood to be embedded in Marxism. My parents had no social connections with anyone from the working class and they looked down on those who were not part of their intellectual, academic, artsy world. Every year at tax time, I heard longing in my father's frustration that as an academic he could not claim the deductions allowed a businessman; he dabbled in the stock market and when he could, bought expensive clothes. A photograph of my family at a wedding in the late 1950s reveals my mother looking elegant and wealthy, wrapped in a fur scarf. "Doesn't look much like a communist," a friend recently commented.

I hid my own exciting, and decidedly non-Marxist desires. I invented a game: I would spend hours, in private, filled with both shame and delight, pouring over the pages of the huge Sears-Roebuck mail order catalogue, picking one coveted item from each page. Zizek (1999b, 2000), captures the flavor of the contradictions in my family, citing the disingenuousness of those in the West who "pursue their well-paid academic careers while using the idealized other [the current communist regimes] as the stuff of their ideological dreams: they dream through the other."

Incongruities between material comfort and Marxist ideals were also fueled by my parents' memories of the hardships and longings for better lives that brought their parents to America. The contradictions between the ascetic life – style implied in Marxism and celebrated by family friends and our wishes for comfort and luxury echo what for my Grandparents must have been ambivalence about leaving their own parents and siblings in poverty and danger while they (my grandparents) fled the shtetl for better lives.[2] I have a photo of my maternal grandfather's parents and brothers, in Vilna, looking poor, over-worked, and sad. I look at it side by side with the wedding photo taken in the 1950s – my mother wrapped in fur. So many dissociated and unexamined selves in conflict!

My father died in 1977. In many ways a realist, he died holding on to the almost psychotic belief that neither Stalin nor Mao had done anything wrong. Holding on to a fantasy of Stalin as a protector – as the man he wished he had been – may have tempered the loss of my father's ideal, that a more humane state would emerge after the revolt of the working class.

My father had once been an aspiring pianist; he married a pianist and had a daughter (me) who was a professional violinist. In 1967, before there was much information available publicly in the West about the ongoing social destruction in China, we read a brief report in the *New York Times* (1967) that the Red Guard (the chaotic and violent bands of mostly teenagers who roamed many areas of China during the cultural revolution destroying what they viewed as the counter-revolutionary cultural and intellectual elite) smashed the wrists of a prominent pianist, a man who was deemed dissident only because he was considered part of the cultural elite. My father dismissed my horror, saying "this kind of thing sometimes has to be done in the service of revolution," seemingly condoning what had happened. A bizarre, confusing, and contradictory statement from a man who was both an academic and a musician, who took pride in being part of the cultural elite and whose rage had always been well hidden.

Now I understand the dogmatism and dissociation as my father's attempt to protect himself from disillusionment and his politics from victimization and destruction; dogmatism was a means to master threats from both within and without. Unprotected himself, he could not be an empathic witness. Rather, he had to maintain his blind identification with his hero (Grand, 2010), and adopt a "rigid, moralizing stance" (Zizek, 1999a) in order to hold on to his political energy in the face of the disappointment of his hopes for radical social change.

My father's response to the story of the Chinese pianist illustrates well how empathy and care-taking can dissolve and dissociated rage emerge in the face of the loss of safety from the social surround. In another example, a blog post written by Lisa Gilford (2009), the daughter of a blacklisted actor, recounts her mother's attempts to avoid being served by FBI agents bearing a subpoena to appear before HUAC. The mother comes face to face with the agents as she is entering her beach cabin, her two young children in tow. In a rage, she grabs her 18-month-old son by the ankles and using him as a club, swings at the FBI agents, terror and rage co-opting mothering. I understand this as the mother's identification with those trying to destroy her as well as a moment when her paranoid fear met external threat; blind terror left her in a state of internal confusion; the space for reflection collapsed.

Nachträglichkeit

My experiences, memories, and identifications have been shaped by my lived reality of traumatic silencing and misplaced speaking, by stories of pogroms, and by the rebelliousness, grief, and powerlessness that belonged to the lives of my parents and grandparents. As I entered adolescence this history, along with my family's elitism, came alive in my internal world, side by side with values from the left that identified the power to create social change with collective action. The summer I was 12, coincidentally or perhaps significantly right about the time the FBI investigation of my father was closed, something akin to my 5-year-old feistiness emerged; I became an outspoken insurgent. While still upholding silence around family secrets, I (briefly) found a voice both as an angry rebel against the covert power of authority and as a believer in the power of collective action. Sticking to my somewhat safe world I became a leader of a protest against the rules at summer camp. Much later, in graduate school (during my first career as a musician), I organized and led a rebellion against the influence of a new dean. These were loud, angry protests, neither thoughtful nor productive. But in both instances, I felt confusedly impelled to persist and unable to stop, driven by a sense of superiority and by a moral imperative to take action according to my beliefs. I was shocked and somewhat shamed to discover that others who agreed with me in private were unwilling to take the risks I was taking. Now, having re-signified many memories of my childhood, I understand my protests to have been expressions of unexplored and dissociated rage and of my contradictory identifications with the oppressed, the oppressors, and the elite, as well as attempts to undo what was then an unreflected story of silence.

I have discovered that each time I go back to look at the fragments of colored glass which prompted this exploration, the patterns and meanings have shifted. This reminds me of experiences with the music of Bach: at each encounter with a well-learned and beloved piece my hearing of the interplay of the multiple voices reconfigures; a different line shifts to the forefront, and a new musical conversation emerges. Re-examining my own history, I now see things I hadn't understood earlier. In my youthful attempts to create change through mobilizing collective action I had felt out of control and in the grips of hopelessly idealistic expectations. I find now I am proud that the multiple threads of oppression and terror in my growing up reconfigured (even though in small ways) as activism. I hadn't understood this when I began this project.

An additional new strand that has emerged with unforeseen nuance as I revisit my history relates to my expanded understanding of how profoundly this history has shaped my psychoanalytic sensibilities. As a younger adult I realized that trying to change a large system felt overwhelming. My activist self has instead found a home and deep satisfaction in the more private world of clinical exploration. Being a psychoanalyst has helped me to re-shape my relationship with concealing and revealing. Not surprisingly, I am drawn to work and theory related to dissociation and trauma.

The ongoing counterpoint of speaking and silence, the multiple ways silence speaks to us in the consulting room and can gradually be undone through the work, and the enterprise of finding and re-connecting severed links between fragments of narrative history and affective responses are compelling for me, and salient to my way of working. Critically, I have come also to value listening with my patients for the internal register of the larger social surround (Dimen, 2011) embedded in the intra-psychic and the relational.

The radical questioning that is at the core of psychoanalysis suits me well. Although the climate in which I grew up draws me toward the comfort of explanatory systems, it has also left me deeply wary of dogma and rigidity. Tangled threads of oppression, social justice, silence, and speaking re-configure continuously in me as I interact with fully formed systems – I question, re-mold, and re-shape. Early imperatives around silence and the threats I both knew and avoided knowing have shaped in me both a risk taking self, the one who led protests as a 12-year-old, and a deeply conservative, cautious self. Psychoanalytic theory and clinical work nurture both these selves, leading me to creative and generative freedom as well as to moments of protective inattention.

A clinical vignette has hovered on the fringes of my consciousness throughout the work on this chapter. As I was looking for a way to bring my narrative into the clinical world of psychoanalysis, this long ago fragment of a session came back to me with fresh clarity. I worked with Hal for several years. He came to treatment when he found himself, in his mid-forties, living house-bound with anxiety. Unable to sleep until daylight, lonely and alone, he was supporting himself with a stock-market windfall that was soon to run out. He wanted a partner and children, and knew that he would have to work again. In his twenties and thirties, although anxious and in an ongoing struggle with the need to shut down his engagement with the world, he worked, dated, and managed to get an advanced professional degree. He was thoughtful and philosophical, and had been spending much of his time in isolation working on a paper about Kabbalah and the transmission of mystical knowledge – a project we gradually came to understand was saturated with metaphors related to pieces of his family history that he both knew and couldn't let himself know, as well as experiences and fears that initially neither he nor I knew we shared. He was sure he couldn't leave his solitary existence until his paper was finished.

From an Orthodox Jewish family, Hal was deeply, although mostly privately, religious. He was however quick to tell me, with pride and awe, that he was a Kohain – a descendant of the priestly tribe from the time of Moses. He viewed this as a sacred heritage and a great responsibility – something that set him apart as both special and other. He felt certain that he could marry only another Kohain, and that he belonged to an elite group destined to be leaders among Orthodox men and scholars. Although often in despair about what he viewed as his inability to follow through on his responsibilities as a Kohain, he was subtly and gently disparaging of those who didn't share this heritage. Looking back, he and I were linked from the start by a sense of belonging to elite and private worlds, and by our embeddedness in families where rigid and narrow identifications had shaped paranoia and defended against loss.

Hal's parents were Holocaust survivors. His mother, blond and as a child looking more Aryan than Jewish, had lived openly in Germany during the war with falsified credentials, in constant danger and fear. Hal's father had been in Auschwitz, something alluded to only in moments when, responding to Hal's distress over childhood hurts and disappointments, he would say "You think that's bad, you should try Auschwitz." An aunt, also a survivor, lived with the family until the end of her life, un-partnered, without a job, and silent about her war-time traumas. In fact, no one in the family talked about the Holocaust or about the siblings, parents, and – in his aunt's case – a husband and child buried in the mass graves and ovens of the camps. The holocaust was a silent presence, felt by Hal mostly through its absence. Night contrasted with the day-time silence; then, horrors came alive. Hal remembered as a child being woken by screams and cries coming from his parents' and aunt's bedrooms. His questions about the nightly terrors were met with silence, as if they too had never happened.

One day, during a session, we were trying to comb through some of the many meanings of Hal's anxiety and his inability to sleep until the sun came up. In a quiet moment, and without any warning, this thoughtful, respectful, and often somewhat paralyzed man suddenly jumped up from the couch, took a long step toward my chair, and, without warning, pounded violently with his fist on the small table next to me. It was over in a few seconds. I was left terrified, heart pounding, dizzy with confusion. We were both stunned and for a few minutes unable to think or talk. "That," he said, "is why I can't sleep when it's dark outside; the knock at the door that might come at any moment."

This clinical moment, an enactment of silent and disowned terror and rage transmitted to a child, and of a shared fear neither of us had previously identified, had lurked in the shadows, just out of my view, throughout the writing of this chapter. Long before I began to explore my own history, Hal and I had worked to untangle the multiple meanings for him of that moment. I knew back then as now about my own childhood fears of a similar knock and about how I had taken in the story of Anne Frank. But as I worked on this chapter, Hal's story, much more recent, was barely in my awareness. What I knew about my own fears and the intensity of my reaction to Hal's pounding on my table remained unlinked, frozen, and unsignified. Now I can understand my reaction. When Hal banged on my table, enacting the feared knock on the door and the social surround of terror that had both traumatized and silenced his family and permeated his experience of the night, he had summoned my own history. Our stories – events we had each directly experienced and events and affective landscapes unconsciously transmitted to us and between us by small gestures, mute responses, tales untold – all these came alive in the transference and counter-transference, narrative and affect linked.

Note

1 National Committee for a Sane Nuclear Policy (SANE) established in 1957.
2 For a lengthy discussion of emotional complexities and enactments related to class mobility, see Layton, 2004.

Acknowledgement

This essay is dedicated to the memory of my father, Alexander Sandow, and to my aunt, Judith Lieb, who revealed many family secrets to me. I am deeply indebted to the many friends, mentors and colleagues who encouraged me to pursue this project and steered me along the way, and I am especially grateful to Jody Messler Davies, Muriel Dimen, and Adrienne Harris.

References

Belafonte, H. (2012). *My Song: A Memoir of Art, Race, and Defiance* (with Michael Shnayerson). Vintage Books, New York.
Benjamin, J. (2012). Beyond Doer and Done To: An Intersubjective View of Thirdness. In L. Aron and A. Harris, eds. *Relational Psychoanalysis: Volume 4: Expansion of Theory*, pp. 91–131. Routledge, New York, London.
Bion, W. R. (1992). *Cogitations*. Karnac Books Ltd, London.
Butler, J. (1995). Melancholy Gender-Refused Identification. *Psychoanalytic Dialogues*, 5:165–180.
Cairo, I. (2004). Psicoanalisis: Revista de al Asociacion Psicoanalitica de Buenas Aires: Abstracts. *Psychoanalytic Quarterly*, 73:863–887.
Davoine, F. & Gaudillière, J-M. (2004). *History beyond Trauma*. Other Press LLC, New York.
Dimen, M. ed. (2011). *With Culture in Mind: Psychoanalytic Stories*. Routledge, New York, London.
Etchegoyen, R. H. (1996). Some views on psychic reality. *International Journal of Psychoanalysis*, 77:1–14.
Federal Bureau of Investigation. (1952–1959). File on XXXXXXXX. FOIPA No.: 1134958. Washington, DC.
Frank, A. (1952). *Anne Frank: Diary of a Young Girl*. Doubleday, New York.
Freud, S. (1917). Mourning and Melancholia. *Standard Edition*, 14:73–102. Hogarth Press, London, 1957.
Freud, S. (1923). The Ego and the Id. *Standard Edition*, 19:12–59. Hogarth Press, London, 1961.
Gerson, S. (2009). When the Third is Dead: Memory, Mourning and Witnessing in the Aftermath of the Holocaust. *International Journal of Psychoanalysis*, 90(6):1341–1357.
Gilford, L. (2009). Blacklist. Blog: Message posted to www.Lisagilford.com.
Gornick, V. (1977). *The Romance of American Communism*. Basic Books, New York.
Grand, S. (2010). *The Hero in the Mirror: From Fear to Fortitude*. Routledge, New York, London.

Hollander, N. C. (2010). *Uprooted Minds: Surviving the Politics of Terror in the Americas*. Routledge, London, New York.
Hollywood blacklist. (2015, March 1). In Wikipedia, The Free Encyclopedia. Retrieved April 12, 2015, from http://en.wikipedia.org/w/index.php?title=Hollywood_blacklist&oldid=649426087.
Holmes, D. R. (1989). *Stalking the Academic Communist: Intellectual Freedom and the Firing of Alex Novikoff*. University Press of New England, Hanover, London.
Hughes, L. (1951). *Dream Deferred*. Retrieved March 7, 2012, from www.cswnet.com/~menamc/langston.htm.
Kaplan, J. & Shapiro, L. (1998). Introduction. In J. Kaplan and L. Shapiro, eds. *Red Diapers: Growing up in the Communist Left*, pp. 1–13. University of Illinois Press, Urbana and Chicago, IL.
Layton, L. (2004). This Place Gives me the Heebie Jeebies. *International Journal of Critical Psychology*, 10:36–50.
Layton, L. (2014). Performing Class, Enacting Distinction: Class, Neoliberalism and Unconscious Process. Unpublished paper.
Lenin, V. (1902). What is to be Done? In R. C. Tucker, ed. *The Lenin Anthology*, pp. 12–114. W.W. Norton & Company, New York, 1975.
Marxism and religion. (2015, April 11). In Wikipedia, The Free Encyclopedia. Retrieved April 12, 2015, from http://en.wikipedia.org/w/index.php?title=Marxism_and_religion&oldid=655973188.
Puget, J. (1989). The State of Threat and Psychoanalysis: From the Uncanny that Structures to the Uncanny that Alienates. Trans. Trista Solous, 1990. Retrieved April 3, 2012, from www.human-nature.com/free-associations/puget.html.
Puget, J. (2003). How to Cope with Social Disasters. *Free Associations*, 10:454–471.
Sane. (2014, November 8). In Wikipedia, The Free Encyclopedia. Retrieved April 12, 2015, from http://en.wikipedia.org/w/index.php?title=Sane&oldid=632922445.
Schrecker, E. (1986). *No Ivory Tower: McCarthyism and the Universities*. Oxford University Press, New York.
Schrecker, E. (1998). *Many are the Crimes: McCarthyism in America*. Princeton University Press, Princeton, NJ.
Shakespeare, W. Sonnet XXX. In G. W. Clark and W. A. Wright, eds. *The Unabridged Shakespeare*. Running Press, Philadelphia, PA, London, 1989.
Soviet says Red Guard broke pianist's wrists. (1967, March 9). *New York Times*. Retrieved April 3, 2012, from http://query.nytimes.com/mem/archive/pdf?res=FA0816F6355F137A93CBA91788D85F438685F9.
Zizek, S. (1999a). The Super Ego and the Act. The European Graduate School website. Retrieved March 9, 2013, from www.egs.edu/faculty/slavoj-zizek/articles/the-superego-and-the-act.
Zizek, S. (1999b). Attempts to Escape the Logic of Capitalism: Vaclav Havel: A Political Tragedy in Six Acts. *London Review of Books*, 21(21):3–7.
Zizek, S. (2000). Ideological Fraud. *National Interest*, Winter. Retrieved March 9, 2013, from http://egs.edu/faculty/zizek/zizek-ideological-fraud.html.

Chapter 11

To Unchain Haunting Blood Memories

Intergenerational Trauma among African Americans

Kirkland C. Vaughans

In this chapter I have several immodest goals that are intricately connected, as well as independently complex and encompassing. First, I will attempt to give representation to the voice of ordinary people who were enslaved and perished. But for a few who wrote narratives of their lives, or wrote letters to their families and loved ones, or who were later interviewed by the Works Progress Administration, they are mostly forgotten. I will represent some of the thematic content from those writings as they are manifested today within the African American community as a sort of "cultural introject" (Moskowitz, 2012). I also intend to differentiate what I refer to as a cultural introject from the notion of internalized racism which is the main construct used to 'explain' negative behavioral patterns within American Black communities today. By cultural introject I mean internalization of something without quite knowing why. It is not quite identification but a disturbing amplification of unknown fears. In addition, I am proposing to describe some of the historical responses to the aftermath of slavery by both Whites and Blacks that inhibited the resolution of its traumatic aftermath. Lastly, I will attempt to describe some of the current impediments to working through the traumatic legacy of slavery within the African American community.

While space will not permit me to elaborate on all of the circumstances of slavery, what I will make note of is the traumatic legacy of American slavery on American White society. Toni Morrison (1992) takes up an aspect of this issue in her study of the impact of Blackness in White literature. While I view this subject matter as extremely important for the psychological well-being of African Americans and our nation, like the

---

Reprinted with kind permission:
Vaughans, K. (2015). To Unchain Haunting Blood Memories: Intergenerational Trauma among African Americans, Chapter in *Fragments of Trauma and the Social Production of Suffering*, edited by Michael O'Loughlin and Marilyn Charles. Lanham, Maryland: Rowan & Littlefield.

historian John Hope Franklin, I claim no more than a glimmer of insight into these powerful dynamics.

History

With very few exceptions (Fanon, 1967; Gump, 2010; Pinderhughes, 2004), psychoanalysis has only tentatively considered the impact of slavery on the psyche of the African American community. Between the sixteenth and nineteenth centuries, Berlin (2010) estimates that at least 11 million Africans were forcibly transported from across the Atlantic through what has come to be known as the Middle Passage. Black scholars have named this Black Diaspora *Maafa*, a Swahili term meaning the "Great Sorrow or Tragedy" (Ani, 1994). Africans identified themselves by tribe and ethnicity, so their treacherous voyage through the Middle Passage would thus constitute both a "death and birth canal." For them, the voyage constituted the death of a whole way of life and the birth of a new culture and racial identity (Gomez, 1998). The American brand of slavery dehumanized the subjects of this predatory system legally, politically, economically, and socially. Sociologist Orlando Patterson (1982) characterized it as a social death, meaning that the enslaved had lost their membership in the universal family of humanity. Until this time, slaves across the world had maintained their identity as human, but the American experience would be qualitatively different. Slaveowners sought not only to enslave them physically, but also to enslave their very souls. This attempt at soul murder is reflected in the writings of Frederick Douglas (1845/2003) who describes his struggle with a slave breaker: "Mr. Covey succeeded in breaking me. I was broken in body, soul, and spirit ... the dark night of slavery was upon me" (p. 75).

Today American slavery is viewed erroneously as that part of American history that occurred solely in the southern states. What is not understood is that America was in fact a slave nation, meaning that its total economic growth was thoroughly dependent upon slavery. Patterson distinguishes nations that hold people in slavery from nations whose economic well-being is dependent upon slavery, he refers to the latter as slave nations. Slavery was such a powerful part of the American credo that most of the Presidents, from the founding of the United States until the Civil War, were large slave holders. This included

Washington, Jefferson, Madison, Jackson, Tyler, Polk, and Taylor. In addition, during this period, a majority of members of the Supreme Court and of the U.S. Congress were also slave holders (Berlin, 2003). Thus, as it is today, those with economic wealth wielded the most political power. American slavery was therefore embedded within the historical and cultural marrow of the United States. It played a significant part in igniting the Revolutionary War, in uniting northern and southern colonies to form one union, as well as serving as a major cause of the Civil War.

Despite the fact that African Americans have historically spent less time emancipated than they did in slavery, the historian Rushdy (2001) warns us that slavery is very distant in the American imagination, and it has remained so because: "slavery is the family secret of America" (p. 2). By calling it "secret," Rushdy does not mean that slavery is concealed from the public. It is a secret because it remains on the periphery of the national imagination. It remains the national paradox, the stain on our founding ideals of freedom, liberty, and justice. The cruel, dehumanizing and violent nature of slavery can no longer be denied as earlier writers had sought to do. It was not just the institution of slavery, and its effects on those who lived through it, that has resulted in a traumatic legacy but also the collective memory of slavery by those who endured it, by their offspring, as well as the national response in its aftermath, that have contributed to the traumatic legacy of slavery (Eyerman, 2001; Morrow, 2003; Vaughans, 2014). Writing from the perspective of cultural trauma, Eyerman (2001) articulates this position: "The trauma in question is slavery, not as an institution or as a personal experience, but as a collective memory: a pervasive remembrance that grounded the identity-formation of a people" (p. 1). This construct in no way negates the individual or group psychological trauma experienced by those who were subjected to it. It simply views the experience from a different vantage point. Nor by examining Black experience through this lens do I mean to suggest that all Africans arriving on American shores came as slaves, as Sertima (1976) has documented, they did not. Eyerman (2001) describes cultural trauma as a "dramatic loss of identity and meaning, a tear in the social fabric" (p. 2a) for a people who previously were cohesive. In addition, it is not necessary for individual members or any member of the group to directly experience or acknowledge the trauma. This view in no way is to be considered a counter assertion of the actual trauma experienced by those who were enslaved.

Voices of the Enslaved

The history of American slavery has largely been told from the vantage point of those who did the enslaving, through their personal records, memoirs, biographies, and public documents. What was missing was the voice of those who had been enslaved. Any documentation that did become available was largely discredited or ignored, and the vast amount of it was lost through years of neglectful storage. During the 1920s, a number of Black scholars began documenting the personal experiences of those who had been enslaved and later, in the 1930s, the Federal Writers Project began interviewing thousands of the formerly enslaved and recording their interviews. The legitimacy of these narratives would be repeatedly contested on the grounds of their subjectivity and supposed bias and inaccuracy, and due to the alleged failing memories of the narrators (Berlin, 1998). The end result was the perpetuation of the benign and humanitarian view of slavery propagated, for example, by the historian Ulrich Phillips (1929). This damaging stereotype would remain dominant and largely unchallenged until the 1960s. As Berlin (1998) noted, the struggle regarding whose memory of slavery would prevail was just about as fierce as the actual conflict over slavery. Almost anticipating this struggle over the legitimacy of the enslaved voices, John Little, who had escaped bondage and fled to Canada, stated in 1855 that "Tisn't he who had stood and looked on, that can tell you what slavery is – tis he who has endured" (Yetman, 1970, p. 1).

The slave narratives and biographies do not always speak with one unified or collective voice, with the possible exception of those written during slavery, that most often made appeals to abolitionists to protest the institution of slavery and to seek its demise. In the narratives, there are discussions of the daily struggles of working on a plantation, whether or not they were worked too hard, and even if they had good or bad masters. Other prominent issues reflected upon were sexual exploitation of young girls by the master and his sons, colorism, loss and longing for family members, and being whipped. Very often the women reported being partially or fully stripped of their clothing on these occasions. As Berlin (1998) points out, their stories reflect a strong capacity for love and forgiveness. In addition, their stories do not reflect the simple dichotomy between the house slave and that of the field Negro, so popular in today's Black culture and as it is depicted in the film *Django Unchained* (Tarantino, 2013) in which the actor

Samuel Jackson, the house servant, was extremely identified with his master. He identified with the aggressor, in opposition to a slave played by Jamie Foxx, who played the role of the rebel or field Negro, who stood in opposition to White supremacy. In some narratives, slaves speak of the "kindness" of their masters. In most instances, however, this referred to reluctance on the master's part to sell them. Priscilla Joiner spoke to this sentiment, stating, "My old mistress was the best woman in the world. She may have owned slaves, but she never sold any. She brought me up just like one of her own children until I was twelve years old. Then she paid for me to go to a colored school with my own people" (Perdue, Barden and Phillips, 1976, p. 90). Other examples of masters who were considered kind were those who allowed their slaves to stay with their chosen mates, those who fed them well, and those who did not beat them. In many instances, the power of the master is acknowledged, something that is also constantly challenged and often renegotiated. Examples of resistance include slaves running away rather than be beaten, and remaining hidden until word from the owner reached them with a report that they would forgo the lash only if they returned within a specified time or the beating would be increased. A second example (Berlin, 1998) of this is where husbands living on different plantations visited their wives despite orders from their owners not to. Martha Spence offers an example. She describes how her father was sold away from the family when she was small and how the rest of the family lived in fear of being sold as well. She explains,

> My father sho did hate to leave us. He missed us and us longed for him. He would often slip back to our cottage at night. Us would gather around him and crawl up on his lap, tickled slap to death, but he give us these pleasures at a painful risk. When his Mars missed him he would beat him all the way home. Us could track him the next day by de blood stains.
>
> (p. 145)

A similar story is related by Vinnie Busby who lived on a plantation in Mississippi but whose father lived on a different plantation and whose owner also refused him permission to visit his family. She reports that at night her father would slip over and visit the family and would sometimes be caught by his owner who was on the lookout for such: "When he would catch him he would beat him so hard till we could tell which way he went back by de blood. But pa, he would keep a coming to see us and takin de beatins" (Berlin, 1998, p. 144).

Another very powerful and frequently reported issue pertained to that of parental authority over the children of the enslaved. The contest between the master and the mother could reach dangerous levels for the enslaved mother, as the master by law had no obligation to respect their parental standing or the marriage, but rather, as Berlin stated, he had preeminent authority. In her autobiography, *Incidents in the life of a slave girl* (1861/1987), Harriet Jacobs shares her personal thoughts on this issue after being threatened by her owner Dr. Flint, who stated, "These brats will bring me a handsome sum of money one of these days ... I thought to myself that, God being my helper, they would never pass into his hands. It seemed to me I would rather see them killed than have them given up to his power" (p. 80). John Boggs, who was formerly enslaved, echoed similar views: "That is what our people dread the most. The idea is like this. When a man goes out in the morning, he may have a wife and a parcel of children, and maybe when he comes back at night, he will find nobody who will tell him anything about them. If a woman ask about her children that had been sold, she would be whipped or knocked and slashed about" (Blassingame, 1977, p. 422). In recalling her childhood, Fannie Moore spoke of the love and protection displayed by her mother. She states, "I never see how my mammy stan sech had work. She stan up for her chillum tho. De ol overseeah he hate my mammy, case she fight him for beatin her chilun. Why she get more whippins for dat den anything else. She had twelfe chillum" (Berlin, 1998, p. 133).

Although they realistically feared the whip, they probably feared being sold away from their families even more. Hence the verbal threat by the master, "I'll put you in my pocket" (Stuckey, 1987), meaning they would be sold off, was more than enough to win obedience. Thomas Jefferson was well aware of these fears and believed the most severe punishment that he could exert over incorrigible slaves was to sell them away from their families (Berlin, 1998). This struggle to maintain family was unrelenting for two and one half centuries, and the odds against doing so were pathetically unforgiving. As Berlin (1998) points out, "Few enslaved parents could expect to nurture their children to maturity, see their grandchildren grow up, or succor their own parents in their last years" (p. xxvi). But the relentless loss of family and community, a half a century before the Civil War, ushered in what Berlin (2010) described as the "second middle passage." This entailed the greatest change in movement that the enslaved had endured since arriving on North America's shore. The vast shipment of millions of enslaved from the eastern seaboard to the Deep South constituted wholesale disruption of families and communities. The civilization that had been developed was now all but lost, and both those left behind and those that were scattered were forced to begin anew. With the end of slavery, four million people were finally liberated. The moment of their emancipation was noted by Booker T. Washington:

> For some minutes there was great rejoicing, and thanksgiving, and wild scenes of ecstasy. But there was no feeling of bitterness. In fact, there was pity among the slaves for our former owners. The wild rejoicing on the part of the emancipated colored people lasted but for a brief period ... there was a change in their feelings. The great responsibility of being free, of having charge of themselves, to think and plan for themselves and their children, seemed to take possession of them.
> (1901/1989, p. 21)

Despite incredible disappointments at the short span of the Reconstruction Period, the newly freed exploited it to their fullest. First and foremost came education, not only as a pragmatic investment but also as a moral crusade to uplift and redefine a people. It also included reconstituting families and searching for long lost members.

Loss, Sorrow, and Cultural Amnesia

As Black newspapers were quickly developed, they contained numerous announcements seeking to reunite families. An example of such an ad appeared in the *Colored Tennessean* in 1865 stating:

> Information is wanted of my two boys. James and Horace. One of whom was sold in Nashville and the other was sold in Rutherford County. I, myself, was sold in Nasville and sent to Alabama, by Wm Boyd.... Ps. Any information sent to the Colored Tennessean office, Box 1150 will be thankfully received.
> (Williams, 2012, p. 186)

Thornton Cope would search for his mother for more than twenty years and Charity Moss ventured to find her sons despite her journey of many miles since she last saw them (Williams, 2012). Despite many years of determined searching, most searches ended in sorrowful disappointment. Much progress was, nonetheless, achieved by Black people and their vision was forward looking, as slavery was now a thing of the past. As Booker T. Washington (1901/1989) noted, slavery was "something to be forgotten and left behind like a dead skin" (p. 19). This forgetting of slavery would quickly become culturally sanctioned and motivated by Blacks and Whites for different reasons that would ultimately cause a revision to the meaning of slavery for the nation. Black churches served as the bedrock for cultural advancement, moral support, and political liberation for Black people, and they were quite insistent that the "ole spirituals" sung during slavery be removed from their hymn books (Berlin, 1998). Du Bois had referred to these as the "Sorrow Songs," which he described as the "...echo of haunting melody from the only American music which welled up from Black souls in the dark past" (1961, p. xiv). Later, this exclusion would also come to include the gospel blues (Harris, 1992) and ragtime blues, constituting a kind of cultural purging of the collective memory of slavery. In interview, Sarah Debro noted, "I's lived near about 90 years, and I's seen and heard much. My folks don't want me to talk about slavery, they's shame niggers ever was slaves..." (Hurmence, 1984, p. 61) The abrupt end and failure of Reconstruction, in effect, was an economic compromise between the North and the South (DuBois, 1935; Foner, 2005). Dreams of full participation in American democracy were violently suppressed by institutional terrorism, including loss of the right to vote, massive imprisonment for those without work, physical destruction of self-sustaining Black communities, birth of the Ku Klux Klan, and the lynching of thousands. Once again, the might of the nation's scientific, religious, academic, and arts establishments was used to denigrate and humiliate Black people as innately inferior. It is this sequestering of the collective memory, together with the abject failure of Reconstruction, as well as its humiliating and terrorizing aftermath, that set the tone for the unresolved trauma of African Americans today. In *Trauma and recovery*, Herman (1992) explains that trauma shatters connections among people and their communities, resulting in a crisis of faith. She insists on three basic requirements for recovery from trauma: the establishment of safety; reconstruction of trauma narrative; and reconnecting survivors to each other and to their community. Herman also describes how silence is the usual response to atrocity and, as is well established in trauma literature, this leads to trauma symptoms and intergenerational transmission. The immediate goals of Black people were physical and psychological survival. Many of those who could, moved north, fearing the re-institution of slavery (Painter, 1976), and the bulk of their energies went into carving out a new racial identity against both the history of their enslavement and against the new national tsunami of racial denigration. One of the ways public opinion was fashioned against Blacks during this period was through the construction of national and state memorials, monuments, and statues honoring their respective military leaders and battlefields (Eyerman, 2001). No monuments were ever built to acknowledge those who were enslaved and their accomplishments. Volkan (1977) views the building of monuments and the like after traumatic events as a psychological necessity. Their perceived indestructibility affords those who were victimized a psychological containing function that also sustains and regulates emotions. Thus, the collective memory of slavery was consigned to entombment as America's "skeleton in the closet" (Fredrickson, 2000).

The crucial importance of collective memory is actively demonstrated in the refusal of Jewish people to allow the Holocaust to fall into a universal amnesia, as expressed in the aphorism, "Never forget," as well as in the construction of Holocaust memorials and museums. Prior to claiming this legacy, Jews who survived the Holocaust were subjected to a conspiracy of silence resulting in additional clinical trauma by having their voices muted. Volkan (1997) suggests that children become the reservoir for unresolved and unacceptable mental representations of the trauma of previous generations who have been unable to come to terms with issues of humiliation and loss. The children absorb their elders' traumatized parts and then bear the burden of completing the task that their forebears were unable to resolve. These mental representations or traumatized self-images are continuously passed from one generation to the next and are constituted by shared feelings, perceptions, fantasies, and interpretations of the calamity. In what may be viewed as a radical approach to generational transmission of trauma, Abraham and Torok (1994) suggest that, during treatment, psychoanalytic inquiry must move beyond the individual patient because they believe that some patients have inherited the "secret psychic substance" of their ancestors. Thus the analyst must listen for phantom voices from different generations in the patient under treatment. The process of therapy includes uncovering shameful secrets and understanding nameless and undisclosed suffering. This, Abraham and Torok believe, will assist the patient in remembering the past, recalling what was taken, and understanding and mourning what was lost, so that healing can begin. The group psychoanalyst Earl Hopper seems to have a similar notion in mind when he asserts, "People and groups must always be located within their foundation matrices. It is necessary to think in terms of horizontal depth. Within the infinite context of time and space, the self belongs mostly to others, who may have lived far away and long ago" (2003, p. 19). Through their narratives, the voices of those who were formerly enslaved speak painfully of loss, shame, and grief as well as of a profound need to develop a positive identity in a "land without sanctuary" due to their "unforgiveable Blackness."

The accomplishments of African Americans are significant, but some aspirations remain unfulfilled to this day. Each succeeding generation has in some form championed these tasks; however, their legacy has not been successfully redeemed. That which remains unclaimed, without a collective narrative, constitutes a breach with our past, and it is filled with haunting blood memories, whose lease must expire for the wellbeing of the African American community to be realized. From a psychoanalytic perspective, I suggest we first appreciate what impediments may deter our thinking about slavery and how that may be made manifest psychosocially. It is also important to understand racism as a major organizing principle in American society, as Pinderhughes (2004) explains. Because of the imperative of survival, we, Black Americans, have colluded in our own invisibility by shrouding painful and degrading aspects of our past and placing our faith in the future. However, it is also important to note as Grand (2000) stated, that "...forgetting is the first condition of evil's dissociative contagion" (p. 153). While teaching at Howard University in the 1950s, the Black sociologist E. Franklin Frazer requested those students who were descendants of slaves to raise their hands. He acknowledged that no student ever raised their hand.

I recall sixty years ago my father's painful confrontation with the past when a picture of my White maternal great-grandfather arrived in the mail. He violently threw it in the garbage, saying that no picture of a White bastard that had preyed on Black women would ever hang in his house. My White great-grandfather had eighteen children by several different Black women, and their descendants are largely divided by color cleavage to this day. Those who pass as White, and those who are very light, go by his surname of Arbuthnot, and the others, including me, are known as Vaughans. It is only now that I am finally able to reach back into that garbage and reclaim that picture as a part of my heritage and as a part of my own identity. One may be tempted to relegate these two examples to ancient history, but please do not. Ten years ago, while conducting research on Black boys, a den mother at Jack and Jill (an upper class social club for Black children), reported the following effort to raise racial consciousness among the Black boys in her care (Vaughans, 2014). She presented them with a very festive lunch, but she divided the group in half, and designated one half as servers, who had to not only serve the other half their lunch, but also could not begin their own lunch until the other half was finished. When it was over, she inquired as to what it was like for them and what social implication it might have. They all agreed that it was totally wrong and unfair and equated it to anti-Semitism and gender bias. None of these children were from economically or academically impoverished backgrounds. A confrontation with my own son challenged my own comforting illusion that I had worked through these issues in my multiple therapies and two personal analyses. The fact of the matter is that the topic of race and the trauma of slavery was never broached in any of those therapies. In chastising my young son David over some misdeed, I asked him "if he was out of his cotton-picking mind." He responded with the perplexed inquiry, "Dad, why would my mind have to be cotton picking?" I apologized to him and assured him that it was my mind that was still "cotton picking," not his; that some injuries just take an awful long time to heal, especially when we are unaware of our wounds. Recall the struggle Black mothers endured over losing parental rights to their own children from having them sold away. For the more economically disadvantaged in the Black community in the United States today, that very struggle continues, as evidenced in the over-representation of Black families in family court, special education, child protective services, as well as the school-to-prison pipeline in the United States. While these agencies can constitute a real threat to the survival of the family and to Black youth, I sense that Black people's fears become confounded by residual anxieties arising from slavery. Often today, when Black parents become highly threatened about their ability to protect or guide their children, you will hear the expression, "I brought you into this world, I will take you out." In the film *The Butler* (Daniels, 2013), the surviving son joins the Black Panther Party and, when the father is unable to dissuade his son, he barks this very threat at him. It is my sense that through this expression Black parents are unknowingly expressing grievances to earlier unacknowledged losses as well as proffering a manic defense against a felt sense of helplessness about the fate of their children, as their forbears had done earlier. During slavery, Black women worked in the fields right beside Black men. However, they were expected to pull double duty by bearing children for the profit of the owner. They continued performing hard labor until the last quarter of the pregnancy. In some of the narratives, enslaved women reported their ability to perform work the equal of any man on the plantation. Today, double duty is still expected of Black Women. They are expected to bear up under any odds and be known as resilient. An analyst colleague of mine commented on "the phantasy that Black women have been through so much, that they are like tempered steel" (Adams, 2001). Clinically, this sometimes appears during the course of treatment with the complaint, "I feel like I am getting weaker."

Treatment Implications

It is paradoxical that Blackness constitutes a most significant element in the lives of Black youth, and that psychoanalytic psychotherapy is the tool for examining one's internal and external world, and yet I am informed by White therapists and by Black boys that race is rarely discussed in treatment. While resistance to such exploration is probably present on both sides of the racial dyad, it is the responsibility of the therapist to acknowledge and invite the oppressed "otherness" into the treatment. Failure to do so constitutes the formulation and maintenance of an "as if" relationship. Hence, the sources of social trauma, degradation, and shame remain outside the purview of the therapeutic situation. This is a modern day version of what Danieli (1984) referred to as a "conspiracy of silence" and is a quiet message to the Black patient that ghosts from past social trauma are too powerful to engage here. These powerful unconscious communications also serve to reinforce stereotypes regarding the toughness of Black males, that Black males should be able to take it if they are man enough. This notion also serves to deny Black boys a crucial developmental stage of "boyhood." Research by Goff et al. (2014) confirms that Black boys in many instances are seen as about four and a half years older than their actual age. Pinderhughes (1989) emphasizes that it is not clinically possible to help patients examine their own cultural identity without therapists having done similar self-examination for themselves. I strongly concur with her definition of race "as entrapment for everyone" (p. 71). I also believe that while the exploration of the impact of living in a racist society is painful and frightening, it is also liberating for the patient, as well as for the therapist.

Conclusion

African Americans proudly celebrate Kwanza, a holiday that combines many African customs and beliefs (Riley, 1995). During this celebration, many Blacks adorn themselves in their finest African garb. This celebration is excellent for acknowledging our African ancestry and the wisdom in its value systems. However, it fails to address the sacrifice, courage, strength, and loss of those who were enslaved on these shores. In order to do so, my colleague Dr. Michael Harris (2006) advises that we would have to adorn ourselves in knapped cotton or burlap in their honor, something my more fashion conscious colleague, Dr. Owens, informs me is not likely to happen, regardless of the worthiness of the cause. While I graciously concede her point, I do not yield on my own point at all. The honoring of our African Heritage appears to highlight a gap in African American consciousness regarding the honoring of those who were enslaved. It is my belief that much stands to be gained from the study of African American slavery, for both Blacks and Whites, that can positively expand how we see ourselves and each other. Fraiberg (1987) talked about ghosts in the nursery, and I have been speaking of ghosts in African American culture whose presence needs acknowledgement in order for us to be truly strengthened by them. Therapeutically, Dimen (1998) describes the psychoanalytic session as an opportunity for the unspeakable to be spoken and the unthinkable to be thought by imagining what was never known and could not be thought. It is time for that silence to be broken and those muted voices be allowed to tell their stories. Examining history from a different perspective can also help facilitate this process. The Black historian John Henrik Clarke (1998) contends that,

> History is a clock that people use to tell their political and cultural time of day. It is also a compass that people use to find themselves on

the map of human geography. History tells a people where they have been, what they have been, where they are, and what they are. Most important, history tells a people where they still must go and what they still must be. The relationship of history to its people is the same as a mother to her child.

Such a perspective can help significantly to alleviate some of the disavowed shame that haunts today's Black youth and can transform the traumatic emotional scars that they bear into a source of new-found strength.

References

Abraham, N. and Torok, M. (1994). *The shell and the kernel*. Chicago: University of Chicago Press.
Adams, M.V. (2001). Personal communication.
Ani, M. (1994). *Let the circle be unbroken*. New York: Nkonimfo Publications.
Berlin, I. (1998). *Remembering slavery*. New York: The New Press.
Berlin, I. (2003). *Generations of captivity: A history of African American slaves*. Cambridge: Belknap Press.
Berlin, I. (2010). *The making of African America: The four great migrations*. New York: Penguin.
Blassingame, J.W. (1977). *Slave testimony: Two centuries of letters, speeches, interviews, and autobiographies*. Baton Rouge: Louisiana State University Press.
Clarke, J.H. (1998). *A great and mighty walk*. (DVD) WBAI Radio 99.5 fm. New York: Dot Media: Cinema Guild.
Danieli, Y. (1984). Psychotherapists' participation in the conspiracy of silence about the Holocaust. *Psychoanalytic Quarterly*, 1, 23–42.
Daniels, L. (Director) (2013). *The butler*. (DVD). The Weinstein Company www.leedanielsthebutlermovie.com.
Dimen, M. (1998). Strange hearts: On the paradoxical liaison between psychoanalysis and feminism. In M. Roth (Ed.), *Freud: Conflict and culture: Essays on his life, work and legacy*. New York: Knopf.
Douglas, F. (1845/2003). *Narrative of the life of Fredrick Douglas: An American slave*. New York: Barnes and Noble.
DuBois, W.E.B. (1935). *Black reconstruction in America*. New York: Russell & Russell.
DuBois, W.E.B. (1961). *The souls of black folk*. New York: Dodd & Mead.
Eyerman, R. (2001). *Cultural trauma: Slavery and the formation of African American identity*. Cambridge: Cambridge University Press.
Fanon, F. (1967). *Blacks skin, white masks*. New York: Grove Press.
Foner, E. (2005). *Forever free: The story of emancipation and reconstruction*. New York: Knopf.
Fraiberg, L. (1987). *Selected writings of Selma Fraiberg*. Columbus: Ohio State University Press.
Franklin, J.H. (2006). Black men, America and the twenty-first-century. Conference keynote address: *Black male youth: Creating a culture of educational success*. Cuny.

Fredrickson, G. (2000). The skeleton in the closet. *New York Review of Books*, 47, 17, 61–66.

Goff, P., Jackson, M., Brooke, A., Cullotta, C. and DiTomasso, N. (2014). The essence of innocence: Consequences of dehumanizing black children. *Journal of Personality and Social Psychology*, 4, 526–545.

Gomez, M. (1998). *Exchanging our country marks: The transformation of African identity in the colonial and ante-bellum South.* Chapel Hill: University of North Carolina Press.

Grand, S. (2000). *The reproduction of evil: A clinical and cultural perspective.* New York: Routledge.

Gump, J. (2010). Reality matters. *Psychoanalytic Psychology*, 27, 42–54.

Harris, M. (1992). *The rise of gospel blues.* New York: Oxford University Press.

Harris, M. (2006). Personal Communication.

Herman, J. (1992). *Trauma and recovery.* New York: Basic Books.

Hopper, E. (2003). *The social unconscious: Speaking the unspeakable: Selected papers of Earl Hopper.* London: Jessica Kingsley Publishers.

Hurmence, B. (1984). *My folks don't want me to talk about slavery.* Winston-Salem: John F. Blair Publisher.

Jacobs, H.A. (1861/987). *Incidents in the life of a slave girl.* Cambridge: Harvard University Press.

Morrison, T. (1992). *Playing in the dark: Whiteness and the literary imagination.* Cambridge: Harvard University Press.

Morrow, A. (2003). *Breaking the curse of Willie Lynch.* Florrissant: Rising Sun Publications.

Moskowitz, M. (2012). Personal Communication.

Painter, N. (1976). *Sojourner truth: A life, a symbol.* New York: Norton.

Patterson, O. (1982). *Slavery and social death.* Cambridge: Harvard Press.

Perdue, C., Barden, T. and Phillips, R. (1976). *Weevils in the wheat.* Charlottesville: University of Virginia Press.

Phillips, U. (1929). *Life and labor in the old South.* New York: Grosset and Dunlap.

Pinderhughes, E. (1989). *Understanding race, ethnicity and power.* New York: Free Press.

Pinderhughes, E. (2004). The multigenerational transmission of loss and trauma: The African American experience. In F. Walsh and M. McGoldrick (Eds.), *Living beyond loss* (pp. 161–181). New York: Norton.

Riley, D.W. (1995). *The complete Kwanza: Celebrating our cultural harvest.* New York: Harper Collins.

Rushdy, A. (2001). *Remembering generations: Race and family in contemporary African American fiction.* Chapel Hill: University of North Carolina.

Sertima, I.V. (1976). *The African presence in Ancient America: They came before Columbus.* New York: Random House.

Stuckey, S. (1987). *Slave culture: Nationalist theory and the foundation of black America.* New York: Oxford University Press.

Tarantino, Q. (Director). (2013). *Django unchained.* (DVD). (Available from Anchor Bay Entertainment, LLC, 9242 Beverly Blvd. Beverly Hills, CA 90210).

Vaughans, K. (2014). Disavowed fragments of the intergenerational transmission of trauma from slavery among African Americans. In K. Vaughans and W. Spielberg (Eds.), *The psychology of black boys and adolescents* (v. 2, pp. 189–208). New York: Praeger.

Volkan, V. (1997). *Blood lines: From ethnic pride to ethnic terrorism.* New York: Farrar, Straus and Giroux.

Washington, B.T. (1901/1989). *Up from slavery: An autobiography.* Williamstown: Corner House Publishers.

Williams, A.H. (2012). *Help me to find my people.* Chapel Hill: University of North Carolina Press.

Yetman, N. (1970). *Voices from slavery.* New York: Holt, Rinehart and Winston.

Part IV

Fragmented Legacies, Healing Narratives

Part II

Introduction

Jill Salberg

The historian Haydon White (1980) considers narrative as much about culture as it is about humanness. He writes, "Far from being a problem, then, narrative might well be considered a solution to a problem of general human concern, namely, the problem of how to translate *knowing* into telling" (pg. 5). Bedtime stories, a classic example, are a cross-cultural ritual, one that may help parents as much as it does children. Parents feel the need to give their children something to last them through the long dark night of separation. They want them to feel safe, to feel loved and cared for. Culture becomes imparted in the stories told. We unknowingly impart our innermost selves hidden in the timbre of our voices, in the choice of stories we pick, where we start and where we end these stories. Children desire a ritual allowing them to extend both the day and the time being close with their parents. But what exactly is the use they make of our stories, both those told and the ones not able to be told?

It is not a stretch to imagine that these early "told" stories help perform the educative work of teaching narrative making to children. They instruct how to organize facts, events and feelings into a coherent story. Slade (1996, 2002) sees the development of self-narratives as universal but also illustrative of the early maturational environment and its capacity to regulate, modulate, organize, soothe and ultimately make meaning of the experiences of the child. She argues,

> What I want to suggest here is that the infant's experience of care seeking and regulation in relation to the caregiver forms the semantic base of the grammar of self-narratives. Arousal and the need for care is the infant's "trouble," and a self-story or self-representation is a way of encoding the dynamic relation between the self, the other, and the resolution of that trouble.
>
> (pg. 5)

However, under traumatic circumstances the "trouble" that Slade is referencing increases exponentially. Under the great stress of trauma, telling becomes difficult, problematic and at times impossible, while *knowing* can become a dangerous enterprise. What undergirds this all is the human need for a narrative that makes sense. Reis (2015) reminds us that: "What's helpful, it turns out, is having a coherent story, a working story – one that hangs together without contradiction" (pg. 343). With trauma it is no longer an easy flow from experience, to thought then to word. Telling one's story becomes fraught.

As we now know, massive trauma disrupts the normal processes of mind by flooding us with affects and experiences that cannot be contained and turned easily into memory stories. To protect ourselves we fragment, dissociate, disavow so as to function and exist.[1] Laub and Podell (1995) provide a compelling example:

> In 1986, an 18-year-old Cambodian boy was referred to an analyst for consultation. In the first meeting he asked for help in writing his memoirs.
>
> When the analyst asked him what he recalled, he came up with very little. He did not remember the names of his family, his own name, his town, or his past. The only clear memory was an execution scene ... Other than the memory of this mass execution; the boy could summon no memories.
>
> (pg. 991)

Remembering and forgetting are intertwined and inter-implicated. Why did he not dissociate the horrific mass execution scene? Why could he not remember much else, his family, his name, the name of his village? I believe he lost his own capacity to keep his personal narrative alive when subjected to such brutal and horrific loss. He survived but at what cost we may ask? And at what cost to the next generation if he grows up and has children of his own?

The resilience involved with surviving massive trauma may also be seen in the ways in which people take the fragmented pieces of what they carry in their minds and attempt to heal and make meaning of the trauma. Sophia Richman (2014) has been researching and writing about how creative arts are crucial ways in which we can heal ourselves. She writes, "It is my contention that through the creation of art it is possible to maintain an attachment to the lost object and preserve meaning and dialogue that has been threatened with rupture" (pg. 87). Further, she argues that all kinds of creative expression – literary, visual/artistic, music and performance – all of them are powerful avenues leading to increased expressiveness and narrative formation.

Another way of framing these polarities might be to see how the capacity to tell a personal story becomes the basis for selfhood. Meares (1998) describes a flat record of events as a *chronicle*, which does not reflect the internal experience or world of the person. If the experience is more of a traumatic one, then the story is even further compromised, has less complexity and Meares refers to it as a *script*. Both, chronicles and scripts, are distinguished from narrative forms which are more complex and reflective stories; true narratives. Grand (2009) portrays it as: "It is *authored* by an agentic self; it is constructed in relationship to the inner and outer worlds" (pg. 16). Repetition of an unhealed wound or re-traumatization will proceed through chronicles and scripts, while true narrative acts to prevent re-experiencing or re-enacting the trauma. True narrative reflects the repair and resilience that the internal work of deep healing has done. In this part of the book we take up the issue of the shattering or breaking of one's ability to tell one's story, seeing chronicles and scripts and the finding of the many forms that healing narratives can take.

One of our aspirations in this book was to give space to and recognition of atrocities and genocides that sometimes can be under-considered. The Holocaust, after many years of denial surrounding the trauma and its legacy, has now begun to be extensively witnessed and studied. We now have these tools from the work accomplished on Holocaust study and it was a goal to give space and recognition to other groups of people who have suffered. Part and parcel of healing from the trauma of war, genocide and the inter-generational transmission effects is when there is recognition of the trauma and its injustice with some mechanism of repair or restitution. Denial of atrocities and the extent that deeply seated hatred can fuel violence has sadly led to further genocides. The massacres that occurred in history keep repeating; be it fueled by nationalistic zeal or religious extremism to name just two sources of genocide in the twentieth and twenty-first centuries.

The chapters in this part of the book focus on some of the less recognized traumas and genocides of Native Americans, Armenians and Koreans. (There are many more but space prevents exhaustive coverage.)

They involve violence perpetrated against a "people" that remain at the heart of genocide: the eradication of the value, culture and humanity of a group of people. The generations that follow the victimization reverberate these horrors and yet we can see in varied ways how children and grandchildren begin and take up the task of healing. This can take many forms, but in its most basic sense it involves creating a narrative that is no longer fragmented. It is the telling of a story that bears the pain and the strength of resilience.

This work can be seen in the ongoing research of Maria Yellow Horse Brave Heart and her co-authors (Josephine Chase, Jennifer Elkins and Deborah B. Altschul) who have for years worked with Native American and indigenous populations to document trans-generational historical trauma and to help revive rituals originally part of tribal life. These healing rituals had been banned during years of governmental control over Native American life and had become forgotten or lost to many tribes. We can see the healing value in Eric V. Hachikian's use of composing music to re-imagine his grandmother and her family's trauma during the awful death march that Turkey enforced on the Armenian people of Amasyia. Hachikian goes further by making a documentary while visiting his family's home, trying to find traces of Armenian life in Turkey as well as writing about the traces of trauma in his family. We see how stories are fragmented, dissociated and secrets are maintained. In Marie Myung-Ok Lee's chapter we can see how a writer who relies on narrative is able to hold her mother's trauma by giving her a fuller story, by becoming a witness to the loss of family, home and country. We can feel the resilience in many of these stories and efforts.

And so the last part of this book brings us up against further genocides and more inhumanity visited against the "other." We hope these chapters stimulate an increase in our readers' empathic responsiveness. We believe this empathic capacity is the necessary bridge to rebuild our human connections and communities. We need to foster and see resilience that people have in the face of trauma and how they creatively work on healing. It can take multiple generations for healing to occur.

Note

1 Much has been written about the break in narrative making that occurs for people who have survived massive trauma (see Laub & Auerhahn, 1993; Laub, 1998; Laub & Podell, 1995; and others).

References

Grand, S. (2009). *The Hero in the Mirror: From Fear to Fortitude*. London & New York: Routledge.

Laub, D. (1998). "The Empty Circle: Children of Survivors and the Limits of Reconstruction." *Journal of the American Psychoanalytic Association*, 46: 507–529.

Laub, D. & Auerhahn, N. (1993). "Knowing and not Knowing Massive Psychic Trauma: Forms of Traumatic Memory." *International Journal of Psychoanalysis*, 74: 287–302.

Laub, D. & Podell, D. (1995). "Art and Trauma." *International Journal of Psychoanalysis*, 76: 991–1005.

Meares, R. (1998). "The Self in Conversation: On Narratives, Chronicles, and Scripts." *Psychoanalytic Dialogues*, 8: 875–891.

Reis, B. (2015). "How Deep the Sky: Discussion of Special Issue on Evolution of Witnessing." *Contemporary Psychoanalysis*, 51 (2): 333–347.

Richman, S. (2014). *Mended By the Muse: Creative Transformations of Trauma*. New York & London: Routledge.

Slade, A. (1996). "A View from Attachment Theory and Research." *Journal of Clinical Psychoanalysis*, 5: 112–122.

Slade, A. (2002). "Moments of Regulation and the Development of Self-Narratives." *Journal of Infant, Child and Adolescent Psychotherapy*, 2: 1–10.

White, H. (1980). "The Value of Narrativity in the Representation of Reality." *Critical Inquiry*, 7 (1): 5–27.

Chapter 12

Historical Trauma Among Indigenous Peoples of the Americas
Concepts, Research, and Clinical Considerations

Maria Yellow Horse Brave Heart, Josephine Chase, Jennifer Elkins, and Deborah B. Altschul

Indigenous Peoples of the Americas[1] are a diverse population, with over 500 federally recognized tribes in the United States and over 400 in Latin America. Indigenous Peoples have experienced pervasive and cataclysmic collective, intergenerational massive group trauma and compounding discrimination, racism, and oppression. There is insufficient data on emotional responses to collective trauma and losses among Indigenous Peoples and how best to intervene in order to alleviate psychological suffering and unresolved grief. A long-term goal of historical trauma intervention practice is to reduce emotional suffering among Indigenous Peoples of the Americas by developing culturally responsive interventions driven by the community to improve behavioral health.

American Indians and Alaska Natives[2] are one segment of the Indigenous Peoples of the Americas. American Indians/Alaska Natives rank higher in health disparities than any other racial or ethnic group in the United States. American Indians face emotional challenges such as depression, substance abuse, collective trauma exposure, interpersonal losses and unresolved grief, and related problems within the lifespan and across generations (Beals et al. 2005; Manson et al. 2005, 1996; Whitbeck et al. 2004a, b; Brave Heart 2003, 1998). Although there is a paucity of research among Indigenous Peoples living within the United States, some studies indicate elevated levels of PTSD and depression among both American Indians and Alaska Natives (Manson et al. 2005) and Indigenous Peoples from Latin America (Sabin et al. 2003). In addition,

---

Reprinted with kind permission:
Brave Heart, M. Y. H., Chase, J., Elkins, J. & Altschul, D. (2100). Historical Trauma Among Indigenous Peoples of the Americas: Concepts, Research, and Clinical Considerations. *Journal of Psychoactive Drugs*, 43 (4): 282–290.

substance abuse is a significant problem (Walters 2004), with death from alcohol-related causes being five times more likely for American Indians than for White Americans. Additionally, suicide rates are 50 percent higher than the national average (U.S. DHHS 2001). Thus, there is an urgent need to reduce racial and ethnic health disparities, which have a significant public health impact, through designing effective interventions with American Indians/Alaska Natives (Wallerstein & Duran 2011). In order to develop culturally resonant interventions for Indigenous Peoples, more information is needed regarding collective as well as individual lifespan trauma, grief, and loss in this diverse population who have faced histories of genocide, colonization, forced assimilation, and exclusion that undermine intergenerational health and well-being.

Despite the array of tribal cultural practices, many Indigenous Peoples share historical and contemporary experiences, intertribal organizations, and often congruent worldviews and values. With increasing migration to urban areas, approximately 60 percent of American Indians live in cities rather than on reservations (U.S. Census Bureau 2006). Trauma among American Indians/Alaska Natives is pervasive, often related to the mass genocide documented in the literature (Jaimes 1992; Stannard 1992; Hoxie 1989; Legters 1988; Thornton 1987; Prucha 1984; Tanner 1982; Brown 1970). The subsequent communal suffering, cumulative trauma, and prevalence of PTSD in some American Indian communities have been addressed by a few studies and clinical articles (Beals et al. 2005; Manson et al. 2005, 1996; Robin et al. 1997a, b; Robin, Chester, & Goldman 1996). For instance, Whitbeck and colleagues (2004a) found evidence of the impact of historical loss on risks for alcohol abuse among American Indians. The collective traumatic past of American Indians and Alaska Natives and subsequent responses merit consideration in the design and delivery of clinical interventions and research with these populations. Although alcohol remains the most prevalent substance abused by American Indians/Alaska Natives, there is increasing abuse of drugs such as methamphetamines, IV drug use, and risks of needle sharing resulting in devastating illnesses such as HIV/AIDS and hepatitis C. Thus, there is a need to target all substance abuse prevention and early intervention efforts for this population.

This article will review the conceptual framework of historical trauma, current efforts to measure the impact of historical trauma upon emotional distress, and research as well as clinical innovations aimed at addressing historical trauma among American Indians/Alaska Natives and other

Indigenous Peoples of the Americas. We will discuss assessment of historical trauma and implications for research and clinical as well as community interventions, and conclude with recommendations.

Conceptual Framework of Historical Trauma and Historical Trauma Response

Primm and colleagues (2010) note the importance of taking a public health approach to addressing mental health disparities for racial/ethnic minorities, specifically examining the prevalence rates, diagnoses, access to care, and sources of care. Collective, communal, and generational trauma for massively traumatized Indigenous Peoples, as well as ongoing racism, oppression, and discrimination, have been described in the literature in relation to their impact on the prevalence of psychiatric disorders among American Indians/Alaska Natives (Duran & Walters 2004; Duran et al. 1998). Elevated chronic trauma exposure and the high prevalence of DSM IV-TR disorders (including both mental health and substance abuse disorders) have been found among large samples of American Indian adults living on reservations (Beals et al. 2005; Manson et al. 2005; Robin et al. 1997a, b).

Historical trauma (HT) is defined as cumulative emotional and psychological wounding across generations, including the lifespan, which emanates from massive group trauma (Brave Heart 2003, 1998). To our knowledge, the concept of historical trauma among American Indians first appeared in the clinical literature in 1995 (Brave Heart 1998). Historical trauma theory frames lifespan trauma in the collective, historical context, which empowers Indigenous survivors of both communal and individual trauma by reducing the sense of stigma and isolation. *Historical loss* is a term utilized by Whitbeck and colleagues (2004a) in a measure of historical trauma.

The *historical trauma response* (HTR) has been conceptualized as a constellation of features associated with a reaction to massive group trauma. *Historical unresolved grief,* a component of this response, is the profound unsettled bereavement resulting from cumulative devastating losses, compounded by the prohibition and interruption of Indigenous burial practices and ceremonies. Whitbeck and colleagues (2004a) found that thinking about historical trauma is associated with emotional distress, specifically depression and anger. These researchers raised additional important questions for consideration such as: what are the psychological characteristics of people with high levels of perceived loss and what tribal differences contribute to responses to historical trauma. Further considerations include diversity in responses related to being a direct descendant of a historically traumatic event or more recent collective trauma. For example, some boarding schools were reportedly more traumatic and attendance was more widespread in some tribal communities. Additionally there may be regional and cultural tribal factors that impact the magnitude of historically traumatic events and responses to them (e.g., there are some regions where tribes may currently be experiencing higher degrees of discrimination and oppression and there is a need to understand how this impacts HTR). Thus, studies are needed to determine the prevalence of HTR and the diversity among tribal groups regarding historical trauma exposure. There has been a groundswell of positive reactions to the concept of historical trauma (Whitbeck et al. 2004a) as evidenced by significant requests for workshops and training on this topic across tribes throughout the United States and Canada, the number of "hits" on the website www.historicaltrauma.com, an increase in literature on this topic, and local as well as national and international conferences about historical trauma and related topic areas. Research is needed about the prevalence and characteristics of HTR as well as the effectiveness of the HT intervention strategies now in use.

Relationship of Current Bereavement and Historical Trauma: Clinical Implications

Many Indigenous communities experience multiple traumatic deaths with great frequency due to elevated morbidity and mortality rates, lowered life expectancy, and high accidental death rates. Most grief research focuses on marital bereavement (Sanders 1989) rather than the extensive premature and traumatic losses faced by Indigenous Peoples. Brave Heart's conceptual model is that HT and HTR are strongly related to the experience of lifetime traumatic events and that both are related to a series of psychological outcomes for individuals including unresolved grief, complicated/prolonged grief, PTSD, and depression, all of which are often comorbid with substance abuse. The major mechanisms for ameliorating these results include developing functional support systems and returning the individual to a sacred path as defined by their particular tribal culture. The hope is to demonstrate that this relationship exists and then develop interventions to alter functional support systems and increase the individual's participation in traditional culture. The eventual outcome will be reductions in behavioral health consequences.

Traditional American Indian/Alaska Native mourning practices and cultural protective factors were impaired due to the federal prohibition around 1883 against the practice of traditional ceremonies, which lasted until the 1978 American Indian Religious Freedom Act. However, parts of Indigenous practices related to traditional burials are still not permitted. Importantly, when members of Indigenous communities experience death of close attachment figures, the intense positive attachment to the deceased may be a risk factor for complicated or prolonged grief (Shear et al. 2011). For American Indian/Alaska Natives, the quality and intensity of interpersonal attachment is of great importance for conceptualizing Indigenous bereavement and providing effective strategies for coping with loss not only in the lifespan but across generations. For example, a tradition in some tribal groups is to cut the hair when a close relative dies, a manifestation of the degree of attachment and a sense of a loss of part of oneself. Addressing grief and loss must incorporate an understanding of traditional normative grief resolution along with modern practices within each tribal community.

The degree of interpersonal losses and trauma exposure in a number of American Indian/Alaska Native communities has been documented (Manson et al. 2005). More research is needed regarding the relationship between this trauma exposure and risk factors for PTSD, prolonged grief, substance abuse, and depression, to elucidate some of these relationships and to facilitate development of interventions to address root causes of behavioral health needs. To date, interventions that reframe symptoms in terms of collective responses have been observed to alleviate a number of the symptoms at least on a short-term basis (Brave Heart 2003, 1998). Such interventions also focus on the cumulative generational impact of compulsory Indian boarding schools which may negatively influence the quality of parental interaction with children, and contribute to unresolved or prolonged grief, depression, substance abuse, and other behavioral health issues (Whitbeck et al. 2004b; Brave Heart 2003, 1998). Addressing parental trauma and generational boarding school issues for parents may help to improve parenting skills and reduce behavioral health risks for children.

Relationship between PTSD, Depression and Historical Trauma

In their studies on PTSD among a Southwestern tribe, Robin, Chester, and Goldman (1996) asserted the need to describe the collective and communal trauma of American Indians related to the historical past and ongoing impact of oppression and racism. Manson and colleagues (1996) posit that American Indian youth may demonstrate higher thresholds for trauma and PTSD due to chronic and severe trauma exposure, cultural manifestations of trauma responses that may be different, and/or PTSD assessment instruments that may be biased. Although this study found a lower prevalence of PTSD than expected for American Indian boarding school adolescents, other studies have found elevated rates of PTSD among American Indians (Beals et al. 2005).

The original intent of HT was to frame current trauma exposure within the context of historical trauma to reduce stigma about emotional distress and responses to individual trauma, as well as highlight intergenerational collective trauma. The intent of HT and HTR is to foster healing by providing a context for the extreme emotional distress found in American Indian and Alaskan Native communities.

Historical Trauma Measures to Inform Clinical and Community-Based Practices

Whitbeck and colleagues (2004a) developed the Historical Loss Scale (HLS) and the Historical Loss and Associated Symptoms Scale (HLAS) and moved the field forward in terms of empirical evidence demonstrating a link between the trauma of a collective historical past and the emotional experiences of the HTR, compounded by lifespan trauma. HLS assesses the frequency with which people think about the historically traumatic events and losses, and HLAS is designed to capture emotional responses to these losses. Whitbeck and colleagues (2004a) found that the higher the score was for perceived historical loss, the more likely was the report of depression and anger associated with the thoughts about that historical loss. Broader use of HLS and HLAS with different tribal groups would increase our knowledge of the prevalence of HT consciousness and HTR among American Indians/Alaska Natives.

Moving Research Forward: Development of the Indigenous Peoples of the Americas Survey

The collective, intergenerational massive group trauma and compounding discrimination, racism, and oppression among American Indians (Whitbeck et al. 2002) as well as unresolved grief and loss (Whitbeck et al. 2004a; Brave Heart 1998) are increasingly a focus of attention in the literature, in the field, and in tribal communities. Whitbeck and colleagues (2004b) examined the impact of discrimination on the collective issues facing a northern Midwest reservation group and identified that perceived historical loss affected American Indian adolescent depression in that tribal community (Whitbeck 2011). Importantly, neither the HLS nor the HLAS include a full measure of depressive symptoms or PTSD. Additionally, the HLS and HLAS both examine perceived loss of family ties as a consequence of boarding schools but do not ask the individual respondent about their own specific boarding school trauma or particular family history related to boarding school attendance. Research would be strengthened by adding these areas.

In the Return to the Sacred Path intervention (Brave Heart 1998), the first Historical Trauma and Unresolved Grief Intervention (HTUG), information was collected from participants regarding their own boarding school attendance, generational boarding school family history, and rating of the quality of these experiences. Additional questions included the distance of the boarding school from the home tribal community and the frequency of visits home per year as well as traumatic experiences such as physical and sexual abuse at the school. Such information was useful in helping participants to process their traumatic experiences within the historical collective context and experience cathartic relief and support. In clinically informed intervention research, more specific questions may facilitate increased tailoring of healing approaches.

Indigenous Peoples of the Americas Survey

The Indigenous Peoples of the Americas Survey (IPS) is an instrument in development, which is designed to inform clinical practice and research on the effectiveness of interventions incorporating HTUG. It is also intended to explore tribal diversity in the experiences of HT and HTR so that healing can be tailored to fit a variety of tribal communities. IPS is an effort to fill some of the gaps and answer some of the questions raised in previous sections of this chapter. With service providers in mind and the kind of information needed for clinical intervention, treatment, and counseling, the IPS consolidates other structured measures and assessment tools into a survey (giving credit to and citing these measures), including the HLS and HLAS, and also adds items that provide more detail about tribal identity, traumatic experiences, depressive symptoms, PTSD symptoms, and Indigenous identity. Further, the IPS asks for more detailed trauma history (both lifespan and collective historical trauma), looks at tribal similarities and differences in the experience, and may be useful in clinical settings for treatment planning and intervention. IPS will also provide a better sense of the prevalence of HTR and symptoms across multiple tribal populations. Identifying constructs that may be generalizable to numerous tribal groups would be helpful in informing the design of culturally responsive clinical practice for this traditionally underserved population. The authors, as clinicians and clinical and services researchers in tribal communities, are concerned with the application of HT concepts to intervention work. The IPS asks about specific losses the individual has experienced themselves as well as the collective past and unresolved, prolonged grief.

IPS will also provide preliminary data on the nature and prevalence of the emotional challenges (depression, collective trauma exposure, interpersonal losses, and unresolved grief) facing Indigenous parents, which is useful in informing the development of an intervention designed to improve behavioral well-being, parental competence, and relationships with children. Earlier versions of the IPS were reviewed by Indigenous clinical graduate students and Indigenous providers. Currently, the IPS is in the process of review by an Indigenous advisory panel and will be piloted and then refined. Preliminary development of the IPS was grounded in prior work, including a qualitative study on the experience of HT and manifestations of HTR (Brave Heart 2000).

The precedent for designing the IPS was to examine collective trauma and commonalities, while simultaneously respecting diversity among Indigenous Peoples across the Americas. This precedent emerged from an orientation that we are relatives, and is consistent with a variety of Indigenous organizations that have developed linkages across the Canada–United States border and extended into Mexico, and Central and South America. These associations include the International Indian

Treaty Council and the Inter-American Indian Institute in Mexico City, as well as global Indigenous organizations and conferences (e.g., the Healing Our Spirit Worldwide Conference, and the United Nations Permanent Forum on Indigenous Issues).

In addition to the work of the National Aboriginal Health Organization in Canada on residential (boarding) school trauma, there has been some research on Indigenous Peoples of Latin American related to historical trauma, including the impact of unresolved grief, collective trauma, and behavioral health issues among Maya survivors and descendants of genocide in Guatemala and parts of Mexico (Sabin et al. 2003; Beristain, Paez, & González 2000). There is a need for further study to inform interventions with these underserved Indigenous populations (Gone & Alcántara 2007). Similarly, Maya Indians from Guatemala and Chiapas in Mexico have been found to suffer from collective and ongoing trauma and prolonged grief symptoms (Sabin et al. 2003; Beristain, Paez, & González 2000). The IPS will contribute to increased knowledge across Indigenous communities and the sharing of clinical healing approaches.

The Historical Trauma and Unresolved Grief Intervention

HTUG Intervention is a short-term, culturally congruent intervention for grief resolution and trauma mastery that has been shown to be effective among a small segment of the American Indian population with elevated psychosocial issues (Brave Heart 1998). Measures include an experimental Lakota Grief Experience Questionnaire (LGEQ) and an instrument exploring respondent's traumatic experiences including boarding school attendance and a self-report assessment of that experience, as well as projective measures. HTUG was selected as a Tribal Best Practice in 2009 by First Nations Behavioral Health Association and the Substance Abuse and Mental Health Services Administration (SAMHSA), and has been incorporated as part of a Lakota parenting prevention intervention and used with Lakota parents on the reservation (Brave Heart 1999b). Qualitative results revealed that self-perceptions of competency in parenting increased after the intervention as did improved relationships with children, parents, grandparents, and extended kinship networks. Increased use of traditional language and enhanced valuing of the tribal culture were also found in this study. The intervention was structured around the view that parents are wounded by HT, specifically the generational impact of boarding schools. Thus, parents need support to address their own trauma before being emotionally present for their children and being able to absorb parenting skill training.

HTUG has been utilized primarily with reservation-based American Indians/Alaska Natives across the U.S. and Canada but little work has been evaluated with urban communities or with Indigenous Peoples of Latin America. The intent of the IPS is to collect data on multiple tribal communities in both reservation and urban settings in order to increase further understanding of the impact of collective group trauma and lifespan trauma exposure on behavioral health symptoms, and to inform culturally responsive interventions with greater scientific rigor. A modification of the Harvard Trauma Questionnaire (HTQ) has been utilized with Maya genocide survivors, including translation into local Spanish dialect and Maya (Sabin et al. 2003). The HTQ items are incorporated into the IPS.

To our knowledge, the only intervention study reported in the literature that specifically focuses on the HTR among an Indigenous population in the United States was a study of the HTUG Intervention (Brave Heart 1999a, b, 1998). However, a number of prevention studies incorporate some consideration of HT in the intervention design. For instance, one tribal-specific prevention intervention includes culturally specific assessment, recognizes historical and cultural contextual factors, and allows for traditional healing approaches (Fisher & Ball 2002). Healing intergenerational pain is perceived as one way to prevent suicide (Strickland, Walsh, & Cooper 2006) and one small qualitative study explored perceptions of effective traditional healing components among Indigenous Peoples in Canada (McCabe 2007). These studies point to the importance of incorporating HT and HTR into treatment and prevention interventions.

Incorporation of Indigenous customs and traditional healing approaches when developing interventions with Indigenous Peoples are increasingly advocated by Indigenous scholars, clinicians, and prevention specialists. Some of the tenets of Indigenous healing practices (Struthers, Eschiti, & Patchell 2004) may be congruent with some methods of evidence-based treatments which could be adapted for application to diverse populations (e.g., Interpersonal Psychotherapy; Markowitz et al. 2009). Thus, incorporation of indigenous customs and traditional healing approaches is also indicated.

Current Practice Concerns

Current Practice Concerns: Addressing Shared Experiences

Although there are tribal differences in the degree of collective generational trauma exposure there is also a similarity among Indigenous Peoples and an emphasis on shared values and traditions. Certainly tribes share a history of colonization, genocide, oppression, and racism. However, some tribal groups have suffered greater numbers of traumatic events. Unifying bodies (e.g., the United Nations Permanent Forum on Indigenous Issues), conferences, and associations that span across borders seek to transcend tribal differences. However, research and interventions must simultaneously respect this collective philosophy and worldview as well as tribal cultural distinctiveness and differing degrees of trauma exposure. The key to effective intervention development is to develop interventions models that may be generalizable to many tribal groups and, at the same time, adaptable for tribal cultural and historical specificity.

Although there are numerous linguistic and cultural differences within Indigenous populations there are some common cultural features that might inform intervention design, including: focus on a collectivist culture; indirect communication styles; focus on harmony and balance; shared traditional beliefs in the existence of animal spirits as guides, ancestor spirits, and feeding the spirits; and attachment to all of creation (Brave Heart 2001a, b; Rousseau, Morales, & Foxen 2001; Beristain, Paez, & González 2000). Thus, interventions must be developed with the involvement of the Indigenous community.

Current Practice Concerns: Multilevel or Systemic Assessment

Historical trauma is a meaningful concept that resonates with Indigenous communities. There is a need for attention to communal oppression, collective trauma, and cultural distinctions in understanding and measuring trauma responses and unresolved grief (Robin, Chester, & Goldman 1996; Lykes 1994; Zur 1994). While group interventions show great promise, there is also a need to develop individual and family interventions.

Steps to doing this would involve gathering more exploratory data, designing interventions in partnership with Indigenous community members as consultants and advisors, testing these interventions, refining them, and then researching these interventions.

Another part of the process in alleviating the emotional suffering of Indigenous Peoples is validating the existence of not only the traumatic history but the continuing oppression. The Lakota, for instance, share the challenges of mourning mass graves, of the lack of proper burials, of massive collective traumatic losses, and of ongoing oppression and discrimination. Other tribal groups deal with traumatic histories as well (e.g., the Sand Creek Massacre of the Cheyenne, the Long Walk of the Navajo, and the Trail of Tears of the Cherokee). The United States was the last member of the United Nations to acknowledge human rights violations through the signing of the UN Declaration on the Rights of Indigenous Peoples (adopted in 2007). Official recognition of genocide is thought to be an important part of the healing process, and should be incorporated in multilevel interventions.

Evans-Campbell (2008) has articulated the need for multilevel assessment and intervention strategies to address HT at individual, family, and community levels. The interrelationship of these levels has significant implications for clinical approaches to healing. A major challenge among clinicians and researchers is the ability not only to discern detrimental effects but also to identify and maximize areas of strengths and resilience.

Current Practice Concerns: Need for Family and Community Level Interventions

Boarding school attendance affected entire family systems; individual and family relationships; family, community, and cultural attachments; and interpersonal communication (Abadian 2008; Barnard 2007; Mooradian, Cross, & Stutzky 2007; Grandbois 2005; Schafor, Horejsi, & Horejsi 1997; Mannes 1995; Morrissette 1994). Chase (2011) found that students who experienced harsh parenting both at home and at boarding schools reported continued difficulty with trust, relationship building, parenting, and communication. Poor parenting fell on a continuum from lack of involvement to neglectful to abusive. It appears that parents who experienced harshness at boarding schools but felt loved at home were either indulgent with their own children in reaction to their own childhood experiences, or they were more balanced in their care and supervision as parents. Likewise, some students who had difficult home situations but positive experiences at boarding school had the experience of "family" with the other students and care from school staff. However, most students failed to develop appropriate nurturing and discipline skills. Clearly, clinical interventions are needed at the family level to address parenting issues that arose from the boarding school experience.

Similar to findings in earlier studies, Chase (2011) found that individuals first identify historical traumatic events, including boarding school, as important factors in the deterioration of American Indian/ Alaska Native values. Earlier studies also found that individuals recognize the validity of traditional Indigenous culture and practices for a path to healing and recovery. Several researchers and practitioners have written about the consideration of intergenerational effects of historical events and historical trauma on American Indian families. For instance, with sibling groups attending boarding school together, older siblings often took on parental and protective roles for younger siblings and relatives, and this relationship continued after boarding school departure. In addition, being separated from parents and other siblings often negatively affected relations with family members when students returned home (Child 1998; Adams 1995; Hultgren & Fairbanks 1994), resulting in alienation and detachment between boarding school alumni and their home community. However, the strong bonds of kinship, the resilience of the individual students, and culture most often supported the adjustment and reintegration of boarding school alumni. This was due to the fact that individuals perceived their relationships with parents and siblings to have changed during their tenure at boarding school (Chase 2011).

Future research should include the examination of the spectrum of trauma in communities, and distinguish historic events that affect individuals, families, and communities, and the array of responses to those events. Cultural groups that have experienced collective trauma, oppression, and racism are recognizing the intergenerational effects of trauma, and that healing must begin within a culture-specific context both at the family and community levels (Schafor, Horejsi, & Horejsi 1997; Williams & Ellison 1996; Xuequin et al. 1998). Thus, it is important to consider culturally appropriate approaches to engaging communities and gaining community buy-in and ownership when developing interventions that can impact communities at the macro level.

Conclusions and Recommendations

American Indians/Alaska Natives have experienced devastating collective, intergenerational massive group trauma and compounding discrimination, racism, and oppression. There is increasing evidence of emotional responses to collective trauma and losses among Indigenous Peoples, which may help to inform ways of alleviating psychological suffering and unresolved grief. Tribal cultural and regional differences exist which may impact how the wounding across generations and within an individual's lifespan are experienced and addressed. A long-term goal of historical trauma intervention research and practice is to reduce emotional suffering among Indigenous Peoples of the Americas by developing culturally responsive interventions driven by the community to improve the quality of life, specifically behavioral health and well-being. Our aim is to restore and empower Indigenous Peoples, to reclaim our traditional selves, our traditional knowledge, and our right to be who we are and should be as healthy, vital, and vibrant communities, unencumbered by depression, overwhelming grief, substance abuse, and traumatic responses. In essence, we strive to transcend our collective traumatic past.

We recommend increased research on the effects of historical trauma in diverse tribal cultural regions, and that such research be driven by Indigenous Peoples and be culturally informed. Further, we advocate for continued development and evaluation of healing intervention models, grounded in Indigenous worldviews, which aim to ameliorate the emotional distress emerging from the legacy of trauma and grief. HT and HTR appear to resonate well with communities. The next step is to determine the empirical effectiveness of related interventions in healing individuals and communities.

Notes

1 *Indigenous Peoples* is the term endorsed by the United Nations Permanent Forum on Indigenous Issues. For the purposes of this article, the term *Indigenous Peoples of the Americas* refers to the original inhabitants of the land area now known as the United States as well as Canada, Mexico, Central, and South America, and their descendants. American Indians and Alaska Natives are included in this larger collective terminology when used.

2 *American Indian and Alaska Native* are the only terms officially endorsed by the National Congress of American Indians and the National Tribal Chairman's Association.

References

Abadian, S. 2008. Trails of tears, and hope. *Harvard Magazine* 3: 39–43, 85–87.
Adams, D.W. 1995. *Education for Extinction: American Indians and the Boarding School Experience, 1875–1928.* Lawrence, KS: University Press of Kansas.
Barnard, A. 2007. Providing psychiatric mental health care for Native Americans: Lessons learned by a non-Native American PMHNP. *Journal of Psychosocial Nursing* 45 (5): 30–35.
Beals, J., Novins, D., Whitesell, N., Spicer, P., Mitchell, C., Manson, S., & AI-SUPERPFP Team. 2005. Prevalence of mental disorders and utilization of mental health services in two American Indian reservation populations: Mental health disparities in a national context. *American Journal of Psychiatry* 162: 1723–1732.
Beristain, C., Paez, D., & González, J. 2000. Rituals, social sharing, silence, emotions and collective memory claims in the case of the Guatemalan genocide. *Psicothema* 12: 117–130.
Brave Heart, M.Y.H. 1998. The return to the sacred path: Healing the historical trauma response among the Lakota. *Smith College Studies in Social Work* 68 (3): 287–305.
Brave Heart, M.Y.H. 1999a. Gender differences in the historical trauma response among the Lakota. *Journal of Health and Social Policy* 10 (4): 1–21.
Brave Heart, M.Y.H. 1999b. Oyate Ptayela: Rebuilding the Lakota Nation through addressing historical trauma among Lakota parents. *Journal of Human Behavior and the Social Environment* 2 (1/2): 109–126.
Brave Heart, M.Y.H. 2000. Wakiksuyapi: Carrying the historical trauma of the Lakota. *Tulane Studies in Social Welfare* 21–22: 245–266.
Brave Heart, M.Y.H. 2001a. Clinical assessment with American Indians. In: R. Fong & S. Furuto (Eds.) *Cultural Competent Social Work Practice: Practice Skills, Interventions and Evaluation.* Reading, MA: Longman Publishers.
Brave Heart, M.Y.H. 2001b. Clinical interventions with American Indians. In: R. Fong & S. Furuto (Eds.) *Cultural Competent Social Work Practice: Practice Skills, Interventions, and Evaluation.* Reading, MA: Longman Publishers.
Brave Heart, M.Y.H. 2003. The historical trauma response among Natives and its relationship with substance abuse: A Lakota illustration. *Journal of Psychoactive Drugs* 35 (1): 7–13.
Brown, D. 1970. *Bury My Heart at Wounded Knee.* New York: Holt, Rinehart & Winston.
Chase, J.A. 2011. Native American elders' perceptions of the boarding school experience on Native American parenting: An exploratory study. Unpublished doctoral dissertation, Smith College, Northampton, MA.
Child, B.J. 1998. *Boarding School Seasons.* Lincoln, NE: University of Nebraska Press.
Duran, B. & Walters, K. 2004. HIV/AIDS prevention in "Indian Country": Current practice, indigenist etiology models, and post-colonial approaches to change. *AIDS Education and Prevention* 16 (3): 187–201.
Duran, E., Duran, B., Brave Heart, M.Y.H., & Yellow Horse-Davis, S. 1998. Healing the

American Indian soul wound. In: Y. Danieli (Ed.) *International Handbook of Multigenerational Legacies of Trauma*. New York: Plenum.

Evans-Campbell, T. 2008. Historical trauma in American Indian/Native Alaska communities: A multilevel framework for exploring impacts on individuals, families, and communities. *Journal of Interpersonal Violence* 23 (3): 316–338.

Fisher, P. & Ball, T. 2002. The Indian family wellness project: An application of the tribal participatory research model. *Prevention Science* 3 (3): 235–240.

Gone, J. & Alcántara, C. 2007. Identifying effective mental health interventions for American Indians and Alaska Natives: A review of the literature. *Cultural Diversity and Ethnic Minority Psychology* 13 (4): 356–363.

Grandbois, D. 2005. Stigma of mental illness among American Indian and Alaska Native Nations: Historical and contemporary perspectives. *Issues in Mental Health Nursing* 26: 1001–1024.

Hoxie, F. 1989. *A Final Promise: The Campaign to Assimilate the Indians, 1880–1920*. Cambridge, MA: Cambridge University Press.

Hultgren, M.L. & Fairbanks, P. 1994. Long rides across the plains: Ft. Berthold students at Hampton Institute. *Journal of the Northern Plains* 61 (2): 10–36.

Jaimes, M. 1992. *The State of Native America: Genocide, Colonization and Resistance*. Boston, MA: South End Press.

Legters, L. 1988. The American genocide. *Policy Studies* 16 (4): 768–777.

Lykes, M. 1994. Terror, silencing and children: International multidisciplinary collaboration with Guatemalan Mayan communities. *Social Science and Medicine* 38: 543–552.

McCabe, G. 2007. The healing path: A culture and community-derived indigenous therapy model. *Psychotherapy: Theory, Research, Practice, Training* 44 (2): 148–160.

Mannes, M. 1995. Factors and events leading to the passage for the Indian Child Welfare Act. *Child Welfare* 74 (1): 264–282.

Manson, S., Beals, J., Klein, S., Croy, C., & AI-SUPERPFP Team. 2005. Social epidemiology of trauma among 2 American Indian reservation populations. *American Journal of Public Health* 95 (5): 851–859.

Manson, S., Beals, J., O'Nell, T., Piasecki, J., Bechtold, D., Keane, E., & Jones, M. 1996. Wounded spirits, ailing hearts: PTSD and related disorders among American Indians. In: A.J. Marsella, M.J. Friedman, E.T. Gerrity, & R.M. Scurfield (Eds.) *Ethnocultural Aspects of Posttraumatic Stress Disorder*. Washington, DC: American Psychological Association.

Markowitz, J.C., Patel, S.R., Balan, I.C., Bell, M.A., Blanco, C., Brave Heart, M.Y.H., Buttacovali Sosa, S., & Lewis-Fernàndez, R. 2009. Toward an adaptation of interpersonal psychotherapy for Hispanic patients with DSM-IV major depressive disorder. *Journal of Clinical Psychiatry* 70 (2): 214–222.

Mooradian, J.K., Cross, S.L., & Stutzky, G.R. 2007. Across generations: Culture, history, and policy in the social ecology of American Indian grandparents parenting their grandchildren. *Journal of Family Social Work* 10 (4): 81–101.

Morrissette, P. 1994. The holocaust of first nation people: Residual effects on parenting and treatment implications. *Contemporary Family Therapy* 16: 381–393.

Primm, A.B., Vasquez, M.J.T., Mays, R.A., Sammons-Posey, D., McKnight-Eily, L.R., Presley-Cantrell, L.R., McGuire, L.C., Chapman, D.P., & Perry, G.S. 2010. The role of public health in addressing racial and ethnic disparities in mental health and mental illness. *Preventing Chronic Disease* 7 (1): 1–7.

Prucha, F. 1984. *The Great Father, Vol. I and II: The United States Government and the American Indians*. Lincoln, NE: University of Nebraska Press.

Robin, R.W., Chester, B., & Goldman, D. 1996. Cumulative trauma and PTSD in American Indian communities. In: A.J. Marsella, M.J. Friedman, E.T. Gerrity, & R.M. Scurfield (Eds.) *Ethnocultural Aspects of Posttraumatic Stress Disorder*. Washington, DC: American Psychological Association.

Robin, R., Chester, B., Rasmussen, J., Jaranson, J., & Goldman, D. 1997a. Factors influencing utilization of mental health and substance abuse services by American Indian men and women. *Psychiatric Services* 48: 826–832.

Robin, R., Chester, B., Rasmussen, J., Jaranson, J., & Goldman, D. 1997b. Prevalence and characteristics of trauma and posttraumatic stress disorder in a southwestern American Indian community. *American Journal of Psychiatry* 154 (11): 1582–1588.

Rousseau, C., Morales, M., & Foxen, P. 2001. Going home: Giving voice to memory strategies of young Mayan refugees who returned to Guatemala as a community. *Culture, Medicine and Psychiatry* 25: 135–168.

Sabin, M., Cardozo, B.L., Nackerud, L., Kaiser, R., & Varese, L. 2003. Factors associated with poor mental health among Guatemalan refugees living in Mexico 20 years after civil conflict. *Journal of the American Medical Association* 290 (5): 635–642.

Sanders, C. 1989. *Grief: The Mourning After: Dealing with Adult Bereavement*. New York: John Wiley & Sons.

Schafor, B.W., Horejsi, C.R., & Horejsi, G.A. 1997. *Techniques and Guidelines for Social Work Practice*. Boston, MA: Allyn & Bacon.

Shear, K., Simon, N., Wall, M., Zisook, S., Neimeyer, R., Duan, N., Reynolds, C., Lebowitz, B., Sung, S., Ghesquiere, A., Gorscak, B., Clayton, P., Ito, M., Nakajima, S., Konishi, T., & Melhem, N. 2011. Complicated grief and related bereavement issues for DSM 5. *Depression and Anxiety* 28 (2): 103–117.

Stannard, D. 1992. *American Holocaust: The Conquest of the New World*. New York: Oxford University Press.

Strickland, C., Walsh, E., & Cooper, C. 2006. Healing fractured families: Parents' and elders' perspectives on the impact of colonization and youth suicide prevention in a Pacific Northwest American Indian tribe. *Journal of Transcultural Nursing* 17: 5–12.

Struthers, R., Eschiti, V.S., & Patchell, B. 2004. Traditional indigenous healing: Part I. *Complementary Therapies in Nursing and Midwifery* 10: 141–149.

Tanner, H. 1982. A history of all the dealings of the United States government with the Sioux. Unpublished manuscript. Prepared for the Black Hills Land Claim by order of the United States Supreme Court, on file at the D'Arcy McNickle Center for the History of the American Indian, Newberry Library, Chicago, IL.

Thornton, R. 1987. *American Indian Holocaust and Survival: A Population History since 1492*. Norman, OK: University of Oklahoma Press.

U.S. Census Bureau. 2006. *We the People: American Indian and Alaska Natives in the United States: Census 2000 Special Reports*. Washington, DC: U.S. Department of Commerce.

U.S. Department of Health and Human Services (DHHS). 2001. *Mental Health: Culture, Race and Ethnicity, A Supplement to Mental Health: A Report of the Surgeon General*. Rockville, MD: DHHS.

Wallerstein, N. & Duran, B. 2011. Community based participatory research contributions to intervention research: The intersection of science and practice to improve health equity. *American Journal of Public Health* 100 (S1): S40–S46.

Walters, K. 2004. *The Impact of Historical Trauma, Microaggressions and Colonial Trauma Response on American Indians/Native American Mental Health and Substance*

Use [powerpoint slides]. Presented at Models for Healing Multicultural Survivors of Historical Trauma Conference, Santa Ana Pueblo, NM.

Whitbeck, L.B. 2011. The beginnings of mental health disparities: Emergent mental disorders among indigenous adolescents. *Health Disparities in Youth and Families* 57: 121–149.

Whitbeck, L., Adams, G., Hoyt, D., & Chen, X. 2004a. Conceptualizing and measuring historical trauma among American Indian people. *American Journal of Community Psychology* 33 (3/4): 119–130.

Whitbeck, L., Chen, X., Hoyt, D., & Adams, G. 2004b. Discrimination, historical loss, and enculturation: Culturally specific risk and resilience factors for alcohol abuse among American Indians. *Journal of Studies on Alcohol* 65 (4): 409–418.

Whitbeck, L., McMorris, B., Hoyt, D., Stubben, J., & LaFramboise, T. 2002. Perceived discrimination, traditional practices, and depressive symptoms among American Indians in the upper Midwest. *Journal of Health and Social Behavior* 43 (4): 400–418.

Williams, E. & Ellison, F. 1996. Culturally informed social work practice with American Indian clients: Guidelines for non-Indian social workers. *Social Work* 41 (2): 147–151.

Xuequin, G., Toubbeh, J., Cline, J., & Chisholm, A. 1998. The use of a qualitative approach in Fetal Alcohol Syndrome prevention among American Indian youth. *Journal of Alcohol and Drug Education* 43 (3): 53–65.

Zur, J. 1994. The psychological impact of impunity. *Anthropology Today* 10 (3): 12–17.

Chapter 13

Growing Up Armenian

Eric V. Hachikian

Throughout my life I've had an implicit, unspoken understanding of what it means to me to be Armenian. Perhaps more specifically I mean how I have always felt as an Armenian who is displaced from his homeland and living in the United States. My identity as an Armenian, including my ancestor's traumas, is woven into my conscious and unconscious mind as strands in the garment of my life.

As a young boy growing up in the suburbs of Boston, I was not aware of why we went to church, why I went to Sunday School, or why everyone around me looked like me, like family. Armenians in the Boston area had gathered in communities, set up schools, churches, and opened restaurants and grocery stores. It unconsciously solidified a feeling in my mind that the world around me was accepting of Armenian culture. My family is unquestionably Armenian; and yet, as I grew older, I began to question the ritualistic gatherings of religion. I began seeing an irony that my parents wanted my brother and I to identify as Armenian and be involved in the Armenian community, but later moved us to a different white, middle-upper class neighborhood. On a surface level, I identified as a white Caucasian male, but we were now living in communities where we were one of four Armenian families in the town. As time went on, I began to wonder what the label Middle Eastern meant. Was it just Armenian, or did it include Turkish and Kurdish, Greek and Israeli?

I didn't fully grasp the concept then, but this assertion of Armenian-ness was one of my first understandings of my family wanting to give a certain presentation of who they were. We were (and are still now) devoted Armenians, strong in culture and religion, and upstanding citizens of the world. Going to church, for lack of a better understanding, was done out of obligation to the previous generations. It is what they did, so it is what we would do. When my grandparents were alive, going to church appeared to be much more important. Later in life I learned that they also had conflicting feelings about religion. The church signified the Armenian community, and as a community we have learned to stay strong by sticking together. When my mother's mother came to this country, they found their relatives on survivor lists in the churches. The church was the essence of connection and in the post-traumatic exile it aided in re-connection. This resulted in an extensive network of relatives, to the point that we joke that all Armenians know each other.

After my family moved from the suburbs of Boston to the suburbs of Chicago, there was very little church in our lives, and very little talk of religion at home. Even amongst my grandparents, it didn't seem like God was the most important part of religion. It had never occurred to me while growing up that we weren't very religious in the traditional sense, because there had been such a ritualistic focus on going to church and Sunday school while we were younger. As my brother and I grew up, being Armenian, that is culturally, felt like its own religion. It was our religion.

As a result, growing up Armenian in the United States meant many things for me: foods with a wide variety of flavors and names, the mixing of more than one language with English, intricate music with rhythms outside of common Western time signatures, and bedtime stories about the Genocide. Each of these segments was engrained in me, creating the whole. And many times, they overlapped: being around my grandparents and their friends meant hearing both Armenian and Turkish spoken, eating whatever delicious homemade delicacy was put in front of me, and listening to them talk about their families while Armenian music played in the background.

The most powerful and enduring stories were about my grandmother Helen. She was forced to leave her home in 1915 when she was 40 days old. I was put to bed with the story of my grandmother being left by the side of the road by Ottoman soldiers for crying too much, only to be saved by her brother and sister who used a piece of candy as a pacifier. Her mother hid gold coins in her diaper as a means of survival, and eventually saved her family's life after three months on a death march by becoming a slave seamstress for the Ottoman army. The moral of this bedtime story was that my grandmother was strong and resilient, and survived, becoming the matriarch of my family. This left me with a complicated understanding of who the Turkish people are, why there is a continued denial of these atrocities, and how I am to grow and identify as an Armenian.

There were paradoxes growing up and ones that continue in my family. My father won't eat at a Turkish restaurant in New York City with me. The menu is almost identical to an Armenian restaurant, with the same names of region specific dishes. But this to him would be a low level of treason against Armenia.

Because this was the culture I grew up in, I didn't fully accept Turkish people or the food myself until I traveled there. As an Armenian, there is a fear and an anger associated against all Turkish people that was taught to me from the moment I was able to understand bedtime stories. Up until traveling to Turkey, my desire was to have the United States, the country my grandmother was forced to relocate to and I subsequently have lived in, recognize that the Armenian Genocide occurred, using the word Genocide to describe accurately the horrific events that resulted in 1.5 million people being massacred.

This remains true, but my understanding of the geopolitical landscape has widened, and I would much rather see the Turkish government recognize the Genocide. The people of Turkey know about the Genocide. There is a large "denialist" and brainwashing regime in place, and if something this horrific can happen once without being officially recognized, it can happen again. Adolf Hitler, in 1939 while preparing to invade Poland wrote: "I have placed my death-head formations in readiness for the present only in the East with orders to them to send to death mercilessly and without compassion, men, women, and children of Polish derivation and language. Only thus shall we gain the living space [*Lebensraum*] which we need. Who, after all, speaks today of the annihilation of the Armenians?"[1]

However, I did not originally find my Armenian identity in politics, or through religion or obligation. I instead found my window into my Armenian soul through the sounds and rhythms of its music, the "different" time signatures and scales. It somehow always felt natural. My formal study of Western music only fueled my desire to learn more about Armenian music. My desire to go back to the birthplace of my grandmother stemmed from the music I wrote to commemorate her life after her death.

My grandmother always encouraged me to pursue my passion of music. I like to think she knew music would help me get in touch with my Armenian soul. During my adolescence, she would often sit and listen to me practice piano for hours. She was my biggest fan, and I often rely on my memory of her for support and inspiration. I continue to marvel at the immense tragedy she survived, and how she could sit peacefully, listening to me practice my music.

Fractures in Our Lives

When Armenians first came to the United States, they needed to find work to support their families. This led to an intense work ethic, which could be easily described as workaholic. They felt that this was the means to survival, and in many ways it was. Most of the men in my family are workaholics, and the women in my family tend to be extremely strong willed, determined, and stubborn. I am sure that my own intense work ethic is something that I learned from seeing the same in my family. However, when I compare it to what my great grandmother and grandmother experienced and had to survive, I am in awe of their survival.

As I grew up, I observed how my family's influence and lives have played out in my own life, from blind acceptance, to rebellion, to repeating the same steps as my ancestors. I often wonder how much is genetic, how much is environmental, how much is learned from the experience itself, and how much I learned from seeing the pain that still existed in my grandmother's bones and soul. I was raised to respect my elders, and I took it upon myself to go beyond that, especially with my grandmother: anything she said was the rule of law. I've subsequently realized that I have a hard time disappointing anyone. I don't always do what I want to do out of a feeling of obligation toward what I was raised to believe as being the "proper" way.

Both my brother and I are happily married to non-Armenian women. We were encouraged to marry an Armenian, but we were encouraged to be happy with our lives. This idea has always struck me as ironic, that the two ideas are related: Armenian-ness and happiness. As an Armenian living in America, I have found happiness inside and outside of my Armenian identity, but they are not mutually exclusive for me.

My wedding took place in an Armenian Apostolic church and was a mostly traditional Armenian religious ceremony. My brother did more or less the same thing, and he's since had a child. My parents, specifically my mother, were mortified by the fact that he didn't baptize his child. I believe the shame my parents feel is that they are not living up to the

Armenian community's standards, and therefore letting down my family's name. My wife and I don't plan to baptize any children we have, but know this will be a difficult confrontation with my mother. For me, this catch-22 of wanting to adhere to an engrained obligation versus what I formulate to be my own opinion and desire are consistently at odds in my life.

Growing up, I thought that my mother worried too much, and my father was too brazen. I still feel that way, but am quite aware as an adult that my own feelings are theirs magnified and grown within me; it is the realization that when we grow up that we carry versions of our parents and their feelings inside of us. Further, it is those feelings that link me back to seeing my parents and grandparents as children of their parents. I always thought of my grandparents as flawless people, but it makes sense that my parents are magnified versions of my grandparents.

I have a great deal of anxiety around separation, and can't help but wonder how the traumas of my ancestors being forcibly removed from their homes shaped my parents, and subsequently me. My grandmother had no home for the first three years of her life with the only thing keeping her alive was her family. Her mother protected her. Family was home. This idea was imparted strongly to my mother, and almost all Armenians I know. It has taken the form of anxiety in everyday life in subsequent generations; home and family mean safety, and without those, my grandmother would have most certainly been killed.

I wish I asked more questions while my grandparents were alive. Did my grandmother feel the same obligation to her mother that I feel toward mine? How could she not feel obligated to the woman who saved her from certain death?

Helen's Story

My grandmother Helen was born Herminé Zorigian in Amasya, Turkey in 1915, several months after her father, Zorig, was beheaded by the Turks in the Genocide. When Herminé was 40 days old, her family was exiled, and in her widowed mother's arms she left Amasya. For three months, the Zorigian family was marched south toward the Syrian Desert with thousands of other Armenians. They survived because they had a hidden cache of 100 gold coins – some wrapped in cloth and sewn as buttons, others stashed in Herminé's diaper – and were able secretly to buy food along the way. They eventually stopped in Furuncu, a village near the city of Malatya where many Armenians were killed. Around that time, the Turks realized that they had limited tradespeople and services in the region. Since Herminé's mother Aghavnie was a dressmaker, she was conscripted to make uniforms for the Ottoman army. Because of this, her family was spared their lives, but not without a cost.

The Turks brought the Zorigian family to Malatya, where Aghavnie supervised 50 women in a makeshift dressmaking shop, which was previously an orphanage. Herminé cried for the milk that her mother, Aghavnie, could not provide because of the privations she had suffered. Because of the crying, Turkish soldiers forced Aghavnie to abandon her baby on the side of the road. That night, Herminé's older siblings, Takouhie and Sarkis, stole back to their infant sister, wrapped her up, and used a piece of candy as a pacifier so that she would not cry. In this way, Herminé was saved from certain death and reunited with her mother. The Zorigians lived in Malatya for three years, keeping Herminé in hiding the entire time.

In 1918, when World War I ended, the first Republic of Armenia was established in part based on borders drawn by Woodrow Wilson. The Zorigians returned to Amasya in 1919, but in 1920, violence against Armenians started anew. In April of 1920, Zorig's brother, who had already escaped to the United States, sent money to Aghavnie. The family left Amasya for Samsun, where they traveled on a ferryboat to Constantinople. Leaving Turkey from Constantinople, they took a boat to Marseille, France, where Aghavnie briefly found work as a seamstress, earning just enough money to allow the family to travel again by boat to the United States. Initially arriving in Providence, RI, they eventually settled in Somerville, MA. In the United States, Herminé became known as Helen. When she was 25 years old, Helen married Dr. Arthur Shushan, moved to Belmont, MA, and subsequently had three children.

Helen became involved in many aspects of community life and was devoted to Armenian causes of all kinds. She was also a great lover of art and was a member of the Ladies' Committee of the Museum of Fine Arts in Boston. My grandmother died in January 2004. During her lifetime, she passed on her particular passion for music to me, and I have pursued music professionally as a composer.

Voyage to Amasia

After my grandmother's passing, I wrote *Voyage to Amasia* to celebrate my grandmother's life and to thank her for the gifts of music and Armenian culture that she passed on to me. The composition premiered to a sold-out audience at Carnegie Hall in January 2005. In *Voyage to Amasia*, I further explored my passion for melding my Armenian heritage with my classical training as a composer. Set in a context of a traditional four movement piano trio, each section expresses a different part of an imagined journey with my grandmother to Amasya. It was a way for me to communicate with my grandmother after her passing, as well as a way for me to cope with the physical separation of her from my life.

Andante, the first movement, allowed me to imagine my grandmother's birthplace from afar, and envision what it would have been like for the two of us to travel to Amasya. I explored the possibility of a new Armenian Amasia, a place we can go together.

Adagio (Homage to Gomidas), movement two, yearns for and mourns the loss of a homeland and birthplace. Basing the melodies on the *Andooni* theme of Armenian composer Gomidas, I set the Zorigian family's personal tragedy in the context of the tragedy of the Armenian nation.

The third movement, *Allegro ma non troppo*, celebrates the endurance of Armenian culture that has survived persecution for millennia. Using traditional Armenian dance rhythms, I first present a melody to my grandmother, who joins my dance gracefully and majestically later in the movement. The two voices finish the movement together by weaving through their cultural tapestry.

Finally, in *Adagio (Requiem)*, I commemorate my grandmother – the tragedies of her early life and my family's ability to triumph over great adversity. By revisiting themes from the first movement, I bring the journey full circle by allowing my grandmother to travel with me to Amasya even after her death.

Going to Amasya

Following the Carnegie Hall premier, a filmmaker friend of mine and I teamed up to make this more than an imagined musical journey, and document a real voyage to Amasya. In deciding to travel to Amasya (my grandmother's birthplace and scene of my family traumas) and film a documentary of this journey I now realize that I was confronting a fear and anger that was lodged inside of me. This journey felt like it was the only way for me to gain clarity on why I even felt fear and anger in the first place.

It was remarkable to see that so many of the people in Amasya physically looked like me. It hadn't occurred to me that this would be the case, and yet it was one of the more powerful, though in retrospect obvious, discoveries for me. My grandmother was also from there: of course we would share the same physical appearances, recipes, and music. The people I encountered were not hate-mongering Turks. They are residents of Amasya, Turkish citizens. Almost all of the villagers were aware of the Genocide and willing to talk about it, despite Turkey's current government's continual denial of the events of 1915; Turkey has made it illegal to speak openly about anything against Turkish-ness, the Armenian Genocide just one of several items included as something "against Turkish-ness."

Traveling through Turkey was a different feeling than when I went to Armenia for the first time. Being in Armenia was a feeling of belonging, surrounding myself with my countrymen and women. I have best heard it described as feeling that there is a gravitational pull on your blood when you walk on the ground of Armenia. There is a feeling of building a better world together, one that we can all live in happily. In Turkey I was an outsider, but it was a window into my ancestors' history. Amasya is a gorgeous artistic center, and I could easily see why my ancestors settled there. Walking the same streets as them made me feel like I belonged; seeing an almost eradicated Armenian history though quickly snapped me back into feeling conflicted as an outsider.

I frequently find that I have a hard time expressing myself with words, and that music is my only true way of communicating, but I kept a journal while traveling through Turkey, Amasya, and Armenia during the filming of the documentary. It was a way of keeping myself grounded, and directly documenting my emotions. What follows are selected writings from this journal:

October 19, 2007

Amasya is gorgeous.

We started the day by wandering, to get a feel for the city, since we only saw it in the dark last night. The mountains are amazing, and there are Pontic tombs from 3200 BC that still exist. We went to the Amasya History Museum this morning and saw many old artifacts from 3200 BC through the twentieth century. There was one display that had items from the Byzantine period, including old crosses, a sculpture of Mary, and several other Christian artifacts. They also had the incense burners we use in our church, though without a cross on them. We walked around the entire city, up and down the river. We have not found anything explicitly Armenian yet, but we have not been trying too hard. Now that we feel comfortable and safe, we will ask more questions. There seems to be some Armenian resemblances in many of the buildings but it is hard to say for sure.

It is a strange feeling, but I feel like I could have lived here.

October 20, 2007

We climbed to the top of one of the mountains, the Kale (castle) from Pontic times, which was later used by the Ottomans. It was a stunning view – we found old tunnels that were used for hiding, as well as a very old canon. After speaking with the owner of our hotel for some time, he drew us a map of what he believed was one of the old Armenian neighborhoods, and where the Armenian churches were (now converted to Mosques). We also went to another museum, which was in an old home on the river. The embroidery on the curtains there looked just like my great grandmother Aghavnie's embroidery.

We then set out for the old Armenian neighborhood. After speaking with a few people, we met a very nice middle-aged woman who showed us the oldest Armenian house still standing in the neighborhood, kept in its original form. The ceiling was beautiful, hand-carved wood. She introduced us to her entire family, with whom we spoke at length. They told us an older man lived up the street and that he would know more of the history of Amasya.

We did not find this old man at first. We knocked on a door near where the previous woman said this man would be, and sure enough, an old man invited us into his home. We had at least five cups of tea with him and his wife (she also gave us homemade cookies which she said she learned to make from her husband's Armenian tailor's wife). There were so many signs of similarity to my family.

He recognized the names Zorigian and Kebabian, though didn't know them personally. We engaged the man about the Genocide, as well as the

US resolution to recognize the Genocide formally. When pressed about 1915, he said, "We don't have a problem with it," but also said we needed to "let the historians decide" what really happened. His wife claimed it was the Armenians who did all the killing. That being said, the man and I shared a pomegranate, and when we went to leave, he said, "My door is open to you always."

I was enraged, and paralyzed at the same time. I wasn't about to get into a physical altercation with this man, but my thoughts were racing: I wanted this man to know what happened to my grandmother. I don't speak Turkish, so the conversation being held through a translator complicated the process, but I was able to ask him directly, "How am I today, when I've heard these horrible stories first hand from my grandmother, supposed to come to terms with this?" His response was, "A few events shouldn't be considered a majority," and "You and I don't have a problem." It was the moment I always feared: direct denial of the Genocide.

We hurried back to the first woman, who told us to come back after we were done with the old man, as they would be baking bread, a ritual done once a month, and that it was happening today. The woman and her daughter baked the bread in front of us, bickering in a very familiar way. They served us several more cups of tea, giving us more bread than we could eat, and put out a spread of Amasya apples, cherries, and peaches, picked from their yard.

We think we found the Armenian churches, but it hard to say for sure, as almost all evidence of Christianity has been erased from this city. There was a building that looked very much like a church right by the Armenian neighborhood we were in today, which must have been Aghavnie and Zorig's church. We also think we found the church my grandmother was baptized in.

I have been feeling so torn today as I reconcile my own feelings of family, tradition, and home mixed with being confronted by the denial and fear I heard and felt.

October 21, 2007

This morning, we climbed up to the Pontic Tombs. It was quite an experience to be standing by something so old (3200 BC); you really get the feeling that a lot of different people have come through Amasya. After that, we went to Merzifon, a neighboring town with a population of about 40,000. We found an abandoned American Missionary School as well as some old Armenian houses. (According to my family's account, American missionaries came to Amasya to build churches and schools, but were rejected by the Turks, so they instead went to Merzifon.) We ate lunch at The Meatball Guy's restaurant, recommended by our Amasya hotel owner, and it was excellent.

We continued on to Gümüşhacıköy – another neighboring village, thought once to be Armenian. After asking several people, we found the one Armenian family left living there. They invited us into their home, where we sat, drank tea, and ate simit (cookies), talking with them for several hours. The older woman reminded me very much of my grandmother. They showed us an Armenian church in town that was turned into a school, and the older woman took us to an Armenian cemetery. Though mostly destroyed – it is used as a field for grazing cows – a few tombstones remained. At the cemetery we were stopped by the police who were "checking up on a report" that some tourists with a big camera were walking around with the Armenian woman. We were eventually able to defuse the situation with our American passports and Turkish speaking guide. I had wondered if we would encounter any problems on our trip with the authorities, and this certainly was a nerve-racking experience. It was again the same conflicted feeling of feeling at home with this welcoming family, but being very aware of the atrocities they had lived through.

October 23, 2007

We visited the Minister of Culture, where we were able to get two very thorough books on the history of Amasya. Being in a government building was not exactly pleasant experience. Though we had no confrontational problems whatsoever, we all felt uncomfortable with the atmosphere. The men in the office we spoke with talked at length about how great Ataturk was, saying that if only he was around now, there would be no problems. After finishing with the Minister of Culture we drove/climbed up the other mountain in town.

We spent the rest of the day with a city architect, who took us to all the Armenian neighborhoods – there were three main sections, and a fourth smaller one. He pointed out which houses Armenians were said to have lived in, as well as the houses Armenians built. Many of the Armenians who lived here back then were carpenters and the Greeks were painters. Though we did not find a house that exactly fit my family's drawing, we found many possible locations and a few houses that looked very close. It was extremely powerful for me to walk in those streets.

I felt compelled to find my family's home, despite being told I never would, given the information I had of its location. Anything that remotely resembled any of the descriptions I had of our home I clung to. It was a feeling of longing and anxiety mixed together; I felt like I was failing myself for not finding the exact home, which brought up feelings of anger and sadness.

At the end of our tour with the architect, he took us to a choreg (sweet bread) shop, where they made Amasya choreg. This was the only place we've been so far that did not allow us to film, as the recipe is a secret, and is only known by the father and son. They said the recipe has been passed down their family since 1901, but that they originally got the recipe from Armenian friends. The architect claimed that all the Armenian churches were destroyed – that what we suspected were Armenian churches were actually not. To be honest, it is hard for me to believe him.

Even though my opinion is surely influenced by the fact that my grandmother was born here, Amasya is one of the most beautiful places I have ever been to. I can find solace imagining happier times here.

October 25, 2007

We arrived safely in Malatya this afternoon. The drive was spectacular, with a never-ending landscape the entire way. It was quite sad though, to reflect on the fact that my family were forcibly marched through these mountains. It was a beautiful backdrop from the car, but would have been treacherous walking through. I honestly don't know how they made it.

Malatya is much bigger than we expected (population is 381,000), and quite cosmopolitan. The center of town reminds me a lot of big European cities (though like Sivas, not as beautiful as Amasya). There are pastry shops filled with baklava everywhere, apricot shops with barrels of overflowing fruit, and a number of simit shops with variations on the name "The Simit Palace" (much like Original Ray's Pizza in New York City).

We found two Armenian churches here, though neither of them are currently in use. One was built in the late 1800s and was closed around

1930. The other, Venk, is from the seventeenth century, and has been closed for some time. Though mostly in ruins, Venk was inspiring to find still standing in the middle of Turkey.

We also found the Armenian cemetery, which was much bigger than we expected, with a lot of tombstones engraved in Armenian – it was really quite beautiful. I looked for any of my family's names, but did not find any. I wasn't sure whether to feel happy or sad about this – had they made it out or were they murdered with no graves? We spoke with the woman who watches over the grounds, who gave us a few clues to find some Armenians to speak with in Malatya, but said that all the ones she knows of do not identify themselves as Armenians, and will likely not respond positively to our filming them.

October 26, 2007

We started the day back at Venk church. Again, the inside of the church was quite serene. There were inscriptions written in Armenian, and we found several engravings of crosses. I felt a great sense of comfort being inside this ancient, ruined but still standing church.

Afterwards, we went back to the Armenian cemetery, where the groundskeeper was incredibly sweet, and seemed genuinely happy about our return. We looked through a book with her of all the names of the people buried in the cemetery. Though we did not find anyone in my family in the book – at least by names that I know – we had a wonderful conversation with her about Armenians currently living in Turkey. We will return to the cemetery on Sunday morning hoping to meet any Armenians, as she said that old people occasionally come on Sundays to pay their respects.

We went to a teahouse for lunch, where we met a man who said he is Armenian. He explained that he is currently follows the Muslim faith, but has Armenian ancestry. He spoke with us for longer than one might expect a stranger to sit and talk with "tourists." He made great comments about human nature, and I agreed with him mostly on his global view of the world.

As soon as the conversation shifted to the Genocide, I sensed my anger rising. The man proceeded to give the stock government answer – saying that it was a war, not a genocide, that the Armenians shot first, and that it is not crimes against humanity. I had heard this a few times now throughout our trip, but hearing it today struck a nerve. I probed the issue with him further, which resulted in more frustration on our end. The Holocaust, he said, was unacceptable, but the events of 1915 were just a war between the Armenians and the Turks.

After lunch, we traveled to Furuncu. By speaking with the Kurdish locals, we confirmed that Furuncu was a "stopping point" for the Armenians, which was saddening. We found the old part of the village, and an empty area that the villagers said was a "type of cemetery" – it was clear to us that this was one of the places where several Armenians were left to die, and where my family would have died had they not been saved.

October 27, 2007

We started our day in search of Kurköz ("40 eyes"). It was hard to find, and we had to ask several locals for directions. We did eventually find someone to confirm the location of the bridge, but the bridge is completed submerged under water. It has been for 20–25 years, and the water is now used as a hydroelectric dam. It was again quite sad to see another area that is essentially a mass grave.

Upon further searching, we found the one café in the area. The owner was very friendly, and immediately opened up, explaining he has Armenian relatives. He showed us old pictures of the bridge while his staff cooked us a mixed grill of kebobs. When we tried to pay for our meal, he said, "Your money is no good here, we are brothers." When we explained that we were looking for traces of my family, he called us into his office where he looked through his phone book and called several of his family members and friends in search of any remaining Armenians in Malatya. He located one, and gave us her address ("She lives in between the church and the cemetery, just go there and ask for Lucia."). We searched for Lucia, and finally found her home, however she had moved to Poland recently.

We have not had any explicit success locating the orphanages that my family stayed and worked in. We have been told this is because most of them were closed in 1919 or shortly after. If any buildings remain, they would just be large old abandoned buildings. We did find one of the oldest streets in town, and the buildings there are large old abandoned buildings.

There were 12 PKK (Kurdish Workers Party) terrorists caught in Malatya today. Three of them escaped into the mountains, and there was a helicopter search party going after them. There were uniformed soldiers in the street with machine guns, and people of all ages lining the streets in protest. We saw demonstrations in Amasya in response to the Turkish soldiers getting killed a few days before, but this is different. There are tanks lining the streets and fighter jets flying above. They are preparing for war.

This modern day conflict mixed with my thoughts and feelings of my family's past has made it hard for me to give any merit to the Turkish government's decisions. The people of Turkey want me to feel like family, but all physical traces have been or are being wiped away.

October 30, 2007

We arrived in Istanbul last night, and got our bearings today. Our guide was excited to show us around her hometown, and helped us explore both the European and Anatolian sides. It's funny being in Istanbul as we definitely come off as tourists, whereas in the smaller cities we appeared to be travelers interested in the country. Istanbul seems a lot like San Francisco on much larger scale – windy streets, crowed city, shops everywhere, but very few tall buildings.

We went to *Agos*, Hrant Dink's newspaper. There is an indescribable energy in that building, though his murder also leaves the place feeling slightly spooked. Even in the short time we were there, you could see that the people there really cared about what they are doing.

Our guide took us to her old Armenian school, where she previously worked as a counselor. We spoke with the principal who is originally from Gümüşhacıköy. She unfortunately could not let us tape her because she is a visible employee of the state, but was able to put us in touch with one of her teachers originally from Amasya.

After lunch, we went to Aras, an Armenian publishing company that was started by Hrant Dink. We met Rober Koptas, who is now the editor-in-chief of *Agos* newspaper, and he allowed us to interview him. He is quite knowledgeable and provided a fantastic interview. He talked about what it was like growing up as an Armenian in Istanbul, what he knows of his family's exile, and the modern situation of recognition of the Genocide.

We also saw two working Armenian churches today, one of which was the main one in Istanbul, and I was able to light a candle there. After traveling through the countryside, seeing such a concentrated group of Armenian people was invigorating.

November 1, 2007

Today was our final day in Istanbul. We searched all over the city, asking questions to just about everyone who would stop and try to understand us. After finding another Armenian church, a middle-aged man directed us to a tea shop where he said an older Armenian man originally from Amasya worked. We eventually found this man – a 60-year-old Armenian man who had lived in Amasya for 40 years, and has lived in Istanbul for the last 20 years. This was the most interesting interview we have done so far, because after about five minutes it took a bad turn. We started with easy questions, and he gave a nice description of Amasya, the residents, etc.

As we started in on 1915, he said he had stories, but wouldn't tell them on camera. He started to tell about the deportation, but was interrupted by his boss, also Armenian, who very angrily accused us of using them, that we were trying to destroy their store and their living, that the Turks were good people, and that we should forget about this "1915 nonsense" and focus on why Armenia has such poverty. We apologized and again explained about my grandmother and Amasya, but ended up getting out of there very soon after the boss's outburst. This was one of the more poignant moments of this trip for me. The fear still exists today: is being an Armenian in Turkey a crime?

We also met with the Armenian teacher, whose grandfather was actually from Merzifon, not Amasya, but had the exact same deportation route as my family – from Merzifon to Amasya to Sivas to Malatya. He was old and has been on and off very sick – but there were moments of clarity in him that were amazing: he said he knew all of our surnames – Kebabian, Zorigian, etc. – even saying he knew a Kebabian who was in Malatya and married a Turkish man to stay alive.

November 5, 2007

We arrived safely in Armenia, and it has been wonderful. It has been great to speak with the people here, and to get such an opposite perspective of that in Turkey. We hit all the tourist spots (Khor Virap,

Zvartnots, Echmiadzin, Garni, Gegherard), and made it to one of the Amasia villages today. We were told more than once that this Amasia is the Siberia of Armenia, so we expected the worst. Despite it being on an extremely rough road, only 7 km away from the Turkish border, and a really run down village, we had the best possible experience here. I finally felt at home. I still battled an internal conflict, that the Armenians living here should have their original homeland, but it was wonderful to see the residents living happy and fulfilling lives.

We met the mayor of the village, who gave us a personal tour for three hours. He introduced us to the only old man left in town, whose parents were from Amasya, Turkey. His story very much matches my family's – his family being exiled to Malatya, and then escaping to France. While in France, Soviet Armenian soldiers found his family after the Genocide, and asked if they would come to Armenia to help repopulate their home country, which is when they relocated to Amasia, Armenia.

November 6, 2007

We went to the second Amasia in Armenia today, and we met another old man whose family was also from Amasya, Turkey. Afterwards, we went to the Genocide museum, and captured some great footage of the memorial, and spoke with the director of the museum. He was able to provide fantastic information about the specifics of Amasyetsi's, the deportation routes, and a great historical perspective of the Genocide.

What was perhaps the most amazing part of this visit to the museum, and maybe even the voyage itself, was finding my great grandmother's picture – Aghavnie – in a book about Amasya history in the archives of the Genocide museum. I was stunned, and again quite moved to see her as a part of the official history of Amasya. The writing around her in Armenian tells her life story as my family knows it. It was the perfect conclusion to this journey, to find a concrete piece of my family in my homeland.

I long to come back to Amasya with my mother and her siblings and my cousins, to show them the land from which our family sprung forth. There is a gravitational pull in the place where your roots began, and I want to share that feeling. I hope that other displaced Armenians can experience this, as I found great hope in finding my homeland.

Note

1 This text is the English version of the German document handed to Louis P. Lochner in Berlin. It first appeared in Lochner's *What About Germany?* (New York: Dodd, Mead & Co., 1942), pp. 1–4. The Nuremberg Tribunal later identified the document as L-3 or Exhibit USA-28. Two other versions of the same document appear in Appendices II and III. For the German original cf. *Akten zur Deutschen Auswartigen Politik 1918–1945*, Serie D, Band VII (Baden-Baden, 1956), pp. 171–172.

Chapter 14

Things They Carried
Leaving Korea

Marie Myung-Ok Lee

This was a summer of refugees, of walls, of border police, of daring journeys, of violence and death, sometimes of rescue, of separated families, each side not knowing what to do.

As Iraqis now join Syrians and Eritreans in a mass exodus out of their home countries on to Europe and beyond, one might wonder, what has to possess someone to leave everything they know for a dangerous unknown? And not just the single and the mobile, but families.

As I read these stories from a comfortable remove, in America, I am reminded of my mother's odyssey and how these movements are not always purely voluntary and how, even in a "successful" escape, the psychic scars from the dislocation last forever. A teenager in Korea in 1945, she had hoped that the defeat of the Japanese in World War II meant that Korea, until then a Japanese colony, could finally have an independent sovereign government. Instead, Korea was given over as a spoil of war to the winners, the Soviet Union and the United States. Two young American officers were given the job of figuring out how to partition the country; after only 30 minutes, they decided to split the country roughly in half at the 38th parallel.

At the time of the partition, my mother lived a privileged life in Pukchong, in what would become North Korea after the formation of the Democratic People's Republic of Korea in 1948. As the Soviet-backed government began descending with a hand that appeared to be just as heavy as that of the Japanese, people in their village whispered of moving south while they still could. She recalls Soviet soldiers moving from house to house, gang-raping the women, stealing, gratuitously trampling on crops. But it was impossible to know if things down south, with a United States military-led government, were any better.

Reprinted with kind permission:
Lee, M. M-O. (2015). The Things They Carried: Leaving Korea. NYTImes online blog: Opinionator Private Lives, September 24, 2015.

My mother's family wavered over what to do. Her grandfather, the patriarch, declared that they needed to protect their ancestral land, an impressive gated compound that included a main house, a house for the in-laws, one for the servants, as well as a strawberry patch, a paddock for pigs and a creek nearby for water. This estate upon a hill was so large, my mother said, you could see it when you got off the train at the station across town.

One of my mother's aunts – not a direct aunt, but in the Korean meaning of aunt, a female relation many times removed – was a widow with two small children who decided to take her chances in the south. By then, both the United States and the Soviet Union had begun fortifying their respective sides of the 38th parallel, and it was becoming increasingly dangerous to cross. But like the Syrians of today, people still went, driven by whatever makes people uproot themselves to risk a life elsewhere. My mother was ordered to accompany the aunt to help with the children. She didn't exactly understand what she was doing, but in the Korean way, didn't question. Her mother packed them some rice balls for lunch and sent them off in the fall of 1945.

That I am here and not living in North Korea is testament to the journey's success. But even though it sounded like the stuff of movies – crossing a heavily fortified military zone to escape an oppressive regime – my mother never talked about that time in Korea and in fact, often became upset if it was ever brought up, say, for a class project.

After years of persistent inquiries, I finally pieced together the story. She and her aunt and the children took a train to a checkpoint where they met smugglers, who took them over mountainous terrain in the middle of the night to evade the soldiers. She was walking and running over the 38th parallel in the dark, over rough terrain full of soldiers with guns, barbed wire and bandits – while carrying a toddler on her back.

My mother eventually ended up in Seoul with nothing but a few gold rings sewn into her clothes. The smugglers had taken all their money and made them abandon their bags. Not really understanding what was happening, she never even said goodbye to her mother.

For most divided Korean families, the fate of their loved ones in the North has been forever blocked by the "bamboo curtain" that is the D.P.R.K., the most secretive regime in the world.

When my siblings and I were growing up in rural Minnesota, oblivious to this history, our mother's obsessions and apocalyptic thinking was something to roll our eyes at: She wouldn't leave the house without taking 10 minutes to stare at the stove to make sure it was off, even if we hadn't cooked all day. It drove me to the edge of impatience when the simplest decisions – which apple had fewer spots? – would leave her paralyzed in a supermarket aisle. In college, one of us kids not returning her call in a timely fashion would result in her not only frantically calling our roommates, but also sometimes the parents of our roommates.

My mother, and my father, adhered religiously to binary certainties that they created: Get into Harvard, and everything will be all right. Wear your seatbelt, and everything will be all right. They would not have torn a tag off a mattress for fear of prosecution. The first time I saw a car change lanes without signaling, I waited for the inevitable fiery crash.

Now that my mother is in her 80s, that the terrible things in her mind have not come to pass have not reassured her at all. Her compulsions and hair-trigger panics appear to outsiders to be the eccentricity of the elderly, but they are basically what I grew up with, unabated. The other day, I left her Minneapolis condo in the early a.m. to catch a flight. The shuttle van arrived in a torrential rainstorm, and the driver was nice enough to throw a T-shirt on his head and run out into the downpour to help me with my bags. I had to jump over a raging mini-river by the curb into the van, that's how hard it was raining. We were pulling out when we heard, over the sounds of the rain, what sounded like a rock hitting the window. It was my mother, having run after the van, and she was frantically knocking on the window. I opened the door to see her soaked, hair streaming. She seemed agitated, but all she said was "Call me the minute you get home."

I didn't call her the minute I returned home. My son, who had missed me, wanted me to take him to the farmers' market, so I did. When we returned, I called, and my mother, still somewhat frantic, said she'd been praying for me all this time. When I asked her to explain, she said she was worried about the masked man she'd seen take me away in the strange looking car – the standard blue airport shuttle van. It was so odd to contemplate that the same things I had seen – the familiar, punctual van, the driver running into the rain – had prompted in me feelings of good will and a desire to generously tip while to my mother it was a potential kidnapping.

Now that I am older and understand the history better, layered by these reprises playing all over the globe, I have come to see the actual logic in her reactions. Her inability to make decisions makes perfect sense when you consider that in the world she grew up in, the "wrong" decision could be fatal. But also the "right" decision – accompanying her aunt – ended with her never seeing her mother again.

A lifetime after the dash across the 38th parallel, now living in a snug condo in Minneapolis, my mother still hardly sleeps at night; she sees a counselor for debilitating anxiety. She's astoundingly healthy – her cardiologist says she has the heart of a 60-year-old – but with every twinge, she's always sure this is "it." She craves company, but is scared to go out. It's a confounding way to live, but now I'm realizing she may not be able to change – the scars that were inflicted on her psyche when she was 14, instead of getting smaller with time have only grown with her.

As our past and present American attitudes toward immigration have shown, countries and their people have differing ways they receive their fellow humans in need. Children, we tell ourselves, are resilient. What we don't think about is that one's worldview becomes formed in this period, and early experiences, even if not understood, maybe especially if not fully understood, become part of the things carried into adulthood, that haunt a person, every day.

Index

Aaron, Soazig 41
Abraham & Torok 87, 234–5
abortion 171
academic psychology and psychiatry 197
African Americans, intergenerational trauma among: Black culture and 229; cultural introject 226; history of 227–8; internalized racism, notion of 226; loss, sorrow, and cultural amnesia 232–7; psychoanalytic perspective of 235; psychological 228; slavery, due to 2, 84, 227; treatment implications of 237–8; voices of the enslaved 228–32
Agamben, Giorgio 30
alienated identification 85
American Civil Rights Movement 70–1
American Indian Religious Freedom Act (1978) 254
American Labor movement 206
American military: epidemic of sexual abuse in 117; gays in the military 117; male-on-male rape in 116–19; Military Sexual Assault Report 117; posttraumatic stress disorder (PTSD) 117
American Psychiatric Association 197
American Psychoanalytic Association 190
American Psychological Association 189, 200
"angels in the nursery," concept of 130, 132, 144
annihilation, trauma of 54–5
anti-Semitic persecution 26
anti-war movements 192–3
anxiety 216
anxiety disorders 126, 139
Anzaldúa, Gloria 181–2
Apprey, M. 2, 84, 86, 171, 173, 184
Armenian genocide 2, 269–70, 273; US resolution to recognize 277

Aron, L. & Starr, K. 82
attachment: interpersonal 254; manifestation of the degree of 254; neo-Darwinian concept of 199
attachment trauma 10, 80, 87–8; transgenerational transmission of 88
Auerhahn, Nanette 52, 82

Barker, Pat 63–4, 120
Bateson, Gregory 69
battered women's shelters 195
bearing witness, process of 179
behavioral health: risks for children 254; and well-being 263
bereavement: historical trauma due to 253–4; marital 253; strategies for coping with 254
Berlin, I. 227, 229–31
Bersani, Leo 110, 113–14, 123
Big history 1–2
Black culture 229
Boggs, John 231
Bois Caïman ceremony 71
Boston Change Process Study Group 83, 88
borderlands hybridity, notion of 181
Bowlby, J. 81, 87, 89, 126, 199
"box of terrible things" 104–5, 144
Brave Heart, Maria Yellow Horse 125, 248, 253
'brick wall of indelibility' 13–14
British Psychoanalytical Society 81
Bromberg, P. 61, 85, 89–90, 93
Butler, Judith 121–3, 216

Chasseguet-Smirgel, J. 113
Chiew, Florence 69
child abuse 197
child–parent psychotherapy (CPP) 104, 127–30; case related to 131–45; client's

sociocultural and historical context in 130–1; posttreatment assessment measures 133, 145; tracking trauma through four generations 139–44
children: behavioral health risks for 254; impact of trauma in *see* traumatized children
civil disobedience 207
Civil Rights Act of 1964 195
civil rights movement 70–1, 193
Civil War 227–8, 231
Clarke, John Henrik 238
Clifton, Lucille 67
Clough, P. 177
Cohen, Jonathan 55
collective group trauma 259
collective memory, importance of 107, 228, 233–4
community based activism 169, 181; creating conditions for new emergence 182–6
concentration camps 13, 22, 39; gas-chambers 44
consciousness-raising, issue of 193, 195
conspiracy of silence 234, 237
contextually congruent interventions 130–1, 146
countertransference analysis: of intergenerational transmission of trauma 33–5; reflections on 35–6
cultural introject 2, 226
Cultural Revolution (1966–1976) 105, 137–9, 142, 144–5
Cvetkovich, A. 174, 184

Danieli, Y. 237
Davoine, F. 2, 11, 82, 84, 87, 89
Dearing, Ronda 201
Debro, Sarah 233
depression 126; relation with historical trauma 255
Derrida, J. 180
developmental trauma 10, 118
Dimen, M. 238
dissociation, phenomenon of 14
dissociative amnesia 201
dissociative attunement 14, 73n2, 91
DNA methylation 64
domestic violence 131–2, 138, 144, 170, 185, 193
Douglas, Frederick 71, 227
Du Bois, W.E. 66, 233

Einsatzgruppe (Death Squad) 22
Elise, Diane 120
empty circle, notion of 83–4
entangled relationality, ecology of 69–71
epigenetics, effects of environment on 79
episodic amnesia 80
Epstein, H. 83
"ethic of translation" 173
ethnic violence 178
Ettinger, B. L. 169
Evans, Sara 193
Evans-Campbell, T. 261
"expendable warriors" 198
extreme trauma, experiences of 19, 63
Eyerman, R. 228

failed empathy, idea of 52
Faimberg, Haidee 68, 78, 85, 153
family trauma transmission 12
fantasy 42, 80, 88, 119, 165, 204–5, 219
fascism 72, 189
Father-Daughter Incest 196
father–daughter relationship 12; incest relations 195–6
fear and anxiety, management of 70
fearful arousal 89
Federal Writers Project 229
female infanticide 171
Ferenczi, S. 80–1
First Nations Behavioral Health Association 258
Fletcher, John 119
Fonagy, P. 81, 88, 152
Fortunoff Video Archive, Yale University 22, 42
Fraiberg, L. 88, 91, 238
Franklin, John Hope 87–8
Frazer, E. Franklin 235
Freire, P. 169, 181
Freud and Modern Psychology 199
Freud, Anna 11–12, 81; definition of trauma 12; 'psychic apparatus' and 'psychic reality,' construct of 9–10; on psychic trauma 12
Freud, Sigmund 9, 12, 20, 80, 106, 114; *Interpretation of Dreams, Three Essays on the Theory of Sexuality, The* 199–200; intra-psychic formulation 216; oceanic feeling, concept of 19; reaction against Ferenczi's ideas 81; *Totem and Taboo* 200
Fugitive Pieces 64

Gampel, Y. 85
gender selective abortions 171
gender-based violence 169, 177, 183, 193, 197
gene expression, alteration of 64
genocide 170, 247, 251; Armenian genocide 2; Holocaust 170; intracountry 125; against the Jews 155–9; Maya survivors 259; trans-generational transmission of 2
Gerson, S. 85, 88, 215
ghostly attachments: analysis of 92–6; haunting quality of 91; notion of 87–91
"ghosts in the nursery," concept of 129, 238
Gilford, Lisa 219
Glennie, Evelyn 60
Gordon, A. F. 180
Grand, Sue 88, 115–16, 123, 235, 247
Great Depression 214, 216
Great Leap Forward 142
Green, Andre 84–5, 109, 161
Greenland, Susan Kaiser 135

Harris, A. 90–1
Harris, Michael 238
Hartman, J. J. 12; father–daughter loyalty, reconstruction of 13
Harvard Trauma Questionnaire (HTQ) 259
Harvey, Mary 197
hauntings 77, 91, 154–5, 166–7, 180, 182, 184, 235
helplessness, sense of 237
Herman, Judith Lewis 80, 166–7, 233
Historical Loss and Associated Symptoms Scale (HLAS) 255–6
Historical Loss Scale (HLS) 255–6
Hoffman, Eva 106–7
Holocaust trauma 2, 10, 12, 35, 160, 170; impact of 13; memorials and museums, construction of 234; survivor's testimonies *see* testimonial narratives, of Holocaust survivors; testimony and psychoanalysis of 21–5
homophobia 82
homosexual imaginary 106, 109, 113, 121
homosexuality 109–10; in cases of war trauma 111–16
Hopper, Earl 235
House Un-American Activities Committee (HUAC) 206, 213, 220
HTUG Intervention 258–9

identity, rhythm of 63–9

imagined reconciliation 67
indigenous peoples of the Americas, historical trauma among: addressing of shared experiences 260; assessment of 251–2; clinical implications of 253–4; conceptual framework of 252–3; current bereavement and 253–4; measures to inform clinical and community-based practices 255; need for family and community level interventions 261–3; prevalence of psychiatric disorders 252; relation with PTSD and depression 255; suicide rates 251; and unresolved grief intervention 258–9; healing practices 259
Indigenous Peoples of the Americas Survey (IPS) 256–8; design of 257; development of 256; intent of 259
infant-parent psychotherapy 129
inter-generational transmission of trauma 60, 81, 152–4, 247; among African Americans *see* African Americans, intergenerational trauma among; analysis of 33–5; CPP case involving 131–45; making of 32; widespread force of 155
internal representations, of reality 149–52
internalized racism, notion of 226
International Indian Treaty Council 257–8
interpersonal trauma 125, 127
Ippen, Ghosh 129–30, 146

Jacobs, Harriet 231
Jacobs, Jane 165
Jefferson, Thomas 227, 231
Jim Crow laws 170, 194
Joiner, Priscilla 230
Jordania, Joseph 70
Junger, Sebastian 118

Kestenberg, J. 83, 153
Kidron, Carol 146
Kleinman, Arthur 139
Kohler, B. 79
Korea: exodus from 286–9; partition of 286–7
Ku Klux Klan 233
Kuriloff, E. 11, 82

Lakota Grief Experience Questionnaire (LGEQ) 258
Langer, Larry 22

Lanzmann, Claude 40
Laplanche, Jean 110, 118–19
Laub, Dori 15, 52, 83, 95; empty circle, notion of 83–4
Lewin, Kurt 181
Lewis, Helen Block 166–7, 189
lifetime traumatic events, experience of 253
Little, John 229
Long Walk of the Navajo 261
Lyons-Ruth, K. 79, 89, 91

Maafa (Black Diaspora) 227
McCarthy, Joseph 166–7, 189, 192, 199, 205–6, 210, 212–13, 217
McDougall, Joyce 118
Mahler, Margaret 19
Mainardi, Pat 194
male-on-male rape: in American military 116–19; male victims, public perceptions of 117; Military Sexual Assault Report on 117; as sequela of unraveled enigmatic messages 118–19
Mao, Zedong 142
marital bereavement 253
mass amnesia 165
mass genocide 170, 251
maternal abandonment 92–3
Matthews, Michael 117, 122
Meares, R. 247
Melrose, David 111
memory and resilience, dialectical relationship of 71–2
Michaels, Ann 64
Middle Passage 72, 227, 231
misogyny 82
Morrison, Toni 226
mother and a daughter, joint video testimony of 39–55; of concentration camp of Auschwitz 39; and dissociative effects of traumatic experience 39; Jolly's dissociation and the concreteness of the maternal body 49–50; mother in the mother (Rosalie's good object) 53–4; mother–daughter relationship and 42–4; traumatic loss of structure and 50–2; mother–child attachment 85, 88

Nachtraeglichkeit 105, 119, 205, 220–4
National Aboriginal Health Organization, Canada 258
National Institute of Mental Health, in Washington, DC 197

Nazis 13, 64

Obama, Barack 114–15
Oliver, K. 179, 181
one-generation model 79, 86

Parens, Henri 13–14, 19
parent–child bonding system 128, 131; disruption and disorganization of 91
Patterson, Orlando 227
Phillips, Ulrich 229
Pinderhughes, E. 235, 237
pogroms, against the Jews 61, 155–9; anti-Jewish legislation and 156; "In the City of Killing" poem 158; Kishinev pogrom (1903) 158; sexual trauma and 159
posttraumatic stress disorder (PTSD) 64, 117, 126, 133, 145–6, 197, 208, 250–1, 253; relation with historical trauma 255; risk factors for 254
Price, June 201
Prince, Robert 11, 82; idea of psychoanalysis 82
'psychic equivalence' of trauma 10–11, 39, 44, 49, 55, 152
psychic holes, notion of 85
psychic trauma 12, 14, 155; construct of 10–11
Psychinfo databases 170
psychological trauma 197, 228
psychosis blanche 84
Puget, J. 217

racism 82, 173, 177, 178, 226, 235, 250, 252, 255–6, 260, 262–3
rape, trauma of: intergenerational transmission of 152–4; rape crisis centers 195; representations of 149–52
Reagon, Bernice Johnson 70
recognition and doing something, conditions for 180–2
Red Diaper babies 206
Reis, B. 2, 86, 172, 246
relational trauma 9–12, 14, 82, 88–9; concept of 12
religious based violence 170
residential (boarding) school trauma 256, 258
resilience 1, 5, 10, 27–8, 61, 66–7, 72, 87–9, 91, 246–8, 261–2
Richman, Sophia 93, 246

Role of Shame in Symptom Formation, The 200
Rosenberg, Ethel 206, 209, 211
Rosenberg, Julius 206, 209, 211
Rushdy, A. 228
Russell, Bertrand 69

St. Aubyn, E. 111, 116
Saketopoulou, A. 121
Salberg, J. 2, 3, 10–11, 13, 15
Sand Creek Massacre of the Cheyenne 261
Schatzow, Emily 201
Schiff, Rivka 159
Schore, A. N. 9, 12, 15
Schwab, Gabriele 65–6
self-endangering behaviors, due to trauma 126
self-narratives, development of 245
Sertima, I.V. 228
sexual abuse 2, 125; of children 177; male-on-male 118; in US military 117; of women 178, 195
sexual crimes, against children 175
shadow of terror, living and growing up in: contradictions 217–20; grief and loss 213–17; history of 205–8; history revisited 208–10; *Nachtraeglichkeit* 220–4; silence revisited 210–13
Shatan, Chaim 120
"Shoah" documentary 40
shtetl life 93
Slade, A. 89–90, 245
slavery 227, 233; abolition of 71; for African Americans 84; Black people's fears of 236; history of 228; institution of 229; as institutionalized genocide 170; memory of 229; re-institution of 234; residual anxieties arising from 236; revolution against 71; traumatic legacies of 84; traumatic legacies of 84, 226, 228; slave narratives 229; and voices of the enslaved 228–32
social justice 4, 205, 221
social trauma 2, 84, 142; sources of 237
South African anti-apartheid movement 71
Spence, Martha 230
Stein, Ruth 114, 118, 121
story holding, internalization of 104
story making, capacity of 104
storytelling, without the words to say it 61–3
stress hormones, chronic activation of 64–5

Substance Abuse and Mental Health Services Administration (SAMHSA) 258
Sullivan, H. S. 82; ideas about defensive operations 82
Symington, Stuart 190

Tapahonso, Luci 63
telescoping of generations, idea of 2, 78, 85, 153
terror, dealing with 30–1
testimonial narratives, of Holocaust survivors 15; emotional connection of a listener to 41–2; of mother and a daughter 39–55; mother's testimony 21–37
testimony and psychoanalysis: being in the lead 23–5; countertransference analysis 33–6; dealing with terror 30–1; of Holocaust survivors 21–8; testimonial event 20; theoretical considerations in 18–20; for understanding of the traumatic damage 18
Three Essays on Sexuality, The 114
Tiananmen Square massacre (1989), China 105, 137
Trail of Tears of the Cherokee 261
trans-generational transmission of trauma 2, 35, 78, 86, 169–70, 185; ghostly attachments and 87–91; haunting quality of 91; model of 3–5; tracing history and emerging themes of 80–3; tracking of 139–44
transgenerational turn 80
trauma: of annihilation 54–5; assessment of 132; complexities of translating 171–4; definition of 12; in early childhood 126; Freudian concept of 12; homosexuality and 110; impact of 83–7; indicators of 41; interpersonal losses, due to 254; one-generation model 86; parent–child bonding system, impact on 91; problem of the dissociating forces of 42; psychoanalytic theories of 170; reparation of 14; sexuality, impact of 109; trans-generational transmission of *see* trans-generational transmission of trauma
Trauma Symptom Checklist for Young Children (TSCYC) 145
traumatic attachment 12–13; texture of 91, 94

traumatized children: child–parent psychotherapy for 127–30; cognitive-behavioral strategies for treatment of 128; dyadic treatment model for 127; and effects of trauma in early childhood 126–7; intergenerational transmission of trauma 152–4; and maladaptive parenting behaviors 129; parent-child relationship and 128; trauma-related disturbances, treatment of 127
Trevarthan, Colwyn 66, 72
Tribal Best Practice 258
Tustin, Frances 16

United Nations (UN): Declaration on the Rights of Indigenous Peoples 261; Permanent Forum on Indigenous Issues 258, 260, 263n1
unthought known, notion of 92

van der Kolk, Bessel 153, 197
vicarious trauma 10–11, 159
Victims of Violence Program 117, 197
violence against women 169–72, 185, 193
vodou cult songs, evolution of 71
Volkan, V. 234

war trauma: as assault on male gender 119–22; gender-threatening conditions 120; homosexuality, cases of 111–16; impact of sexuality on 109; male-on-male rape 116–19; psychotherapy for 122–3
Washington, Booker T. 232–3
Weinberg, R. 156
White, Haydon 245
Whitehead, Alfred North 69
Wilson, Woodrow 273
Winnicott, D. W. 19, 50, 84
witnessing, psychoanalytic theories of 170, 173
women's caretaking role, feminist re-valuation of 199
Women's Rights 206
Women's Studies and Psychology 199
Wood, James 104
Works Progress Administration 226
World War I 82, 93, 120, 273
World War II 23, 41, 43, 82; memory of 2

Yale University: Fortunoff Video Archive 42; Genocide Studies Program 83
Young, J. E. 87

Zizek, S. 218

Taylor & Francis eBooks

Helping you to choose the right eBooks for your Library

Add Routledge titles to your library's digital collection today. Taylor and Francis ebooks contains over 50,000 titles in the Humanities, Social Sciences, Behavioural Sciences, Built Environment and Law.

Choose from a range of subject packages or create your own!

Benefits for you
- Free MARC records
- COUNTER-compliant usage statistics
- Flexible purchase and pricing options
- All titles DRM-free.

Benefits for your user
- Off-site, anytime access via Athens or referring URL
- Print or copy pages or chapters
- Full content search
- Bookmark, highlight and annotate text
- Access to thousands of pages of quality research at the click of a button.

REQUEST YOUR FREE INSTITUTIONAL TRIAL TODAY

Free Trials Available
We offer free trials to qualifying academic, corporate and government customers.

eCollections – Choose from over 30 subject eCollections, including:

Archaeology	Language Learning
Architecture	Law
Asian Studies	Literature
Business & Management	Media & Communication
Classical Studies	Middle East Studies
Construction	Music
Creative & Media Arts	Philosophy
Criminology & Criminal Justice	Planning
Economics	Politics
Education	Psychology & Mental Health
Energy	Religion
Engineering	Security
English Language & Linguistics	Social Work
Environment & Sustainability	Sociology
Geography	Sport
Health Studies	Theatre & Performance
History	Tourism, Hospitality & Events

For more information, pricing enquiries or to order a free trial, please contact your local sales team:
www.tandfebooks.com/page/sales

Routledge — Taylor & Francis Group
The home of Routledge books

www.tandfebooks.com

CPSIA information can be obtained
at www.ICGtesting.com
Printed in the USA
BVHW030216191222
654530BV00010B/314

9 781138 807501